LINCOLN AND

THE BORDER STATES

Abraham Lincoln. Courtesy of the Abraham Lincoln Library and Museum of Lincoln Memorial University, Harrogate, Tennessee.

Lincoln

AND

the Border States

PRESERVING THE UNION

William C. Harris

University Press of Kansas

© 2011 by the University Press of Kansas

Published by the University Press of Kansas (Lawrence, Kansas
66045), which was organized by the Kansas Board of Regents and is
operated and funded by Emporia State University, Fort Hays State
University, Kansas State University, Pittsburg State University,
the University of Kansas, and Wichita State University

Library of Congress Cataloging-in-Publication Data

Harris, William C. (William Charles), 1933–
Lincoln and the Border States : preserving the Union /
William C. Harris.
p. cm.
Includes bibliographical references and index.
ISBN 978-0-7006-1804-0 (cloth : alk. paper)
1. Border States (U.S. Civil War) 2. United States—History—Civil
War, 1861–1865—Political aspects. 3. United States—Politics and
government—1861–1865. 4. Slavery—Political aspects—United
States—History—19th century. 5. Slavery—Political aspects—
Border States—History—19th century. 6. Slaves—Emancipation—
United States. 7. Slaves—Emancipation—Border States. 8. Lincoln,
Abraham—1809–1865—Views on slavery. I. Title.
E459.H29 2011
973.7'1—dc23
2011024072

British Library Cataloguing-in-Publication Data is available.

Printed in the United States of America

10 9 8 7 6 5 4 3 2 1

For Jim Cotner and the memory of Rick Sauer

Contents

Illustrations

Acknowledgments

Many people have contributed to the preparation of this book. Alexander J. De Grand, a colleague at North Carolina State University, while enjoying his retirement, read the manuscript in its initial stage and offered many helpful suggestions. David Zonderman, also a colleague, critically read several chapters and provided numerous corrections and suggestions. John David Smith of the University of North Carolina at Charlotte carefully read the manuscript and made useful recommendations for its improvement. He also sent me important materials and information on the recruitment of black troops in the border states. Michael Burlingame of the University of Illinois at Springfield, whose knowledge of Lincoln is unsurpassed, read several chapters and offered suggestions. Joe A. Mobley, a colleague at North Carolina State University and an authority on the South during the Civil War, encouraged me in the project and also asked penetrating questions about Lincoln and the border states. Anne E. Marshall of Mississippi State University generously provided me with several typescript pages from her forthcoming book, *Creating a Confederate Kentucky: The Lost Cause and Civil War Memory in a Border State* (Chapel Hill: University of North Carolina Press).

Librarians and curators of manuscript and photographic collections are often the unsung heroes of research and writing. In all of my scholarly efforts, I have received splendid help from the staff of the D. H. Hill Library,

North Carolina State University. Mimi Riggs of the library's Interlibrary Loan department has gone the extra mile in obtaining important published materials for me. As always, Darby Orcutt, collections manager, has aided my research. Jacob Lee of the Filson Historical Society and the staff of the William T. Young Library, University of Kentucky Libraries, have provided useful assistance to my project. The staffs of the Perkins Library, Duke University; the Davis Library, University of North Carolina at Chapel Hill; and the University of Chicago Library have also aided the study.

Illustrations for the book have been expertly provided on digital format by Michelle Ganz of the Abraham Lincoln Library and Museum, Harrogate, Tennessee; Jaime Bourassa of the Missouri History Museum, St. Louis; Jennifer Duplaga of the Kentucky Historical Society, Frankfort; and Jonathan Eaker of the Prints and Photographs Division, Library of Congress, Washington, D.C. My wife Betty provided the print of a photograph of George D. Prentice from an 1876 book of his poems. Cartographer George Skoch of Fairview Park, Ohio, skillfully drew the map of the border states for the book. Elias Nithianandarajah of Raleigh, North Carolina, brought his exceptional computer skills to the task of reformatting the final manuscript. I am especially grateful to Fred Woodward and his excellent staff at the University Press of Kansas for their efficiency and dedication in bringing this book to fruition. A special word of thanks is extended to Kathy Delfosse, who meticulously edited the final version of the manuscript, and saved me from some embarrassing mistakes.

Finally, my wife Betty G. Harris performed innumerable tasks in the preparation of the manuscript, not the least of which was helping me navigate the esoteric and changing world of computer technology. After fifty years of marriage, I owe her a great deal.

William C. Harris
Raleigh, North Carolina

LINCOLN AND

THE BORDER STATES

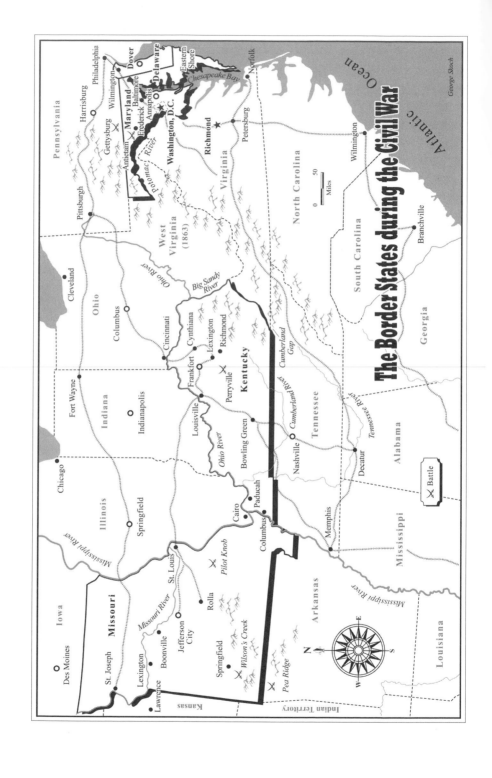

The Border States during the Civil War

Introduction

In 1861 Abraham Lincoln was thrown into a crisis of epic proportion. He correctly concluded that the suppression of the southern insurrection depended on securing and maintaining the loyalty of the border slave states of Delaware, Maryland, Kentucky, and Missouri. In all the border states, though only marginally so in Delaware, Lincoln had to deal with divisions over secession and loyalties and contentious issues relating to constitutional and states' rights, military interference in civil affairs, control of state militias, and factionalism among Unionists. Nothing, however, exceeded the difficulties Lincoln faced in the border states over his antislavery policies and the enlistment of blacks in the army. Although far from perfect in his conduct of border state affairs, Lincoln proved equal to the task of retaining the loyalty and cooperation of these states in the war, and ultimately, in the cases of Maryland and Missouri, to the task of securing emancipation.

The history of Lincoln and the border states offers insights into the president's leadership and the unique and daunting problems he faced in the Civil War. It also provides a window into federal-state relations, military-civil affairs, the ongoing struggle for the Union in the border states, and the relationship of Lincoln with Unionists, army commanders, and others in those states. An intriguing aspect of the study is the Unionist leadership's views of the Civil War president and his management of affairs in their states. Although Lincoln realized he needed the support of border state leaders in the suppression of the rebellion, he at times found them to be more of an obstacle to success than a loyal opposition in achieving his objectives in the war, especially emancipation.

Historians, in giving their reasons for the border states' adherence to the Union, have often cited their close proximity to the North, their diverse populations, their fears of becoming battlegrounds in the war, and the location in these states of three important industrial and commercial centers (Saint Louis, Missouri; Louisville, Kentucky; and Baltimore, Maryland) that rejected southern sectionalism. In addition, historians have pointed out the border region's relatively weak identification with slavery (only 14 percent of border state families owned slaves) and its traditional loyalty to the Union and to sectional compromise.

These were all logical reasons for the border states to remain in the Union. On the other hand, there were also countervailing tendencies that, particularly at the beginning of the war, could have propelled the border states into the rebellion. These included traditional white ties to southern kin and culture, a profound hostility to the antislavery "Black Republican" Party, and the belief that Lincoln and his government posed a threat to constitutional rights. Although slavery was not as extensive in their states as in the Confederate South, border state whites, consisting of one-third of the southern white population, strongly defended the institution as important economically and as essential to social stability and racial control. Even tiny Delaware, with only 1,798 slaves according to the 1860 U.S. census, rejected Lincoln's antislavery efforts during the war, mainly because of emancipation's foreboding social and racial implications for the state.

Lincoln's western Whig background enabled him to understand the political, constitutional, and racial realities in the border states. He realized the necessity of accommodating the sensitivities of whites in these states regarding federal-state relations, slavery, and constitutional rights, as long as there was no threat of secession and military operations were not hindered. When border state governors at the beginning of the war refused to honor his call for militiamen to suppress "combinations" in the lower South "too powerful to be suppressed by the ordinary course of judicial proceedings," Lincoln declined to challenge their decision. Instead, he permitted the governors to raise militia forces to maintain order at home, and, in the case of Missouri, he allowed Claiborne F. Jackson, the secession-leaning governor, to organize state troops to protect the "sovereignty" of the state. Lincoln, however, later insisted that the militias should serve the Union cause and should be under the command of overall federal commanders. Many of the border state militiamen, particularly those in Kentucky and Missouri, ultimately went south and, along with other border state volunteers, joined the Confederate army. These troops, however, never made up a majority of the soldiers from their states who fought in the war.

Lincoln even acquiesced in Kentucky's declaration of armed neutrality during the early months of the war. Governor Jackson and the Missouri legislature briefly attempted an armed neutrality policy that, however, favored the Confederacy. A Union military force under General Nathaniel Lyon drove Jackson and his militia, under General Sterling Price, into southern Missouri, where they merged with the Confederate army. Maryland also toyed with the idea of neutrality in 1861 but soon abandoned it when faced with federal military intervention. Lincoln viewed neutrality as virtually equivalent to rebellion, but he accepted Kentucky's action as a temporary necessity until he believed the state was safe for the Union. "I think to lose Kentucky is nearly the same as to lose the whole game," Lincoln wrote on September 22, 1861. "Kentucky gone, we can not hold Missouri, nor, as I think, Maryland. These all against us, and the job on our hands is too large for us," he concluded. "We would as well consent to separation at once, including the surrender of the capitol [sic]."[1]

This gloomy assessment came in sharp response to a letter from his Illinois friend Orville H. Browning criticizing Lincoln for countermanding the antislavery provision in an August 30 proclamation by General John C. Frémont. The proclamation had ordered the confiscation of rebel property, including the freeing of slaves, in Missouri and in parts of Kentucky. The Bluegrass State had only recently, after the Confederate occupation of Columbus, Kentucky, abandoned its policy of neutrality and officially joined in the war on the Union side. It did so on the condition that the federal government leave slavery alone. As Lincoln informed Browning, the news of Frémont's proclamation had reversed loyal sentiment in the Kentucky legislature and caused Union army recruits in the state to throw down their arms and disband. Under the circumstances, the president told his friend, as well as others, that he had no choice but to countermand Frémont's emancipation decree.

Abolitionists and antislavery elements in Lincoln's party did not view his repudiation of Frémont's proclamation in a similar light. They denounced the president's border state policy and his appeasement of slavery, not only in Kentucky but also in the other border slave states. Antislavery zealots and supporters of a hard war against the rebels attacked the president for his acquiescence in Kentucky's neutrality and his refusal to "throttle" secessionist sympathizers in the border states. The silver-tongued orator Wendell Phillips of Massachusetts became Lincoln's harshest critic. In a speech at Tremont Temple, Boston, in January 1862, Phillips announced that the nation was burdened by a "President who could not open his eyes any wider than to take in Kentucky."[2] Black spokesman Frederick Douglass concluded that Lincoln's coddling of the border states to keep them in the Union was a criminal waste of time. Douglass naively claimed that if Lincoln acted against the slave institution in Kentucky, slavery and the rebellion would come tumbling down in the South.[3]

James Russell Lowell, literary lion, editor, and commentator on public affairs, in 1861 criticized Lincoln's "Little Bo Peep policy" toward the border states and cried out to a friend after the president revoked Frémont's antislavery proclamation, "How many times we are to save Kentucky and lose our self-respect?" But by the end of the year Lowell agreed with Lincoln that the border states must first be saved before the war could become a crusade against slavery.[4] Few radical leaders in Lincoln's Republican Party, however, ever acknowledged the wisdom of his border state strategy. The president's misguided policy, Senator Benjamin F. Wade sneered, "could come only of one born of 'poor white trash' and educated in a slave State" (which Lincoln was not).[5]

Despite what his antislavery critics and some historians have claimed, Lincoln firmly believed in the immorality of slavery, a view that he had notably expressed in a speech at Peoria, Illinois, on October 16, 1854, and repeated on other occasions. Despite his moral abhorrence of slavery, Lincoln believed that the institution should be confronted and ultimately eradicated within the political and constitutional framework established by the Founders. As president, in addition to recognizing the political necessity of retaining the support of border state whites and northern conservatives, he had trouble in finding the constitutional authority to take steps against slavery. In his first inaugural address, on March 4, 1861, he promised not to interfere with the institution in the southern states. But once the war began, Lincoln sought a way to act against it.

Lincoln first proposed a compensated emancipation plan for the border states that would require state approval and would be funded by Congress. This strategy, the president reasoned, would not violate these states' authority over slavery and, by extension, over freed blacks. Later, when he issued his Emancipation Proclamation, Lincoln argued that, as commander in chief, he had the constitutional duty to suppress the rebellion in the South. He explained that freeing the slaves in the rebel states had become a military necessity in order to win the war and preserve the Union. That does not mean that Lincoln's antislavery policy was solely tactical and without an important moral dimension to it. Not only did Lincoln view slavery as an evil, but he also saw it as a danger to republican institutions. In closing the Emancipation Proclamation, the president also expressed the belief that his decision was "an act of justice" in which he invoked "the considerate judgment of mankind and the gracious favor of Almighty God."[6]

The president introduced his compensated emancipation plan for the border states in December 1861 as a trial balloon for Delaware's consideration and then in March 1862 for all the border states. The proposal, as described in chapter 5, became the focus of much of his antislavery efforts in 1862. Lincoln insisted that the plan could achieve two important objectives: it could abolish slavery in these Union states and produce an early end to the war. The approval of his plan, Lincoln contended, would deprive the rebels of the expectation that the border states would join them in the war, thereby dashing their hopes for independence and causing them to cease their rebellion.

Lincoln's proposal would permit and even urge the cooperating states to develop a timetable for gradual emancipation. This reflected his long-held position (as well as that of his idol Henry Clay) that gradual emancipation was preferable to immediate abolition because, Lincoln announced, it would "greatly mitigate [southern] dissatisfaction" over the loss of slavery. Furthermore, he said, "The time spares both races from the evils of sudden derangement."[7] Lincoln expected the border states and Congress to work out the details of the compensation plan. During the period of transition from slavery to freedom, the president indicated, an apprenticeship system for young blacks would be acceptable. Despite Lincoln's repeated appeals for the approval of his compensation proposal, all the border states, including Delaware, rejected the plan.

After he issued the Emancipation Proclamation on January 1, 1863, which applied only to the rebel states, Lincoln urged the border states to end slavery, with or without compensation. Earlier he had dangled the prospect of voluntary black colonization outside the country before these states partly in order to gain support for emancipation, but probably also to lessen northern conservative and Democratic opposition to the proclamation. The colonization scheme, which actually was disastrously attempted on an island off Haiti, was an unrealistic and unworthy effort that Lincoln, in principle, had favored before the war.

Due to a considerable extent to Lincoln's prodding, Maryland in October 1864 became the first border state to abolish slavery, followed by Missouri in January 1865. (In 1863 West Virginia, as a congressional requirement for statehood, had abolished slavery in its constitution.) Both Kentucky and Delaware refused to change their constitutions or repeal their laws protecting slavery, and they also declined to ratify the Thirteenth Amendment to the U.S. Constitution. Freedom for the last slaves in Kentucky and Delaware did not occur until several months after the war, when the Thirteenth Amendment became a part of the Constitution.

Few problems during the Civil War created more anguish for Lincoln than the factionalism among Unionists in the border states and the often-related conflict between military commanders and civil officials. He lamented that he was "tormented . . . beyond endurance" by the factionalism. The president believed that the "pestilent factional quarrel," as he characterized these disputes, threatened the course of emancipation, weakened support for the Union and for civil government, and thwarted the suppression of guerrillas and other lawless elements in the border states.[8] The renewal of old party antagonisms between Whigs and southern rights Democrats and the heightened tensions of war contributed greatly to the divisions in these states. In Missouri, radical Unionists, sometimes referred to as "Charcoals" (they preferred "Unconditional Unionists"), gained control of the state government late in the war and enacted proscriptive legislation against rebels and their sympathizers. Because Lincoln was insufficiently radical for them and supported conservative Unionists, they attempted unsuccessfully in 1864 to prevent his renomination by the National Union (Republican) Party.

At the other end of the political spectrum, Kentucky conservatives, whose reasons for opposing Lincoln were different from the radicals', sought a coalition with national Democrats in the 1864 election on a platform supporting the suppression of the rebellion but leaving all other issues, including slavery, to the states. The Democrats, however, controlled by the party's peace wing or "Copperheads," adopted a war-failure platform and called for a cease-fire preparatory to negotiations with the Confederates. Bitterly opposed to Lincoln and the Republicans, most Kentucky conservatives swallowed their disappointment and voted for the Democratic candidate, General George B. McClellan, who had promised to restore the Union despite the party's platform. The general easily captured Kentucky's electoral vote; he also won Delaware but lost Missouri and Maryland to Lincoln.

Governors Hamilton R. Gamble of Missouri, Augustus W. Bradford of Maryland, and Thomas E. Bramlette of Kentucky repeatedly reminded Lincoln that their states were loyal and that therefore the federal government should treat them the same as the northern states. They, along with border state senators and representatives in Congress, demanded that their state laws and the constitutional rights of their citizens should be respected by the military and federal government. Their governors and congressmen often protested against arbitrary arrests and imprisonments without due process of law.

Lincoln on occasion directly acted to curtail civil liberties in the border states. Shaken by the virtual siege of Washington after Fort Sumter and by rioting in Baltimore on April 19, 1861, the new president suspended the writ of habeas corpus in Maryland and gave General in Chief Winfield Scott carte blanche to impose martial law in the state. He later approved the military arrests of suspected secessionist legislators and Baltimore officials. In 1864, prior to the August state elections in Kentucky, Lincoln suspended the writ of habeas corpus in the Bluegrass State. Nonetheless, he frequently attempted to satisfy border state officials when they brought violations of civil liberties to his attention, particularly in cases where commanders had violated state election laws and exceeded their authority in suppressing loyal political dissent. Lincoln, however, always reserved to army commanders the right to intervene in order to combat "traitors," guerrillas, and those obstructing military operations.

Historians have concluded that by December 1861 the border states were secure for the Union.[9] However, Confederate military campaigns in those states in 1862–1864 and the insecurities caused by guerrilla activities in

Missouri and to a lesser extent in Kentucky kept the border region in turmoil. Political and social conditions remained volatile, and in the Bluegrass State, the Union cause continued to be at great risk. The Union success in the border states during the first months of the war, although tenuous, did establish a foundation for the growth of loyalty and for the suppression of the rebellion. Nonetheless, Lincoln's patient and judicious management of border state affairs, though not free from error (for example, his vacillation in removing controversial military commanders), proved crucial in keeping the border states in the Union, gaining their support for the war effort, and ultimately securing the end of slavery. The failure of Lincoln's border state policies would have ensured the independence of the southern slave republic, dealt a serious blow to the Republican Party in the North, and greatly complicated emancipation, even to the extent of postponing indefinitely the death of slavery. It also would have forever tarnished Lincoln's reputation and his presidency.

The late William E. Gienapp has written that Civil War historians lost interest in the border states after these states supposedly "unequivocally cast their lot with the Union" in 1861. Historians, Gienapp wrote, "have concentrated on the opening months of the struggle, from the call for troops to Lincoln's first annual message in December, and except for his efforts to get them to adopt a program of gradual emancipation have given only limited attention to Lincoln's policies concerning the border states during the remainder of the war."[10] Professor Gienapp's premature death prevented him from writing the history of Lincoln and the border states during the Civil War.

In this book, I attempt to fulfill the long-standing need for such a study. I have benefited not only from primary sources but also from state and local accounts on the Civil War and related works (for example, on emancipation). Biographies have also proved useful. These works are cited in the endnotes. My book begins with an account of the region's early influence on Lincoln and describes the role of the border states' political leadership in the presidential election of 1860. It explores the often-troubled relationship of Lincoln and the Unionists of Maryland, Kentucky, and Missouri in their efforts to maintain state authority while sustaining the Union in the secession crisis and during the war. Political attitudes and divisions, conflict over emancipation and black troops, control of state military forces, civil liberties in the border states, and military interference in state and local affairs, including elections, are described. Lincoln's relations with the border state governors and regional military commanders and his handling of the serious factionalism among Unionists are interwoven in the account.

Because of Delaware's small size and its relative unimportance in the war, I do not devote separate chapters to the state. Where appropriate, I integrate its story into the narrative. Delaware's material and other interests lay to the north, and it declared for the Union early in the war. However, Delawareans in the beginning were divided over the state's participation in the conflict, and the majority remained hostile to Lincoln and the Republicans. Most Delawareans felt a kinship with southerners, due to a great extent to the presence of slavery in the state and to their opposition to abolitionists who, they believed, were intent upon establishing racial equality in the South. In 1860 they gave their electoral votes to John C. Breckinridge, the Southern Rights Democratic candidate for president (Lincoln received 3,815 popular votes out of 16,039 cast in Delaware). Conceivably, Delaware could have gone with Maryland had that state joined the Confederacy. The editor of the *Wilmington Journal and Statesman* fairly accurately described the state's situation when he wrote, soon after Lincoln's election, "We of Delaware live in the South. It is a Slave State; and yet there is no man within her boundaries who dares utter seriously the word *secession*. We are all for the Union."[11] That editor, however, probably exaggerated the unanimity of Union sentiment in the state. During the war Delaware's Democratic senators in Congress, though Unionists, proved a constant thorn in Lincoln's side on issues relating to the purpose of the war, constitutional rights, and slavery.

West Virginia, although it became a border state during the war, is not included in this study. Granted statehood in 1863 after seceding from Virginia, the state had an unusual history. In the beginning of the war, Unionists in western Virginia, backed by the federal army, secured the president and Congress's endorsement for the creation of a loyal government for the state of Virginia. Called the Restored Government of Virginia, it gave permission for the formation of a separate state to be known as West Virginia. The new state consisted mainly of the mountain and Ohio Valley counties of the Old Dominion. West Virginia lacked the importance of Kentucky, Missouri, and Maryland in the Civil War, though, like these border states, it remained divided over Lincoln's antislavery policies and the enlistment of black troops in the Union army.[12] In Congress, the rump Virginia and the West Virginia senators and representatives usually voted with the border state members while dependent on Lincoln to sustain their governments.

The role of border state members of Congress in opposing Lincoln and the Republicans is one of the important themes of the book. Historians have usually referred to these senators and representatives as Democrats, a designation that many of them as former Whigs would have resented. Regardless of past political affiliations, the border state members, often in spirited exchanges with Republican colleagues and even with President Lincoln, usually reflected the public sentiment and concerns at home and also those of conservative northerners.

CHAPTER I

■

The Border States and
Lincoln's Election

Abraham Lincoln was a product of the border country between the North and the South, first as a small child in middle Kentucky, then during his youth and early adulthood in southern Indiana and central Illinois. He lived in communities populated overwhelmingly by settlers from the upper South and the border slave states. As a young man in New Salem, Illinois, Lincoln aligned with the Whig Party of Kentuckian Henry Clay and read the conservative *Louisville Daily Journal*, the Whig newspaper organ of the region. The *Journal*, edited by George D. Prentice, wielded considerable influence in Kentucky and adjacent states, and it would continue to do so into the Civil War.

Most of Lincoln's associates in his rise to prominence were Whigs and natives of the border states, especially Kentucky. These included his three law partners, John Todd Stuart, Stephen T. Logan, and William H. Herndon, and Circuit Judge David Davis, Orville H. Browning, and Richard Yates. They also included Mary Todd Lincoln's family in Springfield and Lexington, and Joshua Speed, Lincoln's closest friend, who lived most of his life on his large family farm near Louisville and only resided in Springfield for a few years. Lincoln spoke in the Kentucky vernacular, and his legendary sense of humor reflected a rural idiom that flourished during the early nineteenth century throughout the Mississippi-Ohio Valley. His father, Thomas, handed down to his son an appreciation for the backcountry humor of the region.

As a Whig in Illinois, where his party was usually in the minority, Lincoln's political instincts inclined him toward a conservative position on issues, including slavery. Nonetheless, he was influenced in his political views by the influx of antislavery Whigs in the northern part of the state and also by his opposition to Democratic senator Stephen A. Douglas's popular sovereignty provision in the Kansas-Nebraska bill. The bill, enacted in 1854, opened the door for slavery's expansion into the territories, particularly the Kansas Territory, where proslavery Missourians sought to control the voters' decision on slavery. Lincoln emerged as the leader of an antislavery coalition in Illinois that opposed the expansion of slavery, but, as a constitutional and political necessity, he recognized the institution in the states where it existed. By 1856 the Lincoln-led coalition had become the state Republican Party. Lincoln had cleverly advanced a conservative antislavery political strategy that he calculated could win the critical central counties of Illinois, even though border state and other southern transplants dominated local politics in those counties. These counties had traditionally favored the Democratic Party of Senator Douglas.

A conservative approach to ending slavery, Lincoln believed, would also appeal to diverse political elements throughout the state, such as nativist Whigs, dubbed "Know Nothings" because of their refusal to divulge the contents of their secret meetings. Paradoxically, the Know Nothings, while calling for restrictions on immigrant naturalization and voting, tended to oppose slavery, partly because their Democratic adversaries defended it. Despite his dislike of nativism, Lincoln avoided public attacks on the Know Nothings, many of whom had formerly associated with him in the Whig Party and were strong in the border states.

During the 1850s, Lincoln proclaimed the immorality of slavery, while opposing its expansion. His position sharply contrasted with Douglas's popular sovereignty doctrine and "care not" attitude toward slavery, which, Lincoln repeatedly charged, would perpetuate the institution. Lincoln insisted that his approach would place slavery en route to "ultimate extinction," a course that he argued had been sanctioned by the Founding Fathers. True to his conservative instincts and his Kentucky and southern Indiana origins, Lincoln rejected any federal action against slavery in the South. Indeed, he went so far as to support the federal Fugitive Slave Act of 1850, a law that the radical antislavery advocates vehemently opposed. Unlike many radicals and immediate abolitionists, Lincoln also refused to label slaveholders as evil people, and he denied that he had any "prejudice against the Southern people." "They are just what we would be in their situation," he declared at Peoria in October 1854. "If slavery did not now exist amongst them, they would not introduce it. If it did now exist amongst us, we should not instantly give it up."[1]

Lincoln hoped that the inhabitants of border states, particularly old Whigs like the prominent Kentucky senator John J. Crittenden, would understand his position on slavery and would reject the inflammatory anti-Republican rhetoric of the Democrats and ultraconservatives in both the North and the South. But this did not happen. Like other southerners, border state political leaders saw little difference between Lincoln's antislavery position and that of radicals like William H. Seward of New York and Salmon P. Chase. Lincoln's House Divided speech, which launched his 1858 senatorial campaign against Douglas, contributed mightily—and mistakenly—to the border state belief that he was a radical who favored direct northern action against slavery in the South. Crittenden, Henry Clay's heir as a Whig leader, encouraged his Illinois friends to support his old Democratic enemy in the election; he viewed Douglas as less threatening to sectional peace. After losing the election, Lincoln wrote Crittenden expressing his mortification that the use of Crittenden's name against him among old Whigs had contributed to his defeat.[2]

Border state leaders played an even more active role against Lincoln and the Republicans in the presidential campaign of 1860. Most border state Democrats, who opposed Douglas's candidacy because of his refusal to endorse slavery's rights in the territories, threw their support behind Southern Rights Democratic nominee John C. Breckinridge of Kentucky. Douglas, however, retained the loyalty of Missouri Democrats. Border region Whigs, including Senator Crittenden, fearful of the sectional consequences of a Republican triumph and unwilling to support either Democratic candidate, provided the leadership for the formation of the Constitutional Union Party. They nominated Senator John Bell of Tennessee for president on a platform that ignored the slavery issue and appealed to voters on the sole issues of support for the Constitution and the Union. They hoped to win enough conservative upper South, border state, and lower North electoral votes to throw the presidential election into the House of Representatives. There, each state had one vote, and Bell's chances for election, they believed, would be good.

But the Republicans, meeting in Chicago, dealt a serious blow to the Constitutional Unionists' strategy. Republicans rejected the reputedly radical Seward and nominated Lincoln on a conservative, albeit antislavery, platform designed to win the key states of the lower North. Lincoln could have written the platform, whose key plank was that there should be no expansion of slavery. The *Louisville Daily Courier*, the most influential southern rights newspaper in Kentucky, wasted no time in denouncing Lincoln and predicting that the election of the "Black Republican" candidate would result in a breakup of the Union and civil war. In a long editorial on May 26, the *Courier* announced, "The mind shrinks" from contemplation "of the triumph of the party of which Mr. Lincoln is the representative and leader." The editor argued, "Lincoln's doctrines are the most subtle and dangerous form of anti-slaveryism," even though Lincoln did not advance the whole cloth of abolitionism. Lincoln, the *Courier* editor told Kentuckians, had supported Senator Seward's radical pronouncement of an "irrepressible conflict" between the North and the South. Furthermore, the editor reminded his readers that Lincoln had preached the pure and alarming doctrine that "slavery is an evil." He professed to know of no winnable arguments with which to oppose Lincoln and the Republicans "except to strike at the very foundation of the whole superstructure of fraud and delusion [that] anti-slaveryism has erected." The editor, along with other border state Democrats, rejected the controversial Douglas as the man to lead an Armageddon campaign against Lincoln and the "Black Republicans." "To nominate Douglas," he contended, "is at once and in advance to give up the fight" to defeat the Republicans.[3]

The *Courier* editor and southern rights activists insisted that Breckinridge was the only candidate who could win enough electoral votes to throw the election into the House of Representatives, where a victory over Lincoln was possible. With some exceptions, southern rights advocates in the border states denied that they supported secession if the "Black Republican" (Lincoln) won the election. Even Breckinridge rejected the charge that he was a disunionist. In a long speech at Ashland, Kentucky, he repeatedly affirmed his devotion to the Union, but with the usual qualifications that northerners should faithfully uphold the constitutional rights of southerners regarding slavery and check the abolitionist assault on the institution.

The *Louisville Daily Journal*, whose principal editor was still George D. Prentice, gave its readers a less ominous view of Lincoln's nomination than did the *Courier*. Nonetheless, it predicted that the Illinois Republican's election would seriously divide the nation and lead to terrible consequences. "We have a favorable opinion of the personal and even the political integrity of Abraham Lincoln," the *Journal* declared. "But he is, as the whole nation knows, a sectional candidate and only a sectional candidate." The editor reminded its readers of Lincoln's House Divided speech of 1858, and he repeated the misleading claim that it expressed the same "irrepressible conflict" and "higher law" doctrines put forth by Senator Seward. "There is reason to believe that Mr. Lincoln still entertains the views to which he gave such vehement utterance in 1858, and that they have probably been strengthened and rendered even more violent since by the wild and powerful and raging partisan influences by which he is now continually surrounded." The *Journal* called upon "the conservative men of the North . . . to ponder deeply" the disastrous implications of Republican control of the government and to "use every honorable means and patriotic exertion to prevent the election of Abraham Lincoln to the Presidency of the United States."[4]

Prentice, Crittenden, and other Kentucky conservatives believed that the key to preventing a Lincoln victory lay in neighboring Indiana. They focused their attention on securing an anti-Republican fusion in the state. At the same time, they had some hopes for a similar movement in Lincoln's home state of Illinois, where Douglas Democrats and Know Nothing Whigs, if combined, could conceivably, though not probably, defeat the Republicans. (Indiana actually had more electoral votes in 1860 than Illinois.) The fusionist success in Indiana depended on gaining the support of the former Whigs in the Know Nothing movement who had cast their ballots for Millard Fillmore, the American Party candidate, in 1856. The Fillmore vote had cost the Republicans the presidential election in the swing states of Indiana, Illinois, and Pennsylvania. Lincoln also recognized that a major threat to his success in 1860 was the border-state-backed effort to arrange an anti-Republican fusion strategy in Pennsylvania as well as in Indiana; Lincoln believed his home state was safe for the Republicans. The October gubernatorial elections in Indiana and, to a lesser extent, Pennsylvania, as Lincoln and others correctly assumed, would foretell the winner of the presidential contest in November.

During the campaign, Crittenden and Kentucky conservatives bombarded Indiana with speeches, printed addresses, and editorials arguing for anti-Republican fusion tickets in both the gubernatorial and presidential elections. Speaking at Louisville on August 2 and echoing the views of Prentice's *Louisville Daily Journal*, Crittenden told his friends across the Ohio River, "Mr. Lincoln may be a very worthy, upright and honest man," but if elected president, "he must be governed by the political influence and voice of his party. Mr. Lincoln is at the head of the great anti-slavery party, a purely sectional party, which, according to all its antecedents, threatens the existence of slavery everywhere." His election, Crittenden warned, "would be, therefore, a great calamity to the country, though he never should do an act positively offensive or injurious to any interest of the country."[5]

To counter the fusionist threat in Indiana, Lincoln dispatched his secretary, John G. Nicolay, to meet secretly with Richard W. Thompson, the leader of the state's Know Nothing Party, and seek his support against the movement. Thompson, an old Whig, had served with Lincoln in Congress during the late 1840s, and despite his proslavery leanings, he promised Lincoln that he would oppose fusion with the Douglas Democrats. Thompson told Lincoln that his "primary object was to beat the Democracy by holding off" Know Nothing opposition "in the doubtful northern states."[6] When the Indiana State Constitutional Union convention met in August, consisting mainly of Know Nothings, the delegates heard a rousing speech for fusion by former Know Nothing governor Charles S. Morehead of Kentucky. Like Thompson, Morehead had been a Whig colleague of Lincoln in Congress, but in 1860 Morehead viewed Lincoln as a threat to the Union and to slavery (Morehead owned a plantation in Mississippi). The Constitutional Union delegates, however, followed Thompson's lead and refused to merge their John Bell electoral ticket with Douglas's. Then, five days before the critical October 9 gubernatorial election, Thompson, irritated by the repeated interference of Kentuckians in the campaign, issued a printed circular, *To the Conservative Men of Indiana*, announcing that he would vote not only for Lincoln but also for the Republican candidate for governor, Henry S. Lane.[7] Thompson's support for the Republicans among conservatives, combined with divisions in the Indiana Democratic Party between Douglas and Breckinridge supporters, produced a victory in Indiana for Lane in October and for Lincoln in November.

Border state pressure on Know Nothings and conservative Whigs in Illinois and Pennsylvania was not as great as that in Indiana. Lincoln's presence on the presidential ticket deflated much of the opposition to the antislavery Republicans among conservative elements in his home state.

John J. Crittenden, U.S. senator and representative of Kentucky. Political heir of Henry Clay and conservative Union leader in the border states who unsuccessfully sought a compromise to restore the Union, he opposed Lincoln's antislavery policies. Crittenden's death in 1863 removed an important border state leader in Congress. Courtesy of the Abraham Lincoln Library and Museum of Lincoln Memorial University, Harrogate, Tennessee.

Still, diehard conservatives of border state Whig antecedents formed a National Union Party and nominated John Todd Stuart, Lincoln's political mentor and first law partner, as their candidate for governor in November. However, they rejected fusion with Douglas Democrats, their old political enemies, in the presidential election. Stuart came in third to Republican Richard Yates in the gubernatorial election; Lincoln easily won the state.[8]

In Pennsylvania, political rivalries also prevented a fusion of the Know Nothings with the Democrats, despite the warnings of Kentucky, Maryland, and Virginia conservatives that a sectional crisis and perhaps civil war would follow the election of Lincoln. On the eve of the election, Prentice made a passionate appeal in the *Louisville Daily Journal* for northerners to reject both Lincoln and Breckinridge. He cried out, "Men of the American Union, if you would have your consciences and your names free from the ineffaceable and damning stain of liberticide, defeat the Republican candidate for the Presidency together with his Seceding accomplice [Breckinridge], and bury the two in one common pit of ruin and shame."[9]

Prentice's plea fell on deaf ears, despite a late desperate effort to arrange an anti-Lincoln fusion in New York. The election returns demonstrated clearly that the Constitutional Union–border state strategy to defeat the Republicans had failed. Lincoln swept the northern states except for New Jersey, where he had to share the electoral votes with Douglas. The Constitutional Union Party won only Tennessee, Kentucky, and Virginia. Breckinridge captured two border states, Maryland and Delaware, and also the other slave states except for Missouri, which was carried by Douglas. Lincoln only polled 26,390 votes in the four border states. Missourians cast 17,028 of those, mainly in Saint Louis, where there was a relatively large antislavery German American population. He won 1,364 votes in Kentucky and 2,294 in Maryland. The *Dover Delawarean* reflected the sentiment in the border states, as well as that of many future historians, when it concluded that Lincoln's victory could be attributed to nothing less than the "folly of his enemies" in their failure to fuse in an anti-Republican ticket.[10] Actually, as historian William E. Gienapp pointed out in 1986, even with fusion in the states where it was possible, Lincoln still would have received twenty-seven more electoral votes than needed to win.[11]

Predictably, Lincoln's election triggered a sectional crisis. Disunion sentiment overwhelmed the lower South and traumatized North Carolina, Tennessee, Arkansas, and Virginia. In these upper southern states, secessionists remained in a minority until after the fighting in Charleston Harbor in April and Lincoln's call for troops to suppress the insurrection in the lower South. Caught in the middle of the furor, border state citizens reacted with dismay and uncertainty to Lincoln's election and to the disturbing news from the cotton states. In Kentucky, Garret Davis, a former congressman who in 1861 would play an important role in saving the state for the Union, feared the worst as a result of the Republican triumph. On December 10, he excitedly wrote Senator Crittenden, "Unless there is some satisfactory indication shortly given by the free states that they intend to permit the fugitive slave law to be executed and to cease their assaults upon slavery, Kentucky with an overwhelming majority will range herself with the South."[12]

Border state political leaders and newspaper editors, even those who had supported Breckinridge, somberly warned against hasty action by their states. While condemning the northern crusade against slavery, they favored a "watch and wait" policy toward Lincoln and the Republicans. Crittenden cautioned Kentuckians to remain calm, and border state representatives in Congress attempted to work out a compromise to save the Union when Congress met in December. The *Lexington Kentucky Statesman*, a Democratic newspaper, advised its readers that "the election of Lincoln *per se*, under all the forms of law, ought not to be made the occasion of severing the present relations of the States and disrupting the confederacy." Its editor admitted, "The principles enunciated" in the Republican platform "are directly opposed to the Constitution, are utterly subversive of the equality of the States, are destructive to all the rights of African slavery, and if enforced, must inevitably upturn our whole social system in the South and destroy the present Union." But as long as Lincoln did not "attempt to carry out the avowed [antislavery] purposes of his party," the editor counseled Kentuckians and other southerners to acquiesce in his inauguration as president: "There is hope that Lincoln will not be so insane as to attempt" to implement the principles of the Republican Party. "Wait, wait, wait, and if we fail to preserve the Union with a Constitution intact, then let us have a UNITED SOUTH."[13]

One week later, that Democratic editor argued that Lincoln could do nothing as president without the consent of Republican opponents in Congress: "[The opposition will] have it in their power to stop the machinery of government, to withhold supplies and vacate the public offices. [Lincoln] will be powerless for evil now as when a private citizen of Illinois, if the opposition to him is concentrated and well directed." The *Statesman* editor perceptively remarked, "All this advantage would be lost if the cotton States secede and withdraw their members" from Congress.[14]

In Maryland, the *Baltimore Sun*, the leading Democratic newspaper in the state, announced, "Lincoln is elected, and it becomes us, as law-abiding and Union-loving citizens to submit quietly and await the result," and added hopefully, "our noble ship of State" would be able to sail "safely through the dark and troublous waters of the present. Should the North attempt to subvert our rights it will be ample time to speak of redress, and even then dissolution will be madness."[15] *Baltimore American* editor Charles C. Fulton, a former Whig and Know Nothing who had earlier referred to the Republican candidate as "a third rate district politician," two days after the election reaffirmed what the editor of the *Lexington Kentucky Statesman* and other border states spokesmen were arguing. Fulton reminded his readers that Lincoln, faced with an anti-Republican majority in Congress, would be powerless to subvert the Constitution and the rights of the people. "While we are in the Union, we are Mr. Lincoln's master," he wrote.[16]

The *Frederick Herald* urged western Marylanders to shun secessionist talk and stand for the Union. The editor proclaimed, with typical hyperbole, that "though we have been taunted and insulted, until every nerve of every limb seemed to cry out for shame or further forbearance, . . . though they [Republicans?] have vilified the bond of our association" and instilled "the venom of their slanderous and corrupting treachery into the whole body politic, we say hold on to the Union! They [southerners] are our brothers still by the ties of common memories, a common glory, and common hopes for the future."[17] Maryland senator James A. Pearce, a former Whig, reminded his constituents, "The Union has given us for seventy years . . . a blessing of inestimable value," and said that Marylanders should not throw away that heritage because of Lincoln's election.[18]

Many in the border states urged President-elect Lincoln to reassure southerners of his good intentions. Joined by conservatives and Democrats in the North, they demanded that he break his policy of public silence and issue a strong statement promising southerners that their rights and institutions would be protected by his administration. Lincoln, however, refused to do so.[19] Nathaniel P. Paschall, editor of the *Saint Louis Daily Missouri Republican*, requested a public statement from Lincoln, who on November

16 wrote in response, "I could say nothing which I have not already said, and which is in print and accessible to the public." Lincoln irritably argued that such a public statement "would do positive harm [because] the secessionists, *per se* believing that they had alarmed me, would clamor all the louder." Furthermore, he told Paschall, it would be "persistently garbled, and misrepresented [by] papers, like yours."[20]

Upset by Lincoln's reaction to his request, Paschall, also a former Whig, wrote the president-elect that it would be impossible "to keep Missouri in her conservative stand" for the Union "if something [was] not done to keep down the excitement now pervading the South." Paschall published his letter in the *Saint Louis Daily Missouri Republican*.[21] Lincoln believed that no matter how much the secessionists in the lower South and their sympathizers inflamed the public mind, the border states and the upper South would not leave the Union on the basis of his election alone. The president-elect, at least publicly, played down the secessionist threat, even as South Carolina and the other lower southern states moved to cut their ties with the Union. He had concluded that quiet firmness on his part as well as on that of his party would restore political sanity in the South. Lincoln's failure to issue a soothing public statement to southerners, however, had made the political situation more difficult in the border states. Without repudiating the Republican platform against slavery, Lincoln could have reassured the border states of his good intentions by making such a statement and reduced the uncertainty of retaining them in the Union once the cotton states seceded.

The border state governors, by virtue of their constitutional responsibilities, assumed the lead in their states' official response to the crisis created by Lincoln's election and the secession of the lower South during the winter of 1860–1861. Like the overwhelming majority of southerners, the four governors, Thomas H. Hicks of Maryland, Beriah Magoffin of Kentucky, Claiborne F. Jackson of Missouri, and William Burton of Delaware, had opposed the Republicans and supported the southern position on slavery. All but Burton were slaveholders, and three of them (Jackson, Magoffin, and Burton) had been elected as Democrats. The governors, as well as their constituents, differed on the courses that their states should take as the crisis unfolded. The political party antecedents of the governors, as well as the circumstances that they faced in their states, influenced their actions.

The geographic position of their states vis-à-vis the free states and neighboring southern states (in Maryland's case, Virginia and Pennsylvania, as well as the District of Columbia) also contributed to how the governors handled the sectional tempest.

Of the four governors, Jackson proved the strongest southern rights supporter and the most determined to resist any effort by Lincoln to coerce the seceded states. Magoffin, however, was not far behind him in devotion to the southern cause, but he was not in favor of secession. Jackson was the only border state governor who ultimately cast his lot with the Confederacy. Elected governor of Missouri in August 1860, Jackson had favored Breckinridge for president, though he endorsed Douglas because, he explained, the Illinois senator was the candidate most likely to defeat the "Black Republican" in the fall election.[22] Shunning a fusion with the John Bell supporters in the conservative Constitutional Union Party, Jackson helped Douglas win Missouri, the only state that the "Little Giant" captured outright (he shared the New Jersey electoral votes with Lincoln).

When Jackson assumed office on January 3, 1861, he devoted much of his inaugural address to a denunciation of Lincoln's election, equating it with an abolitionist triumph. Jackson announced that Missouri had "ever been devoted to the Union, and she will remain in it so long as there is any hope that it will maintain the spirit and guarantees of the Constitution." His denial stretched the truth about his own commitment to the Union. The governor assumed that Lincoln would inevitably violate his presidential oath to protect the constitutional rights of Missourians, as Jackson interpreted these rights. Furthermore, he plainly announced that any attempt by Lincoln to coerce the seceded states would justify Missouri's immediate withdrawal from the Union. Meanwhile, Jackson recommended that the legislature call for the election of delegates to a state convention whose purpose would be to determine Missouri's course in the crisis.[23]

Missouri Unionists, however, feared that the convening of a state convention would lead to secession. The convention method, as the Unionists knew, was the constitutional procedure used by the lower South secessionists to take their states out of the Union, and without the ratification of the voters. Jackson's southern rights faction controlled the Missouri state legislature, and it dutifully followed the governor's recommendation by authorizing an election for convention delegates, who were to convene on February 18. At the same time, Jackson moved to activate the militia for the purpose of maintaining order and defending Missouri in case of federal intervention.

CHAPTER ONE

Much to Governor Jackson's disappointment, conservative and stead-fast Unionists handily won the election of delegates to the state convention. When the convention met in late February 1861 in Jefferson City, it adopted a series of resolutions designed to keep Missouri in the Union. The convention resolved that "at present there is no adequate cause to impel Missouri to dissolve her connection with the Federal Union, but on the contrary she will labor for such an adjustment of existing troubles as will secure the peace, as well as the rights and equality of all the States." The delegates urged the calling of a national convention to adopt constitutional amendments for the protection of slavery. One amendment would permit the extension of slavery into the territories, which, the delegates optimistically—and naively—claimed, would "successfully remove the causes of difference forever from the arena of national politics." The convention also passed a strongly worded resolution opposing the use of military force against the seceded states. An attempt by Lincoln to coerce the South, the delegates predicted, would "inevitably plunge this country into civil war, and thereby entirely extinguish all hope of an amicable settlement of the fearful issues now pending before the country." They recommended the withdrawal of federal troops from the southern forts in order to avoid an armed collision that would result in war. Finally, the delegates to the Missouri convention provided for the selection of a thirteen-member committee, chaired by Hamilton R. Gamble, a conservative Whig, with the authority after adjournment on March 22 to call the convention into special session in case "the public exigencies require" it. The committee was also to provide the convention with a report on the existing relations of the state and the federal government when it reassembled in regular session in December.[24]

Beriah Magoffin, a southern rights Democrat like Jackson, had been elected governor of Kentucky in 1859 on a platform advocating slavery in the territories and denouncing the abolitionists. Although a firm supporter of Breckinridge in the presidential election, Magoffin wanted to keep Kentucky in the Union. Ten days after the election, he announced in a letter to the *Frankfort Tri-Weekly Yeoman* that Lincoln's success was not a reason to secede. Like many border state spokesmen who expressed support for the Union, Magoffin pointed out that those opposed to the Republicans would control Congress and the Supreme Court; furthermore, the president would be bound by the Constitution not to commit any overt action against the South.[25] The governor's letter, however, contained an ominous threat. He warned that if Lincoln adopted an aggressive policy against the seceded states, "then Kentucky can and will join her sister Southern States" in secession. Magoffin thought that Kentucky's continuance in the Union also depended on southern unity, including the border states, that would force Lincoln and the Republicans to respect southern rights in the territories and would insist on the return of slaves escaping to the North.

With that in mind, Magoffin on December 9 wrote all the slave state governors and proposed a southern convention. Its purpose, he said, was to save the Union. He outlined a plan that he believed would reverse the secessionist tide in the lower South. Magoffin argued that if most of the slave states agreed with his plan, Lincoln and the Republicans would have no choice but to accept it. The proposal called for the division of the western territories along the thirty-seventh parallel; above the line, the territory would be free; below it, slavery would exist. Magoffin also proposed a constitutional amendment that would invalidate the personal liberty laws of the northern states that had been enacted to prevent the enforcement of the Fugitive Slave Act of 1850. Another amendment would prohibit the federal government from interfering with slavery in the states, though Lincoln had never contested individual states' rights to allow slavery.[26] The territorial concession to slavery constituted a sticking point in the governor's plan. Even if it could derail secession in the lower South—a highly unlikely prospect—Lincoln would not accept any proposal permitting the expansion of slavery. The nonextension of slavery had been the centerpiece of his and the Republican platform in 1860. Furthermore, any plan involving concessions to the South had to come from Congress, not from the southern governors.

The governors immediately rejected Magoffin's call for a southern convention to propose a compromise. Instead, deep South disunionists dispatched "commissioners" to the border states and to the upper South (Virginia, North Carolina, Tennessee, and Arkansas) seeking support for secession. Most of the commissioners were natives of the states they visited. David Clopton of Alabama, while still a member of Congress, appeared in Dover to lobby for Delaware's secession. Clopton told Governor Burton that the "Black Republicans" intended "to circulate insurrectionary documents and disseminate insurrectionary sentiments among [the] hitherto contented servile population." The ultimate objective of Lincoln's party, Clopton claimed, "was the establishment of an equality of races" in the South.[27] Although Burton partly agreed with Clopton's characterization of the Republicans, he refused to recommend secession to the Delaware legislature.

Other southern commissioners repeated Clopton's racialist argument as they sought support in the border states and the upper South. Alabama commissioner Stephen F. Hale, a native of the Bluegrass State, arrived in Frankfort on December 26, 1860, and immediately wrote a long letter to Governor Magoffin in which he covered all the grounds for secession.[28]

Partly influenced by Hale's appeal and disturbed by cascading events, Magoffin on December 27 called for a special session of the Kentucky General Assembly on the crisis. He proposed that the legislature provide for the election of a state convention to consider "the future of Federal and interstate relations of Kentucky." Spokesmen of the John Bell Constitutional Unionists and Stephen A. Douglas Democrats expressed alarm at what they believed was the governor's intention to take Kentucky out of the Union. They met in Louisville on January 8 and formed the Union State Central Committee to oppose immediate secession. Led by conservatives George D. Prentice of the *Louisville Daily Journal,* former congressman Garret Davis, and James Speed, the older brother of Lincoln's close friend Joshua, the Union coalition resolved that although Kentucky had been provoked by the Republicans, it had no cause for secession because of Lincoln's election. At the same time, the Unionists announced their determination to oppose any federal policy by which the country would be "held together with the sword, with laws to be enforced by standing armies; it is not such a Union as our fathers intended, and not worth preserving." They stopped short, however, of threatening secession if Lincoln attempted to use force against the seceded states. Instead, they called for the adoption of a proposed compromise on slavery that Senator Crittenden had introduced in Congress when it met in December (see below).[29]

When the Kentucky legislature assembled on January 17, Governor Magoffin issued a strong warning to President-elect Lincoln and the Republicans that Kentucky "[would] not be an indifferent observer" to any effort to coerce South Carolina and the lower southern states. "The people of Kentucky," he declared, "will never stand by with arms folded while those States are struggling for their constitutional rights and resisting oppression, or being subjugated to an antislavery government." Magoffin denied the charge by the Unionist coalition that his words placed him on the side of the secessionists.[30] Rather, he sought to impress upon Lincoln that unless the Republicans avoided a policy of coercion, events could quickly get out of control and, tragically, Kentucky would be drawn into the vortex of secession.

Even so, the governor's recommendation for a state convention was a red-flag issue for staunch Unionists. These Unionists, as in Missouri, feared that a convention, elected in the heat of the crisis and with the encouragement of the seceded states and the governor, would be controlled by extreme southern rights advocates and would adopt a secession ordinance. Kentucky, the Unionists claimed, would have seceded before Lincoln had an opportunity to demonstrate a conciliatory policy toward the South. Prentice's *Louisville Daily Journal* reported, "The chief secession [newspaper] organs of Kentucky intimate quite clearly, that, if the Legislature fails to call a State Convention for the passage of an Ordinance of Secession, rebellion and civil war in the State shall be the consequence."[31] The *Journal* increased its attacks on the "Southern conspirators" after southern rights Democrat Breckinridge, recently elected to the U.S. Senate by the General Assembly, announced his support for a state convention. The *Journal* charged that Breckinridge, Magoffin, and the other "conspirators [aimed] to precipitate Kentucky into war with our friends along the Ohio river," despite their pretensions of support for the Union.[32]

While the Kentucky General Assembly was meeting on the crisis in early 1861, and before Lincoln's inauguration in March, Unionists held rallies throughout the state. They filled the columns of the state press with appeals for the legislators to vote down Governor Magoffin's request for a state convention. Their statements, however, revealed that support for the Union was not unconditional. Almost all the rallies and newspaper articles demanded that Lincoln and the Republicans disavow their antislavery platform, support a compromise on the territories and on other issues troubling the South, and reject any policy designed to coerce the seceded states.[33] Gradually strong public sentiment in favor of a "watch and wait" policy toward Lincoln developed, strengthening the hand of the Unionists in the legislature. On February 11, the last day of the session, the members of the General Assembly, having heard from their constituents, disapproved the resolution calling for a convention. But the struggle to keep Kentucky in the Union was far from over and would critically divide the state when the war began in April.

CHAPTER ONE

During the secession winter of 1860–1861, no state except Virginia had a greater, more immediate importance for the Union than Maryland. This border state virtually surrounded the national capital and contained America's third-largest city, Baltimore, with a population of 212,418 in 1860. As in Missouri and Kentucky, political divisions in Maryland over the course the state should take in the crisis developed soon after Lincoln's election. The relatively large slaveholding counties of the southeast were a hotbed of southern rights sentiment, with many supporting secession if Lincoln showed the cloven hoof or if neighboring Virginia seceded. Zealous southern rights leaders predicted that the fence-straddlers and lukewarm Unionists like the editors of the *Baltimore Sun* would eventually abandon their "watch and wait" policy toward Lincoln and support secession. Contributing to the tension in the state, particularly in the eastern counties, was the presence in Baltimore of a large free black community. The city's white population, with a troubling number of recent immigrants, had dramatically increased during the 1850s, producing racial and ethnic conflict in the city. Free blacks alone numbered 25,680 of the city's population in 1860; 2,218 blacks were still held in slavery. Baltimore had voted for Breckinridge in 1860 by the slender margin of 1 percent over Bell, the Constitutional Union candidate. At the same time, the state had reelected a Democratic legislature that supported southern rights. No one knew which way Maryland would go if the secession fever afflicting the lower South reached Virginia.

The man that Lincoln and Maryland Unionists depended on to save the state was Thomas H. Hicks, a former Whig. Elected governor in 1857 as a Know Nothing, Hicks had supported Bell for president. A devotee of deceased Whig icon Henry Clay and governor of a state with a slight Democratic majority in 1860, Hicks naturally reacted cautiously to Lincoln's election. Furthermore, the state's strategic and vulnerable position between Virginia and Pennsylvania, as well as its close proximity to Washington, necessitated a careful approach by Hicks to the secession crisis. Although a Unionist and, paradoxically, a supporter of southern rights, Hicks realized that he had to walk a tightrope if he hoped to save Maryland for the Union while also preserving its "sovereign" rights, including those relating to slavery.[34]

After Lincoln's election in November 1860, Governor Hicks assumed that his task as a Unionist would be virtually impossible if he called the Democratic General Assembly into a special session to consider the state's position. Even though many southern rights Democrats might be unwilling to jump into the secessionist frying pan without provocation, the legislature, the governor believed, could still take steps that would spark a confrontation with the Republican administration in Washington and lead to secession. Hicks, ever wary of his old Democratic adversaries in the General Assembly, did not want to take that risk if the legislature met.

Hardly had the votes been counted in the fall election when southern rights supporters demanded that Governor Hicks summon the legislature to Annapolis to consider Maryland's position in the crisis. On November 27 Hicks, as expected, rejected out of hand their demand and announced that though he supported southern rights, a meeting of the General Assembly unfortunately would intensify, rather than defuse, the excitement and divisions in the state. Like other Union leaders in the border states, he argued that Lincoln would be restrained by the Constitution and laws in his policy toward the southern states, including Maryland. Southern grievances against the North, Hicks insisted, could be handled within the Union.[35]

Hicks followed this announcement with an address to the people of Maryland in early January, after South Carolina's secession and while other lower southern states prepared to leave the Union. He reminded the people that Maryland was "a conservative Southern state" and that they should take no part in the effort to pull down the Union. "The whole plan" of those demanding the convening of the General Assembly was "to fully commit this State to secession," Hicks charged. "I firmly believe that a division of this Government would inevitably produce civil war," an eventuality that "the secession leaders in South Carolina, and the fanatical demagogues of the North have alike [predicted]." Nonetheless, Hicks promised, Maryland would stand with her southern neighbors in demanding that northerners purge their laws of the "offensive, unconstitutional statutes" that interfered with the return of fugitive slaves. Slaveholding Marylanders keenly felt the issue of escaping slaves because of their proximity to the free states and the easy access of militant abolitionists to their communities. John Brown's shocking raid at Harpers Ferry, Virginia, in 1859, from a base in Maryland, was fresh in their minds.[36]

If the southern appeals were "in vain," Hicks announced, Maryland "would make . . . common cause with her sister border States in resistance to tyranny." Such a course, "if need be," would be determined "more effectively by the people themselves, in their meetings, than by the Legislature" that had been chosen before the crisis, the governor declared. At the same time, Hicks decried any effort by federal authorities to coerce South Carolina or any other state to remain in the Union.[37]

Governor Hicks flirted with the idea of a central confederacy of border states in case Lincoln and the Republicans violated southern rights and made war on the seceded states. On January 2 he wrote Governor Burton of Delaware suggesting the formation of a central confederacy of border states if the Union was disrupted. Burton replied on January 8 that Delaware had too many commercial ties with the North to leave the Union, though he admitted that the two lower counties sympathized with the South. The third county, New Castle, containing Wilmington, was staunchly Union. When other border states showed little interest in a separate confederacy, Hicks dropped the matter.[38] Meanwhile, in early 1861, the compromise movement in Congress to preserve the Union gained the governor's support, as well as that of other border state leaders. Hicks himself attended the much-heralded but futile Peace Conference in Washington in late February that sought to resolve the controversy over slavery and save the Union.

As occurred in Kentucky, both southern rights and Union supporters in Maryland held large rallies during January and February 1861. Gradually the tide of opinion turned in favor of the Union and in opposition to the assembling of the legislature. No one was more important in influencing opinion for the Union than Reverdy Johnson, a longtime conservative Whig leader, former U.S. attorney general, and former senator who had voted for Douglas in 1860 as the only candidate likely to defeat Lincoln. In meetings in Baltimore and elsewhere, Johnson backed Governor Hicks's decision not to call the legislature into special session. On January 10 Johnson, who was almost blind, addressed a huge rally in Baltimore and outlined the case for a conservative Union policy for Maryland. Though he proclaimed his support for southern rights on slavery and condemned the "heresies of political abolitionism," Johnson argued that Maryland's Union tradition and its political and economic interests dictated that the state shun the excitement afflicting the lower South. He reminded Marylanders that the state had played a leading role in the establishment of the republic and should not now desert it. Like Hicks, Senator James A. Pearce, and other Unionists, Johnson argued that Lincoln as president would be impotent to do harm. He also urged the border states to get together and propose constitutional amendments safeguarding slavery. However, unlike other border state spokesmen, he insisted that Fort Sumter in Charleston Harbor, which had become a flashpoint in the crisis, "must at all hazards be defended, [and] the power of the National Standard preserved."[39]

Far away in Springfield, Illinois, Lincoln remained determined to pursue a policy of "masterly inactivity in both word and deed" until he became president on March 4, in the words of George Ashmun of Massachusetts who had chaired the Republican convention that nominated Lincoln. But privately, Lincoln stated his opposition to secession and declared that the government possessed "both the authority and the power to maintain its own integrity."[40] The president-elect wrote Worthington G. Snethen, a rare Baltimore Republican, on December 17 and expressed his views. Although the letter has not been found, its substance is suggested in Snethen's reply on December 21. Apparently taking his cue from Lincoln, Snethen told Lincoln that "the real object of the politicians of the States . . . in forming this excitement, and pretending to go with that nest of tories [secessionists]," was "to try the nerves of the Republican party and this President whom they have elected." He informed Lincoln, "The poison of rebellion has seized upon many of our merchants and lawyers" in Maryland. Snethen, however, predicated that Governor Hicks would not "yield to the pressure upon him [and] call the legislature together" for the purpose of arraying Maryland with South Carolina and other states that plotted to leave the Union.[41]

Two important Republican visitors in the state did not share Snethen's confidence in Governor Hicks's ability to resist the secessionists. Joseph Medill, editor of the *Chicago Tribune* and a political associate of the president, confidentially reported to Lincoln on December 26, 1860, that in Baltimore "loyal sentiment [was] gradually giving way, and the vicious rabble [were] getting control." He continued, "If things go on thus for the next 60 days as they have for the last 30, the city will be under the complete control of Disunion vigilance committees and a reign of terror will domineer over that city." Medill told Lincoln that when Baltimore was "stormed by the enemy and in their hands, Maryland [would] go the same way [since] the city rules the state." He wrote, "It is the intention of the dis-unionists . . . to 'clean out' the Republicans" in Washington and to "take possession of the capitol and proclaim the Southern Confederacy."

CHAPTER ONE

"At all events," he continued, "they will call a southern convention" in Washington "to 'reconstruct' the Constitution, as they term it."[42]

On January 15, 1861, Alexander K. McClure of Pennsylvania reported to the president-elect, "The pressure upon Hicks is fearful; & if he should be compelled to yield," which McClure suggested that he would, "you could never get to Washington except within a circle of bayonets."[43] Not until Lincoln arrived in Pennsylvania on February 21 en route to his inauguration did he seem to realize the seriousness of the situation in Baltimore and eastern Maryland. This awareness would influence his reaction to events in the Old Line State and particularly in Baltimore during the first critical months of the war.

Although he refused as president-elect to issue an address on the crisis, Lincoln sought to reduce southern, including border state, opposition by appointing southerners to his cabinet. He first approached Edward Bates, a conservative Republican of Saint Louis, and offered him the office of either secretary of state or attorney general; the position, he said, would depend upon Seward's acceptance of the secretary of state office. Bates agreed, and Lincoln later appointed him attorney general. Lincoln also wanted another southerner in his cabinet. When James Guthrie of Kentucky, a former secretary of the treasury in Franklin Pierce's Democratic administration, showed no interest in joining the new administration, Lincoln asked John A. Gilmer, an old-line Whig congressman and large slaveholder of North Carolina, to visit him in Springfield with the understanding that a cabinet position would be offered. Gilmer, probably fearing severe repercussions at home if he accepted an appointment from a Black Republican, turned down the invitation. Lincoln then selected Montgomery Blair, the scion of a prominent Maryland political family and a founder of the Republican Party, as postmaster general. He admitted, however, that the appointment of Blair did not really satisfy the need for a true southerner in the administration.[44] The Bates and Blair appointments might have helped somewhat to assuage border state concerns, but they did little to reduce apprehension regarding Lincoln's future policies or that of his party toward the seceded states and slavery.

When Congress met in December 1860, border state senators and representatives took the lead in an effort to find a compromise that, they hoped, would reverse the secession momentum in the South. The House of Representatives immediately set up a committee of thirty-three—one member from each state, including the lower South states—to recommend a solution to the crisis. Two weeks later, the Senate formed a similar committee of thirteen members. Lazarus W. Powell, a Kentucky southern rights Democrat, chaired the Senate "Union Saving Committee," as Seward, a committee member, facetiously dubbed it. However, border state and southern Unionists, as well as northern Democrats like Douglas, who was also on the committee, looked to Crittenden, Powell's seventy-four-year-old colleague, for a compromise plan that Congress would approve. Since the new Republican administration would need to endorse the plan for it to succeed, the committee adopted a rule, offered by Senator Jefferson Davis of Mississippi, that only by a dual majority of the five Republicans and of the other eight members could a proposal receive the committee's approval. This meant that Lincoln, if he chose to do so, could have an important influence on the votes of the Republican members of the committee and thus on the fate of any compromise plan. It was soon clear that the president-elect intended to play that role.[45]

From the beginning of the congressional session, Lincoln worried that the forces of compromise, backed by lame-duck president James Buchanan, would prevail in Congress on the critical issue of slavery's expansion. The Republicans had won the election on a platform opposing the extension of slavery in the territories, and that position, Lincoln insisted, should not be surrendered. On December 10, 1860, he wrote Senator Lyman Trumbull, "Let there be no compromise on the question of *extending* slavery." If slavery was permitted to expand, he continued, "all our labor is lost, and, ere long, must be done again." "Stand firm," he admonished the Republicans in Congress. "The tug has to come, & better now, than any time hereafter."[46]

The president-elect's refusal to compromise on the territorial issue greatly distressed Crittenden and other border state members of Congress, who desperately sought to prevent the disruption of the Union. Nonetheless, the Kentucky senator as a member of the Union Saving Committee proposed a border state plan that would restore the Missouri Compromise line, thereby providing for the protection of slavery below 36 degrees, 30 minutes north latitude in the West. The Crittenden Compromise, as it became known, also proposed a constitutional amendment prohibiting any federal interference with slavery in those states where it already existed and a congressional resolution calling on the northern states to repeal their per-

CHAPTER ONE

sonal liberty laws. The part of the proposal permitting the expansion of slavery into the territories doomed the compromise package. Taking their cue from Lincoln, Republican members of the Senate committee rejected Crittenden's plan.[47]

The venerable Kentucky senator, however, did not give up the fight for the compromise. Encouraged by concerned northeastern merchants and other conservatives, Crittenden in January, as the lower southern states moved toward secession, introduced his proposals on the Senate floor as a personal bill.[48] Upper South and border state Unionists pleaded with Lincoln to throw his weight behind the compromise. Samuel T. Glover, a Missouri friend, grimly wrote Lincoln, "Much of the Union feeling in Mo is deceptive." "Disunionists put on the 'livery of Union' everywhere," he wrote, but unless the Crittenden Compromise was approved, he feared that the state under Governor Jackson's leadership would leave the Union. Others in the upper and border South during the winter of 1860–1861 foretold a similar gloomy outcome if the compromise were to fail.[49]

These Unionists exaggerated the political situation in their states, partly to frighten Lincoln and the Republicans in Congress to support the Crittenden Compromise. Approval of the compromise was not essential to keeping the border states in the Union, or even to maintaining upper South loyalty. If Lincoln refrained from a policy of aggression against the lower South and gave assurances regarding slavery, these southern states, though traumatized and divided by events, would not abandon the Union. Lincoln, however, believed that if the suppression of the secessionists in the lower South became necessary to preserve the Union, the border states would rally to his call for troops. On December 24, 1860, an anonymous article in the *Springfield Illinois State Journal*, probably written by the president-elect, predicted that if armed forces were needed to put down the secessionists, "the border Slave States, whose tranquility and interests [were] more imperiled than those of any part of the country, [were] just as likely to furnish [troops] as any other part of the Union."[50] Lincoln was overly sanguine.

Despite the president-elect's opposition to any compromise of the Republican platform that had produced victory in the fall, some concerned members of the party in early 1861 wavered on the territorial issue, including Senator Seward, who was also secretary of state–designate. When Crittenden's bill reached the Senate floor, Lincoln again admonished his friends in Congress to hold firm against any proposal that would permit slavery to expand.[51] Although the Republicans in Congress also defeated the latest Crittenden effort to arrange a compromise, Lincoln still had to face another challenge to his policy when the so-called Peace Conference assembled in Washington before his inauguration.

The Virginia legislature had issued a call for a convention of all the states to meet in the capital in February and recommend a compromise for congressional approval. The border states quickly endorsed the move and dispatched delegations to the meeting. Several northern legislatures also appointed delegates to the Peace Conference. Privately, Lincoln seethed with anger at the call. He agreed with Orville H. Browning, a close Illinois associate, that "no good results would follow the border State Convention, but evil rather, as increased excitement would follow when it broke up without having accomplished any thing."[52]

Lincoln's prediction that the Peace Conference would fail to resolve the crisis proved correct. The conference's recommendations were similar to the Crittenden Compromise, and, as expected, Congress rejected the plan, except for a proposed constitutional amendment forever prohibiting federal interference with slavery in the states. Lincoln had no serious objection to the amendment, though he concluded that it was redundant because under the Constitution as it stood the federal government had no authority over slavery in the southern states. When the war began, the proposed amendment failed at ratification. Despite Lincoln's fear that the Peace Conference would increase sectional passion, the mere fact that it met helped break the secessionist momentum in the upper South and bolstered Unionists' morale in the border states. It also provided time for the political excitement to weaken and give Lincoln a better chance of gaining border state support after he assumed office.

No compromise proposal or soothing statements by Lincoln would have persuaded the lower southern states to return to the Union. They had cast their lot with secession, and there was no turning back. When Lincoln traveled to Washington in mid-February to take the oath of office on March 4, the real issue had become the military coercion of the seceded states, not compromise. At Indianapolis, on February 11, the president-elect launched a trial balloon on the question. He suggested to an audience that it was not coercion if the federal government "simply [insisted] upon holding its own forts, or retaking those forts which belong to it."[53] Although he quickly said that he had decided nothing in the matter, the remark rekindled secessionist talk in the upper South and the border states, upset northern conservatives, and caused Lincoln concern. The *Louisville Daily Courier* excitedly proclaimed it "a war proposition . . . without a declaration of war, waged under false pretenses, and justifiable only to that fanaticism of which Mr. Lincoln is at once the embodiment and representative." The *Saint Louis Daily Missouri Republican*, a conservative Unionist newspaper, denounced the Indianapolis speech and declared that it heralded the beginning of a civil war—"the North against the South, and the latter to be subjugated at all hazards."[54] Border state Union leaders, however, generally refrained from publicly criticizing Lincoln's coercion remark at Indianapolis in order to avoid unduly inflaming sentiment before the new president had an opportunity to reveal his southern policy.

Twelve days after his Indianapolis speech, Lincoln arrived in Washington, but only after he had secretly slipped through Baltimore and into the national capital to avoid an assassination plot. The southern rights press excoriated him for his furtive trip through Maryland and were joined by newspapers elsewhere. Denying that any violence awaited the president in the city, the *Baltimore Sun* declared, "Had we any respect for Mr. Lincoln . . . the final escapade by which he reached the capital would have utterly demolished it, and overwhelmed us with mortification." The *Sun*, reflecting the sentiments of many in Maryland, contended that the people of the state had "much cause to fear that such a man, and such advisers as he has, may prove capable of infinitely more mischief than folly when invested with power." Even the ardent Unionist *Baltimore American* was embarrassed by the president-elect's secret ride through the city. It expressed the opinion that the Baltimore police had made "ample precautions" to protect Lincoln, though the newspaper admitted that his appearance would have "excited a spirit of stern opposition."[55] Governor Hicks, quick to protect the reputation of his state, publicly expressed his belief that there had been no plot against the president-elect's life. Baltimore mayor George W. Brown, writing years later, also denied that "a formidable conspiracy existed to assassinate" Lincoln. Brown maintained that the incident unnecessarily inflamed the people of Baltimore against the new president and contributed to the later violence against northern troops passing through the city. Furthermore, Brown wrote, "fearful accounts of the conspiracy flew all over the country, creating a hostile feeling against the city, from which it soon afterwards suffered."[56]

The question should be asked, was there a real conspiracy to assassinate Lincoln in Baltimore? Most historians have accepted the account, supposedly by Ward Hill Lamon, that no serious plot existed. In a book later ascribed to him but which he did not write, Lamon, an old friend of the president-elect who had accompanied him through Baltimore, quoted Lincoln as saying, "You . . . know that the way we skulked into this city [Washington] . . . has been a source of shame and regret to me, for it did look so cowardly." A more reliable account, however, was that of Illinois congressman Elihu B. Washburne, who later wrote, "I was the first man to see him after his arrival in Washington, . . . and I know he was neither 'mortified' nor 'chagrined' at the manner in which he reached Washington." Washburne insisted, "There can be no reasonable doubt" of a plot in Baltimore to kill Lincoln.[57] The preponderance of evidence, as compiled and published by Norma B. Cuthbert in 1949, strongly suggests that Lincoln's midnight ride through Maryland did indeed avert an attack on his life.[58]

In the national capital, President-elect Lincoln held several meetings with border state and upper South senators and representatives. On these occasions, border state men, including Governor Hicks of Maryland, impressed upon Lincoln the difficult political situation they faced at home and forcefully warned him against any hostile action against the seceded states. Such action, they insisted, in addition to causing the upper South to leave the Union, would swing public opinion dangerously close to the secessionists in their own states. Furthermore, a coercive policy, they argued, would end any hope of restoring the lower South to the Union. After meeting with Lincoln and other Republicans, Hicks wrote Seward and expressed his concern that they did not understand "the condition of things here, and in the border states." His state, Hicks reported, was on tenterhooks over the crisis, and, as he told Seward, if the legislature met without the governor's constitutional approval, as had occurred in Texas, it might take the state out of the Union. Hicks made it clear to Seward that he was "a union man and supporter of your Administration," but not a Republican. Seward forwarded the letter to Lincoln, who was receiving a quick lesson on the crisis in the border states as well as in Virginia.[59]

In his long-awaited inaugural address on March 4, Lincoln laid down a policy designed, in part, to allay concerns about him in the border states and the upper South but that did not recognize secession. He announced that all rights would be protected in the southern states, including the right of slaveholders to own slaves. He also promised that the Fugitive Slave Act, a bone of contention for border state Unionists as well as other southerners, would be enforced. At the same time, the new president declared that it was his constitutional duty to enforce the laws and protect federal property in the southern states, including military installations. "But beyond what may be necessary for these objects," Lincoln promised, "there will be no invasion—no using of force against, or among the people anywhere."[60] Repeating what he had said on February 11 at Indianapolis, Lincoln maintained that his policy would not constitute "coercion," a definition of the term that most southerners rejected.

The new president concluded his inaugural address with a stirring appeal to the spirit of American patriotism. "In *your* hands, my dissatisfied fellow countrymen, and not in *mine*," he exclaimed, "is the momentous issue of civil war. The government will not assail *you*. You can have no conflict, without being yourselves the aggressors. . . . We are not enemies, but friends. We must not be enemies. Though passion may have strained, it must not break our bonds of affection. The mystic chords of memory, streching [sic] from every battle-field, and patriot grave, to every living heart and hearthstone, all over this broad land, will yet swell the chorus of the Union, when again touched, as surely they will be, by the better angels of our nature."[61]

These patriotic sentiments resonated well with many leading border state Unionists, such as Governor Hicks and Reverdy Johnson of Maryland and Senator Crittenden of Kentucky. Johnson told a friend that Lincoln's inaugural address meant no war.[62] John Pendleton Kennedy, Maryland literary icon, brother of Senator Anthony Kennedy, and a former member of President Fillmore's cabinet, pronounced the speech "conciliatory and firm—promising peace, but breathing a purpose to resist aggression against the Government" and the Union of the Founding Fathers. Kennedy found it encouraging that Lincoln was "beginning to perceive the realities of the case" and was "growing more and more conservative" in his approach to the crisis.[63]

Border state newspapers that were owned and edited by conservative old-line Whigs echoed Kennedy's statement. These included Prentice's *Louisville Daily Journal*, Fulton's *Baltimore American*, and Paschall's *Saint Louis Daily Missouri Republican*. The Republican *Saint Louis Missouri*

Democrat announced, "We can only say this morning" that Lincoln's inaugural address "meets the highest expectations of the country, both in point of statesmanship and patriotism, and that its effect on the public mind cannot be other than salutary in the highest degree."[64] The president's speech, the *Louisville Daily Journal* insisted, meant peace. This newspaper predicted that Lincoln and his cabinet would "not undertake the adoption of any policy calculated to give to the country war." Such a policy would be "an insane enterprise." The administration, the *Journal* sanguinely—and naively—argued, might "continue to hold the forts now in the possession of the government, but this would be neither war nor coercion," and business in the seceded states would continue uninterrupted. The *Journal* pointed out that Congress before adjourning on March 4 had rejected a Republican "Force bill" authorizing the military suppression of the seceded states. The editor probably did not know that Lincoln, working behind the scenes, had helped secure the defeat of the bill.[65]

Fulton's *Baltimore American* joined Prentice's *Louisville Daily Journal* in maintaining that "the tone" of Lincoln's inaugural address was "pacific." "Mr. Lincoln," the *American* declared, "avows his determination to preserve peace, so far as it may be done, in the performance of his duty as he understands it. . . . While he announces his intention to collect the revenue and to possess and defend the forts, he distinctly declares that he will do these things in such a manner as to avoid the necessity for strife." But even Fulton admitted that Lincoln's promise to enforce the laws and hold federal properties in the South created the chilling prospect of a violent confrontation with the seceded states.[66]

Southern rights leaders like former vice president Breckinridge, who would soon briefly replace Crittenden in the Senate (the aging senator did not seek reelection), and Governors Jackson of Missouri and Magoffin of Kentucky predictably saw the mailed fist in the inaugural address. They believed that Lincoln's remarks revealed his intentions to use military force against the seceded states. However, they preferred to let their party press take the lead in publicly criticizing the speech. In Maryland, the *Baltimore Sun*, with readers not only in the state but also along the middle Atlantic seaboard, characterized the speech as "sectional and mischievous" and added, "If it means what it says, it is the knell and the requiem of the Union, and the death of hope" for peace.[67] A Frankfort friend of Crittenden summed up sentiment in Kentucky regarding Lincoln's inaugural address when he wrote the now former senator, "As a matter of course all secessionists denounce it. Our friends to some extent are divided in opinion."[68] For the moment, however, border state conservatives had the upper hand in their states. The real test would come, the *Saint Louis Daily Missouri Republican* predicted, when Lincoln attempted to put his policy into practice, specifically whether the forts could be "held or retaken and revenues collected without bloodshed."[69]

One month later, the test that border state men and women, as well as other Americans, had dreaded became a reality. On April 12 Confederate batteries at Charleston opened fire across the harbor on Fort Sumter after news arrived that Lincoln had dispatched a relief expedition to sustain Major Robert J. Anderson's small garrison. On April 15 Lincoln issued a proclamation calling on the states for 75,000 militiamen to suppress "combinations" in the lower South "too powerful to be suppressed by the ordinary course of judicial proceedings." The quota of troops for federal service for Missouri, Kentucky, and Maryland was four regiments, or more than 3,000 men each, and for Delaware was 2,000. The wording in the reply of Governor John W. Ellis of North Carolina to the request for troops was almost verbatim the same as that of his fellow governors in the upper South. Ellis informed Secretary of War Simon Cameron that he would be "no party to this wicked violation of the laws of the country, and to this war upon the liberties of a free people." He promised, "You can get no troops from North Carolina."[70] North Carolina, Virginia, Tennessee, and Arkansas moved quickly to leave the Union and join the Confederate States of America that had been formed by the lower southern states in February.

A similar response to Lincoln's call for troops came from Governors Jackson and Magoffin. Jackson wired Cameron that Missouri would supply no troops "to make war upon the people of the seceded states." He pronounced the requisition for troops "illegal, unconstitutional, and revolutionary in its objects inhuman and diabolical, and cannot be complied with." He too insisted, "Not one man will the State of Missouri furnish to carry on any such unholy crusade."[71] Governor Magoffin "emphatically" replied that Kentucky would "furnish no troops for the wicked purpose of subduing her sister Southern States."[72] Instead of answering by telegram, Governor Hicks hurriedly met with Lincoln to protest the call for troops and warned him of Maryland's strong opposition to the decision to use force against the seceded states.[73] Even Governor Burton of reliably safe Delaware refused to provide the War Department with the 2,000 requisitioned troops from his state, though he called for the organization of a militia to protect "against violence of any sort." Burton announced, however, that these troops would "have the option of offering their services to the general government for the defense of its capital and the support of the Constitution and the laws of the country."[74] In his special message to Congress on July 4, 1861, Lincoln lamented the fact that only Delaware of the slave states had organized a regiment in response to his call.[75]

John Pendleton Kennedy of Maryland pronounced Lincoln's call for troops a "wicked blunder" because its purpose went far beyond defending the national capital to include a dreadful policy of coercing the southern states back into the Union. After having praised Lincoln's inaugural address for its patriotic and pacific spirit, Kennedy now sorrowfully concluded, "We are driven into extremities by a series of the most extraordinary blunders at Washington, which I think must convince everybody that there is no ability in the Administration to meet the crisis. They have literally forced the Border States out of the Union, and really seem to be utterly unconscious of the follies they have perpetrated."[76] Such were the gloomy pronouncements of many border state men after the fighting in Charleston Harbor and Lincoln's call for troops to suppress the insurrection.

Although border state defiance after Fort Sumter and the administration's requisition for troops boded ill for Lincoln's determination to suppress the rebellion, it would be inaccurate to conclude that no support for the decision existed in the border states. As early as January 10, 1861, Reverdy Johnson had declared that Fort Sumter must be defended "at all hazards" as a symbol of Unionism in the seceded states.[77] German Americans in Saint Louis and a scattering of Republicans elsewhere in the border states agreed and quietly applauded the president's action to hold Fort Sumter and use troops to save the Union. A Presbyterian pastor in Wilmington, Delaware, came out boldly for the coercion of the seceded states after Fort Sumter and exclaimed to his congregation that the conflict should become a holy war against the rebellion.[78]

We know today that the border slave states remained in the Union. But this outcome was far from certain during the months after Fort Sumter and Lincoln's call for troops. Events and developments, both political and military, could have tilted the border country into the Confederacy in 1861; and in these states, particularly Kentucky, the struggle for the Union continued almost until the end of the war. A sizable minority of the people in the border states sided with the South, though many of them were unwilling to show their Confederate allegiance because they might be subject to arrest. Some men, however, went south and joined the Confederate army; others, as the war became long and hard, engaged in violence and guerrilla activities at home, tactics that were often returned in kind by armed Unionists and federal forces. Political leaders and newspaper editors who contributed to the passions generated by the war sought to protect the rights of their states and loyal citizens against federal encroachments and at the same time maintain security in their bitterly divided communities. When the war began, Lincoln focused much of his attention on the crisis in the border states in an effort to prevent the region from falling to the "traitors." Despite his ultimate success, Lincoln at times mismanaged border state affairs, for example, in Maryland during the early months of the war. There, after violence occurred in the streets of Baltimore and the national capital underwent a virtual siege, Lincoln associated southern rights supporters with secessionist conspirators, and he either approved of or acquiesced in their suppression. The first crisis of the war for the Union occurred in Maryland, and it would severely test Lincoln's presidential leadership and the strength of Unionism in the state.

■

After Fort Sumter: Crisis in Maryland

The crisis in Maryland began immediately after Lincoln's April 15 call for troops to suppress the southern insurrection. On the next day, rioting erupted in Baltimore. Crowds of southern rights and Union supporters confronted each other in the streets. Lawless gangs, a longtime social menace in the city, took advantage of the political strife and roamed the streets, stealing and intimidating merchants. The police force of 398 men, though armed with revolvers, found it virtually impossible to maintain any semblance of order. "There was a deep and pervading impression of impending evil," Mayor George W. Brown wrote years later about the events of mid-April in his city.[1]

When Governor Thomas H. Hicks met with Lincoln on April 16, the day after the call for troops, he informed the president of the opposition, even among Maryland Unionists, to furnishing state troops for military action against the South. He strongly appealed to Lincoln and also to Secretary of War Simon Cameron and General in Chief Winfield Scott, who attended the meeting, to exempt his state from the requisition. They refused; but Lincoln did promise Hicks that the four regiments of state troops, if tendered to the War Department, would only be used to protect federal property in the state and to defend Washington. Immediately upon his return home, Hicks asked and received confirmation from Cameron of the president's pledge regarding the deployment of the Maryland regiments. Satisfied with the secretary of war's response, the governor issued a proclamation to the people of the state calling for troops and promising that none would be "sent from Maryland, unless it be for the defence of the national capital." The governor also told Marylanders, "The emergency is great, [and] the consequences of a rash step will be fearful. It is the imperative duty of every true son of Maryland to do all that he can to arrest the threatened evil" of civil war.[2] However, when conflict in the streets of Baltimore continued and tension mounted, Hicks postponed raising the regiments for the federal government. He notified the War Department that the men would be needed to quell disorders at home.[3]

The political strife and lawlessness in Baltimore, triggered by Lincoln's call for troops, proved only a prelude to the greater violence in the city that erupted on April 19. Known as the Baltimore Riot—actually the first skirmish of the Civil War—it severely threatened the Union cause in the state and had important repercussions elsewhere. The day before the riot, Baltimore authorities received reports from Harrisburg, Pennsylvania, that two regular companies of U.S. artillery and four militia companies (probably Pennsylvanians) would go through the city en route to Washington. The troops were commanded by Major John C. Pemberton, who, ironically, later joined the Confederate army and rose to the rank of lieutenant general, only to experience the ignominy of surrendering Vicksburg and 30,000 men to U. S. Grant in 1863. When the troops from Pennsylvania arrived, a large, hostile crowd followed them through the streets, hurling abuse and threats at the militiamen but leaving the regulars alone. The timely action of the Baltimore police under the command of Marshal George P. Kane prevented a mob attack on the men before they took the train to Washington.[4]

That night, April 18, amid growing excitement in the city, a boisterous Southern Rights Convention was held in a downtown building. News that Virginia's state convention had voted for secession, though still subject to an expected voter approval in May, greatly increased opposition to the Lincoln government in the city. The Baltimore Southern Rights Convention unanimously denounced the president's intention, announced in his April 15 proclamation, to recapture the forts in the seceded states. It charged that such a design would "inevitably lead to a sanguinary war, the dissolution of the Union, and the irreconcilable estrangement of the people of the South from the people of the North." The Baltimore convention "delegates" hotly protested against "the quartering of militia from the free

Thomas H. Hicks, governor of Maryland during the secession and early war crisis of 1860–1861; U.S. senator, 1862–1864. Caught in the middle of events, he sought to protect Maryland's rights in the Union while preventing secession. Hicks's acquiescence in the Baltimore decision to burn the bridges leading from the North into the city after April 19, 1861, rioting led to federal intervention and Lincoln's suspension of the writ of habeas corpus in the state. Courtesy of the Brady-Handy Collection, Prints and Photographs Division, Library of Congress, Washington, DC.

States in any of the towns or places of the slaveholding States" and declared, "The massing of large bodies of militia, exclusively from the free States, in the District of Columbia, is uncalled for by any public danger or exigency." Such a military deployment, they charged, was "a standing menace to the State of Maryland, and an insult to her loyalty and good faith." Finally, the Southern Rights Convention called on Marylanders "to obliterate all party lines . . . and present an unbroken front" in order "to avert the horrors of civil war, and to repel, if need be, any invader who may come to establish a military despotism over us." Clearly, the "in vader" the delegates had in mind would come from the North, not from the South.[5] As everyone knew, eastern Maryland was the only convenient route for northeastern troops to reach Washington.

The resolutions adopted by the Baltimore Southern Rights Convention did not advocate armed resistance to northern troops that might pass through Maryland. But the resolutions were highly inflammatory and contributed to a mob atmosphere in the city. Fearing the worst if more northern militia attempted to go through Baltimore, Governor Hicks and Mayor Brown hurriedly telegraphed Lincoln and demanded that the president send no more troops through the city.[6] At the same time, Brown, with the governor's endorsement, dispatched a delegation of prominent Baltimore citizens to Washington; they carried a letter from Brown to Lincoln that further described the ominous situation in the city. "Under these circumstances," Brown wrote the president, "it is not possible for more soldiers to pass through Baltimore unless they fight their way at every step." If the attempt should be made by the federal government to send the troops, the mayor solemnly warned, "The responsibility for the bloodshed will not rest upon me," or, by implication, upon the people of Baltimore.[7]

When the tragic events of April 19 occurred, Lincoln had not yet responded to the urgent messages from Hicks and Brown, nor had he talked to the mayor's delegation. On the morning of that day, seven companies of the Sixth Massachusetts Regiment, armed with muskets, and an unarmed regiment of Pennsylvania militia arrived unexpectedly at the President Street train station. Marshal Kane and his police had not been notified of their arrival. The troops moved down Pratt Street toward the Camden Street train station, preparatory to boarding the Baltimore and Ohio train for Washington. An angry crowd quickly gathered, infuriated by the presence of armed "abolitionist" troops and acting not by plan but by impulse. Things soon got out of control. Many in the crowd began hurling rocks, bricks, and debris at the New England troops. The mob increased in strength, and mayhem ensued as the soldiers moved at double-quick time to escape the fury of their assailants. Mayor Brown, hoping to quell the attacks, rushed to the front of the marching column and attempted to face down the mob. At some point, shots rang out, and men on both sides fell. During the fighting, the mayor himself shot and killed a rioter. Marshal Kane and a police unit soon arrived on the scene. Outnumbered, they bravely stationed themselves between the attacking mob and the troops, enabling the soldiers to reach the Camden Street station, where most of them took the train to Washington. Stragglers found safety in the police station, and the wounded received treatment at the Baltimore Infirmary. The unarmed Pennsylvania militiamen were later sent home.

Passions in Baltimore became further inflamed when a prominent local merchant, while standing by the tracks, was shot and killed by an infuriated soldier from a car window on the Washington train. His offense: he had raised a shout for Jefferson Davis and the Confederacy. By nightfall, however, a modicum of peace had been restored to the Baltimore streets. The riot—or skirmish—left four soldiers dead and three dozen wounded; twelve citizens lay dead and many were injured.[8]

News of the Baltimore Riot soon reverberated throughout the country, adding to the excitement and divisions following the fighting in Charleston Harbor and Lincoln's call for troops to suppress the insurrection. In nearby Wilmington, Delaware, Anna M. Ferris expressed the fears of many in her state and in Maryland when she recorded in her diary, "The excitement & suspense are almost intolerable, & the circumstances transpiring around us seem incredible. . . . All at once the flames of Civil War seem raging around us. . . . We seem threatened not only with war but anarchy, as the Capital & the Government are in great danger, & the means for their defense very much obstructed & cut off—Baltimore is in possession of the mob & under martial law." Ferris wrote, "All other interests are suspended & everybody is absorbed by the anxiety prevailing for the welfare & existence of our country."[9]

Late in the afternoon of the nineteenth, "an immense public meeting" was held at Monument Square in Baltimore. Guarded by the city's entire police force, Governor Hicks and Mayor Brown pleaded with the crowd for calm and for an end to the lawlessness. Both men also proclaimed their support for the Union. At the same time, Hicks sought to appease the hostile throng by dramatically announcing, "I love my State and I love the Union but I will suffer my right arm to be torn from my body before I will raise it to strike a sister State." Angry cries of defiance, however, greeted his statement of support for the Union. Baltimore Unionists, intimidated by the pro-Confederate mob (many were simply disorderly gangs), remained quiet.[10]

Faced with an ungovernable situation in Baltimore, Governor Hicks called out units of the Maryland militia to help restore order, despite the fact that the men had few firearms and little discipline. Hardly had the governor issued the order when news arrived that additional troops were on their way from Harrisburg and Philadelphia. Still having received no response from President Lincoln to their earlier messages on the crisis, the governor and Baltimore officials held an urgent, late-night meeting in Mayor Brown's house to determine what to do. The day's ordeal had taken a toll on Hicks's delicate health, and he was sick in bed at the mayor's house and unable to stand for the meeting. The critical conference was held in his bedroom.

The Baltimore officials concluded that the only way to avoid further violence was to take immediate and dramatic action to prevent the movement of northern troops through the city. They vigorously pressed the sick governor to order the burning or disabling of the bridges on the railroads connecting Baltimore with the North. Hicks, with great reluctance according to the later accounts of Brown and three of the participants in the meeting, gave his consent, though he issued no written order for the destruction. By the next afternoon, Baltimore police and Maryland militiamen, joined by local rowdies, had burned or partially destroyed the railroad bridges north of the city, thereby blocking the arrival of the troops from Pennsylvania. Brown later insisted that the order to burn the bridges was given "with no purpose of hostility to the Federal Government," but only to save the city from terrible bloodshed and destruction. He maintained that the intent was not to destroy the bridges; it was only to disable them temporarily.

When criticism erupted, both in Maryland and in the North, over the destruction of the bridges, Hicks denied that he had given his approval for the action. In a public letter to the people of Maryland on May 4, Hicks claimed that the bridge-burning incident was a secessionist "conspiracy, of which an attempt was made to make me a participant [in] its diabolical designs." Yet the governor contradicted himself; he admitted that the disabling of the bridges, "unlawful as though it was, seemed to be the only means of averting threatened bloodshed." Hicks also testified that he had told Brown at the meeting in his house that the state had no authority over the city, and the mayor "could act as he pleased" in the matter.[11]

While the bridges burned, a crisis atmosphere continued to grip Baltimore. On the morning of April 20, Lincoln finally met on the situation with the mayor's delegation. The Baltimoreans pleaded with the president to permit no more troop movements through their city. Lincoln, "half playfully," according to his secretary, John G. Nicolay, responded, "If I grant you this, you will come to-morrow demanding that no troops shall pass around" Baltimore. Nonetheless, the president told the delegation and repeated in a letter to Governor Hicks and Mayor Brown, "[Though] troops *must* be brought here, . . . I make no point of bringing them *through* Baltimore. Without any military knowledge myself, I must leave the details to Gen. Scott." The general, who was in the meeting, immediately interjected, "March them *around* Baltimore, and not through it." Lincoln then assured the Maryland delegation, "By this, a collision of the people of Baltimore with the troops will be avoided, unless they go out of their way to seek it."[12] The president also sent a dispatch to Hicks and Brown asking them to come immediately to Washington for consultation "relative to preserving the peace of Maryland."[13]

On the same day, April 20, U.S. District Attorney William Meade Addison in Baltimore sent a troubling "Memorandum" to Lincoln. He anxiously reported to the president that he had received creditable information about a secret organization of 3,000 men who were plotting insurrection in the city. The district attorney wrote Lincoln that public authorities could not control such a large militant force. Since the fighting in Baltimore, "the sentiments of Maryland had undergone a great change," he informed the president. "There is now a fearful majority against the U.S. Govt," he wrote, and Unionists faced constant intimidation at the hands of secessionists. Addison probably had in mind the hundreds of partly armed Maryland militiamen, summoned by Hicks to restore order. Many of these men leaned toward secession, and most of them blamed Lincoln and the "Black Republicans" for the troubles in the city. Others were simply ruffians, or "Plug Uglies," who sought to take advantage of the chaos in the streets.[14] Colonel Isaac R. Trimble, who commanded the militia, favored the secessionists; he later served as a major general in the Confederate army.

CHAPTER TWO

Reports spread on April 20 that an attack on Fort McHenry at the harbor's entrance was imminent, causing Captain John C. Robinson, the commandant, to promise that if the mob approached the fort he would direct cannon fire against it. With this warning, along with the vigilance of Marshal Kane's police in blocking the routes to the fort, pro-Confederate elements decided that the better part of valor would be to remain in the city. However, for several days, as Brown later wrote, "it looked as if Baltimore had taken her stand decisively for the South."[15]

Not all the men who volunteered to defend the city, however, favored the South. From 300 to 400 Baltimore free blacks offered their military services to city authorities, but Brown turned them down. He feared that the presence of armed blacks in the city containing the largest free black population in the nation would spark racial rioting and greater mob violence. Baltimore authorities had enough trouble putting down white-on-white violence and checking a secessionist surge without igniting a racial conflagration. Nonetheless, attacks on blacks, though unnoticed in the white press and in other reports of the rioting, must have occurred during this turbulent period.[16]

On the morning of April 21, Mayor Brown, accompanied by three associates and in response to Lincoln's summons of the previous day, arrived in Washington by special train and immediately went to the White House. Governor Hicks, who had returned to the state capital at Annapolis on April 20, did not attend the conference. The governor had learned that General Benjamin F. Butler, then in Philadelphia, had sent a detachment of Massachusetts troops by railroad to Perryville at the head of Chesapeake Bay. There the troops embarked on a steamer to Annapolis, where, according to the plan, they would board a train for Washington. Hicks, fearing that secessionists would contest the federal occupation of the state capital, remained in Annapolis hoping to control the situation. Almost as an afterthought, Hicks authorized Brown to argue Maryland's case, and specifically that of Baltimore, in the conference with Lincoln. Brown, a skilled lawyer, was clearly capable of explaining the crisis in Baltimore and the need of at least temporarily forbidding the movement of northern troops through the city. He was not as well versed, however, as Hicks on political conditions in other areas of the state. In the conference, Brown emphasized the situation in Baltimore and not federal-state relations per se.

President Lincoln, who must have been perplexed by the intelligence he had received from Baltimore, had also asked his cabinet and General Scott to attend the important conference. Brown quickly came to the point in the meeting. He described the seriousness of affairs in Baltimore and urged Lincoln to prevent the passage of any more troops through the city. A long discussion ensued, an account of which Brown wrote on the same day and had immediately published. According to Brown, Lincoln vowed that he wanted "to avoid the fatal consequences of a collision with the people" of Baltimore, but he insisted on having "a transit through the State for such troops as might be necessary for the protection of the Federal capital." "None of the troops brought through Maryland," he said, "was intended for any purposes hostile to the State, or [for] aggressive [action] against the Southern States." Lincoln told Brown and the Baltimore delegation that because of the lack of security for troop-carrying vessels coming up the Potomac River to Washington, he "must either bring them through Maryland or abandon the capital," the latter of which he refused to do.[17]

The president then asked General Scott for his opinion on whether troops, coming through Maryland, could be sent around Baltimore, though he seemed to have decided this point the previous day in his meeting with the mayor's delegation. Scott answered by saying that it could be done over two possible routes: one completely by rail circling several miles north, west, and southwest of the city, and the other by rail to Perryville on the Chesapeake, then by boat to Annapolis, and finally by train to Washington, the route planned by General Butler. Brown agreed that either of those two routes would be acceptable, and he assured Lincoln that he "would use all lawful means to prevent [his] citizens from leaving Baltimore to attack the troops in passing at a distance." However, the mayor told the president that he could not give a similar promise for the people elsewhere in Maryland. "The President," Brown later wrote, "frankly acknowledged this difficulty, and said that the Government would only ask the city authorities to use their best efforts with respect to [people] under their jurisdiction."[18]

During the conference, Secretary of War Cameron asked Brown under what authority a bridge on the Northern Central Railroad in Baltimore's jurisdiction had been disabled? The mayor turned to the president and replied that it had been done as an emergency measure by local and state authorities to prevent the bloodshed anticipated if the troops were to enter the city. He told Lincoln that the people of Maryland, though "deeply attached to the Union," bitterly opposed the administration's decision to make war on the South. Therefore, "it was not surprising," he said, "that [they] should resent the passage of Northern troops through their city." Irritated by the mayor's explanation, Lincoln sprang from his chair, "walked backward and forward through the apartment," and declared, "with great feeling, 'Mr. Brown, I am not a learned man!'" After repeating the phrase, whose relevance to the discussion was not clear, Lincoln insisted that his proclamation had been misunderstood. He had no intention of bringing on war; rather, his purpose in calling for the troops was to defend the capital, which, he contended, was in danger of bombardment from the heights across the Potomac. The president ended the conference by giving his "distinct assurance . . . that no more troops would be sent through Baltimore, unless obstructed in their transit in other directions."[19]

When boarding the train to return to Baltimore, Brown and his companions received an urgent dispatch from John W. Garrett, the Unionist president of the Baltimore and Ohio Railroad, informing the mayor that 3,000 Pennsylvania troops were at Cockeysville, about fourteen miles north of Baltimore, on the Northern Central Railroad. "Intense excitement prevails," the telegram read. The people were "arming in mass," and "terrific bloodshed" was expected. The mayor and his colleagues immediately returned to the White House and asked to see the president, a request that Lincoln promptly granted. Surprised and disturbed by the information in Garrett's message, Lincoln again summoned General Scott and members of his cabinet to his office. According to Brown, "the President at once, in the most decided way, urged" Scott to withdraw the troops to Pennsylvania. Although this was not an order to him, the general agreed, and he issued the necessary directive to the Pennsylvania troops.[20]

General Scott, however, had no intention of continuing the agreement with Brown once the crisis had passed and a military force sufficient to provide security for the railroads had gained control of Baltimore. The day after the White House conference and without notifying Maryland authorities, Scott wrote General Robert Patterson, commanding Pennsylvania troops, "The fact renders the railroad from Harrisburg to Baltimore of no value to us here without a force of, perhaps, ten thousand men to hold Baltimore—to protect the rails and bridges near it. This shall be done as soon as we shall have a surplus force over above what is necessary for the security of Washington."[21] Whether Scott consulted with the president before sending this message to Patterson is unknown; but conceivably he did not,

Reverdy Johnson, a former Whig member of President Millard Fillmore's cabinet, an influential conservative Unionist in Maryland, and U.S. senator, 1864–1868. Johnson, a leading authority on constitutional law, at Lincoln's request wrote a defense of the president's suspension of the writ of habeas corpus, but later opposed many of the administration's policies, including military interference in state elections and the Emancipation Proclamation. Courtesy of the Brady-Handy Collection, Prints and Photographs Division, Library of Congress, Washington, DC.

since Lincoln had turned over military operations in Maryland to the general's direction.

On the same day, April 22, prominent Unionist Reverdy Johnson expressed his concern to the president regarding the administration's purpose in bringing troops through Maryland. "The existing excitement and alarm of the public mind of my own State and of Virginia," Johnson informed Lincoln, were "owing . . . to an apprehension that it is your purpose to use the military force you are assembling in this District for the invasion of, or other hostile attack upon, these States." He told the president, "It is all-important therefore . . . that this misapprehension be corrected at once."[22]

Lincoln, who had a myriad of serious problems to deal with after Fort Sumter—and some not so serious, such as demands for office—waited two days before replying, and then answered only after receiving a reminder from Johnson. He wrote the Maryland Unionist, "I forebore to answer yours of the 22d because of my aversion (which I thought you understood,) to getting on paper, and furnishing new grounds for misunderstanding." Lincoln assured Johnson, "The purpose of bringing troops *here* is to defend this capital. I *do* say I have no purpose to *invade* Virginia, with them or any other troops, as I understand the word *invasion*." But Lincoln asked three questions: First, "suppose Virginia sends her troops, or admits others through her borders, to assail this capital, am I not to repel them, even to the crossing of the Potomac if I can?" Second, "suppose Virginia erects, or permits to be erected, batteries on the opposite shore, to bombard the city, are we to stand still and see it done?" Third, "are we not to hold Fort Monroe (for instance) if we can?"[23] Johnson did not respond, at least in writing, to Lincoln's questions regarding the use of troops in the District of Columbia.[24]

The president in his reply to Johnson ignored the intention, as announced in his April 15 proclamation, to employ the militia regiments for the suppression of the southern insurrection. When the president wrote Johnson on April 24, he saw an immediate need to placate Maryland on the federal use of its troops. At that time, Lincoln was also receiving threatening reports from the South about plans for an immediate rebel march on the "abolitionist" capital to remove, as the *Richmond Examiner* announced, "the filthy cage of unclean birds." William Woods Holden, the editor of the *Raleigh Standard*, who had supported the Union until Lincoln's call for troops to put down the rebellion, now promised, "North Carolina will send her full quota of troops to unite in the attack on Washington City." The Union capital would "soon be too hot to hold Abraham Lincoln," Holden boastfully predicted.[25] Even General Scott believed, as he expressed in an order on April 26, that an attack on Washington by "numerous hostile bodies of troops [was] expected at any moment."[26] Such an assault never came. A Confederate operation to take the city at this time proved impracticable because of the poorly organized rebel forces and the tactical problems involved, particularly the crossing of the Potomac.

During the spring of 1861, the necessity for protecting the national capital delayed any presidential plan to invade and reclaim the seceded states. For Lincoln, the defense of Washington had the highest priority. The rebel capture of the city would scatter his government and possibly ensure the success of the southern secession. In late April, he could truthfully promise Marylanders that their troops, if tendered, would be used only for the defense of the capital. If the troops were deployed elsewhere, Lincoln believed that the secessionists, whom he equated with the southern rights faction, would use the issue to gain the upper hand in Maryland and would succeed in severing the state's ties with the Union.

Another Baltimore delegation—this one consisting of church leaders and representing the Young Men's Christian Association—visited Lincoln on April 22 and pleaded for peace with the South. Their spokesman, a Baptist minister, bluntly demanded that the president recognize Confederate independence. Although seething inside at such impertinence, Lincoln calmly remarked that neither the president nor Congress had the constitutional power to recognize a secessionist government. He declared that the delegates asked for "peace on any terms" and yet had "no word of condemnation for those who are making war on us." He continued, "You express great horror of bloodshed, and yet would not lay a straw in the way of those who are organizing in Virginia and elsewhere to capture this city." Furthermore, Lincoln told the Baltimore clergymen, "the rebels attack Fort Sumter, and your citizens attack troops sent to the defense of the Government, and the lives and property in Washington, and yet you would have me break my oath and surrender the Government without a blow. There is no Washington in that—no Jackson in that—there is no manhood or honor in that."[27]

Lincoln assured the Baltimore delegation, as he had Reverdy Johnson, that he had "no desire to invade the South" but said he "must have troops to defend this capital." Washington, he pointed out, was surrounded by Maryland. "Mathematically the necessity exists that [the troops] should come over her territory. Our men are not moles," Lincoln famously said, "and can't dig under the earth; they are not birds, and can't fly through the air. There is no way but to march across [the state], and they must do it.

But in doing this, there is no need of collision." He admonished the delegation, "Go home and tell your people that if they will not attack us, we will not attack them; but if they do attack us, we will return it, and that severely."[28]

Meanwhile, the White House agreement of April 21 between the president and Mayor Brown not to send troops through Baltimore had reduced tension in the city. As a result, the mayor and local authorities had restored a semblance of order, and by April 30 communications between Baltimore and Philadelphia had been reestablished. John C. McGowan, a Baltimore Unionist, reported to Lincoln on May 6 that the state militia in the city had been disbanded and the railroad bridges to the north had been largely repaired.[29] Northern troops had again begun their movement into the state, but not through Baltimore. Nonetheless, as Lincoln had predicted, Hicks wrote the president demanding that "no more troops be ordered or allowed to pass through Maryland" and that "the troops now off Annapolis [under General Butler] be sent elsewhere." Remarkably, the governor suggested to the president that Lord Lyons, the British minister in Washington, "be requested to act as mediator between the contending parties of our country."[30]

Lincoln refused Hicks's demand to prohibit the landing of Butler's men, though he assured the governor that they were "intended for nothing but the defense of this capital." Taken aback by the suggestion of British mediation, Lincoln directed Secretary of State William H. Seward to inform Hicks "that no domestic contention whatever, that may arise among the parties of this Republic, ought in any case to be referred to any foreign arbitration, least of all to the arbitratment of an European monarchy." He also wanted Seward to remind Hicks that there was a time when U.S. troops had been cheerfully welcomed in Maryland—during the American Revolution and the War of 1812—to repel the British army.[31]

When Butler's troops landed at Annapolis, Hicks met the Massachusetts general at the U.S. Naval Academy and strongly protested against the "occupation" of his state. He told Butler that all Maryland stood ready to take up arms against his troops if they remained. This proved an empty threat. On April 25, Butler's men at Annapolis began an uncontested movement by train to lift the siege of Washington.[32]

Hicks admitted that he had largely lost control of events in Maryland.

Faced with the possibility that the General Assembly would call itself into special session and take matters into its own hands without his input, the governor summoned the legislators to meet at Annapolis on April 26. He immediately changed the site of the meeting away from the military-occupied state capital and to the more Union-friendly environs of Frederick in the west. In explaining the change, Hicks informed a friend that if the legislature met in Annapolis he feared that it would be intimidated by General Butler's troops.[33] The governor advised members of the General Assembly that Maryland's "only safety" lay "in preserving a neutral position between our brethren of the North and of the South," a position, he contended, that had the support of "a large majority of the people" of the state. Still, Hicks announced, "I cannot counsel Maryland to take sides against the general Government until it shall commit outrages on us which would justify us in resisting its authority. As a consequence, I can give no other counsel than that we shall array ourselves for Union and peace, and thus preserve our soil from being polluted with the blood of brethren." Hicks hoped that by establishing a neutral position in the war, the state could "force the contending parties to transfer the field of battle from [its] soil."[34]

News of the General Assembly's pending meeting, along with recurring threats of a rebel attack on Washington, caused the president to fear that the legislature's southern rights majority would align the state with the Confederacy. For the moment, however, he hesitated to intervene. On April 25 Lincoln wrote General Scott, "The Maryland Legislature assembles to-morrow at Anapolis [sic], and, not improbably, will take action to arm the people of that State against the United States. The question has been submitted to, and considered by me, whether it would not be justifiable, upon the ground of necessary defence, for you . . . to arrest, or disperse the members of that body. I think it would *not* be justifiable; nor, efficient for the desired object." Lincoln explained that the Maryland legislators had "a clearly legal right to assemble," and added, "We can not know in advance, that their action will not be lawful, and peaceful." Furthermore, "We *can* not permanently prevent their action. If we arrest them, we can not long hold them as prisoners; and when liberated, they will immediately re-assemble, and take their action." However, Lincoln instructed General Scott "to watch, and await [the] action" of the legislators, and if they attempted "to arm their people against the United States," he directed him "to adopt the most prompt, and efficient means to counteract, even, if necessary, to the bombardment of their cities—and in the extremest necessity, the suspension of the writ of habeas corpus."[35]

Historian and Lincoln scholar Mark E. Neely Jr. has correctly pointed out that the president in the holograph original of this directive to Scott deleted the words "of course" immediately preceding the phrase about the suspension of the writ of habeas corpus. He replaced it with the qualification "in the extremest necessity." Lincoln, according to Neely, made the change to de-emphasize the suspension of the writ, an action that restricted civil liberties in Maryland and would have immediately raised red flags in the North.[36] Although Lincoln had softened the directive to Scott regarding the writ, he left intact the startling statement authorizing the bombardment of the Maryland cities "if necessary."[37]

The president's consent for "the bombardment of their cities" and the suspension of the writ, if General Scott found it necessary, reflected the confused and threatening situation that Lincoln found himself in during the early days of the war. It also demonstrated the pressure from the North for him to take drastic action against Maryland. Historians have usually failed to relate the importance of the northern reaction to the Baltimore Riot in rallying support for Lincoln and the war. They have tended to focus on the Confederate assault on Fort Sumter and its surrender as triggering a virtually unanimous sentiment in the North for the suppression of the southern insurrection. However, the reaction in the free states to the fighting in Baltimore and the danger posed to the national capital from Maryland and Virginia also contributed to northern outrage and unity in the beginning of the war.

The attack on Union troops in Baltimore, the disorders in the city, the bridge-burning episode, and what many northerners believed was the state's rapid descent into secession had produced a demand in the North for military intervention in the Maryland city and against secessionists everywhere in the state. "The North and its millions are cut off from their capital by the mob of Baltimore," New Yorker George Templeton Strong recorded in his diary three days after the riot. Baltimore "seems in absolute anarchy," he wrote. "The city should receive a severe lesson." It should be plainly told, "So many thousand Northern troops will march through her streets on such a day; and . . . if they are molested, they will withdraw until Fort McHenry shall have wiped out the city, and then resume their march."[38] An unidentified "abolitionist" newspaper declared that Baltimore, in addition to Richmond, must "become a heap of cinders and ashes," and that its inhabitants ought "either to be slaughtered, or scattered to the winds, on account of the mob ascendancy that recently prevailed there."[39] In a similar vein, Andrew Reeder, a prominent Pennsylvania Republican, thundered that if "Baltimore was laid in ashes the North would rejoice over it and laud the Spirit that dictated the act."[40]

In Lincoln's hometown of Springfield, Senator Lyman Trumbull on April 21 wrote the president, "Every body is greatly excited over the news from Baltimore, & extremely solicitous about the condition of Washington." Coming on the heels of the rebel firing on the flag at Fort Sumter, the rioting by the secessionists in Baltimore, Trumbull reported, had even rallied Lincoln's old Democratic foes in Springfield, such as Charles H. Lanphier, editor of the *Illinois State Register*, to the administration's support. The senator told Lincoln that the "proper course would have been to order the New York, Mass, R.I. & Pa. troops to take possession of Baltimore at once." Without strong action, Trumbull told the president, "we do not see how it will be possible to hold Washington with Baltimore against us; besides, the Union men of Baltimore need assistance."[41]

Lincoln's friend Orville H. Browning reported from Quincy, Illinois, that, though enthusiasm for the Union "was unbounded" in the western part of the state, many were "fearful for the safety of Washington." He noted, "The fall of Fort Sumter has been of great advantage" in rallying support for the war, but "the fall of Washington would be most disasterous [*sic*]. . . . Baltimore must not stand in the way" of protecting the national capital. The city "should be seized and garrisoned, or, if necessary to the success of our glorious cause, laid in ruin."[42]

Attorney General Edward Bates, not known for his passion, excitedly wrote Lincoln on April 23 that the people of Maryland, as well as those of Virginia, were "in open arms against us, &, by violence & terror, [had] silenced every friend of the Government." Bates contended, "In Maryland there is not even a pretence of State authority for their overt acts of treason." Secessionists in Maryland and Virginia were "daily winding their coils around us," while Unionists made "no bold effort to cut the cord that is soon to bind us in pitiable impotence." The distraught attorney general, however, could only advise Lincoln to take "active, aggressive measures" to defend Washington and the Union.[43]

Lincoln perhaps agreed with Nicolay, his secretary, who pronounced

Baltimore a "nest of treason" and its citizens "barbarians." At any rate, he did not hesitate to act against the secessionists in the area.[44] On April 27 he suspended the privilege of the writ of habeas corpus along the railroad corridor from Philadelphia to Washington.[45] Fortunately, despite Lincoln's authorization of it two days earlier, General Scott did not order the bombardment of the Maryland cities. Instead, he directed General Butler's forces to move into Baltimore after occupying Annapolis, and on May 13, without resistance, they assumed control of the city. The open recruitment of Confederate soldiers that had begun after the April 19 riot, however, continued in Baltimore. For the time being, Mayor Brown, the city commissioners, and Marshal Kane remained in office, but under military oversight. Military arrests soon occurred. General Butler on May 14 ordered the arrest and incarceration in Fort McHenry of Ross Winans, a prominent Baltimore legislator and industrialist, on a vague charge of treason. The arrest probably occurred without Lincoln's knowledge, but it should be remembered that he had earlier granted area commanders carte blanche to apprehend and hold those who, they judged, posed a threat to the Union. Although federal authorities soon released Winans, his detention became a prelude to a later purge of staunch southern rights legislators by the military.[46]

On May 25 General William H. Keim, commanding Pennsylvania troops in Maryland, ordered the arrest and confinement in Fort McHenry of one John Merryman of Baltimore County, who had allegedly been involved in the burning of the railroad bridges after the Baltimore Riot. Attorneys for Merryman immediately petitioned Chief Justice Roger B. Taney, whose federal circuit court included Baltimore, to issue a writ of habeas corpus directing General George Cadwalader, commander of military forces at Fort McHenry, to produce the prisoner in court to hear the charges against him. The next day, Taney issued the desired writ and ordered Cadwalader to appear before him in court and deliver Merryman to him. Instead, Cadwalader sent a subordinate officer to the federal courtroom to read the general's statement outlining the treason charges against Merryman and to announce that he would not surrender the prisoner. Cadwalader explained that his suspension of the writ had been authorized by President Lincoln on April 27 as essential for the protection of public safety.[47]

Taney, the author of the proslavery *Dred Scott* decision, immediately went to work writing an opinion that sharply criticized the president for his usurpation of the judicial process and constitutional law. He sent the opinion to Lincoln. On May 30 Lincoln asked Attorney General Bates to confer with Reverdy Johnson, Maryland's most distinguished constitutional lawyer, and obtain his aid in "preparing [the] argument for the suspension of the Habeas Corpus."[48] Both Bates and Johnson rendered long, laborious papers defending the right of the president to suspend the writ and to hold without trial Merryman and other enemies of the Union. They maintained that it was the president's responsibility to suppress the insurrection and ensure public safety, even if, by implication in their argument, he had to ignore the courts. Bates wrote, "In a time like the present, when the very existence of the Nation is assailed, by a great and dangerous insurrection, the President has the lawful discretionary power to arrest and hold in custody, persons known to have criminal intercourse with the insurgents, or persons against whom there is probable cause for suspicion of such criminal complicity."[49]

In his opinion to the president, Johnson, who after the war unsuccessfully defended Mary E. Surratt in the Lincoln assassination plot, affirmed Bates's reasoning. He specifically argued that though the suspension of the writ was listed in the constitutional article concerning the powers of Congress, the president could issue a general suspension of the writ during a period of national crisis. The president's authority in suspending the writ, Johnson contended, was "measured and limited by the exigency of each arrest." He added, "In each instance, if the grounds of the arrest involved in any way the success" of the president's armed forces, "he has a right to hold the party until all danger to that object is at an end. This being a military question, it must be for him, as the commander-in-chief, or his agents to decide it."[50] Such an interpretation could easily open the door for the abuse of civil liberties at the hands of the executive branch of the government; and it was especially remarkable coming from a conservative like Johnson, who was a stickler for constitutional rights.

Reinforced by Bates's and Johnson's opinions, Lincoln disregarded Taney's ruling and the criticism of others, including many in Maryland and in other border states. The president refused to surrender Merryman to the courts, and, furthermore, he continued the suspension of the writ in Maryland. (Bates did not give his written opinion until the day after Lincoln's decision on the issue; however, he had earlier discussed it with the president.) In his message to a special session of Congress on July 4, Lincoln de-

CHAPTER TWO

fended his suspension of the writ. After explaining to Congress what he had done, Lincoln gave his justification for his action. He declared, "To state the question more directly, are all the laws, *but one*, to go unexecuted, and the government itself go to pieces, lest that one be violated?" He thought not. However, Lincoln said that he would accept any legislation that Congress chose to enact in the matter.[51]

At the time, the Republican-controlled Congress, deeply troubled by the activities of "traitors" in Maryland and elsewhere, refused to intervene in the habeas corpus controversy. In Merryman's case, his fate was not onerous; military authorities released him in July 1861 to a Baltimore court to face charges on conspiracy to commit treason. Granted bail, Merryman never came to trial.[52]

The Maryland General Assembly that convened at Frederick on April 26, 1861, while contentious, did not prove to be the threat to the Union that Lincoln had feared. Although southern rights Democrats controlled both houses (by only a single vote in the lower chamber), many of these members, despite their bitter opposition to Lincoln's policy of military coercion against the South, had been chastened by the violence in Baltimore, the bridge-burning episode, and the feared economic disaster if the state were to leave the Union. Only a few of the delegates favored secession. A number of Democratic delegates, perhaps influenced by the moderate position of their party's *Baltimore Sun*, wanted the legislature to call for the election of delegates to a state convention to consider "federal relations." The *Sun* denied charges that it had ever supported secession, and it bluntly told the legislators that the General Assembly had no power over federal-state relations and should leave such matters to a state convention.[53] The *Sun* assumed that a Unionist majority would be elected if a convention was called and that it would defeat any movement toward secession.

Pressure also mounted in the western part of the state, where the legislature met, for the members to oppose secession. In addition, Johnson appeared in Frederick to plead with the legislators to avoid any rash action that would "precipitate us into irreparable ruin." He argued that because of Maryland's geographic position between the contending forces, the state would suffer an "immediate and total ruin" if it seceded.[54] The New York diarist George Templeton Strong wrote on April 28 that though Maryland leaders wanted "to rebel and to have Jefferson Davis rule over them," they would not secede because they were "terrified by the great unanimous rising of the North" against them "and by the certainty that Baltimore [would] be razed if necessary."[55]

Three days later, the Maryland General Assembly in secret session voted down a secessionist plan to establish a Committee of Public Safety, reminiscent of similar organizations during the American Revolution.[56] This committee, if approved, would have had extraordinary powers and conceivably might have attempted to align the state with the Confederacy. Instead of a movement toward secession, the General Assembly appointed a three-member commission to see President Lincoln, express the majority's concerns to him, particularly regarding the federal military's presence in eastern Maryland, and ascertain his intentions toward the state.

The Maryland commissioners, according to their report to the General Assembly, were "received by the President with respectful courtesy" and were joined in the meeting by Secretary of State Seward and Secretary of War Cameron. The conference at times, however, became testy when the commissioners, whom John Hay, Lincoln's assistant secretary, referred to as "the Maryland Disunionists," expressed the hostility of Marylanders to the passage of troops through the state. The commissioners reported that "a large portion of our people" sympathized with "our Southern brethren in the present crisis," a comment that must have rankled Lincoln. Nonetheless, the commissioners assured Lincoln that the legislature would take no immediate steps toward secession. On his part, the president announced that "as long as Maryland has not taken, and was not about taking, a hostile attitude to the Federal Government, . . . the military occupation of her ways of communication, and the seizure of the property of her citizens, would be without justification." However, he did not say that he would withdraw Butler's troops from eastern Maryland. The commissioners also appealed to Lincoln "not to act in any spirit of revenge for the murdered [Massachusetts] soldiers" in the April 19 riot. "The President," Hay wrote, "coolly replied that he never acted from any such impulse." Lincoln later told the commissioners that his policy toward the state "must necessarily be contingent" on events.[57]

The president's failure to give the commissioners an unqualified promise to end federal control in eastern Maryland strained the General Assembly's support for the Union, but not to the breaking point. Angered by Lincoln's response, the lower chamber, or House of Delegates, by a vote of 43 to 13 denounced the federal government's policy of coercion against the seceded states and its military presence in the state. Furthermore, it called for the recognition of the Confederate States of America on the ground that the restoration of the Union was impossible. The House of Delegates also declared that Maryland, while loyal to the Union, should remain entirely neutral in the war.[58]

The final resolution, with stronger language, passed the state senate on May 10. The joint resolution pronounced "the war against the Confederate States unconstitutional and repugnant to civilization" and predicted it would "result in a bloody and shameful overthrow of our institutions." Although the people of the state recognized "the obligations of Maryland to the Union," the resolution went on, "we sympathize with the South in the struggle for their rights. For the sake of humanity we are for peace and reconciliation, and solemnly protest against this war, and will take no part in it." The Old Line State implored "the President, in the name of God, to cease this unholy war," at least until Congress could assemble and act on it. Furthermore, "Maryland desires and consents to the recognition of the independence of the Confederate States." The resolution pronounced the military occupation of Maryland unconstitutional; at the same time, it "discountenanced . . . the violent interference with the transit of Federal troops" through the state. Finally, the resolution declared that the vindication of the rights of the state should "be left to time and reason, and that a Convention, under existing circumstances, [was] inexpedient."[59]

In a separate action that historians have missed, the General Assembly dispatched a commission to Montgomery, Alabama, and selected another delegation to visit Lincoln for the purpose of obtaining an end to the war. The legislature called for negotiations to "arrange for an adjustment of the existing troubles" between the two sides. The commission to the Confederate States, headed by Coleman Yellott, a Douglas Democrat who had introduced the bill in the state Senate to create a Committee on Public Safety, arrived in Montgomery in late May and received a cordial welcome from Jefferson Davis. The Confederate president informed the Maryland commissioners that he had supported a cessation of hostilities but that recent efforts to negotiate with the Lincoln government had failed. Davis, however, expressed great pleasure in "the assurance that the State of Maryland [sympathized] with the people of the Confederate States in their determined vindication of the right of self-government." He hoped that "at no distant date the State, whose people, habits, and institutions [were] so closely related to the South," would unite with the Confederacy. The commissioners declined to speculate on what Maryland would do if the war continued. The Maryland commission to confer with Lincoln never reached Washington; they aborted the mission when federal forces invaded northern Virginia.[60] Without taking any further action, the Maryland legislature adjourned on May 14 and agreed to reconvene later.

On June 13, 1861, a test of political sentiment in the state occurred when voters went to the polls to elect six members of the U.S. House of Representatives in time for a special session of Congress summoned by Lincoln to meet on July 4. In an election remarkably free of irregularities, 67,097 voters went to the polls, 25,405 fewer, however, than in the 1860 presidential election. Maryland voters selected all conservative Unionists—and slaveholders—though at least one, Henry May of Baltimore, was a strong southern rights supporter who demanded an end to the "war of aggression" against the South.[61] John W. Crisfield, elected from the southeastern, plantation district, became a diehard proslavery spokesman in the House and a thorn in Lincoln's side throughout the war.

General Nathaniel P. Banks, who had replaced General Butler in command in Maryland, failed to see a silver lining in the election results, particularly in Baltimore. He reported to Washington that the success of the Unionists in the election was not "a just indication of the [loyal] spirit of the city." Banks found Confederate sympathizers silently lurking behind doors in Baltimore, waiting for an opportunity to take to the streets. He informed his superiors, "Active demonstrations on the part of secessionists can only be suppressed by [the] constant readiness of our forces. We need greatly some assistance here." Banks specifically wanted arms for a "home guard" to be recruited among true Unionists (by his definition) and a federal cavalry corps "to suppress the contraband trade on the back roads leading southward."[62] Few federal troops, however, could be made available for Maryland. General Irvin McDowell in northern Virginia needed all the soldiers that he could scrounge to confront General P. G. T. Beauregard's Confederate army in the vicinity of Manassas Junction. With Baltimore as its center, southeastern Maryland continued until late in the war to be a corridor and the Chesapeake a waterway for supplies and intelligence going to Richmond.[63]

During June, Union zealots in Baltimore began sending disturbing reports to Secretary of War Cameron and General in Chief Scott that treason was rampant at the highest levels in the city. These radicals, who soon styled themselves Unconditional Unionists (presumably, loyal conservatives like Reverdy Johnson were conditional Unionists), insisted that the arrest of rebel officials and the suppression of "disloyal" newspapers in Baltimore were necessary to sustain the Union and restore peace. The main purveyor of this exaggerated and damaging intelligence was one Worthington G. Snethen, erstwhile correspondent of the *New York Tribune* in Baltimore and a Republican. Beginning during the 1860 presidential campaign, Snethen had sent Lincoln self-serving reports on political conditions in Maryland.[64] Posing as an expert on conditions in Baltimore after the April riot, he also ingratiated himself with Scott and others in the administration, as well as with General Banks in Baltimore.

In late June, Snethen rushed to Washington and laid out charges that Marshal Kane and members of the Baltimore police board had hidden weapons for the use of secessionists in the city. Based on Snethen's testimony, Scott drafted an order for Banks to seize and hold Kane and the police commissioners. The ageing general in chief told Banks, "Mr. Snethen, a gentleman of standing, will deliver to you this [order]." He explained that Snethen had "just given to the Secretary of War and myself many important facts touching the subject of [the] Union" in Baltimore. "It is confirmed by him that, among the citizens, the secessionists, if not the most numerous, are by far more active and effective than the supporters of the Federal Government." Scott informed Banks, "It is the opinion of the Secretary of War, and I need not add my own, that the blow should be early struck, to carry consternation into the ranks of our numerous enemies" in the city.[65] The wording in Scott's statement suggests that Lincoln was not consulted before issuing the order. As Scott knew, the president in his April 25 directive had given him the authority to take "the most prompt, and efficient means to counteract" any Marylanders who attempted "to arm their people against the United States."[66] The general needed no further instructions from Lincoln before purging Baltimore of its "secessionist" officials.

Early in the morning of June 27, 1861, Banks's soldiers arrested Kane and threw him into Fort McHenry. Banks, at Scott's suggestion, immediately appointed a provost marshal for Baltimore and ordered a detachment of troops to garrison the city. The Massachusetts general, however, denied that he had any intention of interfering with "the ordinary municipal affairs of Baltimore." He promised the people that no other troops would be permitted in the city except under the proper orders of the provost or himself, a pledge that did little to minimize the anger at the military's presence.[67] (Earlier, Butler, after entering Baltimore, had stationed troops on Federal Hill, but they did not actually occupy the city, despite the claims of state officials.) Upon news of Kane's seizure and the appointment of Colonel John R. Kenly as provost marshal, the board of police commissioners met in secret session and declared that the responsibilities of the police under state law had been forcibly suspended. The board summoned the police captains to their meeting and informed them that they were disbanding all police functions in the city.

Snethen immediately reported these events to Scott and charged that the commissioners in suspending the police force sought "to inaugurate anarchy" in the city. He alleged that the commissioners, encouraged by Chief Justice Taney, "whose loyalty is no longer a secret," were "concocting further rebellion." "There is no telling," he went on, "how soon they may rally their old police and precipitate the city into convulsion. Their new place [should be] Fort McHenry." Snethen also told Scott that a stash of 800 arms had been found at Jackson Hall in the city, half of them "stolen from the 6th Mass. Regiment" on the day of the April rioting. Kane and the police commissioners, Snethen claimed, "must have been cognizant of their secret deposit there." Scott approvingly forwarded the Baltimore Republican's letter to Lincoln, who, however, left the matter to the military's discretion.[68]

Banks needed little prompting to carry out the earlier order from Scott to take into military custody the police commissioners themselves, including its chairman, Charles Howard. He had his troops arrest the four men and imprison them in Fort McHenry. Banks immediately organized a new police force consisting of "the best men in the city"; they soon found a cache of "secreted arms" that a Colonel Thomas of Virginia had collected. These weapons presumably were destined for the Confederate army.

Predictably, reaction to the arrests of Kane and the commissioners was swift. While the military prevented violent protests, the southern rights press assailed Lincoln, Banks, and the Republican administration in Washington. Banks even charged that Francis Key Howard, the editor of the *Baltimore Exchange*, the son of arrested commissioner Charles Howard, and the grandson of Francis Scott Key, had recommended assassination as a means to right the wrongs supposedly committed by the Republicans. Howard had printed in his newspaper, "It is difficult to determine whether the country needs a Brutus or a Washington," clear evidence, according to Banks, that the Baltimore editor sought the death of Republican leaders.[69]

Conservative Unionists Johnson and John Pendleton Kennedy rushed to Washington and appealed to Lincoln to order the release of Commissioner Howard, who, they claimed, had done nothing to warrant arrest. Johnson and Kennedy told Lincoln that Howard was a true Unionist, despite the fact that three of his sons were in the Confederate army and his fourth son, Francis, was the militant southern rights editor of the *Exchange*. Lincoln, however, again refused to intervene; instead, he instructed Seward, who was present in the meeting, to inform Banks that he had "entire confidence in [his] discretion and in the sufficiency of the motives which led to [Howard's] arrest."[70]

Sustained by Lincoln, Banks continued to hold Howard and the other political prisoners in Fort McHenry. He justified his action to Seward on the ground that Howard, "without being, perhaps, a bad man at heart," was "one of the worst influences here." He maintained, "The wrong he commits is prospective and the safety of the govt requires his detention for the present." Banks further explained, "The government must make . . . men" like Howard "feel its power just as a matter of argument—They do not comprehend the condition of things at all—They read nothing but their own papers. . . . They live & move in small coteries into which no ideas can penetrate except their own distorting medium. . . . If the govermnt [*sic*] makes them feel its power they will immediately understand the condition of things and think and talk and act as the rest of the world does." The arrests of Howard and the police commissioners "did them good," Banks crowed. As a result, the Massachusetts general and former speaker of the U.S. House of Representatives happily reported that the city was "now very quiet" and in "no fear of an outbreak."[71]

Banks's actions, with Lincoln's sanction, no doubt had a chilling effect on those in the Baltimore area who openly favored the Confederacy or even expressed southern rights or antiwar views. However, the arrests came at an ominous price for civil liberties, and they would serve as a troubling precedent for future military arrests in Maryland and in the other border states, including Delaware, where fifty-two military arrests alone occurred between June 1863 and January 1864.[72] But the arrests and detentions had some plausibility in view of the real threat to the government in nearby Virginia and the uncertainty of loyalty in Baltimore and southeastern Maryland.

In mid-July, 1861, the imprisoned commissioners, Mayor Brown, and members of the City Council appealed to Congress for their release and demanded that "the military render obedience to the civil authority." The commissioners repeatedly proclaimed their loyalty and denied that they had stockpiled weapons for use by pro-Confederates. They explained that the arms in their possession had been distributed to militiamen during the April rioting and then recalled when order was restored. When General Butler entered Baltimore, they said, he had gained control of the weapons.[73] In their petition to Congress, the Baltimore officials failed to mention the secret cache of weapons that Snethen had reported to General Scott and that General Banks's new police force had seized after the arrests.

The detained police commissioners told Congress that they had asked Banks for an investigation of the charges against them, but he had refused. They asserted that Banks's order for their arrests and incarceration "was founded upon false information, communicated to him by designing persons," and could not "be sustained by credible evidence of any sort." The commissioners insisted that at the time "it was only necessary for General Banks to furnish the board of police with the slightest evidence" of a secessionist conspiracy and that if he had done so, they would have acted against the plotters.[74]

On July 24, 1861, the U.S. House of Representatives took up the case of the imprisoned commissioners and Marshal Kane. Since the withdrawal of representatives from the seceded states, the Republicans now had a comfortable majority in the House. They were divided, however, on issues involving civil liberties. As a result conservative Republicans joined northern Democrats and border state representatives to secure the passage of a resolution asking President Lincoln to inform the House immediately on "the grounds, reason, and evidence" for the arrest and imprisonment of the Baltimore officials. Lincoln refused the request. He explained that it "[would] be incompatible with the public interest at this time to furnish the information."[75] Having been rebuffed, the House majority let the matter die, though individual members both in the House and the Senate continued (unsuccessfully) to ask for the reasons why Maryland citizens were being held in federal "Bastilles."

When the Maryland General Assembly reconvened on July 30 for its third session since April, angry members overwhelmingly passed a series of resolutions denouncing the military arrests and imprisonment of the Balti-

CHAPTER TWO

more officials. The resolutions claimed that federal authorities had failed to prove that Kane and the police commissioners had attempted armed resistance to the Union. Furthermore, the resolutions charged Banks and the military with "a gross and unconstitutional abuse of power" that had revolutionary implications for the federal system of government. After approving the resolutions on August 7, the legislature adjourned to await events before reassembling on September 17.[76]

Meanwhile, Governor Hicks had abandoned any pretense of supporting the state's neutrality in the war. He agreed to raise the regiments that Lincoln had called for on April 15, which in effect nullified the General Assembly's action of May 10 declaring neutrality. The president, as he had promised, acquiesced in the governor's demand that the regiments serve only in Maryland and for the protection of the District of Columbia.[77] The restrictions were later quietly lifted, and the state's Union troops took their places in the battle lines in Virginia and at times across from their Maryland neighbors in the Confederate army. Although the exact numbers of Marylanders serving in the two armies during the war will never be known, one estimate has placed the figure of white Union troops at 35,000 and that of Confederates at 20,000. Some men served in a hodgepodge of units that are difficult to classify (for example, the irregular Baltimore militia of 1861). By the end of the war, 8,718 Maryland blacks had enlisted in the Union army.[78] (See chapter 8 for black recruitment in the state.)

By the summer of 1861, the Confederate concentration at Manassas Junction in northern Virginia had again placed Washington in harm's way. On July 21 the Confederate forces defeated the federal army under General McDowell in the first battle of Bull Run near Manassas Junction. Republicans feared that the victorious rebel army would soon descend upon the city and trigger a rebellion in Maryland. General George B. McClellan, who replaced General McDowell as the commander of the Army of the Potomac, gave credence to Republican concerns when he informed Secretary of War Cameron on September 8 that "the ultimate design of the enemy" was to occupy the capital, but he noted, "The first efforts will probably be directed towards Baltimore, with the intention of cutting our line of communications and supplies as well as to arouse an insurrection in Maryland."[79] Lincoln and members of his administration concluded that emboldened secessionists in the Maryland General Assembly, if permitted to meet on September 17, would aid the anticipated rebel invasion and would attempt to take the state out of the Union.

Seward, Cameron, Salmon P. Chase, and other members of the cabinet urged the president to purge the Maryland legislature of the "traitors" and their influential supporters before it assembled. Concerned Unionists in Maryland joined in the demand for federal action against the "secessionists." Frederick Schley, editor of the *Frederick Examiner*, reported to Seward, who had assumed control of the campaign to suppress disloyal elements in Maryland, that a "Tory" majority, if seated, would control both houses of the legislature. The risk to the Union was too great, Schley told Seward, to permit these men to participate in the legislative session scheduled to convene in his town. In Baltimore, Snethen wrote Seward demanding that the government prevent the sitting of the legislature and stating that the "traitors" in it, as well as prominent secessionists throughout the state, should be arrested and dispatched immediately to the Dry Tortugas off Florida or to another inhospitable federal prison.[80]

Seward agreed. In addition, interviews with a number of Maryland Unionists—probably including Hicks—reinforced in the minds of Seward, Lincoln, and the military commanders the need to act swiftly and without the niceties of the Bill of Rights or civil law to apprehend the "traitors" in the General Assembly and leading secessionists elsewhere in the state. The military order came from Secretary of War Cameron on September 11, following a "full consultation" with the president, cabinet members, and McClellan.[81] Lincoln, who was sometimes reluctant to give written instructions in a sensitive matter lest the matter become a national political issue, must have orally approved the order. Cameron's directive to Banks, however, did not specifically order him to purge the legislature, though that clearly was its intent. Cameron said that "the passage of any act of secession by the Legislature of Maryland must be prevented" and that "if necessary all or any part of the members must be arrested." He told Banks, "Exercise your own judgment as to the time and manner, but do the work effectively."[82]

Cameron and McClellan immediately dispatched Allan Pinkerton and his detectives to Baltimore to begin the arrests; they were to be supported by the military under General John A. Dix, who commanded in the city. The first roundup of suspected secessionists occurred under cover of darkness on September 12. Within hours, ten prominent citizens had been arrested and placed in Fort McHenry, preparatory to their transfer by steamer to the federal-controlled Fort Monroe in Virginia. The prisoners included Congressman Henry May and several members of the General Assembly who resided in the city. The War Department released May from imprisonment in Fort McHenry in time for him to take his seat in Congress on December 2. Editors Thomas W. Hall of the *South* and Francis Key Howard of the *Baltimore Exchange* were also arrested by federal authorities.[83]

On the same day, Mayor Brown was taken from his country home seven miles from Baltimore by a squad of soldiers and incarcerated in Fort McHenry. The charge, as Brown later found out, was that he had defied an order by General Dix to quit paying the salaries of the policemen who had been replaced by the military. The mayor claimed that he did not receive the order until after he had made the payments, which, he insisted, were done in accordance with state law.[84]

On September 17, 1861, the scene of the military arrests shifted to Frederick, where the General Assembly was scheduled to reconvene. General Banks, in overall command in Maryland, sent a list of legislators and clerks to Lieutenant Colonel Thomas H. Ruger and directed him to take into custody the men on the list if they appeared in Frederick. Ruger immediately implemented the order; he apprehended seven members of the House of Delegates and four officers or clerks, including several private citizens who had violently interfered with the arrests. They were sent to Fort McHenry for confinement.[85] The military arrested other legislators in late September in their home districts, including E. G. Kilbourn, the southern rights speaker of the House of Delegates. Altogether, twenty-seven legislators—one-third of the General Assembly members—were arrested and jailed. Since a quorum could not be obtained, the General Assembly did not convene.[86] Of the 509 known military arrests nationally in 1861—mainly in the border states—116 were of Marylanders. Arrests would continue and occurred with greater frequency in 1863–1864, when federal authorities jailed 136 citizens of the Old Line State.[87]

Soon after Brown's arrest, Lincoln received an inquiry from unidentified persons as to the reason for the mayor's detention. He declined to comment on the case. However, he took the occasion to make a public statement on all the arrests; it was printed in the *Baltimore American* on September 21. Lincoln announced, "The public safety renders it necessary that the grounds of these arrests should at present be withheld, but at the proper time they will be made public. Of one thing the people of Maryland may rest assured," he said, "no arrest has been made, or will be made, not based on substantial and unmistakable complicity with those in armed rebellion against the Government of the United States. . . . In all cases the Government is in possession of tangible and unmistakable evidence, which will, when made public, be satisfactory to every loyal citizen."[88] Neither the president nor his subordinates, however, ever revealed the "unmistakable evidence" for any of the arrests.

It was hardly the case, as Lincoln asserted, that no arrests had been made on "mere suspicion, or through personal or partisan animosities." Some of the detainees, including Brown and several members of the General Assembly, were held on false claims of disloyalty and plotting secession. Others were placed in custody for "precautionary" reasons to prevent their participation in the state's fall elections. Secretary of State Seward, probably with the president's knowledge if not approval, became a sort of political commissar in overseeing the detentions. In early November, 1861, he admitted to Lord Lyons, that "the recent arrests . . . had almost all been made in view of the Maryland elections."[89] Seward, if quoted correctly by Lord Lyons, overstated this motivation for the arrests. Lincoln and members of his administration, acting out of fear for the Union and for the security of the government in Washington, genuinely believed that at this critical time, when a Confederate invasion seemed likely, the state would collaborate with the rebels if the dissidents remained free to incite the people.

Actually, most of the arrested legislators, as well as others, despite their support for southern rights, had remained loyal to the Union while opposing Lincoln's war to suppress the South. They wanted Marylanders to maintain their neutrality in the conflict, and at the same time, they demanded the protection of their constitutional rights, including slavery. The dissident legislators, as well as their supporters, saw nothing inconsistent with a state policy of neutrality and support for the Union, a position that Hicks had originally favored and that was endorsed by many conservatives in other border states in 1861 after the war began. It proved to be an untenable position, but for a time the chimera of neutrality had a large following and contributed to keeping Maryland safely in the Union when the state was most susceptible to secession.

From their cells in the federal "Bastilles," the Maryland political prisoners vehemently challenged Lincoln's statement in the *Baltimore American* that

CHAPTER TWO

only those complicit in armed rebellion against the government had been arrested and imprisoned. Francis Key Howard, in a letter to the *Baltimore Times* from Fort Monroe, condemned the president's "statement as a baseless & atrocious lie," so far as it applied to him; and he continued, "From the knowledge I have of my fellow prisoners I am persuaded they would . . . contradict it in as emphatic a manner as I have done." Howard maintained that "whatever may be the character of my political opinions, I have not for the purpose of advancing them violated any law State or Federal."[90] He was not completely candid about his political actions. In addition to the veiled assassination threat that he had made in his newspaper, immediately after Fort Sumter and Lincoln's call for troops, Howard had circulated a petition in Baltimore declaring that if Virginia seceded, those signing the document would be "in favor of direct co-operation with that State in secession." The petition, containing more than 100 signatures, was found in Howard's papers at the time of his arrest.[91] Howard, however, seemed content to fire political broadsides at Lincoln and the Republicans without actually calling, at least publicly, for Maryland's secession.

Brown, also imprisoned in Fort Monroe, reacted with "great astonishment" when he read Lincoln's statement in the *Baltimore American*. He wrote the editor denouncing the president's assertion of his guilt: "As I am included by name in a charge of complicity with those in armed rebellion against the United States, it becomes both my duty and my right thus publicly to record my emphatic and unqualified denial of the accusation, and to demand the proof, if any exists, on which it is founded."[92]

Both Howard's and Brown's denials in the Baltimore press were sent to the president; neither received a response. Lincoln, however, drafted a statement that Seward completed and sent in answer to an appeal from Baltimore's police commissioner, John W. Davis, for release from prison. The president wrote, "He deeply commiserates the condition of any one so distressed as the writer seems to be." But he stated, "[Mr. Davis could] at any time since [his arrest], and can now, be released by taking a free oath of allegiance to the Government of the United States; and . . . Mr. Davis has not been kept in ignorance of the condition of release." Lincoln went on to say, "If Mr. Davis is still so hostile to the Government and so determined to aid[?] it's [sic] enemies in destroying it, he makes his own choice."[93] Like the other commissioners, Davis insisted that he had never been unfaithful to the Union, despite opposing the war. To be asked to take an oath of loyalty was insulting, Davis declared, and he refused to do so.

He remained a prisoner in Fort Warren, Boston Harbor, until November 1862, though he was granted an extended parole by the commandant.[94]

Hicks remained publicly silent when the arrests and imprisonments occurred. He had long battled his Democratic opponents in the General Assembly, and he had come to believe the worst about them. Privately, he approved the military arrests and confinements. The governor wrote Banks on September 20, 1861, "We see the good fruit already produced by the arrests" of the southern rights legislators. "We can no longer mince matters with these desperate people," he told Banks. "I concur in all that you have done."[95] When reports reached Hicks after the November election that the Lincoln administration planned to release the legislators, he pleaded with Seward to keep the main leaders in custody lest they give Maryland "much trouble here." "We are going on right in Maryland, and I beg that nothing be done to prevent what I have long desired and labored for, viz. the identification of Maryland with the Government proper." On the other hand, Reverdy Johnson, soon to be elected to the U.S. Senate, asked Seward to release all the prisoners, except Brown and the police commissioners, provided they took the oath of allegiance to the Union. Johnson also testified to the loyalty of several of the imprisoned legislators. The danger to the Union in Maryland having passed, Seward, probably after consulting with Lincoln, in late 1861 ordered the release of the rank-and-file prisoners, including some legislators, after they had taken the oath.[96]

Brown, despite a record of support for the Union, remained in prison until November 1862, which, not by coincidence, corresponded to the end of his term as mayor. At the same time, Francis Key Howard, his father Charles, Kane, and ten other political prisoners were released unconditionally. After his release, Francis Key Howard wrote a pamphlet that he defiantly entitled *Fourteen Months in American Bastilles*. When the publisher of the *Catholic Mirror* sold the pamphlet in his Baltimore bookstore, he was arrested and his store padlocked.[97]

The fall 1861 elections signaled the triumph of Unionism in the state. General Dix, commanding in eastern Maryland and following the orders of General McClellan, had directed his troops not to interfere with the state's election. The state at this time required no loyalty oath for its voters. Dix, however, had opened the door for a voter purge at the polls when he announced that election judges should "detect traitors [and] prevent the pollution of the ballot boxes by their votes." He ordered that "traitors" should "be taken into custody" if they showed up at the polls. The general's instructions caused many fearful southern rights and Confederate sympathizers to stay at home on election day. Some arrests of alleged traitors occurred when they sought to vote.[98]

For most of the state, military intimidation at the polls proved more feared than real. Indeed, voter turnout was high, particularly in view of the absence of hundreds of Marylanders in the armies and of others who remained at home out of concern that they would be arrested. The total vote was only 10 percent less than that of the 1860 presidential election. Some voters, who had not gone to the polls in 1860, cast ballots in 1861; most were motivated by a desire to sustain the Union in the state. During the campaign, Johnson and other Union Party champions either avoided mentioning slavery or reassured the voters that Lincoln was not a threat to the "peculiar institution." Congressman Francis Thomas, a former governor, announced at a rally in Baltimore that "there was nothing in the designs of the Chief Magistrate, or any of his Cabinet, to lead any person in Maryland to believe that they proposed interfering with the institution of slavery." Thomas, a slaveholder from the hilly western part of the state, applauded Lincoln's determination to put down secession and compared it favorably with Andrew Jackson's firm action in preserving the Union during the South Carolina Nullification crisis of 1832.[99]

In the election, Augustus W. Bradford, a former conservative Whig, swept to an overwhelming victory as the Union Party candidate for governor. He won 68 percent of the vote over his opponent, who had run under several party labels in the counties. The opposition to the Union Party, an offshoot of the old Democratic organization, mainly called itself the States' Rights Party. It professed loyalty to the Union while opposing the war and assailing Lincoln's violations of civil liberties.[100] Bradford received 57,502 votes to his opponent's 26,070. The Union Party easily won control of the House of Delegates, but held only twelve of the twenty-two seats in the new state senate after the election (only eleven senate seats were at stake in the November election).[101]

The news of the Union Party's victory delighted Lincoln. On November 15 he confidently told a Union delegation of Baltimore citizens that he regarded the results of their state elections "as auspicious of returning loyalty" not only in Maryland but also "throughout all the insurrectionary States." He recalled "the calamities which the sympathies of some misguided citizens of Maryland had brought down upon" Baltimore in April. "The prosperity of Baltimore up to the 19th of April last," Lincoln declared, "was one of the wonders produced by the American Union, [but] in a single night [Baltimoreans] destroyed" the railroads leading into the city and thus their prosperity. "From the day when that mad transaction occurred," Lincoln said, "the Government of the United States has been diligently engaged in endeavoring to restore those great avenues to their former usefulness, and, at the same time, to save Baltimore and Maryland from the danger of complete ruin through an unnecessary and unnatural rebellion." Success, Lincoln announced, had crowned the efforts of the government and Maryland loyalists to save the state for the Union. He heartily congratulated the people of Baltimore and the state for their "declaration . . . of enduring loyalty to the Union."[102]

A few weeks after the November 1861 election, someone, probably Secretary of State Seward, drafted a presidential proclamation directing that "all political prisoners" in Maryland should be freed in view of the voters' emphatic decision for the Union in the contest. The document was later found in the files of the State Department.[103] No record exists that the president actually issued the proclamation. However, about this time a policy of freeing those prisoners deemed less dangerous to the government and who agreed to take the loyalty oath began under Seward's supervision.

The Union Party victory in November did not represent a vote of confidence in Lincoln. In addition to their traditional attachment to the republic of the Founders, many who supported the Union ticket did so out of necessity. They concluded that if Maryland remained loyal, they would be able to avoid the terrible consequences of the war. Many Marylanders, though supportive of the Union, continued to oppose Lincoln's "war of aggression" against their neighbors to the south. Governor Bradford was not one of them. On December 4, 1861, he charged the new legislature to place the state firmly behind the Union cause in the war, and, as evidence of its commitment, to provide for the arming and equipping of Maryland's full quota of volunteers for the army. Although he had a son in the Confederate army, Bradford called for legislation to punish those persons aiding and abetting the rebellion.[104]

Bradford devoted most of his important inaugural address on January 8, 1862, to denouncing the secessionists but at the same time warning that Maryland's Unionism could be quickly reversed if emancipation became a purpose of the war. A slaveholder himself, like his predecessor Hicks, Brad-

CHAPTER TWO

ford declared that a federal policy to end slavery would constitute "treason" and would be "far more potent for mischief" than "any assistance that Secession is likely to receive from abroad, nor the aid and comfort which treason at home may convey to it." The governor, however, reminded Marylanders that President Lincoln in his inaugural address had assured Americans that he had "no purpose directly or indirectly to interfere with the institution of slavery in the States where it existed" and, furthermore, that "he had no lawful right nor inclination to do so." Bradford rejoiced that Lincoln's "whole subsequent course has justly confirmed us in the conviction that he means to conduct this war with the single purpose of preserving the nation." In addition, he said, Congress in its war resolution in July 1861 (the Johnson-Crittenden Resolution) had endorsed this goal.[105]

The new General Assembly approved Governor Bradford's recommendations for the suppression of rebels and the limited Union purpose in the war. It also pointedly ratified the proposed thirteenth amendment prohibiting the federal government from interfering with slavery in the states.[106] Maryland thus became one of the few states to approve the proslavery amendment, which had passed Congress in early 1861 as part of the ill-fated compromise package to save the Union. Ironically, the Thirteenth Amendment that became a part of the Constitution in December 1865 ended rather than perpetuated slavery in all the states.

Despite the continuing dissatisfaction of southern rights supporters and also despite the Confederate recruitment of soldiers in the state, Maryland by early 1862 had clearly cast its lot with the Union. The emancipation issue would later trigger a vigorous debate in the state, but it did not seriously threaten Union control. However, if Lincoln had inaugurated his emancipation policy during the first year of the war, when support for southern rights was strong, it would have inflamed Maryland whites, both slaveholders and nonslaveholders, to the point of resisting the Union rather than supporting it. Conservative Unionist leaders like Governor Hicks and Reverdy Johnson would conceivably have joined with their old political enemies, states' rights Democrats, in rallying the state against Lincoln and the "abolitionist fanatics." Marylanders would have concluded that the president and his party were determined not only to destroy slavery but also to establish black equality in all the slave states. Lincoln, of course, did not impose federal emancipation upon the South until January 1, 1863, and then only in the Confederacy. He never sought black equality, though in his last public speech, on April 11, 1865, Lincoln acknowledged that he favored "the elective franchise [for] the very intelligent" blacks and for "those who serve our cause as soldiers." Still, he stopped short of declaring that he intended to require black suffrage in the defeated South.[107]

Political developments and conflict in the trans-Appalachian border states after Fort Sumter followed a pattern similar to Maryland's, though differing in particulars and occurring with greater intensity. The outcome for the Union remained uncertain for most of 1861 in Missouri and for even longer in Kentucky. In Missouri, where a bitter border conflict over slavery in Kansas had raged before the war, a secessionist-leaning governor, Claiborne F. Jackson, and a Democratic legislature controlled the state during the spring of 1861. However, an emerging German American population and other newcomers in Saint Louis provided a counterweight to Jackson's designs. The U.S. arsenal at Saint Louis and the headquarters nearby of the Department of the West under pro-Union officers also served to prevent a secessionist coup. Despite formidable opposition, the governor, along with his zealous supporters, mainly outside Saint Louis, labored in a zigzag fashion in 1861 to take the state out of the Union.

In Kentucky, Lincoln depended on the old Union Whig leadership, joined by Douglas Democrats, to sustain the Union. Although Governor Beriah Magoffin and the majority of the legislature, elected before the crisis, were southern rights Democrats, the Bluegrass State had a strong Union tradition that owed a great deal to the influence of Whig icon Henry Clay, who had died in 1852. When the war began, Lincoln turned to the "Great Commoner's" Kentucky disciples, such as John J. Crittenden, George D. Prentice of the *Louisville Daily Journal*, and Garret Davis for Union leadership. In addition, the president could depend on his close friend Joshua Speed and his older brother James, both Whigs, for support and as reliable sources of intelligence on Kentucky. All were conservative Unionists who, like Hicks and Johnson in Maryland, had no love for antislavery Republicans and, in the beginning, clearly agonized over Lincoln's war to suppress their southern neighbors. Not only were Kentuckians bound to the South by their proslavery sentiments, but they also had important commercial and transportation ties with Tennessee and the lower South. In dealing with Kentucky, Lincoln had to tread carefully in order to keep the state in the Union.

Despite differences in their economic interests and political party tradi-

CHAPTER TWO

tions, the two overarching concerns of the white people in all the border states in 1861 and later were the need to protect slavery and the fear of being caught in the middle of an internecine war. Lincoln realized that to be successful despite the growing radical demand he faced within his party and among abolitionists for a more vigorous war against southern society, including emancipation, he would have to satisfy border state concerns and pursue a flexible and patient policy toward each state. He wisely understood that the first step toward preserving the Union in 1861 would be to save the border country, and no state was more important politically and strategically than his native Kentucky.

CHAPTER 3

■

Kentucky: Experiment in Neutrality

On April 18, William "Bull" Nelson, a native Kentuckian and U.S. Navy lieutenant visiting in Louisville, excitedly wrote a friend, "The people have absolutely gone mad. Some of the best Union men are talking secession and acting as officers of secession meetings." His letter was forwarded to President Lincoln. After years of sectional conflict and bitter political recrimination, civil war had become a reality when Confederate guns opened fire on Fort Sumter in Charleston Harbor and Lincoln called for troops to suppress the southern insurrection. Nelson, who would later secure federal arms for local Unionists and raise federal troops in the state, misleadingly reported, "Gov. Magoffin is here doing all he can to encourage secession, damn him!"[1]

Lincoln agreed with Lieutenant Nelson's grim assessment of political conditions in Kentucky. He announced to a group from the Bluegrass State, "Kentucky must not be precipitated into secession. She is the key to the situation," adding, "She is now in the hands of those who do not represent the people. The sentiment of her State officials must be counteracted" at once. Lincoln told the Kentuckians, "We need only to organize against Governor McGoffin's [sic] followers to beat them." He expressed confidence that with Kentucky "faithful to the Union the discord in the other States [would] come to an end."[2] Although Governor Beriah Magoffin was a peace and southern rights advocate, he stopped short of backing secession, so long as Lincoln remained true to his promise to respect the rights of the states under the Constitution, including slavery. Despite the president's understandable concerns about the governor's loyalty, Magoffin, who served in office until August 1862, never cast his lot with the rebels.

Nonetheless, the crisis in Kentucky was real and could easily have deteriorated into secession. Lieutenant Nelson reported to his Unionist friend—and thus to Lincoln—that already hundreds of men had enrolled in rebel units and that others had left for the lower South to enlist in the Confederate army. One ray of hope for the Union, Nelson wrote, was that John J. Crittenden and other leading Unionists planned to stump the state in an effort to calm the passions of the people and to urge them to remain loyal.[3] However, both Crittenden and George D. Prentice of the *Louisville Daily Journal* at this time agreed with Magoffin and most Kentuckians that the state should provide no troops for the suppression of the seceded states.[4]

Frightened by the real prospect of the state being caught in the middle of the impending war, the Union State Central Committee, formed in January 1861 to resist secession, on April 17 issued an address to the people of Kentucky on the crisis. The committee, consisting of both Whigs and Democrats, announced, "The alliance between party spirit and the sectional question of slavery has at length produced the legitimate fruit of such a combination. Disunion and war are upon the land." The committee endorsed the governor's refusal to provide troops for the "wild and suicidal" policy of coercing the seceded states to return to the Union. The duty of Kentucky, the committee declared, was "to maintain her present independent position, taking sides not with the Government and not with the seceding States, but with the Union against them both." This was the bipartisan committee's idea of neutrality in the war, and for more than four months, with some variation, it would be the accepted policy of the state. The committee maintained that Kentucky's "soil [should] be sacred from the hostile tread of either [army]." In order for the state to be "fully prepared," the committee "would have her arm herself thoroughly at the earliest possible moment."[5] Like the Maryland General Assembly, the members of the committee saw no contradiction between a policy of neutrality and continued loyalty to the Union. Such a position, they believed, was constitutional, and the only possible way to save Kentucky from becoming a battleground in the war.

On April 19, two days after the Union State Central Committee issued its address, Unionists held a huge rally in Louisville. Called to order by James Speed, the participants heard stirring Unionist speeches by James Guthrie and Archibald Dixon, after which they endorsed the policy of neutrality and affirmed its consistency with support for the old Union. Guthrie, President Franklin Pierce's secretary of the treasury and president of the Louisville and Nashville Railroad, told the crowd that only ruin would follow if Kentucky separated itself from the states north of the Ohio River. At the same time, he castigated Lincoln for speaking with a forked tongue in calling for peace in his inaugural address and then bringing on war and bloodshed with his call for volunteers to invade the seceded states. Kentuckians, Guthrie insisted, should not permit Lincoln's action to influence their loyalty to the American flag.[6]

Dixon, a former Whig senator, in his speech did not blame the new president for the troubles. He reminded the Louisville throng that Lincoln had denied any intention of interfering with slavery and had repeatedly proclaimed his commitment to the enforcement of the Fugitive Slave Act. Still, Dixon declared that Kentuckians would not "submit to Lincoln" if he sent troops into the state. Dixon promised, "Kentucky will stand firm with her sister Border States in the centre of the Republic, to calm the distracted sections" and restore peace. "The contest," he exclaimed, "should be with Mr. Lincoln" and his policies, "and not with the flag [or] the Union." Dixon charged, "Demagogues at the North and demagogues at the South have divided the country [and] inaugurated civil war." He told Kentuckians, "If we give up the Union, all is lost. There will then be no breakwater, but instead, Kentucky will be the battle-ground . . . in a [bloody] conflict as no country has yet witnessed." A neutral stand in the conflict, Dixon assured the crowd, would roll back on both sides "the tide of war and desolation."[7]

Meanwhile, former Whig congressman Garret Davis, who would soon assume a leading role for the Union in the state, made "a hurried run" to Washington in order to find out Lincoln's position "on public affairs" and on Kentucky in particular. Davis, "a spry, peppery, gray-haired little man of about sixty," met with Lincoln and members of the cabinet during the week of April 23.[8] Although Washington was virtually under siege by secessionists and Maryland's position was uncertain, Davis, who in December 1861 would replace John C. Breckinridge in the U.S. Senate, "found the President frank and calm." But, while hoping for peace, Lincoln was "decided and firm" in his determination to save the government, Davis reported.[9]

Lincoln, according to Davis's account written a few days later, told the Kentuckian that he "greatly regretted" that the state had not complied with his requisition for troops to sustain "the principle of her great statesman [Henry Clay]" in supporting the Union and the Constitution. Despite the fact that he deplored Kentucky's refusal to aid the cause, Lincoln promised that he would not invade the state—or any border state—"unless she or her people should make it necessary by a formidable resistance of the authority and laws of the United States." Furthermore, Davis reported, "he contemplated no military operations that would make it necessary to move any troops over her territories, though he had the unquestioned right at all times to march United States troops into and over any and every state." Finally, Lincoln reassured Davis that he intended "to make no attack, direct or indirect upon the institutions or property of any State"—he meant slaves as well as other property—"but, on the contrary, would defend them to the full extent with which the Constitution and laws of Congress have vested the president with the power."[10] In essence, Lincoln agreed to respect traditional federal-state relations in the border states, a promise that he would find difficult to keep as the war assumed a magnitude and intensity that he probably had not anticipated.

Davis expressed satisfaction with Lincoln's explanation of his intentions toward Kentucky. He left Washington determined to support a policy of neutrality for the state, as long, paradoxically, as its people remained true to the Union.[11] After returning home, Davis wrote General George B. McClellan, commanding in Ohio, "We will remain in the Union by voting if we can, by fighting if we must, and if we cannot hold our own, we will call on the General Government to aid us."[12] Davis hoped, however, that there would be no need to abandon the state's neutrality or to seek federal intervention.

In late April, Governor Magoffin moved to secure legislative sanction for a policy of armed neutrality for Kentucky. He issued a call for the General Assembly to meet on May 6 in a special session to provide for the state's defense and to formalize Kentucky's neutrality. He also prohibited citizens from aiding either side in the war, a prohibition that soon fell victim to the bitter divisions in the state.[13] The governor specifically wanted the legislature's approval for the organization and arming of the Kentucky militia and for his control over it. Though Magoffin remained loyal to the Union, he faced an important concern and dilemma: to protect Kentucky as long as the "Black Republicans" controlled the federal government and made war on the seceded states. Conservative Unionists, mainly old Whigs like Garret Davis, though supporting neutrality, opposed arming a militia that would be under the Democratic governor's control. Ever suspicious of their old political foe's intentions, they believed that Magoffin would suppress those loyal to the national government.

The governor justified the need for action, not on the ground of a secessionist threat but on the likelihood that troops from the North would soon march into the state and violate Kentucky's neutrality.[14] Magoffin reasoned that if the state had a force ready to resist the northern troops, Lincoln and the Republican governors above the Ohio would think twice before invading the state. An armed state militia, Magoffin believed, would also be available to put down disorders at home, including those created by radical Unionists and slaves whom northern abolitionists might inspire to revolt.

After the legislature met, the House of Representatives on May 16 overwhelmingly passed a resolution declaring that the state and its citizens "should take no part in the civil war now being waged, [and] should, during the contest, occupy the position of strict neutrality." It also approved a resolution by a vote of 89 to 4 endorsing the governor's refusal to provide troops for the federal government.[15] Magoffin did not wait for the state senate to act; on May 20 he issued a proclamation of neutrality and again warned all citizens against "any hostile demonstrations" for either side in the war. The governor also announced that he was raising the militia, known as the State Guard, "to resist and prevent encroachment" on Kentucky's "sovereignty by either of the belligerent parties." At the same time, he expressed the hope that "Kentucky [would] become a successful mediator" between the belligerents in the war.[16]

A few days before the legislature assembled, an election was held for delegates to a border state convention to meet in Frankfort on May 27. The purpose of the May convention, which had been called by an earlier session of the Kentucky General Assembly, was to put pressure on Lincoln and the Republicans to accept the Crittenden Compromise. Bluegrass State Unionists, like those in Maryland, had held on to the fantasy of a compromise settlement of the sectional conflict, even after Lincoln called for troops to suppress the southern insurrection and the upper South prepared to leave the Union. On May 4 Unionists, and those leaning in that direction, turned out in large numbers at the polls. They elected twelve Unionists as delegates to the Frankfort convention, including Crittenden, who had recently retired from the U.S. Senate. Much to the disappointment of the Kentuckians, only Missouri of the other border states sent accredited delegates (four) to the convention. Maryland and Delaware Unionists were too remote to send representatives; furthermore, in the case of Maryland, an immediate crisis of loyalty existed at home. An east Tennessee Unionist appeared at Frankfort and was granted a seat in the convention.[17]

After a session of several days in late May, the Border Slave States Convention, chaired by Crittenden, issued an address, "To the People of the United States." The address described the horrible "spectacle . . . exhibited in our distracted land" and proclaimed, "The cry to arms resounds throughout our borders." The only hope to prevent "the horrors of civil war," it stated, was for the free states to approve the constitutional proposals contained in the Crittenden Compromise, measures that Republicans in Congress had earlier rejected. The convention admitted that the northern ratification of the proposals might not "have the effect of reconciling any of the seceded States to the Government" of the Union, but predicted, "The masses in those States will, in time, learn that the dangers they were made to fear were greatly exaggerated. They will then be disposed to listen to the calls of interest and of patriotism, and return to the family from which they had gone out." At any rate, Kentucky and Missouri would "take no part in this war," leaving them in a good position to mediate the strife and bring about peace.[18]

The Bluegrass State delegation in the convention issued a separate statement, "To the People of Kentucky," explaining why they should remain neutral in the war. The conflict, the address contended, "resulted from the ambition of men, rather than from the wrongs done the people. There was a remedy for every thing, already provided by the Constitution, which, with wise foresight, provided against the trials to which it might be subjected." Congress, with a majority in opposition to the Republicans, could have controlled the "sectional President," Lincoln, and obtained redress for southern grievances. But, the Kentucky statement declared, the lower southern congressmen abandoned their seats and left the government in the hands of Lincoln and his sectional party. Their leaving "was a great wrong for which they must answer to posterity." Kentuckians had "had no hand in" bringing on such an unnecessary war and therefore should remain out of it. Otherwise, it warned, "the hostile armies will meet on our soil, and it will matter but little to us which may succeed, for destruction to us will be the inevitable result." Even slavery, for which "this wretched war was undertaken, will be exterminated in the general ruin."[19]

This sober document was signed by some of the most prominent men of both old parties, including the venerable Charles A. Wickliffe, a former governor and southern rights Democrat. It went far toward steeling Kentuckians in support of remaining neutral while continuing to be loyal to the Union and sending their representatives to Congress. The statement, however, did not endorse Magoffin's support of armed neutrality as a means to protect Kentuckians from "hostile armies."[20]

Some Union leaders in 1861 feared a civil war within the state more than an invasion by federal troops, especially if Magoffin's State Guard became a viable military force. Crittenden wrote General Winfield Scott on May 17, in a letter forwarded to Lincoln, that if Kentucky had responded to the president's April 15 call for troops, "she would have been overwhelmed by the Secessionists at home, and severed from the Union." Thus, "it was to preserve, substantially & ultimately, our connection with the Union" and to avoid civil strife that Kentuckians were induced "to acquiesce in . . . [her] Governor's refusal of the troops required" by the president. In this way, Crittenden insisted, Kentucky was "rendering better service, in her present position" of neutrality "than she could by becoming an active party in the contest."[21]

Crittenden also reported to Lincoln that serious damage was being done to the Union cause in Louisville by a circular of May 2, issued by Secretary of the Treasury Salmon P. Chase to his agents in the field prohibiting the transportation of goods to the South through the state. Crittenden called on Lincoln to revoke the directive and permit trade to flow unimpeded.[22] Former governor Charles S. Morehead, who had a large plantation in Mississippi to sustain, reached demagogic heights when he charged that Chase, with Lincoln's approval, was "daily preventing supplies of food to the . . . slaves of the South, in order . . . to [excite] servile insurrection." This was hardly Chase's intention. The circular, however, was more often ignored than enforced. On June 12 Lincoln, in order to satisfy Kentuckians and despite the vigorous opposition of the Republican governors of Illinois, Indiana, and Ohio, directed Chase to relax the trade rules. As long as Kentucky maintained its neutral position, trade with the lower South on the

Louisville and Nashville Railroad and the rivers, including the Mississippi, moved virtually unchecked.[23]

The governor's policy of "strict neutrality" proved untenable almost from the beginning, as did his desire that the combatants accept his offer to mediate the crisis. Even before his proclamation of May 20, bitter political conflict erupted in the state over the war. The Southern Rights Party had formed in early 1861, and during the spring it repeated its demand for a state convention. Ostensibly, a convention could put pressure on Congress to reverse Lincoln's policy of coercion of the South, but it could also enact an ordinance of secession, as had happened in the seceded states. Former vice president John C. Breckinridge led the Southern Rights campaign for a convention. Breckinridge's family reflected the growing divisions within the Bluegrass State elite over the war: His uncle, Robert J. Breckinridge, a nationally prominent Protestant minister, was an ardent Union spokesman, though two of his sons would soon join the Confederate army. A similar division occurred within the Clay, Crittenden, and Prentice families, and even within Mary Lincoln's Todd family in Lexington. The divisions in Kentucky over the war were greater than in any state.

John C. Breckinridge, who earlier in 1861 had been elected to the U.S. Senate, told a large gathering of supporters in Louisville on April 20 that a policy of neutrality would not work because eventually Kentucky would be forced to choose a side in the conflict. If Lincoln persisted in his war against the seceded states, Breckinridge declared that Kentucky should "unite her fortunes with the South."[24] The reassembled legislature, as it had done prior to the outbreak of hostilities and faced with renewed pressure from Unionists, rejected the Breckinridge faction's demand for a convention. It also went a step further in disassociating the state from the southern rights forces and the governor's State Guard, though its action had little immediate effect.

Staunch Unionists feared that if Magoffin succeeded in his quest to secure arms for the State Guard, the weapons would be turned against them.[25] State Inspector General Simon Bolivar Buckner, a West Point graduate, southern rights supporter, and, ironically, a prewar friend of U. S. Grant, commanded the State Guard. Its officers and recruits favored the Confederate States, and once the guard was organized, it would probably intimidate Unionists. Kentucky Unionists, while supporting neutrality, bombarded Lincoln during the

George D. Prentice, long-time proprietor and editor of the Louisville Journal, *the most influential old-line Whig newspaper in Kentucky. As a youth, Lincoln read Prentice's newspaper. A critic of President Lincoln until after his re-election in 1864, Prentice provided important political guidance to conservative Unionists in the state. Portrait of Prentice in* The Poems of George D. Prentice *(Cincinnati: R. Clarke and Co., 1876).*

spring and summer with frantic appeals for arms to counter Buckner's forces. Lieutenant Nelson, after visiting Kentucky, went to Washington in early May to seek arms for the protection of the state's Unionists, who were forming Home Guard units to counter Buckner's State Guard. He met with Lincoln, who at first seemed reluctant to grant the weapons lest it appear that the federal government was intervening in the state. Nelson, however, impressed upon the president the urgency of the situation and persuaded him that the Unionists needed the arms to prevent Kentucky from falling to the secessionists. Lincoln agreed to issue 5,000 muskets to Nelson with instructions for him to meet with Joshua Speed and coordinate the secret distribution of the arms to Kentucky Unionists.[26]

On May 7 Nelson (who would later be appointed a brigadier general in the federal army) found Speed in Louisville. They immediately went to Frankfort, where, along with Crittenden, Garret Davis, and three other Unionists, they formed a Union Defense Committee for the distribution of the weapons. Within ten days the 5,000 muskets had been delivered to Home Guard units; three weeks later they received another shipment of weapons.[27]

In a letter to Lincoln on May 27, Speed reported that the distribution had "had a most salutary influence upon the [Union] party in Ky." It had given "strength and confidence to our friends—and weaken[ed] our foes." Speed added, "If the good work can go on, without bloodshed or violence, we will have Ky all right." He informed his old friend that the "secessionists" had had no such success. Speed, who believed that Magoffin was a secessionist, ridiculed an effort by the governor to buy arms in New Orleans. Before the arms arrived, Speed told Lincoln, "each secessionist looked to be a foot taller, [and] talked loud and boastfully of what they intended to do" with the weapons. When they arrived, "lo & behold, they were old flint lock muskets altered to percussion, [but] in altering them they had omitted to bore a touch hole. They could load them very well" but could not fire them. Speed thought that Lincoln would enjoy the "joke," which he must have, though he had little else to laugh about at this time.[28]

On the other hand, Breckinridge's southern rights friends, while still purporting to support neutrality, found nothing amusing in the surreptitious delivery of federal arms to their opponents. When they discovered what had happened, the *Frankfort Kentucky Yeoman* denounced Lincoln's "arming one class of men in Kentucky by the lawless instrumentality of clandestine agents."[29] Confederate sympathizers sarcastically referred to the weapons as "Lincoln guns," a label that ardent Unionists proudly adopted.[30]

At the same time, the president sent Colonel Robert J. Anderson, the hero of Fort Sumter and a native Kentuckian, to Cincinnati, Ohio, with instructions to consult with Speed in order to facilitate the transportation of the arms to Kentucky. (Anderson, a major at Fort Sumter, only briefly held the rank of colonel; on June 17 he was appointed a brigadier general.) Lincoln also "empowered," not ordered, Anderson "to receive into the Service of the United States, as many regiments of volunteer troops from the State of Kentucky and from the Western part of the State of Virginia" as were willing to serve for three years. These troops, unlike those from the North, would be organized by the federal government and not by the states.[31] Speed and his Union associates persuaded Anderson not to alienate Kentucky's conservatives by becoming involved in the distribution of the weapons to the Unionist Home Guard or in the recruitment of federal troops within the state.[32] Anderson, however, opened a camp in Ohio, named Camp Holt after Kentucky Unionist leader Joseph Holt, for the organization of Kentucky regiments in the Union army. On May 28 Lincoln appointed Anderson to command the newly organized Department of Kentucky but did not give him the authority to move into the state.

Western governors faulted Lincoln for his failure to act forcibly against Kentucky and its self-proclaimed neutrality. On May 24 Governors Richard Yates of Illinois, Oliver Morton of Indiana, and William Dennison of Ohio met in Indianapolis to discuss the uncertain situation existing in the Bluegrass State and Lincoln's acquiescence in Kentucky's neutrality policy. Fearing that the rebellion would be brought to their borders, they sent army General in Chief Winfield Scott a memorial demanding that he order federal troops to occupy strategic points in Kentucky before it was too late to save the state. These positions, the governors contended, would also serve as bases for operations against the "more Southern States."[33] Scott refused, evidently after conferring with Lincoln, and he warned the governors against interfering in Kentucky affairs. The western governors, particularly Morton, continued their criticism of Lincoln's border state pacification policy, even after Kentucky had abandoned its neutrality stance in September 1861.[34]

Lincoln's conservative friend Orville H. Browning joined the chorus of criticism when he wrote the president that Kentucky's neutrality was "both ridiculous and puerile." Kentucky, Browning's native state, "must either be for us or against us," he told Lincoln. "No state has a right to interpose between your armies and the rebels. If she does, crush her down. Ask no permission to march where duty calls."[35]

Anxious Kentucky Unionists also called for stronger federal action, including military intervention, to suppress secessionist sentiment in their state. In Washington, Joseph Holt played an important role in bolstering the Union cause in his home state and in seeking federal military assistance. Holt was a former member of President James Buchanan's cabinet and had taken a hard-line stand in the Fort Sumter crisis. On May 31, in response to an appeal from Joshua Speed, he wrote a long letter, designed for publication, condemning Kentucky's neutrality policy. Speed had 30,000 copies of Holt's letter printed in Louisville and immediately distributed. Holt compared his state's neutrality with "being neutral in a contest between an officer of justice and an incendiary arrested in an attempt to fire the dwelling over [one's] head." The refusal to take sides in the struggle to save the Union, he wrote, was a delusion and could not be sustained; it served only to provide aid and comfort to those seeking to destroy the nation. Holt denounced Magoffin's declaration prohibiting the U.S. government from marching its troops across the state. "This is, in no sense, a neutral step," Holt argued, "but one of aggressive hostility. The troops of the Federal Government have a clear constitutional right to pass over the soil of Kentucky as they have to march along the streets of Washington, and could this prohibition be effective it . . . would, in all its tendencies, be directly in advancement of the revolution [rebellion]."[36]

Holt unabashedly defended the president's policies to suppress the insurrection, despite the strong anti-Lincoln sentiment in his state. (Like most leading Kentucky Unionists, Holt was from a slaveholding family.)[37] Holt contended that Lincoln, beginning with his inauguration, had actively sought to obtain "a peaceful solution of our unhappy political troubles," even to the extent of agreeing to a constitutional amendment forever prohibiting the federal government from interfering with slavery in the states. But the rebel states of the lower South, Holt charged, had sought a clash of arms in Charleston Harbor in order to produce a war that would bring Kentucky and the other slave states to their side. President Lincoln had met their plan "with promptitude and fearlessness" and, by following a conservative course, had succeeded in maintaining the loyalty of the border states. Holt cited the president's "fidelity" to the enforcement of the Fugitive Slave Act as evidence of his good will toward the institution of slavery, a proslavery concern that Speed, Crittenden, and other Unionists had earlier expressed to Lincoln.[38]

Finally, Holt warned Kentuckians that a continuation of the state's armed neutrality, as approved by the legislature and proclaimed by Governor Magoffin, would inevitably lead to secession and the destruction of slavery. He also warned that if Kentucky joined the new slaveholding confederacy, the state would "virtually have Canada brought to her doors in the form of Free States, whose population, relieved of all moral and constitutional obligations to deliver up fugitive slaves, [would] stand with open arms inviting and welcoming them." Holt predicted, "Under such influences, slavery will perish rapidly away in Kentucky, as a ball of snow melts in a summer's sun." He implored Kentuckians to organize every neighborhood for the defense of the Union before it became "everlastingly too late."[39]

Holt's public letter had a salutary effect on wavering Kentuckians, and it also emboldened Unionists. Holt's popularity in the state, especially among old Democrats, proved important in swaying public opinion away from Magoffin's "aggressive neutrality" and toward a strong Union commitment. His letter, as well as campaign speeches by Crittenden and other ardent Unionists, contributed greatly to the success of the state Union Party in congressional contests on June 20. These elections became necessary after Lincoln's call for a special session of the new Congress to meet on July 4; the old Congress had expired on March 3. Many activists in the Breckinridge-led Southern Rights Party refused to participate in an election to "Lincoln's Congress"; as a result, the Union Party won nine of the ten congressional contests. The nine Union victors were conservative on constitutional rights and the preservation of slavery. Crittenden, who had retired from the Senate, was one of the congressional winners. The Southern Rights Party's sole victor, Henry C. Burnett, took his seat in Congress but, without resigning, left in November to preside over the convention that formed the Kentucky state provisional government; it aligned with the southern Confederacy. In December, the U.S. House of Representatives formally expelled Burnett from its membership.

The important success of the Union Party in the congressional elections did not mean that the state had abandoned its neutrality policy. But Magoffin's armed version of neutrality, backed by his southern rights–leaning State Guard, had suffered a major defeat. Lincoln had seemingly accepted the state's neutrality, but he was only biding his time, waiting for Unionists to gain strength and replace Magoffin's supporters in the Kentucky government. From the beginning, Lincoln had privately viewed neutrality as little better than hostility to the federal government. Finally, encouraged by the June 20 congressional election results in Kentucky, he vented his disapproval of border state neutrality in his July 4 message to the special session of Congress that he had called, the first session since the war began. Without naming the states, though he mainly meant Kentucky, the president came down hard on the policy of armed neutrality in particular. "In the border States," he told Congress, "there are those who favored a policy which they call 'armed neutrality'—that is the arming of those states to prevent the Union forces passing one way, or the disunion, the other, over their soil. This would be disunion completed." He argued that "under the guise of neutrality, it would tie the hands of the Union men, and freely pass supplies from among them, to the insurrectionists, which it could not do as an open enemy." The armed neutrality policy, Lincoln said, "recognizes no fidelity to the Constitution, no obligation to maintain the Union, and while very many who have favored it are, doubtless, loyal citizens, it is, nevertheless, treason in effect."[40]

Disturbed by the president's criticism, Magoffin dispatched Simon Bolivar Buckner of his State Guard to Washington for a clarification of the administration's position. On July 10 Buckner met with the president at the White House. Lincoln gave the Kentuckian a written statement declaring that, as president, his duty required him to suppress the insurrection but that he would do so only "with the least possible disturbance, or annoyance to well disposed people anywhere." He told Buckner, "So far I have not sent an armed force into Kentucky; nor have I any present purpose to do so. I sincerely desire that no necessity for it may be presented; but I mean to say nothing which shall hereafter embarrass me in the performance of what may seem to be my duty."[41]

Lincoln's answer obviously was not the unequivocal statement of approval of Kentucky's neutrality that Buckner wanted. However, one month later, in an attempt to placate Buckner and Magoffin, the president offered Buckner a commission as a brigadier general of volunteers in the federal army.[42] The Kentuckian refused the commission. After Kentucky's neutrality strategy collapsed in September, Buckner led most of the State Guard militiamen into the Confederate army; he eventually became a lieutenant general in the rebel forces. Ironically, Buckner's son, by the same name, also served as a lieutenant general, but in the U.S. Army during World War II. He had the unfortunate distinction of being the highest-ranking American general killed in the war. His father met no similar fate: he survived the Civil War and in 1914 became the last senior officer of the Confederacy to die.

The recruitment and organization of Kentuckians in the Union regiments at Camp Holt in Ohio during the spring of 1861, which Lincoln permitted, had not technically violated the state's neutrality. However, pressure soon mounted on the president to authorize the formation of federal regiments within the state. Aware of the sensitivity of Unionists like Prentice on the issue, Lincoln moved cautiously. On July 29 Lincoln called members of Kentucky's delegation in Congress to the White House and announced, "I somewhat wish to authorize my friend Jesse Bayles to raise a Kentucky Regiment; but I do not wish to do it without your consent." Five of the nine Union members consented.[43] One notable dissenter was Crittenden, who argued that the organization of the federal regiment would violate Kentucky's neutrality and would gain support for the rebels. With the approach of another critical election in the state on August 5—this one for membership in the General Assembly—Lincoln postponed giving his approval for the regiment.

Meanwhile, Bull Nelson and other Unionists, apparently at first without the president's knowledge, had established recruiting camps in central Kentucky and organized units commanded by federal officers. When Governor Magoffin found out about the camps, he angrily dispatched a commission to Washington, along with a letter to Lincoln, protesting what he considered a clear violation of Kentucky's neutrality and of "the peace and tranquility" of the people. He urged Lincoln to order the disbandment of the federal camps in order to avert "the horror of a bloody war" in the state.[44]

Lincoln could hardly conceal his anger at the governor's demand and pusillanimity in support of the Union war effort. He told Magoffin's commissioners, according to his secretary John Hay, that "professed Unionists," presumably southern rights men like Magoffin, "gave him more trouble than rebels." Hay noted in his diary that the Kentucky commissioners "put their case strongly but gained no commitment" from the president. The young secretary probably expressed Lincoln's opinion when he wrote, "It is a deep scheme of Magoffin's to put the responsibility of the first blow upon the Govt." in order to gain support in Kentucky for secession. "The President," Hay said, "cannot consent to what they ask for," and he predicted, "neutrality won't continue long."[45]

Nonetheless, Lincoln exercised restraint in his language when he replied to Magoffin on August 24. He admitted, "I may not possess full and precisely accurate knowledge upon this subject; but I believe it is true that there is a military force in camp within Kentucky, acting by authority of the United States, which force is not very large, and is not now being augmented." This military unit, Lincoln said, "consists exclusively of Kentuckians, having their camp in the immediate vicinity of their own homes, and not assailing, or menacing, any of the good people of Kentucky." Lincoln informed the governor that he had consulted with the state's delegation in Congress, and he did not remember that "any one of them, or any other person, except your Excellency and the bearers of your Excellency's letter, has urged me to remove the military force from Kentucky, or to disband it." The president was somewhat disingenuous, because four of the nine members of the state's congressional delegation, including Crittenden, had opposed the organization of the Bayles regiment. Lincoln wrote Magoffin, "I do not believe it is the popular wish of Kentucky that this force shall be removed beyond her limits; and, with this impression, I must respectfully decline to so remove it." The president closed his letter by expressing his cordial support for the governor in his efforts "to preserve the peace of my own native State, Kentucky," but he pointedly and sadly remarked, "It is with regret I search, and can not find, in your not very short letter, any declaration, or intimation, that you entertain any desire for the preservation of the Federal Union."[46]

Throughout the summer of 1861, members of the Kentucky delegation in Congress held on to the illusion that the state could remain neutral in the war. At the same time, most of them demonstrated their devotion to the Union in July by supporting the Johnson-Crittenden Resolution that affirmed Lincoln's announced purpose in the war. This resolution, sponsored by Andrew Johnson in the Senate and Crittenden in the House of Representatives, declared that the war was being fought "to defend and maintain the supremacy of the Constitution and to preserve the Union, with all the dignity, equality and rights of the several states unimpaired," which implicitly included the institution of slavery.[47] In the House, only two border state representatives opposed the Johnson-Crittenden Resolution. In the Senate, Breckinridge and Lazarus W. Powell of Kentucky and Waldo P. Johnson and Trusten Polk of Missouri voted against the resolution, and the Maryland and Delaware senators supported it. The Kentucky and Missouri senators—all had been Democrats—opposed the resolution, as Powell announced, because it unfortunately authorized a "war of subjugation on the Southern States." The Kentucky senator, a large, bluff, sandy-haired man who violently waved his arms when he spoke, defended his state's neutrality policy while expressing the hope that "this Union may be maintained." The preservation of the Union, he unrealistically insisted, "cannot be done by force of arms; it must be done by compromise and conciliation if it can be done at all."[48]

When Kentucky abandoned its neutrality policy in September, Powell remained in the Senate as an unrelenting critic of Lincoln and the Republicans. An earlier appearance by Powell at a Southern Rights Party convention in Kentucky came back to haunt him when Congress met during the winter of 1861–1862. The convention, attended by leading secessionists, passed resolutions denouncing Lincoln's war on the seceded states as a "stupendous usurpation of constitutional liberties." On February 20, 1862, Republican senator Morton Wilkinson of Minnesota submitted a resolution to expel Powell from the Senate on the grounds that he had encouraged secession.[49] Garret Davis, who had replaced Breckinridge in the Senate, made a long speech supporting the expulsion of his colleague.[50]

Illinois Republican senator Lyman Trumbull of the Judiciary Committee, however, reported against the Wilkinson Resolution. Trumbull argued that Powell, unlike Breckinridge, Johnson, and Polk, who had joined the insurrection, continued to fulfill his duties in the Senate. Furthermore, he said, after Kentucky abandoned its neutrality policy, Powell did nothing to support the rebellion. In defending Powell's right to retain his seat, Trumbull made a strong appeal in favor of freedom of speech in the Senate, notwithstanding the unprecedented problems, bitter political divisions, and questions of loyalty created by the war. He explained, "[Senator Powell] does not agree with me in sentiment; his opinions are not my opinions; I do not agree with the views that he has so often announced here; but he is entitle to his own opinions; and no man is to be expelled from this body because he disagrees with others in opinion."[51]

The roll call on Wilkinson's resolution to expel Powell from the Senate immediately followed Trumbull's report. By a vote of 28 against and 11 in favor, the expulsion resolution failed to pass. Only Davis of the border states voted in favor of the resolution; he was joined by some strange bedfellows—Charles Sumner of Massachusetts and other radical Republicans.[52] Davis's opposition to Powell probably reflected old political animosities in Kentucky more than differences over the war and constitutional rights. Ironically, in early 1864 Davis faced a similar—and also unsuccessful—expulsion attempt for criticizing the war and Lincoln's subversion of constitutional liberties. At that time, Davis admitted that he had been wrong in seeking his colleague's expulsion in 1862.[53]

CHAPTER THREE

The Johnson-Crittenden Resolution of July, supported by the majority of border state men in Congress, provided the Union Party in Kentucky with an important boost in the campaign to elect a new legislature on August 5. Joseph Holt returned to the state during the summer to stump for the Union and to encourage support for Lincoln in the war against the "revolutionaries." Speaking to a large crowd in Louisville, his hometown, Holt contended that the rebellion was "a gigantic conspiracy"—a common theme of border state Unionists. He likened it to "some huge boa [constrictor]" that "had completely coiled itself around the limbs and body of the republic." But, Holt declared, Abraham Lincoln had acted "to baffle the machinations of [the] wicked men" who had formed the conspiracy. "If this rebellion succeeds," Holt exclaimed, "it will involve necessarily the destruction of our nationality, the division of our territory, the permanent disruption of the Republic. It must rapidly dry up the sources of our material prosperity, and year by year we shall grow more and more impoverished."

Holt in his Louisville speech explained further the ominous consequences of a secessionist success in the war. He maintained that, unless checked, "disunion once begun [would] go on and on indefinitely." Reflecting a concern that Lincoln had expressed in his inaugural address, Holt predicted, "Under the influence of the fatal doctrine of secession, not only will States secede from States, but counties will secede from States also, and towns and cities from counties until universal anarchy will be consummated." Holt, as before, insisted that the Lincoln government had been "faithful to all its constitutional obligations." He told Kentuckians, "There cannot be any neutral ground for a loyal people between their own Government and those who, at the head of armies, are menacing its destruction."[54]

Demoralized by the erosion of support for armed neutrality and the overwhelming strength of the Union Party, the state Southern Rights Party did not conduct an active campaign in most of the legislative districts for the August elections. As expected, the Union Party, consisting mainly of Whig conservatives like Crittenden and of Douglas Democrats, won an easy victory in August. In each of the three Kentucky elections in 1861, beginning on May 4 for delegates to the border state convention, support for the Union had grown, despite the continuation of important concerns about Lincoln and his party's intentions in the war. Seeing the handwriting on the wall for their cause, many avid southern rights' supporters, particularly young men, abandoned any pretext of loyalty to the Union and went south to join the rebellion. Other southern rights men, usually of the older generation, followed the example of Senator Powell and maintained their loyalty to the Union, hoping that the state's neutrality policy might still prevail.[55] Kentucky Unionists, however, remained determined to hold Lincoln's feet to the fire and challenge any transgressions he might attempt on state and individual rights (for whites) and on slavery.

Lincoln soon discovered the fragile nature of the Union triumph in the Kentucky elections. Less than four weeks after the legislative elections, General John C. Frémont, commanding the Department of the West (mainly Missouri but also areas in Kentucky along the Mississippi River), tossed a firebomb into the Unionist ranks in Kentucky and the other border states. On August 30, 1861, Frémont, faced with what he described as a desperate military and political situation in Missouri, issued a proclamation declaring martial law throughout his command and directing the confiscation of rebel property, including slaves, who would then be set free. Furthermore, the proclamation ordered, "All persons who shall be taken with arms in their hands within [occupied] lines shall be tried by court-martial, and if found guilty will be shot."[56]

Protests immediately erupted in Kentucky and elsewhere over Frémont's startling proclamation, particularly the part pertaining to slavery. Garret Davis wrote Secretary of the Treasury Chase that the proclamation came at a "most inopportune [time] for the Union party," since "the leading members of the legislature & other prominent union men of the State" had recently gained the upper hand in the government and hoped soon to end support for the rebellion in the state. "The slavery feature of the proclamation is greatly objected to by our friends," he told Chase. "We should have passed all our measures but for it; now I have serious doubts if we pass any of them."[57] In the minds of the people, Davis reported, the proclamation gave credence to the secessionists' argument that the war for the Union would inevitably become a war to end slavery. He obviously wanted Chase to urge the president to revoke it, an intercession that the antislavery treasury secretary refused to do.

Inflamed by Frémont's proclamation, the southern rights press in Kentucky pronounced it "an abominable, atrocious, and infamous usurpation, by a military subordinate of the President." The *Louisville Daily Courier* labeled the proclamation a violation of the Constitution that was "approved . . . by the President" and that thus "*must* open the eyes of the people of the entire country and the whole world of the designs of the Administration at Washington" to end slavery.[58] Unionist newspapers like Prentice's *Louisville Daily Journal* joined the hew and cry against Frémont's order. It called on the administration in Washington to overturn it immediately.[59]

Lincoln's Kentucky friends also bombarded him with urgent demands that he revoke the proclamation. None was more vociferous than that of his close friend, Joshua Speed, who lived near Louisville. On September 1 Speed excitedly wrote the president, whom he familiarly addressed as "Dear Lincoln," "I have just seen Frémonts proclamation—it will hurt us in Ky. The war should be waged upon high points and no state law be interfered with. Our Constitution & laws both prohibit the emancipation of slaves among us—even in small numbers. If a military commander can turn them loose by the thousand by mere proclamation, it will be most dificult [*sic*] matter to get our people to submit to it." Speed reminded his friend, "All of us who live in slave states whether Union or [dis]loyal have great fear of insurrection," and asked, "Will not such a proclamation read by the slaves incline them to assert their freedom?"[60] The answer for Speed was an unequivocal yes.

Two days later, Speed expressed an even greater sense of urgency. He reported to Lincoln that if Frémont's proclamation stood, it would "crush out every vestage [*sic*] of a union party in the state" and cause Kentucky's "entire people to resist—for the loyal slaveholder & the non slaveholder would all be alike interested in resistance." Under these circumstances, Speed, himself a slaveholder, painted a dark future for both races: "Cruelty & crime would run riot in the land & the poor negroes would be almost exterminated." Such an overblown forecast of life in Kentucky without slavery was typical of white border state arguments against emancipation. Although Lincoln had long believed that sudden abolition would create serious adjustment difficulties for both races, he probably doubted his friend's gloomy prediction of the results of emancipation. However, the immediate problem for Lincoln was the danger to the Union that Frémont's order created in Kentucky and, to a lesser extent, in Maryland and Missouri.[61]

Both General Robert J. Anderson, commanding in the area, and Joseph Holt reported to Lincoln that the proclamation would have a chilling effect on loyalty in Kentucky. From Louisville, Anderson informed the president that Frémont's action was "producing most disastrous results in this State," including a reduction in the number of army recruits. He told the president, "Kentucky feels a direct interest in this matter, as a portion of General Frémont's force is now upon her soil."[62]

Holt, though a hard-liner in the prosecution of the war, wrote Lincoln that Frémont's proclamation violated the Confiscation Act (1861) recently passed by Congress. He correctly argued that the legislation limited the confiscation of slaves to those "actually employed in the service of the rebellion." Frémont's action, he said, exceeded this requirement for the seizure of property. Holt further contended that "instead of emancipating [rebel] slaves," the congressional act "left their status to be determined either by the courts of the United States or by subsequent legislation." Frémont's proclamation, he insisted, "violates this law in both these particulars, and [it] declares that the property of rebels whether used in support of the rebellion or not, shall be confiscated, & if consisting in slaves that they shall be at once manumitted." Holt, whom Lincoln would appoint to the important position of judge advocate general in 1862, reminded the president that the Confiscation bill, when enacted, "was believed to embody the conservative policy of your administration upon this delicate & perplexing question" of slavery. He told Lincoln, "You may therefore well judge of the alarm & condemnation with which the Union loving citizens" in the border states "have read this proclamation."[63]

At the same time, Frémont's edict generated a wave of strong support in the North. Radical antislavery men and women, including Protestant clergymen and the church press, hailed Frémont's action as the first step toward ending slavery in America. Leading Republican newspapers, such as the *Chicago Tribune*, the *New York Times*, and the *New York Evening Post*, praised the proclamation because, they argued, it struck an important blow against the rebellion. The *Washington National Intelligencer* and the *Saint Louis Daily Missouri Republican*, conservative border newspapers, while concerned about the proclamation's social and political impact, approved of it on military grounds, seeing it as designed to undermine the ability of the rebels to conduct the war. They were joined in their approval by some Douglas Democrat newspapers in the North. However, other northern Democrats, troubled that the object of the war would be changed from solely the preservation of the Union to include emancipation, opposed Frémont's proclamation. The self-styled independent *New York Her-*

ald, with what was probably the largest circulation of any American newspaper, condemned the proclamation. In the excitement immediately following the news of the general's order, both Secretary of War Simon Cameron and Postmaster General Montgomery Blair endorsed the proclamation, but they yielded when they discovered Lincoln's opposition to it.[64]

Even before he had heard from Speed, Holt, Anderson, and other Kentuckians, Lincoln grasped the calamitous significance of Frémont's action for the Union cause in Kentucky and in the other border states. Although he believed that slavery was morally wrong and should be placed en route to ultimate extinction, as he had repeatedly said before the war, Lincoln understood that, particularly at this critical early stage of the conflict, he could not permit his antislavery sentiments to control his actions. He could not ignore his primary constitutional responsibility to save the Union, which clearly meant retaining the allegiance of the border states. He immediately concluded that he must secure a modification of the proclamation. As he explained to Browning, who favored the proclamation, "to lose Kentucky is nearly the same as to lose the whole game. Kentucky gone, we can not hold Missouri, nor, as I think, Maryland. These all against us, and the job on our hands is too large for us. We would as well consent to separation at once, including the surrender of this capitol."[65]

On September 2, soon after receiving a copy of Frémont's proclamation, Lincoln wrote the general and warned him, "There is great danger . . . in relation to the confiscation of property, and the liberating of slaves of traiterous [*sic*] owners." The proclamation would "alarm our Southern Union friends, and turn them against us—perhaps ruin our rather fair prospect for Kentucky." Lincoln asked Frémont to modify, "of your own motion," the problematic paragraph in the proclamation so that it conformed to the Confiscation Act. The president also directed that the general "allow no man to be shot, under the proclamation, without first having my approbation or consent." He explained his reason: "Should you shoot a man . . . the Confederates would very certainly shoot our best man in their hands in retaliation"—and the cycle of retaliation would continue. Marking the letter's contents *Private and confidential*," Lincoln dispatched a special messenger to deliver it to the general.[66]

With the praises of antislavery men ringing in his ears, Frémont refused to alter the proclamation to conform to the Confiscation Act and the president's wishes. He admitted to Lincoln that his decision to issue it had been made overnight and "without consultation or advice with anyone." Frémont contended that the proclamation "was as much a movement in the war as a battle is," and he insisted that he had acted with that in mind. He told the president, "If upon reflection, your better judgement still decides that I am wrong in the article respecting the liberation of slaves, I have to ask that you will openly direct me to make the correction." He explained, "If I were to retract of my own accord" that part of the proclamation relating to slavery, "it would imply that I myself thought it wrong and that I had acted without the reflection which the gravity of the point demanded. But I did not do so. I acted with full deliberation and upon the certain conviction that it was a measure right and necessary," a point contradicting his statement that he had issued the proclamation immediately after determining to do so during the previous night. The general also defended "the shooting of men who shall rise in arms, within its lines, against an army in the military occupation of a country." The execution of guerrillas, he said, was "merely a necessary measure of defence and entirely according to the usages of civilized warfare." It did not "at all refer to ordinary prisoners of war." In conclusion, Frémont pleaded with the president to permit him "to carry out upon the spot" the shooting of guerrillas.[67]

Placed in a difficult position by his foolish and stubborn general, Lincoln felt that he had no choice but to order the revocation of the inflammatory parts of the proclamation. On September 11 he wrote Frémont informing him that the clause "in relation to the confiscation of property and the liberation of slaves" must be changed in order to conform to the Confiscation Act. This act, as Lincoln correctly interpreted it, freed only those blacks of rebel masters employed against the Union, and such action would be subject to federal judicial review. By revoking this part of the general's proclamation, Lincoln satisfied border state Unionists and reaffirmed his commitment in the inaugural address not to interfere with slavery in the states. Acknowledging that Frémont, "upon the ground, could better judge of the [military] necessities," the president let stand the other parts of the proclamation, including the provisions for military courts and the summary execution of rebels caught in arms within Union lines.[68]

As Lincoln probably expected, he received a pounding from northern anti-slavery activists, hard-war advocates, and Protestant clergymen for his modification of Frémont's proclamation. Joseph Medill, a *Chicago Tribune* editor and erstwhile political associate of Lincoln, reported to Secretary of the Treasury Chase that the president's directive to Frémont had "cast a gloom over the state and the intire [*sic*] west"; he called the directive "a heavier calamity than the battle of Bull run" in July. He contended that if "the letter to Frémont was written to placate Kentuckians," it was "a stupid blunder, as it will have the opposite effect. It will embolden the rebel slave holders by removing the most dreaded penalty of their treason:—the loss of their slaves." Medill reminded Chase, who agreed with him, "This is a slave-holders rebellion," and he added, "[It] was inaugurated to expand and strengthen the [slave] system. . . . And until [Lincoln] sees the contest in its true light the blood of loyal men will be shed in vain and the war will come to naught." Medill declared, "When the rebel Slave-holder raises his dagger against his Country let one of the penalties be the confiscation and liberation of his slaves: This strikes at the root of the disease."[69]

Black spokesman Frederick Douglass, who had not warmed to Lincoln's leadership, lamented in his magazine, "Many blunders have been committed by the Government at Washington during this war, but this, we think, is the greatest of them all."[70] Massachusetts abolitionist Maria Childs denounced Lincoln's action and cried out, "O Lord! O Lord! How we do need [an Oliver] Cromwell!" who would act on the side of right. Jane Grey Swisshelm condemned Lincoln for his "imbecility, or treachery" in revoking the proclamation.[71]

Antislavery proponents flooded the White House with letters and resolutions denouncing Lincoln's action. Illustrative of this correspondence was a letter from Andrew Peck of central New York contending that "at least eight tenths of the people" of the area "sympathise with General Freemont [*sic*], most deeply, in the spirit and tone of his late Proclamation." Peck told the president, "An overwhelming majority of these worthy citizens . . . will experience a *fatal chill*, in support of the administration" if he did not reverse his decision regarding the proclamation. An Ohio writer pleaded with Lincoln not to permit the influence of Kentucky or any other "doubtful state [to] darken the true Loyal men in other States" in the prosecution of the war. He angrily informed Lincoln that many people in his community now believed that Frémont's "*temperament*" was better suited for "the present emergency than *your own decisive action*" in revoking the proclamation.[72] A Hillsboro, Illinois, writer warned the president "to consider whether you can afford to alienate the great mass of your supporters in the North in order to propiciate [*sic*] a few quasi Union men in Kentucky and Mosouri [*sic*]."[73] Since secretaries John Nicolay and John Hay usually selected the letters for Lincoln to read, it is questionable how many of these critical missives he actually read.

Letters from clergymen repeatedly expressed their pain upon learning that Lincoln had repudiated Frémont's "righteous proclamation" against slavery. A group of Hamilton, Illinois, ministers wrote the president, "The God of justice will *take no part* with us in our present fearful conflict so long as the inhuman relation of human chattelhood [*sic*] is thus recognized & sacredly protected by our national government." Frémont's policy, they declared, "should be adopted in all the rebel states, as far & as fast as the government has the means & opportunity of enforcing it." Like other dismayed antislavery correspondents, these Illinois ministers called on Lincoln to reverse his decision on the proclamation.[74]

Unlike the clergymen and radicals who emphasized a moral opposition to slavery in their protests, northern conservatives and Democratic critics of the president's action justified Frémont's proclamation on the grounds of military necessity and as a means to punish the rebels for secession and war. (Lincoln would later adopt the military necessity justification when he issued his Emancipation Proclamation, but he did not justify it specifically as a weapon to punish the rebels.) John L. Scripps of the *Chicago Tribune* probably exaggerated his region's backing of Frémont when he wrote the president on September 21, 1861, "The fact cannot be disguised that the Northwest is, as near as such a thing is possible, a unit in support of Frémont's proclamation." He claimed that "the most conservative of the old Democratic politicians were, or at least they professed to be, entirely satisfied with it." Scripps reported, "The modification of the proclamation has everywhere been regarded as a backward step" in the war effort and said, "[It] has cast a gloom over the entire community, has engendered doubts and impaired confidence, has checked enlistments [in the army], and will show its fruits earliest, in the Northwest, in a meager subscription to the National loan." Scripps took issue with the president's contention that Frémont's proclamation exceeded the property provisions in the recent Confiscation Act. "The law was not made for the regulation of or for the purpose of limiting the Military Authority," he told Lincoln. In this instance, "the proclamation was purely an exercise of Military Authority, irrespective of any law," and, Scripps concluded, "It met the necessities of the situation, *and no more.*"[75]

Browning wrote two letters to the president praising Frémont's proclamation and, like Scripps, defending it on legal and constitutional grounds. On September 17, 1861, Browning, who had replaced Stephen A. Douglas in the Senate, told Lincoln, "The proclamation had the unqualified approval of every true friend of the Government within my knowledge . . . and it was accomplishing much good." Browning argued, "War is never carried on, and can never be, in strict accordance with previously adjusted constitutional and legal provisions." He contended, "Traitors who are warring upon the Constitution and laws, and rejecting all their restraints, [have no] right to invoke their protection." In addition to defending the military seizure of rebel property, Browning also justified the legality and propriety of Frémont's order that rebels found in arms within Union lines should face a court-martial and, if found guilty, be shot.[76]

Browning's letter startled Lincoln. On September 22 he replied to his conservative friend's criticism. "Coming from you," the president wrote, "I confess it astonishes me. That you should object to my adhering to a law, which you assisted in making," as a U.S. senator, "and presenting to me, less than a month before, is odd enough." Lincoln admitted that a commander out of military necessity could seize and temporarily hold property, including slaves, but, he wrote, "When the need is past, it is not for him to fix their permanent future condition. That must be settled according to laws made by law-makers, and not by military proclamation."[77]

The president told Browning that Frémont's assumption of military authority in his proclamation was "simply 'dictatorship.'" "It assumes," he wrote, "that the general may do *anything* he pleases—confiscate the lands and free the slaves of *loyal* people, as well as disloyal ones." Lincoln emphatically declared, "I cannot assume this reckless position; nor allow others to assume it on my responsibility. You speak of it as being the only means of *saving* the government. On the contrary it is itself the surrender of the government." Lincoln explained, "Can it be pretended that it is any longer the government of the U.S.—any government of Constitution and laws,—wherein a General, or a President, may make permanent rules of property by proclamation?" Lincoln conceded, however, that Congress might pass a law, similar to Frémont's proclamation, that would pass the test of "propriety" and added, "What I object to, is, that I as President, shall expressly or impliedly seize and exercise the permanent legislative functions of the government."[78] This was good, old-line conservative Whig doctrine that should appeal to Browning, who, like Lincoln, had been nurtured in the political faith of Henry Clay.

On September 30 a somewhat contrite Browning responded to Lincoln's reproach in a more elaborate letter, justifying the legality of Frémont's proclamation and, by extension, the imposition of military authority over an enemy population. The proclamation, he said in refutation of Lincoln's argument, "has no reference whatever to the class of cases provided for by the Statute," that is, the Confiscation Act. Frémont's edict, he argued, "rests upon the well ascertained, and universally acknowledged principles of international political law as its foundation—upon the laws of war as acknowledged by all civilized Nations, and is in exact harmony with them." Browning maintained that "the rebel States, by making war upon the United States, [had] dissolved the state of society which previously existed between them." Those who acknowledged "allegiance to the Confederate States, or [took] part with them," were *"public enemies"* and should be treated as such, and their property, including slaves, could under international law be taken from them. Browning told Lincoln that Frémont's proclamation was limited to public enemies in Missouri, "and had no more application to or operation in Kentucky than in Australia." (Actually, it also applied to a sliver of territory in Kentucky.) The Illinois senator admitted that the political expediency of exercising military power in Missouri was "another question, and one about which men may well differ," and he said, "Upon that I do not now propose to express any opinion." Although he suggested that Lincoln reconsider his revocation of the disputed part of the proclamation, Browning promised his friend that he would sustain him in whatever decision he made.[79]

Despite the widespread criticism in the North over his repudiation of Frémont's action on slavery, the president remained firm in his position. Even had Lincoln accepted Browning's constitutional argument, political considerations involving Kentucky and the other border states trumped any reasons for not overriding Frémont's proclamation. Indeed, his modification of the proclamation came at a critical time. The Kentucky General Assembly, meeting in Frankfort, was reevaluating the state's neutrality policy; these proceedings did not escape the president's attention. On September 3, less than a week after Frémont issued his proclamation, a Confederate force under General Gideon Pillow occupied strategic Columbus, Kentucky, on the Mississippi River. Federal troops had seized Belmont, Missouri, across the river, on the previous day, and General Leonidas Polk, the overall Confederate commander in the area, correctly believed that General Frémont had plans to occupy Columbus. He immediately—and foolishly, in view of the political significance of his action—ordered Pillow to move into the town before the federals took it.

The General Assembly reacted quickly to the Confederate "invasion." On September 9 resolutions were introduced into the state senate declaring that "Kentucky's peace and neutrality had been wantonly violated . . . by the so-called Confederate forces." The resolutions demanded that Governor Magoffin "call out the military force of the State to . . . drive out the invaders" and asked for federal military aid in the effort. However, as Lincoln later wrote Browning, the legislature "would not budge" in approving the resolution, "till [Frémont's] proclamation was modified."[80] Assured that the president would repudiate Frémont's action, which he did on September 11, the General Assembly on the twelfth passed the resolutions. Magoffin opposed the resolutions because they failed to demand the withdrawal of both Confederate and federal forces from the state. However, the governor did not advocate resistance to either armies. Magoffin and other Democratic members of the state administration probably would have kicked in the traces and gone with the secessionists if Frémont's antislavery decree had been permitted to stand. The action of the General Assembly on September 12 marked the state's official abandonment of neutrality.[81] Thomas Ewing, a former Whig cabinet member of Ohio and foster father of General William Tecumseh Sherman, concluded that if Lincoln had not forced a modification of Frémont's proclamation, Kentucky would have been lost, and "the war would be now raging on the banks of the Ohio."[82]

Even so, a new wave of southern rights men, including Breckinridge and Buckner, who commanded the State Guard, went south and joined the rebellion. At Russellville, Kentucky, on November 18–20 representatives from sixty-eight counties met in a convention and went through the motions of severing the state's connection with the Union, an action that Governor Magoffin in Frankfort and other Kentucky officials denounced. The delegates organized the Provisional Government of Kentucky to work for the redemption of the state from the Washington and Frankfort "despotism." The convention designated Bowling Green as the new government's capital, selected George W. Johnson as provisional governor, and successfully applied for admission to the Confederate States.[83]

The formation of the provisional government, along with the Union legislature's abandonment of neutrality, spurred recruitment of the forces under Buckner. General Sherman, commanding the Department of the Cumberland, which included Kentucky, reported to the U.S. War Department on November 6 that rebel units had been reinforced by volunteers "while ours [had] to be raised in the neighborhood, and [could] not be called together except at long notice."[84] Sherman reported that "the young men were generally secessionists and had joined the Confederates, while the Union men, the aged and conservatives, would not enroll themselves to engage in conflict with their relations on the other side."[85] Nonetheless, as the war progressed, the Union far exceeded rebel recruitment, mainly by virtue of holding more-populated territory, including Louisville, Frankfort, and Lexington. Before the end of the war, as many as 90,000 men, including about 23,703 blacks (beginning in 1863), had served in either federal or state Union units, whereas an estimated 25,000 to 40,000 whites had donned gray uniforms.[86]

The military situation in Kentucky became increasingly bleak for Unionists in late 1861, threatening the political gains they had made during the summer. Governor Oliver P. Morton of Indiana wrote Lincoln on September 26 that the rebel forces were preparing to march on Louisville and other points in the state. On October 10 General Sherman ignored military channels and appealed directly to the president for help. He informed Lincoln, "My own belief is that the Confederates will make a more desperate effort to join Kentucky than they have for Missouri. The [Union] force now here or expected is entirely inadequate."[87] After a visit to the state, Secretary of War Cameron telegraphed Lincoln, "Matters are in a much worse condition than I expected to find them. A large number of Troops & arms are needed here immediately."[88]

Joshua Speed and other Unionists also frantically called on the president to increase federal forces in Kentucky. George D. Prentice, James Guthrie, and James Speed telegraphed Lincoln on November 5 that unless General Sherman was "promptly reinforced," he might "meet the fate of [General Nathaniel] Lyon in Missouri," and, they told the president, "the consequences of such a result you can see."[89] Adjutant General Lorenzo Thomas and Joseph Holt, both traveling in the state during the fall, reported that the Confederates were planning a major military invasion of Kentucky, augmented by troops from Virginia.[90]

Lincoln branded such reports as exaggerations of the military situation in the state; furthermore, he said, he had his hands full elsewhere and could not send reinforcements. "As to Kentucky," he wrote Governor Morton in response to his September 26 letter, "you do not estimate that state as more important than I do; but I am compelled to watch all points. While I write this I am, if not in *range*, at least in *hearing* of cannon shot, from an army of enemies more than a hundred thousand strong," an inflated number apparently given to him by a concerned General George B. McClellan, commander of the Army of the Potomac. "I do not expect them to capture this city; but I *know* they would, if I were to send the men and arms from here, to defend Louisville, of which there is not a single hostile armed soldier within forty miles, nor any force known to be moving upon it from any distance."[91] Lincoln may have underestimated the threat to the state, since Confederate troops under General Albert Sidney Johnston had entered Kentucky, captured Bowling Green, and occupied large areas in the southern part of the state. Remarkably, the president, at the same time, insisted upon a Union movement from Kentucky through the Cumberland Gap to liberate the hard-pressed Unionists in east Tennessee. This operation in remote and difficult terrain was doomed to failure from the beginning. However, in January 1862, a Union force under General George H. Thomas routed Confederate General Felix Zollicoffer's small army at Mill Springs, ending the immediate rebel threat to central Kentucky.

Contributing to the resurgence of secessionist strength in the state during late 1861 was the hostile public reaction to the arrests and detention of Kentuckians charged with conspiracy to commit treason. On September 19 A. H. Sneed, U.S. marshal for Kentucky, on a warrant issued by a Jefferson County (Louisville) justice of the peace, arrested former Know Nothing governor Charles S. Morehead; Reuben T. Durrett, acting editor of the *Louisville Daily Courier*; and Martin W. Barr, a telegraph agent at Louisville. As advised by Governor Morton of Indiana, Sneed immediately sent the prisoners to Indianapolis, ostensibly for "the safety" of their persons but most likely to avoid habeas corpus proceedings in Louisville. On September 21 Sneed wrote Lincoln, "The effect of these arrests has had a beneficial effect here & it would be disastrous to have the [prisoners] released." Sneed later testified that Secretary of War Cameron, on the president's authority, had ordered troops in Indiana to take control of the men and immediately convey them to Fort Lafayette in New York Harbor for confinement. In October, the military transferred the three prisoners to Fort Warren in Boston Harbor.[92]

Federal authorities charged that Durrett had written a secessionist editorial and that Barr had "used his position as telegraph agent of the Associated Press to advance the insurrectionary cause." It was later demonstrated that Durrett had not written the incriminating editorial and that Barr was an unoffending secessionist. Morehead, the biggest fish, was accused of "stirring up and promoting rebellion and . . . treason." Leslie Coombs, self-styled Unconditional Unionist and court clerk in Frankfort, labeled Morehead "the most specious, plausible, dangerous of all our Kentucky traitors."[93]

Although some ardent Unionists like Coombs applauded the arrests, the detention of Morehead, Durrett, and Barr immediately created serious opposition in Kentucky and caused unnecessary problems for federal authorities. The imprisonment of the former governor particularly threatened to become a cause célèbre in the Bluegrass State. On September 23, 1861, Morehead's attorney in Louisville petitioned U.S. Associate Justice John Catron, who was "riding circuit" in the district, for a writ of habeas corpus in behalf of Morehead. Catron, though sympathetic to southern rights and owner of at least four slaves in Tennessee, supported the war to preserve the Union. The justice issued the writ of habeas corpus, only to be told by Marshal Sneed that he no longer held Morehead and that Morehead could not be returned to the state.[94] Catron made no further effort to execute the writ.

Guthrie, Prentice, Crittenden, and other prominent Kentucky Unionists immediately appealed to the president for the release of Morehead, Durrett, and Barr. They argued that the arrests, particularly that of Morehead, had damaged the Union cause in the state. Guthrie informed Lincoln that the former governor's arrest had been "the pretense for many to leave the state" and join the rebellion. Prentice wrote Lincoln, "[Though Morehead's] feelings lately had been with the South, I have heard him say twenty times and with great vehemence that he would give all he has in the world, life included, to restore the Union on what it was before the Southern States seceded." The *Louisville Daily Journal* editor and proprietor further claimed that Morehead, a long-time friend, had "uniformly condemned secession," and had "contended warmly for peace on the ground that war could never restore the Union." Editor Durrett, Prentice said, "is a bitter personal enemy of mine, but I am extremely anxious for his release," adding, "[although] he is a secessionist, he has never done any harm in our community."[95]

In seeking the release of Barr, Prentice appealed to Lincoln's well-known compassion for the plight of helpless women. He cited the wretched condition of Barr's wife, who, Prentice said, was completely dependent on him. She was "on the verge of delirium on his account," he informed Lincoln. "I do believe . . . that if he be kept from her [for] many days she will go utterly and hopeless mad." Crittenden used strikingly similar language on behalf of Morehead, claiming that the former governor's wife was "on the verge of insanity, on account of his imprisonment," and predicting, "If it shall be necessary to continue his imprisonment much longer, I believe it will result in the settled derangement of her mind."[96]

Lincoln, who had known Morehead in Congress, refused to rush to judgment in the cases of the three Kentuckians. On receipt of Prentice's letter of September 24, the president wrote regarding the Morehead case, "It would be improper for me to intervene without further knowledge of the facts than I now possess." Lincoln gave the letter and his response to Secretary of State William H. Seward, who had assumed control of matters relating to federal political detentions. On October 2 Seward replied to Prentice by repeating Lincoln's statement. Two days later, however, Morehead's Unionist son-in-law, Samuel J. Walker, appeared at the White House and made a personal plea for the former governor's freedom. Lincoln now concluded, as he informed Seward, "[Since] the Kentucky arrests were not made by special direction from here, I am willing if you are that any of the parties may be released when James Guthrie and James Speed think they should be."[97]

Despite the president's intercession, the wheels of justice still moved slowly for Morehead and the other two Kentucky prisoners in Fort Warren. No record has been found that Seward contacted Guthrie or Speed about the men, though on October 25 Guthrie appealed to Lincoln himself for Morehead's release.[98] Crittenden also wrote Lincoln from Frankfort, reporting that two sessions of the federal court in the state had refused to indict the former governor. He asked the president, "Have Mr. Morehead's case attended to, & such examination made into it as you may think proper, immediately—and in order to his discharge." Having heard nothing by late December regarding Morehead, Crittenden, then in Washington, apparently talked to Lincoln on the twenty-eighth about the case, since on that day, the president sent a note to Seward, inquiring, "Might we not let Gov. Moorehead [sic] loose?" Crittenden also wrote Seward—probably reporting what he had told Lincoln—that federal grand juries in both Louisville and Frankfort, after "extensive inquiries," had found nothing against Morehead. He asked the secretary of state to release Morehead on his parole rather than requiring that he take an oath of allegiance. Crittenden explained to Seward that the former governor stood to lose his property in Mississippi to the Confederates (including his slaves) if he swore allegiance to the Union. Seward agreed to the release, and on January 6 Morehead was granted a parole "on condition that he neither enter Kentucky or any other state in insurrection nor act or correspond against the authority of the U.S." Durrett and Barr were likewise freed on their parole.[99]

On parole, Morehead went to New York, where he worked for his discharge from all federal custody. His effort paid off when Secretary of War Edwin M. Stanton on March 18, 1862, authorized his unconditional release.[100] Morehead left for Canada, then England, where on October 9 he delivered a searing speech in Liverpool attacking the Lincoln government. He sharply criticized Lincoln and also Seward for deceiving him and other border state men in early 1861 regarding the new administration's intentions toward Fort Sumter. Morehead recalled a meeting with the president and several border state men, including himself, in which Lincoln promised, "If Virginia will stay in" the Union, "I will withdraw the troops from Fort Sumpter [sic]." The Kentucky expatriate told his Liverpool audience that he "was led to believe from this that Mr. Lincoln . . . would not attempt to make war to bring back the States which had seceded. . . . But I was soon undeceived."[101] When Lincoln was asked in January 1863 about the report that he had made such a promise, he authorized his secretary Hay to reply that it was "substantially correct, but that, for the present," he preferred it should be withheld from the public.[102]

Before he left England for Mexico in 1864, the irrepressible Morehead had one final volley to fire at Lincoln. He issued a pamphlet denouncing the Emancipation Proclamation as unconstitutional and certain to create racial warfare.[103] After the war and a brief stay in Mexico, Morehead settled on his plantation in Mississippi. In 1867–1868 he participated in the conservative movement against the military reconstruction policy imposed by Congress on the former Confederate States. His health broken and his wealth greatly reduced, Morehead died in 1868.

CHAPTER THREE

Other arrests of "traitors" also occurred in Kentucky during the fall of 1861, creating more disaffection in the state. In Lexington, where many families were divided over the war, including the Clays and the Todds (Mary Lincoln's family), Ohio troops on September 24 suspended the vitriolic *Lexington Kentucky Statesman*; they also arrested and sent to Louisville fifteen men, including James B. Clay, the son of Lincoln's "beau ideal." On that day, the commanding officer ironically marched his troops out to the tomb of Henry Clay in order to pay their respects to James's father.[104]

The alleged Kentucky "traitors" were placed in the custody of General Anderson. They immediately sought and secured writs of habeas corpus from Associate Justice Catron in Louisville. Anderson reported to Lincoln that he intended to honor the writs unless instructed otherwise. Unlike in the case of John Merryman in Maryland, in which Lincoln had refused to honor the writ of habeas corpus issued by Chief Justice Roger B. Taney, in the case of the Kentucky detainees he chose not to intervene. It should be remembered that in the Merryman case the government in Washington was under an immediate threat from armed secessionists, prompting Lincoln to declare martial law in Maryland. Justice Catron immediately discharged Clay on his giving bond for $10,000, and he released all but one of the others on the condition that they take the oath of allegiance to the Union. The lone prisoner, a man named Carny, was indicted for conspiracy to commit treason and was dispatched to Fort Lafayette in New York Harbor for confinement.[105]

Federal circuit court proceedings continued through the fall term of 1861 in Louisville and Frankfort with Justice Catron and U.S. District Judge Bland Ballard presiding. On October 9 Catron wrote the clerk of the U.S. Supreme Court, William T. Carroll, that "indictments for Treason are rife" in Kentucky, and he would probably have to return in January to complete the trials. Carroll forwarded the letter to Lincoln.[106] In November alone, the court at Frankfort brought in thirty-two indictments. Almost all those charged were beyond the reach of federal authorities. They included John C. Breckinridge, now a Confederate general, and John Hunt Morgan, a Lexington hemp manufacturer who was soon to become a famous Confederate raider. Not to be outdone by the federal court, state circuit courts controlled by Union zealots began handing down their own indictments, mainly against men who had left to join the rebel army. Although the judges were deadly serious, the indictments largely proved to be formalities; only a few convictions occurred, and these apparently resulted in no capital sentences, as the law provided in the case of treason.[107]

During 1862 attitudes in Kentucky hardened, and divisions over the war and over federal interference in the state mounted. Fearful of a Confederate invasion and of enemies within the state, federal military authorities began to round up and, without benefit of trials, imprison rebels or suspected rebels. They sent some Confederate sympathizers, including women and children, into exile in the South. Federal authorities opened an encampment at Newport, Kentucky, across the river from Cincinnati, for women who were charged with being rebels or, in some cases, with having relatives in the Confederate army.[108]

Upset by the military's growing violations of civil liberties, the Kentucky legislature, controlled by conservative Unionists, in March 1862 passed a resolution calling on Secretary of War Stanton to provide information on the state's citizens who had been arrested and held in prison. (Rebel soldiers had been "expatriated" by act of the Union legislature and no longer counted as citizens of Kentucky.) Stanton in his reply to the Kentucky legislature followed Lincoln's earlier language in which he had refused to give the U.S. House of Representatives information on Marylanders who were arrested and confined by federal officers. The secretary of war declared, "It is not deemed compatible with the public interests, at this juncture, to furnish the information desired."[109]

On April 21, 1862, Senator Powell took the matter to the floor of the U.S. Senate, where he offered a resolution directing Secretary of State Seward "to inform the Senate how many residents or citizens of the State of Kentucky have been arrested or removed from the State." He wanted Seward to include their names, the reasons for their confinements, and the camps where they were being held.[110] Senator Sumner of Massachusetts offered an amendment to Powell's resolution, which became a watered-down substitute motion for it. Sumner's motion asked the president, not Seward, to communicate to the Senate information on the Kentuckians arrested and imprisoned but with the important qualification "if in his opinion" the information was "not incompatible with the public interests."[111] After a brief debate on May 14, the Sumner substitute passed by a vote of 26 to 7. All the border state senators who were present opposed the motion because of its failure to demand compliance by the president. Probably to no one's surprise, Lincoln refused the request by referring the Senate to Stanton's statement that it would be incompatible with the public interests to provide the information.[112]

The military arrests and violations of civil liberties increased during the summer of 1862 after General Jeremiah T. Boyle assumed command of federal forces in the state. A Kentucky lawyer and slaveholder, Boyle was an ardent Unionist who had participated "with conspicuous gallantry" as a brigade commander in the battle of Shiloh in April.[113] Soon after assuming command in his home state, Boyle directed that anyone who had joined the rebellion, given aid to it, or even visited within rebel lines must report to a local provost marshal, take an oath of allegiance, and give a bond for good conduct. Anyone failing to do so would be arrested and sent to a federal military prison outside the state. At the bottom of the required oath was the harsh warning "The penalty for a violation of the oath is *death*." Boyle further announced that anyone doing anything to incite rebellion would be arrested and tried, presumably by military commissions and not by the state courts. Finally, where rebel guerrillas attacked loyal citizens or their property, military commissions would assess damages and enforce compensation by the disloyal people of the community or county.[114]

A wave of military arrests followed Boyle's draconian decree. Many "traitors," though probably no more than a few hundred, soon found themselves incarcerated in Camp Chase, Ohio, and other inhospitable northern prisons. Some Kentuckians who refused to take Boyle's oath were simply banished to the South or were granted paroles in the North provided they did not return to the state. Several Protestant ministers were arrested, and two denominational newspapers were suppressed by the military, with the concurrence of Kentucky's most famous clergyman, Robert J. Breckinridge. This Union champion justified the arrest of his fellow ministers on the grounds that, while "pretending to be horrified at every mention of political affairs by professing Christians," they were "themselves at the same time, such turbulent traitors, that the peace of society [required] their own incarceration."[115] Of those taking the oath and violating it, apparently none except guerrillas faced death at the hands of a military commission.

Before the end of the summer, conservative Unionists were complaining about Boyle's military arrests. On August 12, 1862, John P. Temple, the president of the state Military Board, reported to Lincoln that "the indiscriminate arrests" made by the general were "producing a dangerous state of things."[116] On September 15 James F. Robinson, who had replaced Magoffin as governor on August 18, anxiously telegraphed the president that he found "great dissatisfaction and," he feared, "injury to the Union cause" in Boyle's system of military arrests. Joshua Speed agreed with the new governor's assessment of the situation. Simultaneous with Robinson's message, Speed telegraphed Lincoln, "The good of the cause requires that you should direct Boyle to leave this whole matter to our loyal Governor." He urged his old friend to "order Boyle to the field," adding, "[Boyle] is a good man there. In his present position he is doing more harm than good. Our cause is weakening under his management."[117]

On the same day that he received the telegrams from Robinson and Speed, the president, through Stanton, directed Boyle to "abstain from making any more arrests except upon the order of the Governor of Kentucky." However, Lincoln did not take all of Speed's advice; specifically at this time, he refused to remove Boyle from command in the state. Stanton informed Boyle of the complaints regarding the "injudicious military arrests" made on his order in Kentucky, and he told the general, "The exercise of military power for such purposes no longer exists."[118]

Offended by the complaints and by Stanton's order, Boyle responded by denying that numerous arrests had occurred. He admitted, however, "Recently during the first excitement of defeat of our forces at Richmond, Ky," some disloyal persons had been taken into custody, but these, he claimed, were the exception. Boyle reminded Stanton that the Confederates had entered the state in August 1862 as a part of a major two-prong campaign to "redeem" Kentucky, and he maintained that the arrests were necessary to prevent aid to the invaders. Boyle angrily insisted, "The representations made to you are false, and made by weak-backed Union men, who hope to so act as to secure rebel protection" as the Confederate forces continued their invasion of the state. The general told Stanton, who probably informed Lincoln, "If the Government does not intend to put down the rebels in our midst and enforce" the Confiscation Acts of 1861 and 1862 requiring the seizure of rebel property, "the war will have to be fought over in Kentucky every year." He found it appalling that "rebel flags" were "thrown [flown] from the windows of houses in this city [Louisville] with impunity."[119]

The Confederate campaign in the state climaxed at the battle of Perryville in central Kentucky on October 8, followed by the withdrawal of Generals Edmund Kirby Smith and Braxton Bragg to Tennessee. The disruptions and fears created by the invasion, despite Boyle's denial, led to more arrests by federal officers and to the military's inevitable conflict with Governor Robinson and civil officials. Two days before the battle of Perryville, the governor again appealed to the president to establish "the true line of demarcation between the Civil and Military authorities of the State." He wrote, "Already we have witnessed great injury to the Union cause by an indiscreet and unjust system of arrests by Provosts Marshals throughout the State." Robinson told Lincoln that he knew of "no other or better remedy for all these evils past, present and future, than a faithful and enlightened administration of the law by the Constitutional authorities." He reminded the president that the jurisdiction of the civil government was "fixed by the Constitution and laws of the United States and State of Kentucky" and should be obeyed by military officers. The governor conceded that "all offenders taken in arms, their aiders and abettors, within the military lines should be dealt with and punished by the military authorities, [but] all others [should be dealt with] by the Civil" authorities. He "earnestly" urged Lincoln to instruct the military commanders "as may seem best" to resolve the conflict.[120]

Robinson dispatched Joshua Speed to Washington with the letter; he also informed Lincoln that his friend would "give you more fully my views upon the entire subject."[121] As a result, the War Department formulated a new system of provost marshals for Kentucky, with clear instructions to the army officers regarding their authority. The new rules, which Robinson endorsed, presumably would reduce, even if not eliminate, the reasons for conflict between the civil and federal military officers. But disagreements over constitutional rights, loyalty, and the enforcement of state laws continued. The differences took on a greater and more serious aspect in 1863 when Lincoln issued his Emancipation Proclamation and authorized the recruitment of black troops in the Union army. A strong resistance arose in Kentucky, especially to the enlistment of African Americans in the army, which deeply troubled Lincoln and caused him concern regarding the state's loyalty. The opposition to the president's policies and to the military interference in the state was led by Unionists like Senator Garret Davis and George D. Prentice, whose conservative Whig antecedents were the same as Lincoln's.

In 1861, in order to forestall the state's secession, Lincoln had wisely acquiesced in Kentucky's policy of neutrality, despite his belief that it was "treason in effect." In his annual message to Congress in December, the president happily reported that Kentucky had abandoned its experiment in neutrality; like the other border states, he reported, it "is now decidedly, and, I think, unchangeably, ranged on the side of the Union."[122] Although at the time he had reason to be pleased with Kentucky's decision to support the war for the Union, the struggle to sustain that decision, as Lincoln would find out in 1863–1864, had not been completely won.

CHAPTER 4

∎

Missouri: A State in Turmoil

A few days after Fort Sumter, the *Saint Louis Daily Missouri Republican*, an influential conservative newspaper, thundered, "The Republican party at the North [has] found the long-sought opportunity for waging a war upon the South and its institutions." Editor Nathaniel P. Paschall charged that Lincoln was attempting to establish a "consolidated Republic" and stated that if he were to succeed, the states would become, like counties, "mere geographic divisions." Paschall, a former Whig who had clashed with Lincoln soon after the November election, wishfully called for the president's impeachment for high crimes and misdemeanors on the grounds that he had violated the Constitution by requisitioning troops without congressional approval.[1]

Governor Claiborne F. Jackson and others who favored secession wanted to move quickly to sever the state's ties with the Union. Democrat William B. Napton, a Missouri Supreme Court justice and a native of New Jersey, wrote his wife, Melinda, upon learning that President Lincoln had called for 75,000 troops to suppress the insurrection, "The wretched set of malignant fanatics who have the control of the government have at last inaugurated war. . . . There is no longer any room for neutrality," as some Missouri leaders were proposing. "The Bl[ac]k. Republicans intend to hold on to power in the North by keeping alive the flame of negro fanaticism and carry fire and sword into the South. The only hope is that the masses of the people will tear down the hideous despotism they have set up." Although admitting, "It is hard to say what [Missouri] will do," Napton thought that the effect of Lincoln's proclamation would be "undoubtedly a speedy secession from [Republican] domination."[2]

Many southern rights advocates, however, faced with strong Union sentiment, particularly in Saint Louis, opposed secession as long as Lincoln did not commit an overt act against Missouri. Along with old-line Whigs like Paschall, they preferred a policy of armed neutrality, the kind that Governor Beriah Magoffin had put forward in neighboring Kentucky. Paschall told his readers, "Let us take the same position that Kentucky has taken—that of armed neutrality. Let us declare that no military force levied in other States, shall be allowed to pass through our State, or camp upon our soil. Let us demand of the opposing sections to stop further hostile operations until reason can be appealed to in Congress, and before the people; and when that fails it will be time enough for us to take up arms."[3] Like their friends in Kentucky, Missouri supporters of neutrality hoped that a nonaligned but neutral stance would force a peaceful settlement between the South and the North.

Faced with both Unionist and moderate southern rights opposition, Governor Jackson at first did not strike for secession. Instead, after the fighting in Charleston Harbor, he called the legislature into special session on May 2 and asked it to take "such means" as might be required "to place the State in a proper attitude of defense" to enforce a policy of neutrality. Jackson viewed the Lincoln government, not the Confederates, as the only real threat to Missouri's neutrality and its constitutional rights. He specifically called for the organization and arming of the militia.[4] In order to secure the necessary arms and equipment for his proposed military force, Jackson demanded control of the federal arsenal at Saint Louis, insisting that it now rightfully belonged to the state. The Saint Louis arsenal, the largest in the slave states, contained 60,000 muskets, forty artillery guns, and machinery to produce weapons. General William S. Harney, a native of Tennessee who commanded the Department of the West, which included Missouri, refused to turn over the arsenal to the state government. The general, whose headquarters was in Saint Louis, explained that he had no authorization from Washington to provide arms for either Jackson's militia or Union zealots in the city, mainly German Americans who wanted to organize for the purpose of opposing the secessionists.[5]

Governor Jackson concluded that if Confederate arms could be obtained, he could force the surrender of the arsenal. On April 17 he sent a secret and urgent message to President Jefferson Davis outlining his plan to take the arsenal and requesting Confederate artillery. (He sent a similar message to Virginia authorities but received no response.)[6] Jackson, however, stopped short of promising to align the state with the Confederacy if the weapons were furnished. On April 23 Davis replied, agreeing to furnish two howitzers and two 32-pounder guns from the Baton Rouge, Louisiana, arsenal for the assault on the Saint Louis arsenal. Davis told the governor that he looked "anxiously and hopefully for the day when the star of Missouri [would] be added to the constellation of the Confederate States of America." Pleased with the Confederate president's response, Jackson on May 5 confidently wrote Davis's secretary of war, Leroy P. Walker, that the recently convened legislature, dominated by southern rights men, would give him the legal authority to put thousands of Missouri troops in the field on the side of the South. The governor, however, reported that he must move cautiously. Missouri, Jackson reminded Walker, "is yet under the tyranny of Lincoln's Government," and, he implied, it could not act until secession sentiment was stronger in the state. He complained to Walker, "We are woefully deficient here in arms, and cannot furnish them at present. But so far as men are concerned, we have plenty of them ready, willing, and anxious to march at any moment to the defense of the South."[7]

In anticipation of the imminent arrival of the Confederate artillery from Baton Rouge, Governor Jackson on May 6 directed the commander of the Saint Louis County militia, General Daniel M. Frost, to establish a training camp near the city for his men. The installation was named Camp Jackson. The governor's intention at this point becomes murky. The question should be asked, did the governor give General Frost orders to prepare for an attack on the Saint Louis arsenal? When later faced with the demand to surrender the encampment, Frost, a native of New York and a graduate of West Point, insisted that he had no aggressive plans for the troops. His purpose, he told Captain Nathaniel Lyon, the commander of the U.S. Army troops in Saint Louis, was purely defensive. He emphatically denied that he or his men were disloyal to either the state or the Union and reminded Lyon, furthermore, that they had sworn an oath to protect the laws and property of the United States.[8] Nonetheless, as Saint Louis Unionists pointed out, the main street in the encampment was named after Jefferson Davis. Jackson at this time, as a political necessity, seemed resigned to follow a policy of armed neutrality and await the actions of Lincoln and federal authorities in Missouri before making a bold move toward secession. The governor clearly expected events to favor the secessionists as the crisis unfolded.

Jackson did not count on the energetic efforts of Francis "Frank" P. Blair Jr. and of Captain Lyon in raising troops and taking preemptive action to control the city. The scion of the politically prominent Blair family of Maryland, Frank Blair had arrived in Saint Louis in 1842 to practice law. Although a Democrat, in 1856 he won a seat in the U.S. House of Representatives on the Free-Soil ticket opposing the expansion of slavery. Defeated for reelection, Blair regained the seat as the candidate of the People's Party (a euphemism for the Republican Party) in the 1860 election. With his brother Montgomery in Lincoln's cabinet and his venerable father, Francis Sr., living across the street from the White House, Frank Blair had powerful voices in Washington to support his Union activities in Missouri.

During the secession winter of 1860–1861, Blair formed a Committee of Safety consisting of leading Saint Louis Unionists. He also organized a paramilitary group of about 1,000 Home Guards to combat the "Minute Men," a militant body of secessionists that marched openly through the city. The Minute Men were not under General Frost's control, though many later joined his militia forces. Lacking arms, Blair appealed to General Harney at nearby Jefferson Barracks for weapons and ammunition from the Saint Louis arsenal. Harney, a long-time resident of Missouri and a hard-bitten veteran of the Indian wars and of Winfield Scott's dramatic march on Mexico City in 1847, refused Blair's request. The general claimed that the Minute Men did not pose a serious threat to the Union and, moreover, that arms in the hands of the Home Guards would spark violence in Saint Louis.[9]

Angered by the general's refusal, Blair went to Washington, where he met with Lincoln on the Missouri situation. Before becoming president, Lincoln had repeatedly cited Blair's courageous free-soil activities in the slave state of Missouri, contrasting Blair's position with that of other Democrats who supported Stephen A. Douglas's "don't care" attitude about slavery.[10] Blair, however, more so than Lincoln, had aggressively promoted the foreign colonization of blacks as a solution to the sectional conflict and race issue.[11] In 1857 Blair met Lincoln in Springfield, Illinois, and the next year he campaigned for him against Douglas; he also visited Lincoln soon after the 1860 election.[12] Lincoln was personally fond of Blair, which fitted in nicely with his need to maintain the support of powerful former Democrats, notably the Blair family, who had become Republicans. Frank Blair also seemed to possess the firm leadership qualities that the Union needed in Missouri.

After Fort Sumter and given Governor Jackson's defiant response to the president's call on April 15 for troops to suppress the insurrection, Lincoln overrode General Harney and gave Blair the authority to organize his Home Guard into regiments to fulfill the state's quota of 3,123 troops. The recruitment of the troops, especially among Saint Louis's German Americans, proceeded rapidly. (Out of a total population of approximately 166,000 in Saint Louis, a remarkable 60,000 were German Americans.) Having escaped autocratic regimes in Europe, German Americans viewed the North, in contrast to the slave South, as democratic and open to economic opportunities. During the 1850s, under the leadership of Blair and activists in their communities, German Americans gravitated to the free-soil Republican Party, despite the presence of old Know Nothings, or nativist Whigs, in the new antislavery party. The influence of Blair, a former Democrat who had opposed the Know Nothings, facilitated the German American association with the Republican Party and staunch Unionists in Saint Louis and elsewhere in Missouri.

Although a member of the new Congress, Frank Blair assumed command of the first regiment. General Harney, however, refused to muster the Unionist Home Guard into the army because, he lamely explained, state authorities had not officially tendered them to federal service under the April 15 call for troops. Furthermore, Harney believed that their acceptance in the army would increase political passions in the state. Many ardent Unionists incorrectly concluded that Harney sympathized with the secessionists and conspired to undermine Lincoln's efforts to raise troops.

Blair quickly went to work in Washington and obtained Harney's recall. In addition, despite Governor Jackson's disapproval, Blair secured the authority to muster his regiment into the U.S. Army. With Harney out of the way—it proved temporary—Blair gained Lincoln's approval, through General in Chief Winfield Scott and Secretary of War Simon Cameron, for Captain Lyon to recruit 10,000 loyal men from the area for "the purpose of maintaining the authority of the United States" and of providing "for the protection of the peaceable inhabitants of Missouri." The president placed Lyon in direct control of the Saint Louis arsenal and the federal troops in the area. He gave the captain the sweeping power, in consultation with Blair and other leading Unionists, to "proclaim martial law in the city" if necessary.[13]

Lincoln and the War Department's actions in recalling General Harney and appointing Captain Lyon to command soon produced bitter fruit. With two partially armed and antagonistic forces—Governor Jackson's Minute Men and Lyon's federal troops—drilling and parading in the streets of Saint Louis, a violent confrontation was almost inevitable. Lyon, whom even Blair found too aggressive, did not have the temperament or the understanding of public sentiment to command troops in such a volatile situation. Born in Connecticut in 1818, Lyon attended West Point, graduating high in the class of 1841. Although he criticized the American decision to go to war against Mexico in 1846, Lyon distinguished himself as a young officer in General Scott's campaign to take Mexico City. After the war, Lyon served on the western frontier, including Kansas, where he opposed the violent tactics of the proslavery "border ruffians" of Missouri.

In February 1861 Captain Lyon arrived in Saint Louis to command a company of U.S. infantry at the Saint Louis arsenal. The secession of the lower South prompted Lyon to write, "It is no longer useful to appeal to reason, but to the sword, and trifle no longer in senseless wrangling" with secessionists. In the conflict to come, "I shall not hesitate to rejoice at the triumph of my principles, though this triumph may involve an issue in which I certainly expect to expose and very likely lose my life," a prophecy, unfortunately for Lyon, that would soon come true.[14]

On April 16, even before he had received the authority to control the arsenal, Lyon acted to reinforce the installation and provide for the safety of the arms against a secessionist attack. Without consulting General Harney, who was still his superior officer, Lyon asked Governor Richard Yates of Illinois to prepare six regiments of state troops for service in Saint Louis. He also asked Yates to send a requisition to Washington for the transfer of "a large supply of arms" from the Saint Louis arsenal to Springfield, Illinois, for safekeeping. Yates agreed to Lyon's request. The governor immediately dispatched an agent to Washington, where he obtained approval from both General Scott and President Lincoln for the delivery of the arsenal arms to Illinois authorities. With the president's authorization, Lyon's men, under cover of darkness, transferred 21,000 stands of arms and ammunition across the Mississippi to Illinois.[15]

The Lyon-Yates request for Illinois state militiamen to serve in Missouri at first was also approved. Immediately, prominent conservative Unionists of Saint Louis, who supported Harney's cautious and conciliatory policy, protested to Attorney General Edward Bates, a Missourian, against the deployment of any outside state troops in their city. W. W. Greene, a friend of Bates, wrote the attorney general, "Rumors of the Government sending twenty-five thousand men from other States to protect the arsenal here have produced immense excitement, and if such order should be issued, I should apprehend much danger would arise, and perhaps the State would be led into . . . secessionism."[16]

Lincoln, who wanted to avoid a repeat of the rioting that had occurred in Baltimore on April 19 when free-state troops entered the city, agreed with Greene and conservative Unionists, including Bates. He immediately reversed the order for the dispatch of the Illinois militiamen to the state. As the president explained to Charles Gibson, Bates's nephew, "If he was compelled to send men from one side of Missouri to the other . . . he would rather send them around than through the State in order to avoid any trouble. No troops will be sent to Missouri from other States. In short everything tending to arouse jealousy of the people will be avoided."[17] Later, when the rebellion threatened to engulf the state, the president changed his mind about the deployment of free-state troops to Missouri. Greene, Gibson, and other conservatives in late April advised that only the dispatch of regular units from the West could reduce the "satanic passions" that had convulsed the state, especially in Saint Louis, after the fighting in Charleston Harbor. Few additional regular troops, however, could be made available for duty in Saint Louis, leaving the city a virtual powder keg of conflict.

Meanwhile, after surrendering his command on April 23, 1861, General Harney left for Washington to explain his actions to the administration and to seek vindication. En route, through Virginia, he was seized by state troops at Harpers Ferry and taken to Richmond. Since Virginia, pending a referendum, had not yet officially joined the Confederacy, its governor, John Letcher, immediately released Harney, apologized for the incident, and urged the Tennessee-born general to accept a command in the southern army. Harney refused but was permitted to continue his trip to Washington. In the national capital, he conferred with General Scott, Secretary of War Cameron, and probably Lincoln. Harney vigorously denounced the claims that he was false to the Union. He also contended, as he wrote a friend at the time, that "any exertion of force" in Missouri would "plunge the State into the vortex of revolution."[18] His arguments for a conciliatory but firm policy in Missouri persuaded the administration to restore him to the command of the Department of the West. Harney returned to Saint Louis on May 11, unfortunately one day too late to prevent the violent and calamitous events in the city that threatened to sweep Missouri into secession.

The establishment of Camp Jackson on May 6 and the arrival by steamboat on May 8 of a large shipment of military stores, including cannons from Baton Rouge, had spurred Captain Lyon to take preemptive action against what he believed was an imminent attack on the Saint Louis arsenal by the governor's forces.[19] After Lyon secretly visited Camp Jackson, disguised as an old woman, he met with the Saint Louis Unionist Committee of Safety on May 9 and, without consulting his superiors in Washington, outlined his plan for capturing the encampment. The committee members, including Blair, agreed that the weapons from Baton Rouge must be seized before the cannons were mounted on their caissons. However, since Camp Jackson had been legally authorized by the state government and the United States flag flew over it, the majority of the committee members proposed that a federal marshal, backed by Lyon's troops, should issue a court writ of replevin, or order, for the seizure of the arms and other U.S. property held unlawfully at the camp.[20]

Supported by Blair, the impetuous Lyon had no time for such legal formalities. Lyon knew that General Harney had been reinstated in command and would arrive in Saint Louis on May 11. Correctly concluding that the general would oppose his plan for the capture of the camp, Lyon decided to act immediately. He returned to the arsenal from the meeting with the Committee of Safety and set in motion his operation against "the nest of traitors" at Camp Jackson.[21] Believing that they needed an officer of general rank to command the force of 8,000 men, regimental officers designated Lyon a brigadier general.[22] Lincoln, faced with a fait accompli, later admitted that he had had no choice but to approve the appointment.

On the afternoon of May 10, Lyon advanced his army to the encampment of the 700 state militiamen. Ironically, two illustrious future Union generals—U. S. Grant and William Tecumseh Sherman—were in Saint Louis and independently witnessed the riveting events of May 10 and later. Confronted by an overwhelming federal force, General Frost, the commander of Camp Jackson, could only protest Lyon's action against "citizens of the United States who are in the lawful performance of [militia] duties . . . under the Constitution." He surrendered without a fight.[23]

Fighting, however, erupted when Lyon insisted on marching his prisoners through the streets of Saint Louis to confinement in the arsenal. Angry crowds gathered along the route and began shouting epithets at the "Dutch Blackguards" (Germans). Hurrahs for Jeff Davis could also be heard in the crowd. Some of the onlookers were armed and not altogether sober. As at the beginning of the Baltimore Riot three weeks earlier, rocks and bricks rained down on the Union troops. Shots soon rang out, and a soldier fell to the ground. The German American regiment, which had been attacked, immediately responded by firing into the crowd. When the fighting ended and the troops had returned to the arsenal with their prisoners, twenty-eight people lay dead, and others were mortally wounded.[24] Rioting continued into the evening, but the police and the Unionist Home Guard prevented the mob from sacking the offices of the radical *Missouri Democrat* and *Anzeiger des Westens*. Excitement continued for several days as false rumors spread that "Black Dutch" troops were shooting women and children in cold blood. Hundreds, if not thousands, fled the city. Lyon in his report on the operation against Camp Jackson denied any responsibility for the events that sparked the violence.[25]

When the members of the legislature, meeting in Jefferson City, received news of Lyon's capture of Camp Jackson and the fighting in the streets, they immediately approved the governor's comprehensive military proposal. They had been debating it since convening on May 2. The legislature also gave Governor Jackson the authority to put down any lawless action against the state. General Harney, upon returning to Saint Louis on May 11 and resuming command the next day, issued a proclamation calling "upon the public authorities and the people" to aid him in preserving the peace. "I trust that I may be spared the necessity of resorting to martial law, but the public peace must be preserved, and the lives and property of the people protected," he announced. Harney promised that if necessary to preserve the public peace, he would use only units of the regular army, not the overwhelmingly German Home Guards controlled by Lyon and Blair.[26]

General Harney also issued a lengthy address, "To the People of the State of Missouri," explaining his views on the crisis and indicating what Missourians could expect from him. Although he did not explicitly support Lyon's action against Camp Jackson, he told Missourians that "no Government in the world would be entitled to respect that would tolerate for a moment such openly treasonable preparations" as, he contended, had been occurring in the encampment. Harney severely condemned the Missouri legislature for its enactment of the military bill to create a state force capable of challenging federal authority in the state. He ignored the fact that the bill had passed only after Lyon's assault on Camp Jackson and the rioting that followed. The measure, Harney declared, "cannot be regarded in any other light than an indirect secession ordinance." He warned the "citizens of Missouri" not to "yield obedience to this military bill," which he said was "clearly in violation" of their "duties as citizens of the United States."

The general plainly had Jackson's militia or Missouri State Guard in mind when he proclaimed that it was his "duty to suppress all unlawful combinations of men, whether formed under pretext of military organizations or otherwise." Harney reminded Missourians (he claimed to be one of them), "[The state] must share the destiny of the Union. Her geographic position, her soil, productions, and, in short, all her material interests, point to this result." Missouri's strategic location as a border state abutting the Mississippi River, he said, "is seen and its force is felt throughout the nation. So important is this . . . to the great interests of the country, that I venture to express the opinion that the whole power of the Government of the United States, if necessary, will be exerted to maintain Missouri" in the Union.[27]

Despite his stern words, and encouraged by prominent conservative Unionists like Hamilton R. Gamble, Harney soon reverted to his policy of conciliation in hopes of avoiding a tragic clash between state and federal authorities. He particularly reassured Missourians that slavery would be protected by the military. When Thomas T. Gantt, a prominent slaveholder, wrote Harney inquiring whether "it was the intention of the United States Government to interfere with the institution of slavery in Missouri," Harney expressed surprise that the issue should even be raised. Nonetheless, he promised Gantt and other slaveholders that the federal government and the army would protect slave property like any other form of property. He maintained that the Lincoln administration would not order him or any other general to do otherwise. As evidence that slavery would remain undisturbed by the war against secession, Harney cited reports that northern generals had returned to their masters slaves attempting to escape from Maryland to the North. (This practice by some northern officers of returning blacks to slavery did occur early in the war, but rarely later.) Furthermore, the general claimed, when abolitionist "incendiaries" had asked the president for permission to invade the southern states to free slaves, Lincoln had warned them "that any attempt to do this [would] be punished as a crime."[28]

Frank Blair remained determined to get rid of Harney, though he admitted that the general had begun "to see the day-light" in his policy toward the secessionists. Blair dispatched his brother-in-law, Franklin A. Dick, to Washington to secure, for the second time, Harney's removal from command. Upon his arrival, Dick went immediately to the White House for talks with the president. Joined by Frank's brother, Postmaster General Montgomery Blair, they found Lincoln with Secretary of War Cameron and Attorney General Bates. In the ensuing meeting, Dick contended that Harney could not be trusted because of his southern background and his many rebel relatives. Actually, the same point could have been made of Joseph Holt, who played an important role in saving Kentucky for the Union. Dick insisted that Lyon would be a more forceful commander in dealing with Jackson and the Missouri secessionists.

During the White House meeting, Montgomery Blair, apparently at Lincoln's direction, drafted a War Department order, in the form of a presidential memorandum, removing Harney and appointing Lyon to command with the rank of brigadier general. Bates, however, persuaded the president to wait before approving the order until he could discuss it with his brother-in-law, Hamilton Gamble, and his associate James E. Yeatman, who were expected to arrive soon from Missouri. When Gamble and Yeatman met the president, they argued for the retention of Harney and also for the creation of a court of inquiry concerning Lyon's rash action in storming Camp Jackson. Lincoln deferred to General Scott on both matters. Scott in turn recommended the removal of Harney but rejected the idea of a military court to investigate Lyon's conduct.[29]

On May 16 Lincoln, despite reservations, approved the order relieving Harney from command. It was sent to Frank Blair in Saint Louis for delivery to the general. The president, however, still vacillated, a characteristic that reflected both his natural caution and his lack of managerial experience. On May 18 he wrote Blair directing him to withhold the order, "unless in your judgement the necessity to the contrary is very urgent." Lincoln explained, "[I] was not quite satisfied with the order when it was made, though on the whole I thought it best to make it" because of the great anxiety in Washington about Saint Louis affairs. "But since then I have become more doubtful of its propriety. . . . There are several reasons for this," he said. "We better have him [Harney] a *friend* than an *enemy*. It would dissatisfy a good many who otherwise would be quiet. More than all, we first relieved him, then restored him, & now if we relieve him again, the public will ask, 'why all this vacillation.'" Nevertheless, Lincoln reiterated, "if, in your judgement, it is indispensable let it be so."[30]

At first, Blair, who must have found troubling the president's wavering on Harney's removal, gave Harney the benefit of the doubt in his efforts to suppress opposition to the Union and restore order in Missouri. However, Blair soon found ample reason, to his satisfaction, to deliver the dismissal order to Harney. Events leading to the general's final removal began on May 21 when, at the urging of conservative Unionists, Harney met with General Sterling Price, commander of Governor Jackson's Missouri State Guard (as distinct from Blair's Unionist Home Guards). The purpose of the meeting was to obtain an agreement on the roles of federal and state forces in preserving the peace and reducing the growing threat of armed confrontations in the state. At the conclusion of the meeting, Harney and Price issued a joint statement announcing their complete agreement to cooperate in "restoring peace and good order to the people of the State in subordination to the laws of the General and State Governments." Price pledged "to direct the whole power of the State officers to maintain order within the State." On his part, Harney promised that, "this object being thus assured," he would have no reason "to make military movements, which might otherwise create excitements and jealousies."[31] In a separate message to Missourians, Harney announced that the accord with Price would be "by both [men] most religiously and sacredly kept, and, if necessary to put down evil-disposed persons, the military powers of both Governments [would] be called out to enforce [its] terms."[32] Harney, believing that he had no other choice in order to avoid war within the state, in effect recognized the armed neutrality of Missouri as adopted by Governor Jackson and the legislature.

Although several conservative Unionist newspapers applauded the agreement, other Unionists immediately condemned it. Samuel T. Glover, a member of the Unionist Committee of Safety and a friend of Lincoln, wrote the president that "the arrangement made between Price & Harney was very unfortunate. At that moment [Harney] had secession down and could have disarmed" the governor's militia. "He would not do it." Jackson and his secessionist lieutenant governor, Glover reported, had been prepared to resign and flee the state, but the Price-Harney agreement gave legitimacy to the expansion of the militia, or the Missouri State Guard, an action that Harney had earlier denounced. Glover reported to Lincoln that Harney, when approached by Unionists for military protection, declared, "By God I am opposed to coercion," and, furthermore, he had insisted, "Price is all right." Harney, Glover charged, only sought "the counsel of the whole brood of semi-secessionists." Glover told the president, "There is no peace here—and temporizing is only a fatal error—nothing but fear of death to [secessionist] leaders will do."[33] He demanded Harney's immediate removal from command.

Lincoln, however, still hoped that Harney would reverse his misguided policy and act forcibly to protect loyalists and save the state from the rebels and "semi-secessionists." With that in mind, the president dictated the substance of a stern letter to Harney that Adjutant General Lorenzo Thomas on May 27 put in final, authoritative form and sent over his own signature. The letter chastised Harney for approving the agreement with Price and demanded that he act to prevent attacks upon Missouri Unionists. "The President," Thomas wrote Harney, "observes with concern that, notwithstanding the pledge of the State authorities to cooperate in preserving the peace in Missouri, loyal citizens in great numbers continue to be driven from their homes. It is immaterial whether these outrages continue from inability or indisposition on the part of the State authorities to prevent them. It is enough that they continue to devolve on you the duty of putting a stop to them summarily by the force under your command." Thomas informed Harney that if he needed aid to prevent the attacks, he could obtain troops from Kansas, Iowa, and Illinois. He warned, "The professions of loyalty to the Union by the State authorities of Missouri are not to be relied upon. They have already falsified their professions too often, and are too far committed to secession to be entitled to your confidence."[34] Whether these were Lincoln's exact words is unknown; however, the letter contained the substance of his instructions to Harney.

Dependent on conflicting counsel for Missouri, Lincoln had probably misjudged the situation in the state. No doubt many Unionists, as Glover reported to him, had suffered at the hands of the secessionists; furthermore, Governor Jackson, whose intentions at any particular time were not always clear, probably longed for the day when he could carry Missouri into the Confederacy. But many state officials, including members of the legislature and Missouri State Guard officers like General Frost and General Price, a former Whig governor and president of the adjourned state convention, were still loyal in the spring of 1861. These conservatives (or moderates in today's political lexicon) had considerable influence and would exercise it, though perhaps timidly, on behalf of the Union as long as no overt act by federal authorities against the state occurred. Notwithstanding the violence of May 10–11 in Saint Louis, they hoped that the policy of armed neutrality, similar to the one adopted by Kentucky, could succeed and that Missouri could avoid federal intervention and a destructive war.

On May 29 General Harney, before receiving General Thomas's stern admonition, dispatched an optimistic report to Washington on political conditions in Missouri. He wrote, "Missouri is rapidly becoming tranquilized, and I am convinced that by pursuing the course I have thus far . . . peace and confidence" in the government "will be fully and permanently restored." Harney warned, "Interference by unauthorized parties"—he mainly meant Lyon and Blair—"can alone prevent the realization of these hopes, and although [their] policy . . . might be more brilliant in a military point of view," it could not sustain "the loyalty now fully aroused in the State and her firm security in the Union." Harney promised his superiors in Washington that he would promptly put down any attempt at rebellion in Missouri.[35]

General Price assured Harney that the state would honor the agreement and suppress the lawless elements that afflicted the interior. When Harney protested to Price that Unionists in several places were still being attacked, the Missouri State Guard commander told Harney that in every case he had "instituted strict inquiry" and assured him, "In no single instance have these acts been instigated or recognized by meetings or organizations of any kind. . . . No effort has been left undone on my part to prevent" such incidents. Furthermore, Price said, he had issued orders positively enjoining "upon all citizens of the State the scrupulous protection of individual property and rights, irrespective of political opinions." He also denied reports that troops from Arkansas had entered the state.[36] Both Harney and Price exaggerated the true conditions in the state and their ability—or commitment, in Price's case—to control events and maintain the peace.

The Price-Harney "treaty," however, was never fully tested. Blair, Lyon, and militant Unionists in Saint Louis had had enough of Harney's appeasement of Jackson and the secessionists. On May 30, and without consulting further with Lincoln, Blair had a subordinate deliver the May 16 order to Harney removing him from command. The general at first contended that the order had been superseded by recent telegraphic dispatches and by Adjutant General Thomas's letter of May 27, which suggested, Harney claimed, "it was not the intention of the President I should be relieved." He angrily wrote Thomas, "Many of the reports which have reached the President relative to the condition of affairs in Missouri have proceeded from irresponsible sources [and] in several instances . . . were groundless or greatly exaggerated." He insisted, "Matters are progressing as satisfactorily in this State as I could expect considering the very great excitement that has [recently] pervaded the community." Before the end of the day, however, Harney had received a confirmation of his removal from command, probably after Thomas had consulted with Lincoln and received his approval. General Lyon replaced Harney as commander of the Department of the West.[37] In forced retirement, Harney did not further participate in the Civil War. After the war, he came out of retirement to play an important role on the Indian Peace Commission of 1867–1868 that negotiated several treaties with the Plains Indians.[38]

Harney's removal and Lyon's appointment upset conservative Unionists. The *Saint Louis Daily Missouri Republican*, a conservative newspaper despite its name, claimed that since the Camp Jackson incident, Harney had been gradually restoring order in the state.[39] In addition, General Price, who at this time supported the conservative Unionists, was disturbed by Lincoln's decision to remove Harney and place the zealous and impetuous Lyon in command of the federal troops in Missouri. Nonetheless, Price attempted to reassure Missourians that his agreement with Harney would remain in effect.[40] John S. Phelps, a member of Congress from Saint Louis and a postwar governor of the state, pleaded with Lincoln to restore Harney to command. "You gain nothing by the appointment of Lyon," Phelps wrote the president. Lyon's "rashness & imprudence may overthrow us."[41] The president refused to reverse the removal order, probably because, as he had written Frank Blair earlier, the public would find troubling his continued vacillation on the issue. Still, Lincoln should not have left the final decision on Harney's removal in the hands of Blair, an ally of Lyon.

As if to confirm the conservative characterization of him as rash and imprudent, Lyon, after he replaced Harney, quickly moved to exercise his authority in Missouri and suppress "traitors." Frightened by the real prospect of civil war in the state, several prominent conservatives arranged for Price and Governor Jackson to meet with Lyon and Blair at Saint Louis for the purpose of negotiating a new arrangement, which, they hoped, would avert hostilities and secession. In the meeting, on June 11, 1861, the governor announced that he was willing to disband the Missouri State Guard and discontinue the organization of new companies if Lyon and Blair would promise to disarm the Unionist Home Guard and cease federal intervention in state affairs. Jackson also pledged to "protect all citizens equally in all their rights, regardless of their political opinions and to repress all insurrectionary movements in the State." If sincere, this was a remarkable concession by the secessionist-leaning governor. Jackson, however, refused to sanction the federal recruitment of Missourians or the introduction of troops from the free states. Price insisted that his earlier arrangement with Harney should be observed by federal authorities as well as by state officers.[42]

Lyon immediately made it clear that he could not accept any compromise of federal supremacy in the state. After four hours of contentious talks, Lyon turned to Jackson and Price and with great emphasis announced, "Rather than concede to the State of Missouri the right to demand that my Government shall not enlist troops within her limits or move its troops at its own will into, out of, or through the State; rather than concede to the State of Missouri for one single instant the right to dictate to my Government in any matter however unimportant, I would see you . . . and every man, woman, and child in the State, dead and buried." Then, looking directly at Jackson, Lyon declared, "This means war. In an hour one of my officers will call for you and conduct you out of my lines." With this pronouncement, the Union general turned and left the room. Even Blair seemed shaken by his associate's belligerent words and action. Blair and the other Union officers in the room with "courtesy and kind[ness]" bade farewell to the men whom, they realized, they would soon face on the battlefield.[43] Without seeking Lincoln's approval, Lyon had issued a declaration of war against the Missouri state government.

Although Jackson earlier had schemed to steer the state toward disunion, by the time of his meeting with Lyon and Blair he seemed to have had second thoughts about secession and its uncertain consequences for Missouri. He now favored a policy of armed neutrality for the state, while insisting on a strict federal observance of Missouri's constitutional rights in the Union. Jackson equated these rights with the principle of state sovereignty in which state and local officials controlled all domestic matters, completely free of federal interference. His concept of armed neutrality was more assertive and uncompromising than that of Governor Magoffin in Kentucky and was thereby more likely to come into conflict with federal authorities, particularly faced with an impetuous and unyielding general like Lyon. Still, Jackson's promise to disband the Missouri State Guard was contingent on the unlikely event that Lyon and Blair would do the same thing with the Unionist Home Guards.

Immediately after the Saint Louis meeting, Jackson, Price, and their staffs left for the state capital at Jefferson City, burning two railroad bridges behind them in order to forestall any pursuit by Lyon's forces. The next day, the governor issued a proclamation to the people of Missouri announcing, "A series of unprovoked and unparalleled outrages have been inflicted on the peace and dignity of this Commonwealth, and upon the rights and liberties of its people, by wicked and unprincipled men, who profess to act under the authority of the United States Government." Jackson then provided a list of "these outrages and indignities." He insisted that it had been his "earnest endeavor under all these embarrassing circumstances to maintain the peace of the State, and avert, if possible . . . the desolating effects of civil war" from Missouri. With that in mind, the governor said that he had earlier authorized General Price to meet with General Harney and "reach the terms of agreement" that they signed on May 21. Jackson maintained that, whereas "the State authorities [had] labored faithfully to carry out the terms of that agreement," the Lincoln government had "not only manifested its strong disapprobation of it by the instant dismissal" of General Harney but had at once begun "a system of hostile operations in utter contempt of this agreement."[44] The governor wrongly assumed that Lyon's antagonistic stance in the Saint Louis meeting reflected Lincoln's position, though the president would hardly have agreed to a compromise of national sovereignty, as Jackson sought.

For the purpose of protecting the liberties of the people, as he defined them, Jackson announced that he had issued a call for 50,000 men to serve

Hamilton R. Gamble, provisional governor of Missouri, 1861–1864. Leader of the state's conservative Unionist or "Claybanks" faction, Gamble often quarreled with Lincoln over antislavery military commanders in Missouri and control of state troops. Courtesy of Missouri History Museum, St. Louis, Missouri.

in the Missouri State Guard. At the same time, he reminded the people, "Missouri is still one of the United States, and . . . the executive department of the State Government does not arrogate to itself the power to disturb that relation." Until the state convention could reconvene and express the sovereign will of the people in the crisis, the governor told Missourians, "it is your duty to obey all constitutional requirements of the Federal Government." But, he added, "First allegiance [is] due to your own State, and . . . you are under no obligations whatever to obey the unconstitutional edicts of the military despotism" in Washington or "its wicked minions in this State." Jackson closed his proclamation with a stirring appeal for Missourians to drive out "the invaders who have dared to desecrate the soil" of the state.[45] This was hardly the language of a governor who wanted to maintain the peace and leave the matter of federal relations to the state convention when it met.

Events now moved rapidly. On June 14, before Jackson and Price could raise an effective force to resist a federal "invasion," Lyon with about 2,500 well-armed troops moved against the governor in Jefferson City. Jackson and state officials abandoned the capital, and on June 16 Lyon's small army entered the town. On June 18 at Boonville, Lyon issued his own proclamation, "To the Citizens of Missouri," announcing that it was his intention to assert the paramount authority of the federal government in the state against the "treasonable purposes" of Governor Jackson and the legislature. Lyon, however, offered amnesty to all of Jackson's militiamen who returned to their homes and remained peaceful. He also promised that he would "scrupulously avoid interference with the business, right, and property of every description recognized by the laws of the State and belonging to law-abiding citizens."[46] Supporters of Jackson did not believe that Lyon would honor the pledge to protect their property and rights if they returned home. Even many Unionists probably doubted that the antislavery general would keep his promise.

After several skirmishes with Lyon's units in central Missouri, Jackson with a lightly armed militia of 4,000 fled to the southern part of the state, where they temporarily found a safe haven and also won time to mobilize their forces.[47] At this point, the governor made the fateful decision to seek Confederate aid for the state's "liberation" and for the restoration of his government in Jefferson City. This action provided the final justification for Unionists to replace Jackson and form a new government for Missouri.

Although some Unionists thought that Lincoln should appoint a military governor for the state, others wanted the state convention to meet and select a provisional government until elections could be held for loyal officials. Earlier, before the Unionist state convention had adjourned on March 22, 1861, a committee of prominent delegates had been authorized to reconvene the convention if necessary. After hostilities in the state had begun in June and Governor Jackson had fled the capital, the committee met and issued a call for the convention to reassemble on July 22, 1861. The convention, despite doubts regarding its authority, vacated the state offices, disbanded the legislature, and repealed the May military act. It then created a provisional government for the state. The convention delegates selected one of their own, conservative Unionist Hamilton R. Gamble, as provisional governor to serve until elections could be held in November. The fact that Gamble's brother-in-law was U.S. Attorney General Edward Bates partly influenced the delegates in making the appointment. Bates, also a border state conservative, could be expected to aid the new state government in the national capital. Gamble had been in the East where he had consulted with Bates—and probably Lincoln also—before taking his seat in the reconvened state convention. He played a leading role in the decision to form the new government.[48]

In creating the Missouri provisional government, the delegates must have known that Lincoln had approved a similar structure for Virginia. That government had been formed by a Union convention at Wheeling in June 1861 to replace the rebel administration in Richmond. Headed by Francis H. Pierpont and known as the Restored Government of Virginia, it later agreed to the separation of the western counties from the Old Dominion. Unlike the provisional government of Missouri, the Pierpont government, a rump affair, did not gain control of Virginia until the end of the war.[49]

Born and educated in Virginia, Gamble came to Missouri as a young man in 1818. He became a prominent member of the Saint Louis bar, and after one term as a Whig in the state legislature, he was elected to the Missouri Supreme Court in 1851. During his tenure on the court, Gamble, though a slaveholder, argued in favor of Dred Scott in his famous futile bid for freedom in the state. He maintained that Scott's residence in the free state of Illinois and at Fort Snelling in Minnesota had legally made him free. Although Gamble was the presiding judge, the other two members of the court rejected his argument and ruled against Scott. Because of ill health, Gamble resigned from the court in 1854 and, a few years later, went into semiretirement in Pennsylvania.[50] Apart from his relationship to Attorney General Bates, Gamble's background suggested that he was a worthy choice to lead Missouri's civil government during this period of unprecedented troubles. Unfortunately, Gamble's health problems became more severe during the war, causing him to be prickly and oversensitive regarding his prerogatives and those of his state when dealing with Lincoln and federal military commanders. Gamble died in January 1864.

Missouri Unionists praised Gamble's appointment as provisional governor. The *Columbia Missouri Statesman* announced, "It is most fortunate for the people that Judge Gamble was prevailed upon to accept the position and to bring his great talents, ripe experience and tried conservatism to the task of restoring peace to the State." From Washington, Bates wrote his brother-in-law, "You better than any extreme man, can tranquillize the State. The internal peace of Missouri and its security in the Union . . . will do more towards the suppression of the insurrection in the border states, than 100,000 of our best men in the army." Even some of Gamble's old political opponents praised his appointment as provisional governor. Uriel Wright, the leader of the southern rights forces in the state convention, declared, "There is no man in the limits of the State upon whom I more readily confer the important trust which must devolve upon a chief executive . . . than Hamilton R. Gamble." As expected, Lincoln immediately recognized the provisional government under Gamble.[51]

Assuming office on August 1, 1861, Governor Gamble in his inaugural address raised the specter of anarchy in Missouri. "We may soon be in that condition of anarchy, in which a man when he goes to bed with his family at night does not know whether he shall ever rise again, or whether his house shall remain intact until morning," Gamble somberly and prophetically told Missourians. "This is the kind of danger, not merely a war between different divisions of the State, but a war between neighbors, so that [when] a man meets those with whom he has associated from childhood, he begins to feel that they are his enemies. . . . It is terrible." Reflective of an old Whig fear of anarchy, which Lincoln had also expressed in his inaugural address, Gamble warned, "The scenes of the French revolution [will] be enacted in every quarter of our State, if we do not succeed in avoiding that kind of war."[52]

On August 3 Gamble issued a proclamation, "To the People of the State of Missouri," announcing his appointment as provisional governor and explaining that his government would be temporary until elections could be held in November. He promised that "the oppressive conduct" of federal troops in violating civil liberties and private property would, "in a short time, be arrested." He had Lyon's troops in mind. Gamble reassured Missourians that his government had "no concern with men's opinions, except to protect all in their undisturbed enjoyment." While, he wrote, "[the] freedom of opinion is the right of all . . . it is plainly the duty of the Government to suppress . . . all combinations [rebels] that violate this right, and all violence arising from a difference of opinion." Gamble ordered the disbandment of Jackson's secessionist State Guard and announced that a loyal militia would replace it as soon as possible. On the sensitive issue of slavery, Gamble promised to protect the institution "to the very utmost extent of [his] Executive power."[53]

As both Gamble and Lincoln knew, the struggle to save the state for the Union and avoid anarchy first had to be won on the battlefield against the Jackson-Price forces encamped in southern Missouri. In preparation for a campaign against the rebels, a major shake-up in the Union command in Missouri and the West occurred in early July 1861. The governors of several western states and conservative Unionists in Missouri wanted someone more prominent than Lyon in charge of the vast Department of the West. Lincoln agreed, and he replaced the New Englander with John C. Frémont, the celebrated "Pathfinder" of the West and 1856 Republican presidential candidate. The War Department reassigned Lyon to field command in Missouri.

At the time, the Frémont appointment seemed to be a good one; the Blairs had strongly recommended him to the president. Before Frémont left Washington to assume command in Saint Louis, Lincoln talked to him and issued sweeping instructions to him. The president directed that he should clear Missouri of rebels and then move down the Mississippi River to Memphis, Tennessee. "I have given you *carte blanche*" in directing operations, Frémont recalled Lincoln as saying; "you must use your own judgment and do the best you can."[54]

Lincoln, however, could hardly have made a worse appointment. As Allan Nevins, the Pathfinder's biographer, has written, a close scrutiny of Frémont's career discloses "an impetuosity that had repeatedly brought him to the verge of disaster, a want of judgment that disturbed his friends." Lincoln, as well as the Blairs, soon had an inkling that he had made a mistake in the appointment when, much to his dismay, Frémont dallied around Washington for three weeks before departing for his headquarters in Saint Louis.[55] For Lincoln, speed in moving against the rebels in Missouri and the Mississippi Valley was essential to success not only in suppressing the southern insurrection but also in maintaining the loyalty of Kentucky and Missouri.

As soon as the Pathfinder assumed command on July 25, 1861, he surrounded himself with favorites, mainly German Americans and old friends from California. Increasingly, Frémont snubbed prominent conservatives like Governor Gamble, who, along with other Unionists, bombarded the president, Attorney General Bates, and Postmaster General Blair with complaints about the general's arrogance and secretiveness. John Howe of Saint Louis wrote Blair, who forwarded the letter to the president, "Oh how badly have we been disappointed, we have got in stead of a General an Egotist—a very ordinary man" who refuses to see his American officers. Yet, Howe reported, Frémont was willing at all times to entertain "California speculators [and] his foreign attachés, who are very objectionable to our Western People."[56] In the general's defense, at least partly, the War Department, with eastern front priorities to satisfy, ignored his many requests for more men and resources to carry out the ambitious military mission that Lincoln had assigned him.

By August, General Lyon in field command with approximately 7,000 troops had advanced into southwestern Missouri and encamped at Springfield, where he awaited reinforcements from the western states. These were slow in coming. At the same time, General Price, commanding Governor Jackson's State Guard, quickly prepared for a showdown with Lyon's forces. To confront Lyon's smaller army, Price had more than 13,000 troops, including approximately 3,000 men from Arkansas and Louisiana under General Ben McCulloch. Concluding that Price intended to attack him at Springfield, Lyon decided to beat him to the punch, despite the fact that he did not have the troops to fight an important battle. Frémont, in Saint Louis, had misjudged the predicament that Lyon faced at Springfield and instead of reinforcing him had sent units to Cairo, Illinois, and to points below on the Mississippi River. Adopting a poorly conceived battle plan, Lyon on August 10 struck Price's army at Wilson's Creek, ten miles from Springfield. The battle proved disastrous for the Union army. When it was over, Lyon lay mortally wounded and his demoralized forces were in retreat.[57]

Panic gripped the Union community in Saint Louis and elsewhere in Missouri after Lyon's defeat at Wilson's Creek. An officer complained to Samuel T. Glover, Lincoln's Saint Louis friend, that "the flight from Bull-run" in Virginia after that Union debacle three weeks earlier "would be nothing [compared] to our disaster if we should be attacked by 3000 real troops" under Price. Another Saint Louis resident wrote Montgomery Blair and blamed the defeat on Frémont for his failure to aid General Lyon.[58]

Price certainly did not want to relieve the fears of Missouri Unionists or, more important, miss an opportunity to redeem the state from Union control. But General McCulloch refused Price's plea to commit his Arkansas and Louisiana troops to a campaign into the Missouri heartland.[59] Without McCulloch's troops, Price, instead of moving on Saint Louis and Jefferson City, as he had wanted to do, marched directly northward to Lexington, Missouri, a pro-Confederate town strategically located on the Missouri River where a Union force of 3,500 men had established a makeshift fort. On September 18, 1861, Price's army surrounded the federal fort. In the face of a superior enemy, Colonel James A. Mulligan, the young commander at Lexington, expected relief columns dispatched by General Frémont to save his garrison. But the federal relief units were poorly coordinated, and those that finally arrived near Lexington proved too few to attempt an assault on Price's army. On September 20 Mulligan surrendered to Price.[60]

Frémont's failure to relieve Colonel Mulligan and his men, combined with his inability to aid General Lyon, put pressure on President Lincoln to remove the general from command. Opposition to Frémont's inflammatory proclamation of August 30 freeing the slaves of rebels (described in chapter 3) only marginally influenced the call for his removal. The proclamation's explosive effect on Unionists was felt less in Missouri than in Kentucky. Glover wrote Postmaster General Blair on September 2 that, though he had been "captivated" at first by the Pathfinder, he had become increasingly dissatisfied with him. Blair apparently gave the letter to Lincoln. The preservation of the Union in the state, Glover asserted, required the general's removal. This Saint Louis Unionist reported, "[Frémont's] troops need discipline—officers & men throng the streets all the time—no regiments are brigaded—no colonel knows his rank—nor can tell his superior." Furthermore, Glover complained, Frémont "don't know his colonels—never visits the camps. . . . Great bitterness of feeling exists on the part of many officers" against him. Surrounded by "foreigners," Frémont refused to see leading citizens, who "come from one to two hundred miles [to] tell him the condition of their section—ask his advice—[and] procure aid."[61] Glover also wrote a brief note to Lincoln condemning the general.[62]

Lincoln soon found other disturbing qualities in his western commander, flaws that he would also see in General George B. McClellan. For one thing, Frémont, like the "Young Napoleon," repeatedly exaggerated the strength of the enemy. On August 17 Frémont excitedly wrote the president, "The force of the enemy which has entered the State is estimated at about sixty thousand." General McCulloch's army alone, Frémont mistakenly reported, was 35,000 strong, and it planned to join with General Price's Missourians for an advance on Jefferson City. At the same time, Frémont told Lincoln that Confederates numbering 25,000 were moving toward Rolla, Missouri, less than 100 miles below Saint Louis.[63] In reality, the Confederate strength was far less than half what the general claimed, a fact that Lincoln probably could have learned from War Department intelligence. Furthermore, because of McCulloch's refusal to cooperate with Price in an invasion of the Missouri interior, the Confederates posed no immediate threat to Jefferson City or Rolla, much less to Saint Louis, where Frémont had retained troops to fortify the city and calm the nerves of fearful Unionists. Lincoln also soon discovered that Frémont, like McClellan, had a case of "the slows." He repeatedly refused to move expeditiously against Price and other Confederate forces operating in the Department of the West.

The most telling complaints about the Pathfinder came from the Blairs. Frank Blair had recommended Frémont for the western command and had dismissed the early criticism of him. But by September 1861 he had changed his mind and blamed Frémont for Lyon's defeat at Wilson's Creek and for other Union setbacks in Missouri. From Saint Louis, Frank Blair on September 1 wrote his brother Montgomery, "Affairs are becoming quite alarming in the northern part of the state as well as in the south—men coming here to give information are not allowed to approach Frémont, and [they] go away in disgust." Frémont, Blair charged, only listened to his officers, who would "prevaricate & shield themselves for neglect of duty."

Blair reported, "[The general] talks of the vigor he is going to use, but I see none of it." He informed his brother that Frémont also refused to impose discipline on his troops and did nothing to keep them out of the whiskey shops in Saint Louis. "My decided opinion is that he should be relieved of his command and a man of ability put in his place. The sooner it is done the better."[64]

As soon as Montgomery received Frank's troubling letter, he rushed over to the White House and insisted that the president remove Frémont from command. Blair declared that Frémont's antislavery proclamation of August 30 had "no share in producing this request," for he approved that document.[65] Although disturbed by the charges in Frank Blair's letter, as well as by other complaints about the Pathfinder, Lincoln, in keeping with his cautiousness in changing commanders, refused to replace Frémont at this time. (A notable exception to this pattern of slow removals was his immediate supplanting of General Irvin McDowell with General McClellan after the battle of Bull Run in July 1861.) Instead, the president decided to ask, not order, General David Hunter, whom he knew personally, to go to Missouri and assist Frémont. "He is losing the confidence of men near him, whose support any man in his position must have to be successful," Lincoln informed Hunter. "His cardinal mistake is that he isolates himself, & allows nobody to see him; and by which he does not know what is going on in the very matter he is dealing with." Lincoln wrote Hunter that Frémont needed "to have, by his side, a man of large experience" and asked, "Will you not, for me, take that place?"[66]

The president sent Montgomery Blair and his brother-in-law, Quartermaster General Montgomery C. Meigs, to deliver the confidential letter to General Hunter in Illinois. After that, they were to visit Saint Louis in order "to see and converse with Gen. Frémont as a friend," as Lincoln later told Frémont's wife Jessie.[67] Hunter agreed to go with Blair and Meigs and undertake the delicate and unorthodox mission that the president had given him. Predictably, Frémont saw Hunter as a threat, which he was, and he kept Hunter at arm's length, thereby creating an even more difficult situation for federal military operations in Missouri.[68]

Meanwhile, Lincoln met with Provisional Governor Gamble, who had come to Washington to complain about the Pathfinder. In addition to criticizing Frémont for his military incompetence, Gamble had another issue to raise with the president about the general. This was Frémont's insistence on appointing and controlling state militia officers. From the governor's point of view, the meeting with the president was a success. Lincoln gave Gamble a letter for Frémont that admonished the general to work with the governor and other civil officials. But when Frémont met Gamble in Saint Louis, instead of promising to cooperate, he launched into a litany of complaints against the governor, including his action in calling out state troops without consulting him. The meeting between Gamble and Frémont ended on a sour note; and the governor's further efforts to see the general ended in failure.[69]

Frémont also sent Jessie to Washington with his September 8 letter declining Lincoln's request for him to withdraw the emancipation part of his August 30 proclamation. Arriving in the capital on September 10, Jessie, the daughter of Missouri icon Senator Thomas Hart Benton, immediately obtained an interview with Lincoln for nine o'clock that evening. It did not go well. According to her account, "The President's manner" at once struck her as "hard—and the tone of his voice [was] repelling. Nor did he offer me a seat. He talked standing, and both voice and manner made the impression that I was to be got rid of briefly." Jessie Frémont reported to friends that Lincoln did not respond directly to her husband's letter but launched into a syllogism on the purpose of the war and on General Frémont's failure to understand it. She quoted the president as declaring, "*It was a war for a great national idea, the Union, and that General Frémont should not have dragged the Negro into it,—that he never would if he had consulted with Frank Blair. I sent Frank there to advise him.*" (Jessie italicized what she said were Lincoln's exact words.) Although these harsh words, as reported by Mrs. Frémont, seem un-Lincoln-like, he might very well have said them. When Lincoln read Frémont's letter in which he refused to modify the critical antislavery order, Lincoln understandably had a reason to be angry and to lash out in the way Mrs. Frémont remembered. In the encounter with the president, Jessie vehemently defended her husband and sharply complained that Lincoln had failed to support him. Whereupon, Lincoln interjected, "You are quite a female politician," a comment that, of course, she did not appreciate.[70] She "left in anger flaunting her handkerchief before my face," the president told Iowa congressman Josiah Bushnell Grinnell less than an hour after the confrontation.[71]

Lincoln's exchange with Jessie Frémont clearly upset him and lingered long in his mind. Two years later, on December 9, 1863, he recalled the meeting to John Hay and others. Mrs. Frémont "sought an audience with me at midnight," he said. The woman "taxed me so violently with many things that I had to exercise all the awkward tact I have to avoid quarrelling with her. She surprised me by asking why their enemy Montg Blair had been sent to Missouri? She more than once intimated that if Gen. Frémont should conclude to try conclusions with me he could set up for himself."[72] The president must have taken this as a threat that if he continued to oppose her husband, Frémont would organize a political movement against him. Lincoln found it ironic that "when this war first began," the Blairs "could think of nothing but Frémont: they expected everything from him and upon their earnest solicitation he was made a general and sent to Mo." Lincoln remembered that the Blairs sincerely "grieved" when Frémont did not succeed, and he admitted that in 1861 he had also "thought well of Frémont," adding, "Even now I think well of his impulses. I only think he is the prey of wicked and designing men and I think he has absolutely no military capacity."[73] Despite his earlier dispute with Frémont over the general's antislavery proclamation, it was the Pathfinder's military incompetence that Lincoln simply could not tolerate.

As expected, Postmaster General Blair and Quartermaster General Meigs, when they arrived in Saint Louis on their mission for the president, found affairs in disarray. Blair wrote the president on September 14, "[General Frémont] seems stupefied & almost unconscious, & is doing absolutely nothing. I find but one opinion prevailing among the Union men . . . & among the officers, & that is that Frémont is unequal to the task of organizing the defences of the State." Blair told Lincoln that the Pathfinder had rejected the advice of his brother Frank as well as that of Governor Gamble and "the best minds in the State." Montgomery Blair further informed Lincoln that Frémont's newspaper in Saint Louis had launched an attack on Frank, proclaiming that "Mr Politician Blair is no longer omnipotent in Missouri." The postmaster general reported that recruiting had come to a standstill in Saint Louis, despite the fact that the city had a large and loyal German American population and, Blair believed, faced a serious threat from General Price's army. "Under Frémont's command we will be kept on the defensive & not be able to do any thing towards suppressing the insurrection from this quarter." He called on the president to replace Frémont immediately with General Meigs.[74] In retrospect, such a move probably

CHAPTER FOUR

would have been wise. Meigs's later Civil War career demonstrated that he was one of the most competent officers in the Union army, a quality that Lincoln soon recognized.

Upon their return to Washington, Blair and Meigs met with Lincoln and the cabinet on September 18 and gave their reports. Despite their arguments for Frémont's removal, Lincoln still was not ready to replace him as the commander of the Department of the West. The president faced strong opposition to Frémont's removal from Secretary of the Treasury Salmon P. Chase, Senator Charles Sumner of Massachusetts, and other prominent radicals in his party. They supported the general's August 30 antislavery proclamation and preferred to believe his self-serving explanations for the deplorable military situation in Missouri.[75] Lincoln revealed to Orville H. Browning that he had "no thought of removing Gen. Frémont on any ground connected with his proclamation." Furthermore, he wrote, "I hope no real necessity for it exists on any ground."[76]

German Americans in Saint Louis, despite Frémont's incompetence and his pomposity, vehemently opposed the removal of their antislavery champion. Gustave P. Koerner, Lincoln's German American friend from Illinois and a member of the general's staff, reported to the president on October 8 that rumors of Frémont's dismissal had produced "tremendous excitement" in Saint Louis, "bordering almost on open outbreaks of mutiny" among his soldiers. "For some reason or another, there is a charm around his name particularly with the Germans and Irish which is astonishing. This element is very largely represented in his department. I undertake to say that of the privates ¾ of all the men belong to those nationalities." Koerner, a former Illinois lieutenant governor, told Lincoln that "to remove [Frémont] just now would be a suicidal policy."[77]

But other Illinois associates of Lincoln clamored for Frémont's dismissal. In a trip to Saint Louis, John G. Nicolay, Lincoln's German American secretary, reported to the president, "The universal opinion is that [Frémont] has entirely failed, *and that he ought to be removed*—that any change will be for the better. I am told that since the surrender of Mulligan" at Lexington, "no one has ventured to even defend him except Gov. Koerner." Senator Browning, who had earlier supported Frémont's proclamation ordering the confiscation of rebel property, in a letter to Lincoln on September 24 deplored the state of affairs in Missouri and despondently wrote that events there had deeply affected Union morale.[78]

Senator Lyman Trumbull also "found a most deplorable state of things" in Missouri after a visit to Saint Louis on September 30, though he did not blame everything on Frémont. "The Western army is demoralized, ruined, & I fear the Union irretrievably gone unless a remedy is speedily applied," he reported, adding, "Thousands of [Frémont's] men have no arms, others are ragged & half clad, & there was yesterday no money at the command of the Western Department . . . and this too at a time when the rebels are pressing vigorously forward to the conquest of Missouri." In Frémont's defense,. Trumbull, who leaned toward a radical or hard-war policy, told the president, "It is cruel to put a man at the head of an army in the face of an enemy & then deny him supplies. I know you do not mean this, yet no man can go to St. Louis without feeling that this is just Gen. Frémont's condition." The Illinois senator insisted that if the government did not have confidence in General Frémont, Lincoln should "in Heaven's name send somebody" who did and who could obtain funds to support the army.[79]

Lincoln's friends Ward Hill Lamon and Congressman Elihu B. Washburne of Illinois, also visited Missouri and provided the president with disturbing reports of conditions in the army. Declaring that "a terribly disorganized state" of military affairs existed in the state, Lamon predicted, "There is about as much likelihood of [Frémont] catching [General] Price as there is of his being struck by lightning."[80] Washburne, who went to Saint Louis as the chair of a congressional committee to investigate corruption in government contracts, wrote Lincoln that after four days of testimony the committee had found "corruption, extravagance, and peculation utterly astounding." He warned, "Unless some competent and incorruptible man shall come here at once and take charge of matters, we all feel that the government must be utterly wrecked." He contended, "It is a singular fact that all the men in this city and state, whom you and I have known for twenty years, as being gentlemen of the highest degree of character and intelligence, and most of them sympathizing with us politically, have no *status* whatever with the powers that rule and control everything." The Illinois congressman lamented, "We now have sixty thousand of the finest soldiers in this State that ever shouldered a musket, and yet we are worsted all the time by roving armies of Price & McCullough [Ben McCulloch], consisting of half armed, ragged, copperas-breeches, water-moccasin ruffians." In conclusion, Washburne told Lincoln that Frémont was "utterly incompetent in all respects" and must be replaced.[81]

CHAPTER FOUR

Aware of the mounting pressure on Lincoln for his removal from command, Frémont determined in late September 1861 to take to the field and "destroy the enemy," as he informed General Scott. On September 23 he asked the general in chief to "please notify the President immediately" of his intention to act. Scott replied, "The President is glad you are hastening to the scene of action. His words are, 'He expects you to repair the disaster at Lexington without loss of time.'"[82]

Before Frémont left to confront General Price and his army in southwest Missouri, he created a new problem for himself. He arrested Frank Blair and charged him with "insidious & dishonorable efforts to bring [Frémont's] authority into contempt with the Government." Frémont knew that Blair had not only written Montgomery Blair—and thus Lincoln—demanding his replacement but had also encouraged the editor of the *Saint Louis Evening News* to publish a series of articles criticizing him. In addition to arresting Blair, Frémont's provost marshal suppressed the *Evening News* and took its editor into military custody. On September 27, after learning of Blair's arrest, Lincoln, through General Scott, ordered Frank's release. He did not know that Montgomery Blair had earlier persuaded Frémont to free Frank and that the editor of the *Evening News* was also subsequently released.[83]

Despite the Pathfinder's promise to "destroy the enemy," he still failed to do battle with Price's army. By early October, the president's patience with him had about run out. Before he acted, Lincoln wanted "an intelligent unprejudiced, and judicious opinion from some professional Military man on the spot" in Missouri regarding the situation. Declaring that he was "greatly perplexed about Gen. Frémont," the president on October 7 wrote General Samuel R. Curtis, commanding near Saint Louis, and asked, "Ought Gen. Frémont to be relieved from, or retained in his present command?"[84] Lincoln dispatched Secretary of War Cameron, along with Adjutant General Thomas, to deliver the letter to Curtis and obtain his response.

The president also sent Cameron with an order, signed by General Scott, removing Frémont from command if he found it necessary. Lincoln could not have expected to receive General Curtis's answer before the secretary of war delivered the order to Frémont. The president, for both military and political reasons, cleverly sought the backing of Curtis, a senior general in Missouri, for the removal. Lincoln must have been concerned about the radical Republican opposition to the replacement of Frémont, particularly after his revocation of the general's antislavery proclamation, and also about the possibility of a mutiny among his German American troops if their champion was removed. However, he had good reason to believe that Curtis would give him the answer that he needed to his question about Frémont.

On October 12 Cameron delivered Lincoln's letter to Curtis. The general, as Lincoln expected, responded by repeating many of the charges made by others against Frémont. Curtis concluded that "the Army in Missouri could not be successful under his leadership—and that the safety of this great and important State could not be secured, unless [Frémont] was superceded in his command." Curtis dispatched a similar but more detailed report to the president.[85] The next day, the secretary of war met with Frémont in the field and showed him the removal order. "He was very much mortified, pained, and, I thought humiliated," Cameron reported to Lincoln. "He made an earnest appeal to me" to retain him in command, since he "had now around him a fine army, with every thing to make success certain; [he said] that he was now in pursuit of the enemy, . . . and that to recall him at this moment would not only destroy him, but render his whole expenditure useless." Moved by the general's plea, Cameron, who had earlier in the cabinet meeting argued against removal, wrote the president that he told Frémont he would withhold the order until he returned to Washington. "The interim," Cameron said, would give Frémont time "to prove the reality of his hopes as to reaching and capturing the enemy."[86]

Cameron and Thomas returned to Washington on October 21. The secretary of war had Thomas prepare a report for the next day's cabinet meeting on "the vexed question of the recall of Genl. Frémont." The report was a comprehensive indictment, in eleven printed pages, of the Pathfinder's failed military leadership, his mismanagement in providing for the army, and the extensive malfeasance of his staff.[87] After reviewing the report, Lincoln, according to Attorney General Bates, announced to the cabinet that "it was now clear that Frémont was not fit for the command." He seemed to agree with Bates that "the removal" had to be made, "and instantly." But, Bates wrote in his diary, Secretary of State William H. Seward "came again, as twice before, to the rescue—and urged delay," probably until Frémont's mettle could be tested on the battlefield against Price. Cameron "gave in and timidly yielded to delay; and the President," Bates wrote, "still hangs in painful and mortifying [sic] doubt" on the issue. Lincoln's "suffering is evidently great, and if it were not connected with a subject so momentous, would be ludicrous." Bates bluntly warned the president that such a "timorous and vacillating course [would] degrade the Adm and make it weak and helpless." If Frémont was kept in command, "the public [would] attribute the fact to a motive no higher than our [political?] fears," the attorney general argued. Finally, Bates "protested against having [Missouri] sacrificed on such motives and in such a cause" as that of Frémont.[88]

Lincoln must have been moved by Bates's fervor and argument for Frémont's removal. Two days later, the president finally threw political and other considerations to the wind and acted. On October 24 he wrote General Curtis, directing him to deliver to Frémont, "with all reasonable dispatch," the original order replacing him with General Hunter. Yet Lincoln instructed Curtis to withhold the order temporarily if the army was engaged or about to be engaged with the enemy. He told the general to convey a separate directive to Hunter, but only after Frémont had received the removal notice.[89]

In order to ensure secrecy and avoid any serious complications that might occur in Frémont's dismissal, Lincoln dispatched an Illinois friend, Leonard Swett, to deliver the two documents and letter to Curtis. After an unavoidable delay, Swett arrived in Saint Louis on October 29 and immediately met with Curtis. The general informed Swett, as well as the president, in a November 1 letter that the Frémont-controlled press, anticipating their favorite's removal, had "done all in its power to excite insubordination and resentment" in the city against the Pathfinder's enemies. "The german people have talked about making him Dictator," Swett excitedly reported to Lincoln. "Some of his officers in quite high standing have talked so too. There is among a great many sober-minded people a feeling of insecurity," he told the president.[90] Even Lincoln had earlier expressed his belief that Frémont was ready to rebel against his authority.[91]

Under these circumstances, and also concerned that the president's orders might fall into rebel hands, Swett and Curtis developed a plan for the clandestine delivery of the documents to Frémont and Hunter. The main problem was getting through Frémont's lines near Springfield without detection and obtaining access to the general, and then safely conveying the appointment order to Hunter at Sedalia, Missouri. General Curtis found a "reliable" junior officer in Saint Louis to deliver the documents. Riding horseback for two days and nights and dressed as a country farmer, the officer reached Frémont's camp and entered his headquarters, much to the surprise of the general. Frémont huffily wanted to know, "Sir, how did you get through my lines?" After reading the order, Frémont still seemed determined to take to the field and do battle with the rebels before Hunter received the order to replace him. However, no enemy force could be found within thirty or forty miles of Springfield that Frémont might attack. Although the Pathfinder's staff tried to prevent Curtis's messenger from leaving the camp and delivering the order to Hunter, Frémont learned that a duplicate of it had been sent to the general. Later that night, he relinquished his command, gave a pompous farewell address to his troops, and abruptly departed for Saint Louis. Frémont reportedly left camp with his "body guard," fifty Indians, and a paymaster carrying between $200,000 and $300,000 in funds. The paymaster was later arrested, and most of the money was recovered.[92]

The feared mutiny of Frémont's German troops did not materialize, though numerous demonstrations of defiance occurred in the camp. In Saint Louis, a large group of cheering supporters, with bands blaring, greeted their hero when he returned. A committee of German Americans submitted to the general a set of resolutions praising him and declaring that "a wise Providence [had] reserved him for a still wider sphere of action in future times."[93] General Curtis, in command at Saint Louis, happily reported to Lincoln on November 16, "All acts of mutiny and insubordination have been suppressed and the possibility of any thing of that sort is entirely removed." Curtis, a West Point graduate and a former three-term Republican congressman of Iowa, informed the president that he "had gained the friendship and *force* of the German element, although their infatuation for General Frémont was and still is excessive."[94]

Frémont never achieved the military glory that he desired and that his wife Jessie thought he deserved. He would be assigned a command in Virginia, where he also failed to distinguish himself. The Frémonts continued to complain of what they considered the general's unjust treatment by Lincoln and the Blairs; Jessie Frémont referred to the president's conduct as "treason," an epithet that was loosely used during the Civil War to denounce opponents. In 1864 Frémont became the presidential candidate of a small faction of disaffected radicals, only to withdraw at the insistence of his supporters when his enemy Montgomery Blair was forced from the cabinet.

General Hunter's command of the Department of the West was only temporary. Lincoln and the War Department needed a more senior officer to manage such a large area, which included all the trans-Mississippi West.

It was renamed the Department of Missouri, which underscored the importance of the state to the Union cause. On November 9, 1861, Lincoln appointed Henry W. Halleck as its commander. Halleck immediately gained the support of Governor Gamble and other conservative Unionists, because, as one of them put it, "his views about Missouri accord entirely with my own." They especially approved of his openness and his willingness to enforce the Fugitive Slave Act. Before leaving Washington, Halleck visited with Attorney General Bates, who recorded in his diary that the general "urged me to write to him and give the names of men with whom he can confer, and to write to *my friends* to call upon him." An obviously pleased Bates wrote his Missouri friends, "You'll find [Halleck] accessible & frank & I think really anxious to do good & be on the best of terms with the true men of the state."[95] These words were music to the ears of Gamble and others in the provisional government who had been ignored by the Pathfinder and his staff.

While Frémont's removal was pending, Governor Gamble in October 1861 called the Union state convention into another session. (It had adjourned in August after creating the provisional government.) Because of the presence of Price's army and rebel guerrillas in large areas of the state, the convention understandably postponed the November elections until August 1862. It also dispatched Gamble to Washington to seek Lincoln's approval for a plan to expand the state militia and provide federal financial support for it. The governor arrived in the capital in early November 1861 and hand-delivered a memorandum to Lincoln outlining the convention's plan. The proposal had already received the endorsement of Bates, Montgomery Blair, and the new general in chief, George B. McClellan. The president gave his approval, but with a condition: when the governor commissioned a major general of the militia, "it shall be the same person at the time in command of the United States Department of the West."[96] This addendum, which Gamble agreed to, was designed to ensure a unity of command in the state. Otherwise, the governor received the authority to appoint all militia officers below the rank of major general.

The militia plan approved by Lincoln represented an important success for Gamble and the provisional government in their effort to maintain state authority and sustain the Union. The president—and the War Department—also agreed to provide the necessary arms and financial support for the militia as long as it was in active service. Under the plan, the state troops, though obligated to cooperate with the federal forces, could not be ordered out of Missouri "except for the immediate defense of the State." As required, Gamble appointed Halleck to overall command of the Missouri State Militia.[97]

Gamble enthusiastically endorsed General Halleck's selection of General John M. Schofield as the immediate commander of the state militia. Schofield, a conservative and a West Point graduate who had taught physics at Washington University in Saint Louis, seemed ideal to coordinate affairs with the civil authorities under the plan that Lincoln had approved. Still, issues relating to the control of Missouri's troops, civil jurisdictions, the pacification of the state, and slavery would resurface and create serious friction between the military and the civil government.

The most critical problem facing Missouri during the winter and spring of 1861–1862 was the continuation of Confederate operations in the state and the outbreak of guerrilla violence, especially along the state's border with Kansas, where old prewar grudges had to be settled. U.S. Senator James H. Lane of Kansas and Dr. Charles R. Jennison were vigorously rallying antislavery "Jayhawkers" for a bloodletting against the proslavery "Border Ruffians" of Missouri. The Missourians, mainly supporters of the Confederacy, prepared to answer in kind.[98]

Immediately upon assuming command in November 1861, General Halleck asked Lincoln for the authority to establish martial law in Missouri. In a letter to General in Chief McClellan, Halleck anxiously reported, "The enemy is moving north with a large force and a considerable part of North Missouri is in a state of insurrection. The rebels have organized in many counties, taken Union men prisoners, and are robbing them of horses, wagons, provisions, clothing, &c." Halleck insisted, "To punish these outrages and to arrest the traitors who are organizing these forces and furnishing supplies it is necessary to use the military power and enforce martial law," since no civil authority could reach them. "The safety of Missouri," he declared, "requires the prompt and immediate exercise of this power, and if the President is not willing to intrust [sic] me with it he should relieve me from the command."[99]

On December 2 Lincoln granted Halleck the authority to suspend the writ of habeas corpus and declare martial law within his command in order "to secure the public safety and the authority of the United States."[100] Halleck had not asked for permission to suspend the writ of habeas corpus, but the president granted it to him anyway. (Generals Lyon and Frémont, without consulting Lincoln or the War Department, had earlier instituted military control in Saint Louis, but they did not suspend the writ. They apparently believed that after having established martial law, the suspension would be superfluous.)

Acting on this authority, Halleck on December 26, 1861, declared martial law along the railroads, where guerrilla attacks had been especially destructive, and in Saint Louis. In January, he ordered General John Pope, commanding on the western border, to drive the Jayhawkers out of the state. "They are no better than a band of robbers," Halleck informed Adjutant General Thomas in Washington. Halleck wrote to General Thomas, "[The Jayhawkers] disgrace the name and uniform of American soldiers and are driving good Union men into the ranks of the secession army." The only way to secure peace along the border, he contended, was to keep the Kansans and the Missourians apart, which had proved exceedingly difficult.[101]

Remote from the scene of the violent raids and influenced by the lobbying of Senator Lane, Republicans in Washington viewed the Kansas invaders as more sinned against than sinning. Missouri congressmen James S. Rollins and Thomas L. Price (no relation to the Confederate general), however, saw the Jayhawkers not only as a major cause of the lawlessness along the border but also as enemies of the Union people whom they professed to protect. They wrote the new secretary of war, Edwin M. Stanton, on February 5, 1862, asking him to inform the president of the outrages "committed against Unionists in Missouri" as well as against rebels "by a force under Colonel Jennison," the leader of the Kansas marauders. Stanton immediately promised Rollins and Price that he would submit their letter to Lincoln. He also assured the congressmen, who were in Washington, "No effort on the part of the Government will be spared to protect the Union men and loyal citizens of Missouri from all illegal force and lawless violence, come from what quarter it may."[102] No record of the president's reaction to Rollins and Price's appeal has been found. However, with Stanton's backing, Halleck and the Missouri State Militia temporarily drove the Jayhawkers from the state. They captured Dr. Jennison, but Senator Lane secured his immediate release and eventual restoration to command, enabling the doctor to resume his violent operations along the Kansas-Missouri border.[103]

Governor Gamble also appealed to President Lincoln to use his "moral" authority to check the "diabolical outrages" committed by "such brutes as Jennison." On May 19, 1862, Gamble wrote Lincoln, "You know that I cannot submit to any such invasion of the rights of the State Government without impairing very materially my power to control the disturbed and excited population" of Missouri. Displaying more optimism than realism about conditions in his state, the governor informed the president, "Gradually the popular mind is becoming calm, and throughout the largest portions of the State, Courts of justice are . . . open and the law is administered." Still, he said, "there is a wide-spread feeling of disaffection" that had been encouraged by the failure of federal authorities to control the Jayhawkers and other lawless groups. Gamble told Lincoln that the best policy for pacifying the state was "to employ gentle means" while maintaining military power to back the civil authorities.[104] Preoccupied with the critical spring military campaigns in Virginia, Lincoln did not respond to Gamble's letter.

On March 13, 1862, Halleck gave his officers in the field the authority "without any formal declaration of martial law to adopt such measures as may be necessary to restore the authority of the Government and to punish all violations of the laws of war" and directed: "This power will be exercised only where the peace of the country and the success of the Union cause absolutely require it."[105] He expected slave property, as well as other forms of property, to be protected in the state and elsewhere in his command.

General James Totten, commanding the state militia in central Missouri, acted in a severe fashion to carry out Halleck's instructions. A West Point graduate who had served as a junior officer under Generals Lyon and Frémont, Totten ordered: "Whenever and wherever bands of guerrillas, jayhawkers, marauders, murderers, &c., are found in arms in open opposition to the laws and legitimate authorities of the United States and the State of Missouri, the miscreants . . . are to be shot down by the military authorities." He included Kansas Jayhawkers in his order because, as he explained, some of "these wretches" came into Missouri "disguised under the uniform of our patriotic army and are pretending to act under and by authority of the United States." For those people who in the future "harbor or in any manner encourage" these outlaws, Totten directed that they should be arrested and tried by military commission.[106]

Even the usually moderate General Schofield, commander of the Missouri State Militia, succumbed to the need for swift and harsh justice to suppress rebel guerrillas and those aiding them. On May 29, 1862, Schofield issued an order announcing, "The time is passed when insurrection and rebellion in Missouri can cloak itself under the guise of honorable warfare." He "enjoined upon all the troops of the State" to exercise "utmost vigilance . . . in hunting down and destroying these robbers and assassins." Like Totten, Schofield directed that when the "outlaws" were "caught in arms, engaged in their unlawful warfare," they were to be "shot down upon the spot." However, he promised amnesty to those rebels who desired "to become good and loyal citizens," saying, "[They] may surrender themselves and their arms at the nearest military post, and will be released upon subscribing to the usual oath and giving bond, with approved security, for their future loyal conduct." Schofield reminded his officers and men that "while punishing with unmeasured severity those who still persist in their mad efforts to destroy the peace of the State," they should not molest or injure loyal and peaceful citizens. He promised to hold all of his men "to a strict accountability for the just and proper execution" of his order.[107] How many armed Missouri guerrillas and Kansas Jayhawkers were captured and summarily executed by Union troops is unknown. When such justice was meted out, almost certain retaliation followed, and the vicious circle of violence and revenge continued.[108]

Tragically, by mid-1862 Missouri had become the scene of vicious guerrilla warfare and unconscionable lawlessness of a magnitude never before seen in America. Only a large and disciplined army could have restored peace and security to the countryside; such a force was not available during the war. Governor Gamble's Missouri State Militia, though commanded by professional officers like Generals Halleck, Schofield, and Totten, proved unequal to the task of suppressing the disorders in the interior and in the counties bordering on Kansas and Arkansas. Confederate guerrilla bands led by brutal commanders like William C. Quantrill and "Bloody Bill" Anderson took the war not only to the Jayhawkers but also to their Union neighbors and the state militia. Plunder became a compelling motivation for both pro-Confederate "bushwhackers" and Kansas Jayhawkers. A reign of terror prevailed in some areas of the state. In the end, peace and security for many communities did not return until after the Civil War; the political enmities and lawlessness would linger much longer.

Despite the surge of rebel activities in the state, Governor Gamble in 1862 assumed that the Missouri State Militia, supported by federal forces and under the leadership of Generals Halleck and Schofield, would soon clear Missouri of rebel troops and check the marauders on both sides. Then law and order could be restored to a suffering and frightened people and civil government would be revived throughout the state. Gamble and state officials believed that elections scheduled by the state convention for August 1862 could be held and that the results would demonstrate to the nation and to President Lincoln that the state was solid for the Union and equal to the task of managing its civil affairs without federal interference.

Lincoln seemed to have reached a similar conclusion regarding Missouri's future. He optimistically reported to Congress on December 3, 1861, "[Missouri] is comparatively quiet; and I believe cannot again be overrun by the insurrectionists." At the same time, Lincoln proclaimed the success of the Union in Maryland and Kentucky.[109] He now thought that the time was ripe to take action toward eliminating the fundamental cause of the war—chattel slavery—which, he calculated, if successful, would undermine the Confederate war effort and bring the conflict to an early end. He envisioned that a step against slavery in the border states, done in a constitutional manner and with the cooperation of these states, would begin the process of eradicating the greatest blight on America. Moreover, its success would demonstrate to the rebels that they had no hope of the border states joining them in their war against the Union.

Lincoln realized that the abolition of slavery would necessarily be slow, troublesome for many people, and politically risky. But upon its completion, he confidently believed, the cause of liberty and equality would be advanced everywhere, and the destruction of slavery would fulfill the enlightened expectations of the Founding Fathers; it would also end the charge of hypocrisy hurled against America by its critics. To launch the process of black freedom and attain his war aims, Lincoln in early 1862 proposed an ambitious plan of federal, compensated emancipation for the border states.

■

CHAPTER 5

Lincoln's Emancipation Initiatives and the Border States

On an autumn day in November 1861, Lincoln called George P. Fisher, Delaware's lone member of the House of Representatives, to the White House for a conference. The president wanted to know if the Delaware legislature would consider a plan of gradual, compensated emancipation, funded by the federal government, for the 1,800 slaves in the state. Lincoln probably knew that Governor William Burton and Delaware senators Willard Saulsbury and James A. Bayard, though Unionists, were vocal Democratic foes of his administration and would refuse to cooperate in any movement against slavery. On the other hand, Fisher, an old Whig who had supported John Bell, the Constitutional Union candidate for president in 1860, was mildly antislavery. Lincoln believed correctly that Fisher would agree to serve as the point man for his emancipation proposal to the Delaware legislature. Although the congressman promised to seek the legislature's approval of the plan, he did not guarantee success.[1]

During the fall, pressure had mounted on Lincoln to act against slavery, despite his repeated promise not to interfere with it in the southern states. Lincoln must have known that radical members of his party like Massachusetts senator Charles Sumner, who had been disappointed with Lincoln's revocation of General John C. Frémont's antislavery decree, were preparing to seize the initiative for emancipation after Congress met in December. America's leading contemporary historian, George Bancroft, whom Lincoln highly esteemed though he was not a Republican, reflected the antislavery fervor of eastern intellectuals and others in support of black freedom when he wrote the president on November 15. "Your administration has fallen upon times, which will be remembered as long as human events find a record," Bancroft told him. "[The] Civil war is the instrument of Divine Providence to root out social slavery," he declared. "Posterity will not be satisfied with the result, unless the consequences of the war shall effect an increase of Free states." Bancroft, however, exaggerated when he declared that the end of slavery was "the universal expectation and hope of men of all parties"; many Democrats and conservatives in the North and border state Unionists strongly opposed adding emancipation to Union war aims. Lincoln assured Bancroft that his sentiment "is one which does not escape my attention." He also wrote, "I must deal in all due caution" with the slavery issue in view of constitutional and political restraints, and "with the best judgment I can bring to it."[2]

Encouraged by Congressman Fisher's willingness to seek approval for his compensated emancipation plan for Delaware, Lincoln went to work drafting a proposal for the small slave state. On about November 26, 1861, one week before Congress met in its regular session, the president completed the draft of two options for such a bill. He gave the draft to Fisher to present to his friends in the Delaware legislature. Both options provided for the allocation of 6 percent federal bonds totaling $719,200, to be distributed in five equal annual installments as the process of freedom unfolded. The first option called for the phased ending of slavery, with one-fifth of the adult slave population becoming free by mid-1862, and the remaining four-fifths by 1867. The second option provided for a far longer period of phased emancipation, extending to 1893. Both options required that the state adopt a system of "apprenticeship, not to extend beyond the age of twenty-one years for males, nor eighteen for females for all minors whose mothers were not free" at the time of birth. The president admitted, "On reflection, I like No. 2 the better," since it expanded the period for the completion of emancipation, though that meant Delaware would not be required to abolish slavery before 1893.[3] As Lincoln had often said, he favored a process of gradual emancipation that would give time for the social and racial adjustments inherent in uprooting slavery. Neither option for Delaware called for black colonization, a provision that Fisher wanted and that Lincoln favored on a voluntary basis for freed blacks.

Lincoln optimistically believed that the Delaware legislature, with

Fisher's backing, would accept his emancipation proposal. Delaware Unionist Benjamin Burton, at Fisher's suggestion, visited the White House and asked Lincoln whether he was sure that Congress would support the plan. The president replied that he was confident that Congress would approve it and, in his quaint way, told the Delawarean, "Mr. Burton, you tend to your end of the swingle tree, and I'll tend to mine. If I can get this plan started in Delaware I have no fear but that all the other border states will accept it. . . . This is the cheapest and most humane way of ending this war and saving lives." Burton, the largest slaveholder in Delaware, assured Lincoln that the state would agree to his plan, provided a fair compensation could be arranged. The president was "delighted" by Burton's response.[4]

The president on December 1 told Senator Orville H. Browning that he had high hopes that the other border states, as well as Delaware, would accept a plan of compensated emancipation. He expressed his belief that these states would be willing to receive "$500 a piece for all the negroes they had according to the census of 1860," provided "a system of gradual emancipation" could be worked out for "the extinction of slavery in twenty years." Lincoln calculated that such an arrangement, financed by the federal government, "would require only about one third of what was necessary to support the war for one year." He predicted, as he later explained to Congress and border state representatives, that the acceptance of a plan of compensated emancipation would shorten the war, since the insurrection could no longer be sustained by rebel hopes of winning border allegiance because of the need to protect slavery. Browning noted that Lincoln agreed with him that emancipation "should be connected with a scheme of colonizing the blacks some where on the American Continent."[5]

Lincoln's hopes that Delaware would lead off by approving his plan of compensated and gradual emancipation were soon dashed. Although Congressman Fisher, as promised, lobbied for a revised version of the proposal, it received a hostile reaction from the state's leadership. Both Delaware's U.S. senators, James A. Bayard and Willard Saulsbury, denounced the plan. Saulsbury characterized it as a plot "to elevate the miserable Negro, not only to political rights, but to put him in [the] Army."[6] With such a powerful opposition, Fisher's friends never brought the proposal to the floor of the legislature. Instead, its opponents secured the lower chamber's approval of a counterresolution denouncing any federal interference with slavery in the state; the state Senate, however, by a 4 to 5 vote, with one senator not voting, did not concur in it.[7] Because slaves constituted only 1.6 percent of the state's population, the action of the Delaware legislature in rejecting Lincoln's proposal strongly suggests that the main issue in its disapproval was not the protection of an economic system or the maintenance of a plantation lifestyle. Slavery was no longer important to the material welfare or white class structure of Delaware. The overriding issue in Delaware's rejection was racial, specifically the state's continued control of blacks. Like Senator Saulsbury, legislators feared that their acceptance of Lincoln's plan would become an entering wedge for antislavery elements in the federal government to impose black equality or rights upon Delaware whites. In 1861–1862 they opposed any departure from the stated purpose of the war, namely, the preservation of the Union.

Although disappointed with Delaware's action, Lincoln by late 1861 had already concluded that a plan of state-controlled and federally funded emancipation could achieve the twin objectives of suppressing the southern insurrection and ending slavery. He assumed that by combining the two objectives, he could satisfy his antislavery critics in the North and divide the border state slaveholders from those in the rebel states. His plan, he believed, would meet the test of constitutionality and also his inaugural address promise not to interfere with slavery in the states. Lincoln's paramount objective would still be to preserve the Union. Emancipation, he thought, would not only be a means to achieve that purpose; it would also strike a blow at the institution that he had long viewed as immoral and that had caused secession and war. As events would demonstrate, the president, in developing this strategy, put too much faith in the border states' acceptance of his compensation scheme.

In early 1862, Lincoln turned his attention to developing a compensation plan for all the border states. The plan would be in the form of a joint resolution by Congress submitted to the states for acceptance. On December 31 Senator Sumner reported to an antislavery friend, "[The president] *now meditates an early Message to Congress* proposing to buy the slaves in the still loyal states . . . and then proclaim Emancipation with our advancing armies."[8] With other matters to contend with in the new year, including the sickness and death of his son Willie and his frustration with General George B. McClellan's hesitancy to launch military operations, Lincoln was slow in preparing the resolution. He first secured slave popu-

CHAPTER FIVE

lation figures from the U.S. Bureau of the Census, and then he asked Secretary of the Treasury Salmon P. Chase to draft a resolution for Congress's consideration. However, Chase in his draft used inflammatory language to assail the "Slaveholding Empire" and the "misled masses" of the South; he failed to provide the reasoned, legal document on compensated emancipation that might have appealed to border state Unionists.[9] Concerned about the language in the Chase draft, the president himself took pen to paper and crafted the resolution that he planned to submit to Congress at an opportune time.

Meanwhile, on February 11, Senator Sumner, who had little faith in state-controlled, compensated emancipation, introduced a series of resolutions designed to abolish slavery and provide a stringent reconstruction plan for the insurrectionary states. Sumner's resolutions ignored Lincoln's desire for a liberal amnesty and mild reconstruction policy for the South, controlled by southern Unionists. In addition, Representative James M. Ashley of Ohio introduced a bill in the House that proposed emancipation, confiscation of rebel property, and proscription of the political rights of most Confederates. Leading Republican newspapers like the *Chicago Tribune* and Horace Greeley's *New York Tribune* joined in the radical demand for party leaders in Washington to take steps to confiscate and free the slaves of rebel masters.[10] Although the passage of such antislavery measures was unlikely in early 1862, border state members of Congress became deeply concerned. With good reason, they feared that support for the Union in their states would be in grave danger if Congress took action against slavery. Lincoln also realized that most Democrats in the North, along with border state loyalists, would vigorously oppose any movement to change the purpose of the war to include emancipation. As it turned out, a coalition of border state Unionists, conservative northern Republicans, and Democrats, with Lincoln's tacit support, defeated the radical efforts to take charge of reconstruction and secure direct federal intervention against slavery in the South.[11]

The defeat of the radical proposals cleared the way for Lincoln on March 6, 1862, to submit to Congress his resolution recommending a voluntary compensated emancipation plan for the border states. The president's resolution read, "Resolved that the United States ought to cooperate with any state which may adopt gradual abolishment of slavery, giving to such state pecuniary aid, to be used by such state in it's [*sic*] discretion, to compensate for the inconveniences public and private, produced by such change of system." As Lincoln biographer Michael Burlingame has pointed out, the word used by the president, "abolishment," was a softer term than "abolition" and, as Lincoln believed, "less likely to raise conservative hackles."[12] Lincoln insisted that if his proposal did not "meet the approval of Congress and the country," that would be the end of it, but, he went on, "if it does command such approval . . . the states and people immediately interested, should be at once distinctly notified of the fact, so that they may begin to consider whether to accept or reject it."[13]

The president's proposed resolution did not contain the statistical argument or timetable for emancipation outlined in his Delaware plan. He assumed that the details of the plan would be worked out by Congress and the border states. Lincoln, however, said, "Any member of Congress, with the census tables and Treasury-reports before him, can readily see for himself, how very soon the current expenditures of the war would purchase, at fair valuation, all the slaves in any named State." He maintained that his proposal was "one of the most efficient means of self-preservation" for the federal government. He argued that Congress's endorsement of the plan, along with that of "all the slave states" north of the "disaffected region" in the South would deprive the rebels of border state support in the insurrection and dash their hopes for success in the war. The plan's adoption, Lincoln confidently asserted, "substantially ends the rebellion. . . . The point is not that *all* the states tolerating slavery would very soon, if at all, initiate emancipation." Rather, the plan's initiation in "the more Northern [states] shall . . . make it certain to the more Southern, that in no event, will the former ever join the latter, in their proposed confederacy. I say 'initiation' because, in my judgment, gradual, and not sudden emancipation, is better for all."[14]

Lincoln attempted to allay the suspicions of border state Unionists, as well as of northern Democrats and conservatives, that his resolution represented a step toward mandatory federal emancipation. He promised that his proposal created "no claim of a right, by federal authority, to interfere with slavery within state limits." The plan, he said, would leave "the absolute control" of slavery in the hands of each state and its people, and it was "proposed as a matter of perfectly free choice with them." Still, Lincoln issued a somber warning. If "resistance continues," he declared, "the war must also continue; and it is impossible to foresee all the incidents, which may attend and all the ruin which may follow it. Such as may seem indispensable, or may obviously promise great efficiency towards ending the struggle, must and will come." Thus, before it was too late, the border states for "pecuniary consideration" should agree to a compensation plan for the gradual abolition of slavery.[15]

A few days later, in a letter to Democratic senator James A. McDougall of California, the president outlined, with mathematical precision, his calculations on the expense of his plan. Based on a $400 compensation price per slave and a total of 432,622 slaves in the border states, including the District of Columbia, Lincoln concluded that it would cost the federal government $173,048,800 to finance emancipation. This, he calculated, was the approximate cost of the war for eighty-seven days. In a deviation from his Delaware proposal, he said that payments could be made in twenty equal installments and that emancipation need not be completed until a distant date, "say January 1st 1882." The president told McDougall, who opposed the resolution, that the expense "would not be half as onerous, as would be an equal sum raised now, for the indefinite prosecution of the war." The adoption of the plan, he insisted, would bring an early end to the conflict and save the federal treasury millions of dollars.[16]

Lincoln's compensation resolution received broad support in the North. The *New York World*, an independent journal at this time, told its readers, "Here, then, is a hand stretched out to the border states to save them from the ruin, which they have half invited."[17] The Washington correspondent of the *World* reported that at the capital the president's proposal was "generally regarded [as] a most ingenious and timely political movement." Lincoln, by striking the golden mean between federal and state emancipation, this writer contended, had undercut the opposition, including the antislavery radicals in Congress.[18] Many radical Republicans—a somewhat amorphous and shifting faction in the party—pronounced Lincoln's plan a step in the right direction against slavery. Horace Greeley's *New York Tribune*, which rarely had a kind word to say about the president, sanguinely predicted that all sides, including rebel slaveholders, would accept the compensation offer.[19] The *Tribune* gave a list of thirty-one conservative and Democratic newspapers that supported the plan; none, however, was a border state paper.[20] George William Curtis, editor of *Harper's Weekly*, applauded Lincoln's action and wrote a friend, "[The president's] policy has been to hold the border states. He has held them. Now he makes his next move, and invites emancipation. I think he has the instinct of a statesman: the knowledge of how much is practicable, without recoil."[21]

Conservative newspapers like the *Washington National Intelligencer*, the capital city organ of old Whig conservatives, called for Congress and the border states to adopt Lincoln's emancipation plan. The *New York Times*, which soon would be closely allied with the Lincoln administration, printed several articles and editorials in support of the plan, concluding, "[It] has hit the happy mean upon which all parties in the North and loyalists in the South can unite." Nonetheless, the *Times* questioned the heavy financial costs involved in compensating owners for their slaves. Privately, editor Henry J. Raymond wrote the president that his March 6 message to Congress was "a master-piece of practical wisdom and sound policy" in moving against slavery and winning the war; it was certain to please all but the extremists. The proposal, Raymond said, "furnishes a solid, practical, constitutional basis for the treatment of this great question, and suggests the only feasible mode I have yet seen of dealing with a problem infinitely more difficult than the suppression of the rebellion."[22]

Despite broad support in the North, Lincoln's compensated emancipation plan immediately ran into trouble in the place where he had to succeed—the border slave states. The influential *Louisville Daily Journal* exclaimed that the proposed resolution would create discord and division among Unionists in the border region, though the writer—probably George D. Prentice—admitted that the plan was constitutional because it did not impose emancipation upon the states. The newspaper further argued that if enacted, the resolution would play into the hands of the rebels who all along had insisted that the aim of Lincoln and the Republicans was to destroy slavery in the South. Furthermore, the *Journal* disputed the president's contention that the rebels had been led to believe that the border states would join the Confederate States because of slavery. The likelihood that the border states would ever consider abandoning the Union, the *Journal* declared, was "exceedingly slender," if it existed "at all."[23] Former Maryland governor and soon-to-be senator Thomas H. Hicks, though privately approving the plan, warned Lincoln, "Some of your friends" in his state "have been alarmed by [his proposal], fearing it to be the precursor of trouble to the Border slave states," which could undermine support for the Union.[24]

Lincoln soon received disturbing reports that many border state members of Congress opposed his compensation resolution. He concluded that these representatives had "misunderstood" the proposal and mistakenly regarded it "as inimical to the interests [they] represented." In hopes of securing their support, the president asked the border congressmen to meet with him at the White House. The conference was held on March 10. Immediately after the meeting, Representative John W. Crisfield of Maryland wrote an account of it; Congressmen John J. Crittenden and John W. Menzies of Kentucky, who also attended, confirmed the accuracy of Crisfield's report. According to Crisfield, the president "disclaimed any intent to injure the interests or wound the sensibilities of the slave States" by his proposal. "On the contrary," he declared, "his purpose was to protect the one and respect the other." Because "immense armies" would be in the field until the rebellion had been suppressed, Lincoln told the border state men that these forces, as they advanced, "must, of necessity, be brought into contact with slaves" in their states. Slaves, Crisfield reported Lincoln saying, "would come to the camps, and continual irritation [would be] kept up." Lincoln informed the delegation that "he was constantly annoyed by conflicting and antagonistic complaints" from both antislavery proponents and slaveholders. Antislavery advocates, the president said, wanted the slaves protected by the army, and they "frequently . . . acted in a way unfriendly to the slaveholders [who] complained that their rights were interfered with, their slaves induced to abscond and protected within [Union] lines." The president indicated that "these complaints were numerous . . . and a serious annoyance to him, and embarrassing to the progress of the war."[25]

Lincoln reminded the congressmen that the division over slavery "kept alive a spirit hostile to the Government" in their communities and, he reiterated, sustained the Confederates' hopes that the border states someday would unite with them. He told them that if his compensated emancipation resolution was adopted by Congress and accepted by the border states, the irritation over slavery and the hopes of the rebels "would be removed, and more would be accomplished towards shortening the war than could be hoped from the greatest victory achieved by Union armies."

The president advised the border state congressmen to confer with each other and take such action as they felt the interests of their constituents required. Several members asked Lincoln questions about the proposal. Crisfield wanted to know what effect a state's rejection of the plan might have, and whether the president had additional antislavery schemes in mind. Lincoln replied, according to Crisfield's account, "that he had no designs beyond the action of the States" on the issue, though he would "lament their refusal to accept" the proposal. Menzies asked if "there was any power except in the States themselves to carry out his scheme of emancipation?" Lincoln answered that "he thought there could not be," but he did not explain why.

Crisfield, a large slaveholder in eastern Maryland, told Lincoln that the people of his state did not look upon slavery as a permanent institution. He maintained that Marylanders probably would be willing "to give it up if provision was made to meet the loss, and they could be rid of the race; but they did not like to be coerced into emancipation, either by the direct action of the Government or by indirection." Lincoln responded that "unless he was expelled" from the presidency "by act of God or the Confederate armies," Maryland would have "nothing to fear, either for her institutions or her interests." Crisfield informed the president that if the people of Maryland could hear what he was saying, "they would consider your proposition with a much better feeling" than appeared likely. Lincoln quickly dismissed Crisfield's suggestion that he publish a statement on the issue. That would "not do," he emphatically declared. "It would force me into a quarrel" with the "Greeley faction" of antislavery radicals "before the proper time." He intimated that a conflict over slavery with this faction was impending, though he hoped to avoid it. Not until after Lincoln issued his preliminary Emancipation Proclamation in September 1862 was Crisfield's account of the meeting published in the newspapers.[26]

In the March 10 meeting, Representative William A. Hall of Missouri asked the president for his personal opinion of slavery. Lincoln replied that "he did not pretend to disguise his antislavery feeling; that he thought it was wrong and [would] continue to think so; but that was not the question" to be dealt with now. "Slavery existed," he said, "as well as by the act of the North as of the South; and in any scheme to get rid of it, the North, as well as the South, was morally bound to do its full and equal share." (Lincoln continued to hold the view of a shared North-South responsibility for slavery; he later expressed it in his second inaugural address.) Lincoln told the border state congressmen that the institution "ought never to have existed; but yet he recognized the rights of property which had grown out of it, and would respect those rights as fully as similar rights in any other property." The president, however, affirmed that he wanted to get rid of the laws protecting slave property, "not by violating the right, but by encouraging [state emancipation] and offering inducements to give up" the institution. He argued that his compensation proposal was designed to do just that. At the end of the meeting, the venerable Crittenden promised the president that the border state members in Congress "would consider respectfully the important suggestions he had made" before voting on the compensation resolution, but he refused to predict that they would support it.

The next day, March 11, the House of Representatives approved Lincoln's proposed resolution by a vote of 97 to 36. The border state members, including their leading spokesmen, Crittenden and Crisfield, voted overwhelmingly against it.[27] Crittenden explained his vote: "Although the president will abstain from interfering" with slavery, "there are many others, who knowing it is a favorite policy of his, [and] desiring to be in his favor, would stir up an emancipation party in Missouri, in Maryland, and in Delaware" if the border states representatives supported the resolution.[28] Crittenden evidently believed that his home state of Kentucky was immune to any such antislavery agitation.

In the Senate, action on the compensation plan became tied to the debate over federal emancipation in the District of Columbia. Lincoln, whose first priority on slavery was to secure the approval of the border state proposal, wrote Horace Greeley on March 24 that he "was a little uneasy about the abolishment of slavery in this District," not because he would not "be glad to see it abolished," but because of "the time and the manner of doing it." Lincoln said that he would be more agreeable to a bill abolishing slavery in the District "if some one or more of the border-states would move fast" toward the acceptance of his compensation plan. Still, if Congress persisted in acting immediately on slavery in the District, as he told Greeley, "I would like the bill to have three main features—gradual— compensation—and vote of the [white] people."[29] The provisions that he wanted in the bill were precisely those of a proposal to end slavery in the District that he had drafted, but did not introduce, while a member of Congress in early 1849.

Despite the president's wishes to delay action on the District of Columbia emancipation bill, Congress continued to debate the issue, with border state members vigorously opposing it. Senators Lazarus W. Powell and Garret Davis of Kentucky led the fight against the District bill. Powell cited the *Dred Scott* decision (1857) proclaiming slaves were property. The Constitution, Powell reminded his colleagues, provided that "no man shall be deprived of his property without due process of law," which, he argued, the bill failed to guarantee.[30] Senator Davis in a speech on March 12 exclaimed, "[Though] the loyal people of the [border] slave States are as true to this Union as any man in the Senate Chamber, or in any of the free States, [they] never, never will submit to unconstitutional laws," as proposed in the District bill. He particularly objected to having the slaves liberated and then remaining among whites. Davis predicted that such an eventuality would "establish a bloody Vendee in the whole of the slave States."[31] Yet in January he had told Lincoln, according to Illinois Senator Browning, that if necessary to save the Union, he "was willing . . . to see slavery wiped out." Browning, however, doubted that the Kentucky senator really meant it, and indeed Davis, who was known for his extreme rhetoric, continued to find reasons to oppose emancipation.[32]

Davis followed his March 12 speech with the introduction of an amendment to the District emancipation bill that required the removal of freed slaves to colonies outside the United States. The amendment, as Davis hoped, greatly complicated the proceedings on the District bill. He knew that several Republican senators, including James R. Doolittle of Wisconsin, as well as some House members, while favoring emancipation in Washington, supported black colonization and wanted to vote for his amendment. Lincoln himself had given credence to Republican support for colonization in his annual message to Congress on December 3, 1861. At that time the president recommended that Congress adopt a plan of voluntary resettlement for free blacks "at some place, or places, in a climate congenial to them."[33] Even Greeley's *New York Tribune*, though opposed to forced removal to colonies, believed, "The Negro race, whenever free, will gradually migrate southward—colonizing the less populous West Indies, Central America, and the adjacent portions of South America. . . . But if Slavery were ended to-morrow, we are confident that even South Carolina would be in no hurry to expel from her soil the most industrious and productive half of her people."[34]

Davis's amendment to the District bill, designed to force black colonization, failed by one vote in the Senate, with Vice President Hannibal Hamlin breaking a tie on the roll call. The final bill, however, satisfied Republican senators—and the president—by approving $100,000 to aid voluntary black resettlement in Haiti or Liberia. It also provided an average of $300 per slave to District slaveholders as compensation for their losses. The bill

Garret Davis, Kentucky Union Leader; replaced John C. Breckinridge in the U.S. Senate in late 1861 where he became a vigorous opponent of Lincoln and Republican policies, especially emancipation and the military recruitment of blacks. Noted for his hyperbolic rhetoric, Davis barely avoided expulsion from the Senate in 1864. Courtesy of the Brady-Handy Collection, Prints and Photographs Division, Library of Congress, Washington, DC.

passed the Senate on April 3 by a vote of 29 to 14; the border state senators, including those of the Restored (that is, Union) Government of Virginia, voted solidly against it. On April 11, after an impassioned speech by Crittenden opposing the bill, the House approved the measure by a 92 to 39 vote. As expected, the border state representatives followed Crittenden's lead and opposed it.[35] Historian Allen C. Guelzo has written that the passage of the District of Columbia emancipation bill "was the first time in the history of the Republic that Congress had taken a direct step against slavery."[36] Antislavery crusaders, both inside and outside Congress, also noted the historical importance of the moment. Frederick Douglass spoke for many of them when he declared after the passage of the District emancipation bill that he could scarcely believe what had happened. "I trust that I am not dreaming," he said.[37]

On Monday, April 14, Senator Browning took the bill to the president for his action. Lincoln told his Illinois friend that he would sign it but that he would send a special message to Congress asking for a supplementary measure to resolve a few of his concerns about the bill. Lincoln, according to Browning, said that he "regretted the bill had been passed" in the form it was, "that it should have been for gradual emancipation—that now families would at once be deprived of cooks, stable boys & they of their protectors without any provision for them." He informed Browning that he would wait until Wednesday, April 16, to sign the bill in order to accommodate Representative Charles A. Wickliffe, the aging former governor of Kentucky. Wickliffe, Lincoln explained, "had two family servants with him who were sickly, and who would not be benefited by freedom." He "could not get them out of the City until Wednesday, and the Gov had . . . asked for time" before the bill went into effect, a request that Lincoln had agreed to.[38] The president's explanation begs the question, if the servants were dependent on Wickliffe, why could they not have been emancipated in Washington and then, if they wished, followed the congressman to Kentucky?

As he had promised to Browning, the president signed the bill ending slavery in the national capital. In a message to Congress approving it, Lincoln announced that he was "gratified that the two principles of compensation, and colonization, [were] both recognized, and practically applied in the act." He expressed regret, however, that no provision was made in the bill for "minors, femes-covert, insane, or absent persons."[39] Lincoln asked for supplementary legislation to correct the flaw; both houses later made the change. The president took the occasion to express his long-held position on the abolition of slavery in the District. "I have never doubted the constitutional authority of congress to abolish slavery in this District," he informed Congress, "and I have ever desired to see the national capital freed from the institution in some satisfactory way. Hence there has never been, in my mind, any question upon the subject, except the one of expediency, arising in view of all the circumstances."[40]

In his message to Congress, the president left unstated his wish that the bill should have provided for gradual emancipation, and also that it should have secured the approval of the voters of the District. Although Lincoln found slavery repugnant and a blight on the republic of the Founding Fathers, he still was more concerned with winning over whites, politically and economically, to emancipation than he was with the interest of blacks in freedom.

Meanwhile, the logjam in the Senate over Lincoln's March 6 resolution for gradual, compensated emancipation in the border states had been broken. Having passed the House, the bill won approval in the Senate on April 2 by a vote of 32 to 10.[41] Garret Davis broke ranks with his border colleagues and voted for it. He favored the resolution because, as he informed his colleagues, it provided "a satisfactory assurance" that slaveholders would be "compensated to something like the reasonable value of their slaves" and, most important for Davis, "a system of [black] colonization [would] be undertaken at the cost of the United States Government."[42] One week after the Senate's approval, Lincoln sent the resolution to the border states for their action. It also went to Tennessee, where Andrew Johnson, soon after the fall of Nashville to Union forces, had been appointed military governor by Lincoln with instructions to launch the process of reconstruction.

Although Congress had approved in principle Lincoln's compensation proposal, the plan faced formidable—and probably insurmountable—obstacles before it could be implemented. Many Democrats and grassroots Republicans, burdened with the expenses of the war, opposed additional taxes to pay for freeing slaves in the border states, blacks who conceivably would move north, create a burden on their communities, and, in some cases, compete for jobs with whites. Furthermore, these northerners, as well as border state Unionists, were highly skeptical—and correctly so—of Lincoln's contention that the adoption of his plan would lead to the end of the rebellion.

In Congress, Republicans and others wanted the states to agree first to Lincoln's plan and provide an early timetable for the completion of emancipation before they approved the federal bonds to finance it. Yet, hopeful of a positive response by the border states, House Speaker Galusha A. Grow on April 14, 1862, formed a committee on emancipation, chaired by Albert S. White of Indiana, to study and report on "whether any plan can be proposed and recommended for the gradual emancipation of all the African slaves, and the extinction of slavery in Delaware, Maryland, Virginia, Kentucky, Tennessee, and Missouri, by the people or local authorities, and how far and in what way the Government of the United States can and ought to aid in facilitating either of the above objects."[43]

Pressure now mounted on the border states to agree to Lincoln's compensation proposal. The conservative *Boston Advertiser*, the leading old-line Whig newspaper in New England, pleaded with the border state legislatures to endorse the federal bailout for slaveholders in their states. This newspaper also praised Senator Davis of Kentucky for supporting the plan and announced, "One vote like his on such a subject is worth more to the country than a dozen from New England or New York."[44] Postmaster General Montgomery Blair urged his friends in Maryland to adopt Lincoln's plan because it provided for "gradual emancipation with compensation, and the separation of the races." Blair predicted that Maryland would approve the resolution.[45] The *Baltimore American* printed Blair's letter and also endorsed its contents, concluding that the people of Maryland should "lose no time in considering the question presented by the President." The editor of the *Washington National Intelligencer* echoed these views and reminded border state men that Lincoln's gradual, compensated emancipation plan conformed to the "Old Southern Platform" to end slavery at some time in the future. This editor, carried away by false nostalgia, concluded, "The [old] doctrine still remained the received opinion among the more thoughtful of the Southern people, and especially among the most intelligent of the slaveholding class."[46]

But before the border states could act on the Lincoln resolution, General David Hunter, commanding federal troops along the coasts of South Carolina, Georgia, and Florida, lobbed a firebomb into the debate. On May 9, Hunter, fresh from his command on the volatile Kansas-Missouri border, issued a proclamation freeing all slaves within his department and, two days later, organized 500 blacks into the First South Carolina Volunteers. As in the case of Frémont's earlier antislavery proclamation in the West,

Lincoln immediately grasped the seriousness of Hunter's action, not only for the Union cause generally but also for the border states' consideration of his compensated emancipation proposal.

If Lincoln needed any evidence of conservative Unionist outrage over Hunter's actions, border state spokesmen provided it. Reverdy Johnson of Maryland expressed the indignation of border loyalists when he wrote the president on May 16, "For Heavens sake, at once, repudiate it, & recall the officer. . . . Unless promptly corrected, it will serve the rebels, nicer than a dozen victories. . . . I look upon the policy thus inaugurated, if to be followed, as fatal to all our hopes." Johnson told the president, "There is but one sentiment—disapprobation" in Maryland regarding Hunter's proclamation. He added, "All, are looking with confident hope, to your arresting [this] treason at once." Another Marylander reported to Montgomery Blair that after learning of the general's proclamation, "there is not a single exception, but that every official" in the state "pronounces the man an 'Abolitionist' who dared [to] second the [compensation] proposition of the President."[47]

In Kentucky, the hue and cry against Hunter's proclamation could be heard throughout the state and read in almost all its newspapers. The outrage was only slightly less in Missouri, where the state convention had reconvened to consider Lincoln's compensation resolution and other matters.[48] Prentice's *Louisville Daily Journal* pronounced Hunter's action "an outrage, not only upon humanity and the constitution, but upon the dictates of sense, both common and military." The *Journal* exclaimed that the emancipation order was "a reckless and guilty violation of policy as well as of principle" and predicted that "such conduct, if unchecked, would neutralize, and more than neutralize, the brightest victories" that had recently been won on the Gulf Coast by Flag Officer David Farragut and General Benjamin F. Butler. The *Journal,* however, expressed its confidence that "the President, as in the heinous case of Frémont, [would] discharge his imperative duty with promptitude and decision" and revoke Hunter's inflammatory proclamation.[49]

Predictably, radicals in Lincoln's party urged him to ignore border state and northern Democratic opposition and sustain Hunter's antislavery decree on the grounds of military necessity. Chase, the only true radical in the cabinet, wrote the president, "It seems to me of the highest importance, whether our relations at home or abroad be considered, that this order be not revoked. It has been made a military measure to meet a military exigency, and should, in my judgment, be suffered to stand upon the responsibility of the Commanding General who made it." Chase told Lincoln that "more than nine tenths of the people on whom you must rely for support of your Administration" would endorse his backing of Hunter.[50] On the other hand, the *Philadelphia Inquirer*, as was the custom of the partisan press, exaggerated when it reported that only a few "ultra Abolitionist" journals supported it.[51]

Carl Schurz, a prominent German American radical, pleaded with Lincoln to approve Hunter's action. He informed the president that if he agreed to the antislavery order on the grounds of "local military necessity," there would not be "a murmur against it a fortnight hence." Schurz perceptively predicted, "The arming of Negroes and the liberation of those slaves who offer us aid and assistance are things which must and will inevitably be done."[52]

Lincoln, however, concluded that he had to revoke General Hunter's order if he expected the border states to agree to his compensated emancipation scheme and, perhaps also, if he hoped to avoid a serious setback for the war effort. But first, he sent a brusque reply to Chase and by extension to his radical friends: "No commanding general shall do such a thing" as Hunter had done "upon my responsibility, without consulting me."[53] Then he issued a proclamation on May 19 revoking Hunter's emancipation decree. The president announced, "Whether it be competent for me, as Commander-in-Chief of the Army and Navy, to declare the Slaves of any state or states, free, and whether at any time, in any case, it shall have become a necessity indispensable to the maintenance of the government, to exercise such supposed power, are questions which, under my responsibility, I reserve to myself."[54] Lincoln thus, in disavowing Hunter's emancipation order, left the door open for any action he might take against slavery, provided he found it necessary to save the Union and it could be justified as constitutional. Astute border state observers and others must have found ominous the president's statement that he reserved the right to take action against slavery if it were required to win the war. However, pleased with Lincoln's repudiation of Hunter's proclamation, they let the matter rest for the moment.

The president devoted the remainder of his May 19, 1862, proclamation to an appeal to the border states to adopt the compensated emancipation resolution that he had recommended on March 6 and that Congress had approved in April. He told the people of the border states, "I do not argue. I beseech you to make the arguments for yourselves." Having said that, Lincoln then, in starker terms than before, made the arguments for them. "You can not if you would," he declared, "be blind to the signs of the times. I beg of you a calm and enlarged consideration of [the signs], ranging, if it may be, far above personal and partizan [sic] politics." Lincoln insisted that the change the resolution contemplated "would come gently as the dews of heaven, not rending or wrecking anything" and asked, "Will you not embrace it? So much good has not been done, by one effort, in all past time, as, in the providence of God, it is now your high previlege [sic] to do." He closed with the admonition: "May the vast future not have to lament that you have neglected" the historic duty to end slavery in the border states.[55]

Having received no official answer from the border states on his compensation resolution, Lincoln again called their congressmen to the White House for a conference. The meeting occurred on July 12 and included not only members from the border states but also four members from western Virginia (representatives of the rump Union government of the Old Dominion) and two Unionists from east Tennessee who had been elected in 1861. The president informed the group that he wanted to address them about his resolution before they returned home after the congressional session. Reading from a paper that he had prepared, Lincoln began by announcing, "You of the border-states hold more power for good than any other equal number of members" in Congress. He appealed to them to support his plan of emancipation. "If you all had voted for the resolution in the gradual emancipation message of last March," Lincoln told them, "the war would now be substantially ended." As before, the president argued that rebel hopes for victory would continue "so long," he said, "as you show a determination to perpetuate the [slave] institution within your own states. . . . You and I know what the lever of [rebel] power is. Break that lever [slavery] before their faces, and they can shake you no more forever."[56]

Lincoln in this second meeting with the border state congressmen insisted that, like them, he had wanted "the constitutional relation of the states to the nation . . . practically restored, without disturbance of the institution" of slavery in the South. "But," he said, "it is not done, and we are trying to accomplish it by war," adding, "If the war continues long . . .

the institution in your states will be extinguished by mere friction and abrasion—by the mere incidents of the war." Slave property "will be gone, and you will have nothing valuable in lieu of it. Much of its value is gone already. How much better for you, and for your people, to take the step which, at once, shortens the war, and secures substantial compensation for that which is sure to be wholly lost in any other event." Moreover, Lincoln argued, the nation would save blood and money by an early suppression of the rebellion, an eventuality that, he felt confident, would follow the adoption of his compensation plan.[57]

The president repeated to the border state men his position on the timing of emancipation: "I do not speak of emancipation at once, but of a decision at once to emancipate gradually." He also reaffirmed his goal for the voluntary resettlement of freed slaves outside the United States. Although Lincoln had not recommended colonization in his March 6 resolution, he had done so earlier in his December 3, 1861, annual message to Congress and again in his support of the District of Columbia emancipation bill. In his second meeting with the border congressmen, Lincoln announced that there was "room in South America for colonization [that] can be obtained cheaply, and in abundance," and he predicted, "When numbers shall be large enough to be company and encouragement for one another, the free people will not be so reluctant to go."[58]

He then brought up the controversy over Hunter's emancipation order. In repudiating Hunter's decision, Lincoln informed the congressmen, "I gave dissatisfaction, if not offence, to many whose support the country can not afford to lose. And this is not the end of it. The pressure, in this direction, is still upon me, and is increasing." He pleaded, "By conceding what I now ask, you can relieve me, and much more, can relieve the country, in this important point."[59]

The president asked the border state congressmen to discuss the proposition among themselves before leaving Washington "and, at the least," to "commend it to the consideration of your states and people." He ended with a stirring appeal to their patriotism and for the perpetuation of the ideals for which the republic stood. "Our common country," he declared in Lincolnesque fashion, "is in great peril, demanding the loftiest views, and boldest action to bring it speedy relief. Once relieved, it's [sic] form of government is saved to the world; it's [sic] beloved history, and cherished memories, are vindicated; and it's [sic] happy future fully assured, and rendered inconceivably grand. To you, more than to any others, the previlege [*sic*] is given, to assure that happiness, and swell that grandeur, and to link your own names therewith forever."[60]

Two days later, the president received a written response from the majority of the border state delegation. It was not what he wanted. The seventeen House members and three senators who signed the document rejected Lincoln's appeal for their support of the compensated emancipation plan. They included Garret Davis, who had voted for the resolution in the Senate but now opposed it because, he explained, it lacked a specific federal commitment to compensate slaveholders and provide for the colonization of freed blacks. Senators Bayard and Saulsbury of Delaware also opposed the resolution but did not participate in the meeting.[61]

In their statement to the president, the border state congressmen argued that the emancipation plan, while proposing "a radical change of our social system," had been "hurried through both Houses with undue haste, without reasonable time for consideration and debate, and with no time at all, for consultation" with their constituents. The president's resolution, they contended, "seemed like an interference, by this government, with a question which peculiarly and exclusively belonged to our respective States." Much of their explanation for opposing Lincoln's proposal, though hardly as important as their racial and social concerns, focused on refuting his financial argument. "Many of us," the majority statement read, "doubted the constitutional power of this government to make appropriations of money for the object designated; and all of us, thought our finances were in no condition to bear the immense outlay which its adoption and faithful execution, would impose upon the National Treasury." Citing U.S. census slave statistics for the four border states and Tennessee and Virginia, a total of 1,196,112, the congressmen, using slightly flawed arithmetic, calculated that compensated emancipation for these states at $300 per slave, as the District emancipation bill had provided, would cost the federal treasury $358,883,600. In addition, they concluded that the expense of deportation and colonization of freed slaves at $100 per person would cost $119,224,533. The total amount of $478,078,113, in addition to the heavy expense of the war, "involves," they said, "a sum too great for the financial ability of this government at this time."[62]

The congressmen dismissed Lincoln's argument that the continuation of slavery in the border states gave the rebels hope that those states would eventually join the Confederacy. The rebellion, the congressmen contended, derived its strength not from the slave institution, as Lincoln had concluded, but from the overwhelming belief by the rebels that their property and society were under assault by the U.S. government. "Remove their apprehensions—satisfy them that no harm is intended to them, and their institutions: that this government is not making war on their rights of property, but is simply defending its legitimate authority, and [the majority] will gladly return to their allegiance." Reunion, they predicted, "[will occur] as soon as the pressure of military dominion imposed by the Confederate authority is removed from them."[63] The congressmen deluded themselves when they argued that the rebel states would voluntarily return to the Union upon a promise by Lincoln to guarantee their rights and institutions. The president had offered such assurances before, only to be ignored by the secessionists. Short of military defeat, the rebels would not have given up the struggle for independence.

These congressmen also took issue with the president's claim that radical antislavery pressure on him could be relieved by the border states' acceptance of the emancipation proposal. They asked, "Can it mean that by sacrificing our interest in Slavery, we appease the [antislavery] Spirit that controls that pressure, cause it to be withdrawn, and rid the Country of the pestilent agitation of the Slavery question?" They told Lincoln that "the liberation of seven hundred thousand Slaves" in the border states would not end the radical agitation over slavery "while three millions remain in bondage," a reasonable conclusion that Lincoln had not been willing to make.[64]

In closing, the congressmen expressed their appreciation to the president for his "earnestness and eloquence" in appealing to them to support his compensation scheme. Although opposed to the proposal, they promised at least to commend it "to the consideration of our State and people," provided that it "assume[d] the shape of a tangible, practicable proposition." They informed Lincoln, "Our people . . . will not consider the proposition in its present impalpable form." Congress, they insisted, must appropriate "sufficient funds" to pay the states that "shall adopt the abolishment of slavery, either gradual or immediate, as they may determine, and the expense of the deportation and colonization of the liberated slaves. [Only] then will our States and people take this proposition into careful consideration."[65]

Seven members of the border state delegation, including Fisher of Delaware and four representatives from Tennessee and western Virginia, issued a minority statement endorsing Lincoln's resolution. They announced that it was necessary for "the whole power of the Government" to be "sustained by all the influences and means of all loyal men in all sections, and of all parties" and that Lincoln's appeal to them "[had] been made for the purpose of securing that result." They contended, "A very large portion of the people in the Northern States believe that slavery was 'the lever of the rebellion,'" as Lincoln had argued. The seven representatives said, "It matters not whether this belief be well founded or not. The belief does exist, and we have to deal with things as they are, and not as we would have them be. . . . The Government cannot maintain this great struggle if the support and influence of the [antislavery] men who entertain these opinions be withdrawn. Neither can the Government hope for early success if the support of that element called 'Conservative' be withdrawn." The president, they declared, rightly "appeals to the *border State* men to step forward and prove their patriotism by making the first sacrifice" in the interest of saving the nation by adopting his emancipation plan.[66]

The day after the meeting, July 13, Lincoln expressed his "deep anxiety" that the border state members had not agreed to his proposal. Meeting with Illinois congressmen Owen Lovejoy and Isaac N. Arnold at his Soldiers' Home retreat in Washington, Lincoln lamented, "Oh, how I wish the border states would accept my proposition. Then . . . you, Lovejoy, and you, Arnold, and all of us, would not have lived in vain. The labor of your life, Lovejoy, would be crowned with success. You would live to see the end of slavery."[67] Unfortunately, Lovejoy, a longtime abolitionist and brother of Elijah, who had been killed by an antislavery mob in Illinois, did not live to see the last slave freed—he died in 1864.

Lincoln agreed with the majority of the border state congressmen that his proposal, which had been approved in principle by Congress, must include a specific funding commitment by the federal government. With that in mind, and still hopeful that such funding would sway the border state legislatures to adopt his plan, Lincoln on July 14 carefully drafted and sent to Congress a bill "to compensate any State which may abolish slavery within it's [sic] limits." The proposed bill provided that whenever any state had "lawfully abolished slavery, . . . either immediately, or gradually," it would be "the duty of the President, assisted by the Secretary of the Treasury, to prepare and deliver" bonds to the state, "equal to the aggregate value at [he left the amount blank] dollars per head" of the slaves in the state. If the state abolished slavery immediately, all the bonds were to be delivered at once. If, however, a plan of gradual emancipation were adopted, the bonds were to be sent to the state in equal annual installments with the interest beginning at the time of delivery. The proposed funding bill provided that if slavery was reintroduced after the bonds had been received, the bonds would "at once be null and void" and the state would "refund to the United States, all interest which may have been paid on such bonds."[68] Notably missing from the proposed measure was any mention of federal aid for the colonization of blacks. On July 16 Representative Albert S. White, chairman of the Committee on Emancipation, rushed Lincoln's bill to the floor of the House so it could be considered before the end of the congressional session. It was too late; the funding bill died when Congress adjourned on the next day.[69]

By this time, Congress had created another heated controversy over emancipation. On July 12, 1862, Congress approved a bill "to suppress the insurrection, to punish treason and rebellion, to seize and confiscate the property of rebels, and for other purposes." The bill included the confiscation of the slaves of rebels. Fueling support for this legislation was the growing northern hostility toward the South in the aftermath of the horrific battles in Virginia and in the Mississippi Valley during the spring and early summer. The bill, when enacted, became known as the Second Confiscation Act; the first one, a weaker measure, had been approved in August 1861.

The history of the Second Confiscation bill began when Senator Lyman Trumbull, who had moved into the radical Republican ranks, introduced it in December 1861. Trumbull's bill provided for "the absolute and complete forfeiture . . . of every species of property, real and personal . . . belonging to persons [who] shall take up arms against the United States, or in any wise aid or abet the rebellion." The bill reflected the desire of the radicals to punish the rebels and free their slaves.[70] When first introduced and debated during the winter of 1861–1862, its success was problematic.

As expected, the Second Confiscation bill created alarm among border state members in Congress. They perceived it as a large entering wedge for comprehensive federal emancipation, even in the Union slave states and even for loyal slaveholders. Border congressmen, despite having few qualms about punishing the rebels, concluded that the proposed confiscation bill was an integral part, along with the president's compensated emancipation proposal, of a determined northern movement to abolish slavery. In addition to the usual proslavery arguments, several border state senators and representatives warned that emancipating the slaves of rebels, as provided in the bill, would dramatically enlarge the free black population in their states, thereby creating major social and racial problems for their communities. Senator Saulsbury of Delaware promised that if Congress enacted emancipation, he would "go before [his] people" and demand the "enslaving [of] the whole race," including the 20,000 free blacks in his state and the thousands from the rebel states who, he predicted, would flood Delaware.[71]

Several northern Republicans in early 1862 joined the border state men and northern Democrats in opposing the Trumbull bill. These opponents condemned the bill's sweeping confiscation provisions and warned that its passage would inevitably increase support for the insurrection in the South. Conservative Republican Senator Edgar Cowan of Pennsylvania exclaimed, "Pass this bill, and the same messenger who carries it to the South will come back to us with the news of their complete consolidation as a man" in support of the rebellion. "We shall then have done that which treason could not do; we ourselves shall then have dissolved the Union."[72]

By July, a more moderate and acceptable version of the Confiscation bill had emerged. The bill still provided for the confiscation of rebel property, including slaves, and for the punishment of six classes of secessionists whom the federal courts would adjudge guilty of "treason." However, persons engaged in armed rebellion could avoid the penalties of this provision, including death, by renewing their allegiance to the Union within sixty days of a presidential warning and proclamation to enforce the new law. The revised bill provided that the president could pardon or grant amnesty to those found guilty under the law. As a practical matter, its enforcement would occur only where Union forces had established control of an area. The bill also provided that the slaves of rebels who escaped to Union lines would be free; other owners of fugitives, upon an affirmation of their loyalty, could reclaim their slaves. Significantly, the bill authorized the president "to employ as many persons of African descent as he may deem necessary and proper for the suppression of the rebellion, and for this purpose he may organize and use them in such manner as he may judge best for the public welfare." The bill did not require Lincoln to enlist blacks in the army, though it was a major step in that direction. In addition, the Confiscation bill empowered the president "to make provision for the transportation, colonization, and settlement, in some tropical country" of those blacks freed by the act who were "willing to emigrate." The president, however, must first obtain the consent of the tropical state to receive the immigrants, and that nation would have to agree to their protection with "all the rights and privileges of freemen."[73]

On July 11 the House of Representatives approved the Second Confiscation bill by a vote of 82 to 42. The Senate agreed to it the next day by a margin of 28 to 13. In the House, only two border state members voted for the measure; they were Jacob B. Blair of the Restored Government of Virginia and Fisher of Delaware. No border state senator supported it. Browning, Lincoln's friend, and two other free-state senators also opposed the bill on both constitutional and political grounds.[74] The sticking point for the border state congressmen and the bill's northern opponents was its antislavery provisions, which, they correctly believed, opened the door for federal emancipation.

As had been the case with the District of Columbia emancipation legislation, Lincoln regretted the timing of the Confiscation bill's approval by Congress. The bill's passage, he reasoned, would again complicate border state action on his compensated emancipation plan. He still hoped that the Union slave states would accept his proposal as an important war measure and realize that they could still save something from the wreckage of slavery. But with the passage of the Confiscation bill, border state endorsement of his compensation offer was now in greater danger than before. On the same day that Congress approved the bill, the members of the border states' delegation, despite the majority's opposition to Lincoln's compensation proposal, had agreed to send it to their states for consideration. The funding measure died when Congress adjourned, but Lincoln did not know that it would fail when the Confiscation bill was passed several days earlier and sent to him for his action.

On July 1 Lincoln, before the passage of the bill, read a hastily drafted paper to Senator Browning expressing his thoughts on the measure. After the meeting, the conservative Browning approvingly wrote in his diary that the president's "views coincided entirely with my own." Lincoln, however, only mentioned the provisions relating to fugitive slaves and the use of slaves or contrabands by the army. He told Browning, "[Though] no negroes necessarily taken and escaping during the war are ever to be returned to slavery, . . . no inducements are to be held out to them to come into our

lines for they come now faster than we can provide for them and are becoming an embarrassment to the government." Lincoln declared that the
arming of blacks, as the bill made possible but did not require, "would
produce dangerous & fatal dissatisfaction in our army, and do more injury
than good."

The president also remarked, according to Browning, "[Since] Congress
has no power over slavery in the states, . . . so much of it as remains after
the war is over will be in precisely the same condition that it was before the
war began, and must be left to the exclusive control of the states where it
may exist."[75] Lincoln in his inaugural address and on other occasions had
made similar statements denying federal authority over slavery in the
South. These pronouncements strongly suggest that, despite what some
historians have concluded, he was not a determined emancipationist from
the beginning of his presidency.[76] Given his reputation for honesty, which
his contemporaries acknowledged, Lincoln could hardly have been deceit-
ful in his earlier statements about his intentions regarding the "peculiar institution." The prolongation of the war, however, caused the president by
mid-1862 to seek constitutional grounds to justify federal emancipation, as
distinct from state emancipation. He concluded that it could be properly
done as a war measure controlled by him as commander in chief and not
by Congress. First, however, Lincoln wanted to pursue his border
state–controlled plan of federal compensation, which, if accepted, he
seemed genuinely to believe, would soon lead to the end of the rebellion
and slavery in the United States.

When he talked to Browning, the president was already thinking about
vetoing the Confiscation bill. He even prepared a veto message prior to the
vote. The bill's Republican managers had become distressingly aware that
Lincoln, on constitutional grounds, disapproved of the bill's provision that
the confiscation of an offender's property could extend beyond the individual's lifetime (which would run afoul of Article III, Section 3, of the U.S.
Constitution). After hurriedly conferring with Lincoln, Republicans
pushed through an explanatory resolution to satisfy the president's principal objection to the bill. The resolution declared that the clause relating to
the punishment and seizure of rebel property should not be construed "as
to work forfeiture of the real estate of the offender beyond his natural
life." Republicans met another Lincoln concern by exempting from punishment rebel state legislators and judges who had never taken an oath supporting the U.S. Constitution, and who thus had not violated any oath.[77]

Lincoln on July 17 signed both the Confiscation bill and the explanatory resolution, noting that they were "substantially one." He also sent Congress the veto message that he had prepared, though it was no longer relevant to the bill's enactment. As historian John Syrett, the leading authority on what became known as the Second Confiscation Act, has written, by "sending his veto message," Lincoln "made clear the division between him and the radicals on confiscation and emphasized how problematic he found the bill to be."[78] Lincoln supported confiscation as a means to undermine the rebellion, provided it could be done in a constitutional and judicial manner.

The president announced that he found much in the Confiscation bill that was unobjectionable. Specifically, he told Congress that in the section punishing "traitors" and rebels, the bill was fair because it "touche[d] neither person or property, of any loyal citizen; in which particular it [was] just and proper." Furthermore, he explained, "by fair construction" of the bill, offenders were "not to be punished without regular trials, in duly constituted courts." They also would be subject to his liberal pardon and amnesty policy. "The severest justice may not always be the best policy," he said. "The principle of seizing, and appropriating the property of [offenders] is certainly not very objectionable; but a justly discriminating application of it, would be very difficult, and, to a great extent, impossible," he added, which suggests that he would not be vigorous in enforcing this important provision of the bill.[79]

As Lincoln had told Senator Browning, he expressed concern in his prepared veto message about the ambiguity in the bill regarding the fate of slaves confiscated by the military from their rebel owners. He found it "startling . . . that congress can free a slave within a state." However, he again, as in the case of his compensated emancipation proposal, found a legal way to overcome the difficulty. "If . . . the ownership of the slave had first been transferred to the nation," he explained, "and . . . congress had then liberated him, the difficulty would at once vanish. . . . The traitor against the general government forfets [sic] his slave, at least as justly as he does any other property; and he forfeits both to the government." The question then, according to Lincoln, was whether the slave was free or was to be sold to a new master. He answered, "I perceive no objection to Congress deciding in advance that [the slave] shall be free." He gave the example of the state of Kentucky, which had become "the owner of some slaves" when no legal heirs to the slave property existed, and which had "sold none, but liberated all. I hope the same," he said, "[will be] true of some other states. Indeed, I do not believe it would be physically possible, for the General government, to return persons, so circumstanced, to actual slavery. I believe there would be physical resistance to it, which could neither be turned aside by argument, nor driven away by force."[80]

In the veto message that he had drafted, Lincoln also pointed out his concern that no provision had been made in the Confiscation bill "for determining whether a particular individual slave does or does not fall within the [offending] classes" of slaveholders. He believed that "this could be easily supplied" by careful legislation, but he failed to recommend how it might be done, and Congress did not act to satisfy him on the matter. In addition, Lincoln told Congress that the bill lacked a provision by which an individual whose property was seized would have a reasonable period of time for a personal hearing in court on the question of his loyalty. Congress ignored this concern in its explanatory resolution, which, in retrospect, further weakened the enforcement of the bill. Finally, the president announced that he approved of the clause in the Confiscation bill authorizing the president, through his military commanders, "to employ as laborers, as many persons of African de[s]cent, as can be used to advantage."[81]

However, until 1863, Lincoln refused to authorize the enlistment of blacks in the army. (Blacks already served in the navy, and by the time he issued his Emancipation Proclamation on January 1, 1863, as many as 4,000 blacks had enlisted in federal units in South Carolina, Louisiana, and Kansas, though without the president's official approval.)[82] According to the *New York Tribune*, Lincoln told a "deputation of Western gentlemen" on August 4, 1862, that the recruitment of black troops would damage the Union cause, particularly in the border states. He argued that "the nation could not afford to lose Kentucky at this crisis" in the war and that "to arm the Negroes would turn 50,000 bayonets from the loyal Border States against us that were for us."[83]

The president gave a similar response on September 13 to a group of Chicago Christians who came to the White House to lobby for an emancipation proclamation. He contended that such a proclamation would be ineffective, comparing it to the medieval "Pope's bull against the comet!" They asked him to authorize the arming of blacks to fight for their freedom. In his reply, Lincoln again expressed the view that if he approved the recruitment of blacks, many of the "fifty thousand bayonets in the Union armies from the Border Slave States [would] go over to the rebels." He added, "I do not think they all would—not so many indeed as a year ago, or as six months ago—not so many to-day as yesterday. Every day increases their Union feeling. They are also getting their pride enlisted, and want to beat the rebels," even, Lincoln implied, if it meant the enrollment of blacks in the army. He took umbrage at the delegation's contention that the northern people needed "a glorious principle for which to suffer and to fight," namely, the abolition of slavery. Lincoln insisted, "We already have an important principle to rally and unite the people in the fact that constitutional government is at stake" in the war. "This is a fundamental idea, going down about as deep as any thing."[84] Lincoln's response should not suggest that his moral opposition to slavery had diminished, that he was a hypocrite, or that emancipation was not a desired goal in the war. He meant that the war to save republican government, rather than abolition, was the unifying inspiration for the North and the border states to make the necessary sacrifices to preserve the Union. Yet his antislavery feelings lacked the passion of the abolitionists and some radical Republicans like Charles Sumner and Wendell Phillips.

Despite all the conservative fears about the Second Confiscation Act, the law clearly fell far short of the intentions of its Republican sponsors. Because of its inherent weaknesses, Lincoln and Attorney General Edward Bates, a Missouri conservative, failed to insist on the law's enforcement. There was also continuing opposition to the bill in the border states and among Unionists like Andrew Johnson in the rebel states. Historian John Syrett has concluded that the Confiscation Act of 1862 "accomplished little. It was a poorly designed measure without an enforcement mechanism, and the administration had little interest in using it to effect change in the South. . . . Moreover, Congress paid almost no attention to whether or not the law was implemented."[85] Nonetheless, Lincoln did not ignore the authority that the law gave him when he drafted his historic preliminary Emancipation Proclamation.

During the second half of 1862 Lincoln still had his mind set on a voluntary plan of gradual, compensated emancipation for the border states. He continued, however, to be disappointed. Reflecting the strong opposition to the plan of their state's congressional delegation, Maryland legislators never really considered the proposal. The Kentucky General Assembly rejected it outright and announced that the plan's approval "would excite the people of the disaffected [rebel] States to still greater exertion to overthrown the Government."[86] In the Missouri state convention, an ordinance to accept the compensation offer was tabled by a vote of 52 to 19.[87] As it had done several months earlier, the Delaware legislature again defeated the proposal.[88] The refusal of Congress to commit specifically to the funding of the emancipation plan contributed to its overwhelming rejection by the border states, though the legislatures of these states probably would not have approved it anyway. Lincoln, however, refused to give up on his compensation plan; it would resurface as part of a broader antislavery strategy in his preliminary Emancipation Proclamation of September 22, 1862.

With his border state compensation proposal stymied, Lincoln turned his attention to slavery in the rebel states. The huge and demoralizing losses suffered by General McClellan in the ill-fated June 1862 Peninsula campaign to take Richmond brought intense pressure from Republicans for the president to take more vigorous measures against the rebels. Lincoln's view of southern resistance also hardened, which increased his determination to find legal authority to move against slavery in the insurrectionary states. He had already concluded that as commander in chief of the military forces, he had the primary constitutional responsibility for suppressing the rebellion. Lincoln also now had congressional authority to act against slavery in section 6 of the Second Confiscation Act. This provision required the president to warn rebels that their property, which included slaves, would be subject to seizure if they persisted in their hostility to the Union.

On July 13 the president, out of the blue, informed Secretary of State William H. Seward and Secretary of the Navy Gideon Welles that he intended to strike a blow against slavery in the rebel states. Lincoln told Seward and Welles that, having given "much thought" to the issue, he "had about come to the conclusion that it was a military necessity, absolutely essential for the salvation of the nation, that we must free the slaves or be ourselves subdued." Welles wrote in his diary, "It was a new departure for the President, for until this time, in all our previous interviews, whenever the question of emancipation or the mitigation of slavery had been in any way alluded to, he had been prompt and emphatic in denouncing any interference by the General Government with the subject." The navy secretary believed that cabinet members also favored military emancipation in the rebel South.[89]

One week later, on July 21, Lincoln startled cabinet members (except for Seward and Welles) by announcing at their regular meeting that he had determined, as Secretary of the Treasury Chase wrote in his diary, "to take some definite steps in respect to military action and slavery." A lengthy discussion took place on the issue and on the situation for blacks once they were free, including colonization and their enlistment in the army. Nothing was decided at the meeting, though Lincoln, as before, expressed his opposition to arming blacks. The next day, when the cabinet again met on the issue, Lincoln began by reading a draft of a proclamation designed to implement his decision in the matter. The two-paragraph draft of the document provided for the issuance of the warning, as required by the Second Confiscation Act, to the rebels to "return to their proper allegiance to the United States, on pain of the forfeitures and seizures" of their property. Although historians have focused on slave property in the president's proclamation, it also included other rebel possessions.

In the second paragraph of the draft proclamation, Lincoln reintroduced his gradual compensation proposal and added a promise of freedom to slaves in the insurrectionary states. He carefully wrote in lawyerly language, "It is my purpose, upon the next meeting of congress, to again recommend the adoption of a practical measure for tendering pecuniary aid to the free choice or rejection, of any and all States which may then be recognizing and practically sustaining the authority of the United States, and which may then have voluntarily adopted, or thereafter may voluntary adopt, gradual abolishment of slavery within such State or States." As a "necessary military measure" for achieving the restoration of the Union, Lincoln's draft proclamation stated that on January 1, 1863, "all persons held as slaves within any state or states, wherein the constitutional authority of the United States shall not then be practically recognized, submitted to, and maintained," would then be free. The president meant those eleven Confederate states or parts of the states still in rebellion after that date. Lincoln did not mean the loyal portions of the Union border states, where, he continued to believe, the federal government had no constitutional authority to intervene directly against slavery.[90] Nonetheless, he had resolved to his satisfaction the ambiguity in the Confiscation Act regarding what to do with the slaves seized by the federal armies from rebels in the border states: they should be free.

After the president completed the reading of the brief draft proclamation to his cabinet, a moment of silence settled over the group. Then Attorney General Bates broke the silence by expressing his approval of the proclamation; his support came as a surprise in view of his conservatism on slavery. Bates, however, believed that emancipation in the rebel states was inevitable. Reflecting border state racial attitudes, he wanted all blacks forcefully deported after emancipation. The attorney general also wanted the president and cabinet to control the process of emancipation, while maintaining due respect for the property rights of loyal slaveholders. Secretary of the Treasury Chase, though supporting the proclamation, expressed reservations about the legality of using the war powers as a justification for emancipation. He also asked the president to delete the compensation provision in the document. Postmaster General Montgomery Blair, who was late to the meeting, opposed the proclamation because of the disastrous political effect it would probably have on the fall elections in the North.[91] Secretary of State Seward indicated his approval but questioned the expediency of announcing the policy at that time because of the great demoralization in the North following the setbacks experienced by General McClellan's army in Virginia. "It would be considered our last *shriek* on the retreat," Lincoln later quoted Seward as saying. Seward advised the president to wait until after a military victory had been achieved before issuing the proclamation. The other three members of the cabinet, including Secretary of War Edwin Stanton, remained silent.[92]

Three days later, on July 25, the president presented to the cabinet another draft of his proclamation. This document, however, contained only the first paragraph of the earlier draft, the paragraph that warned rebels to return to their allegiance or face the seizure of their property. As Chase had suggested, Lincoln did not include the part of the first draft expressing his intention to recommend to Congress, when it met in December, the adoption of a plan of compensated and gradual emancipation for those rebel states willing to approve it. He also took Seward's advice to withhold the proclamation until the Union could claim a military success. Although the battle of Antietam on September 17 did not give Lincoln the victory that he wanted, he deemed it enough of a success to issue his so-called preliminary Emancipation Proclamation.[93]

The events between July 22 and September 22, when Lincoln announced his preliminary Emancipation Proclamation, are familiar, and their story is best told by historian Allen Guelzo,[94] who has pointed out that "the tone in the preliminary Emancipation Proclamation was noticeably different from that of the first draft. . . . It was entirely a military pronouncement, not a civil proclamation about an act of Congress attached gingerly to a war-power proclamation."[95] Yet the September 22 proclamation can also be seen as a civil decree. The president combined the military and civil purposes in the proclamation by quoting two sections of the Second Confiscation Act. In the first sentence of his proclamation, Lincoln announced, in his capacity as president and commander in chief of the army and navy, "Hereafter, as heretofore, the war will be prossecuted [sic] for the object of practically restoring the constitutional relation between the United States, and each of the states, and the people" where that "relation is, or may be suspended, or disturbed." Furthermore, Lincoln sought to move the people of the rebel states toward self-reconstruction by promising that if they held congressional elections and sent the victors to Washington before January 1, 1863, their states or districts would be exempted from the final Emancipation Proclamation.[96] As it turned out, two congressional districts in the New Orleans area and one on Virginia's Eastern Shore—all under federal military occupation—held elections to the House of Representatives before the deadline. The president, as promised, exempted them from the proclamation; however, Congress only seated the two representatives from Louisiana. Lincoln did not require emancipation in these districts until December 8, 1863, when he issued his Proclamation of Amnesty and Reconstruction.

Despite the opposition of Chase and other radicals in his party, Lincoln included in the preliminary Emancipation Proclamation the provision from his July 22, 1862, draft for the gradual, compensated, and state-controlled abolition of slavery. He also added another important provision. In addition to his recommendation that Congress provide "pecuniary aid" for states adopting "practical measure[s]" to end slavery, the president promised that he would renew his request for money "to colonize persons of African descent, with their consent, upon this continent, or elsewhere."[97] Thus he would have Congress extend to the rebel states the colonization provision included in the District of Columbia emancipation bill.

By including his compensation plan in the preliminary Emancipation Proclamation, Lincoln sought to make black freedom as palatable as possible to its opponents. He also wanted to satisfy, in part, his own constitutional concerns regarding federal interference with slavery and with the property of slaveholders in the states. Moreover, Lincoln probably thought that a federal commitment to black colonization, though impractical on a large scale, would gain finicky northern approval for emancipation. (Chapter 6 gives a fuller account of Lincoln's support for colonization.) If Congress agreed to fund colonization, according to this thinking, blacks would not move north and create a threat, however far-fetched that seemed, to white society.

By the fall of 1862, Lincoln had made emancipation, on whatever conditions or constitutional justification, a Union purpose in the war. He had played the emancipation card to save the Union, as he explained. But his hatred of slavery also influenced him to take such an important and politically risky step against an institution that he had long contended represented a moral blot on the nation and had caused the sectional conflict. He found a constitutional means—in this case, military necessity—to move, though tentatively, against slavery. But even with a sound constitutional justification, Lincoln knew that if he acted precipitously against slavery, without seeking a voluntary state-controlled system of compensation for slaveholders, his antislavery effort could backfire and jeopardize the Union cause. This could occur not only in the border states but also in the North, where Democrats and conservatives, including some in his own party at this time, opposed any change away from the original purpose of the war, to restore the Union, and away from the traditional rights of the states, even those pertaining to slavery. In issuing the preliminary Emancipation Proclamation, Lincoln combined military emancipation in the rebel states with his voluntary compensation proposal for those states that might be persuaded to end slavery in order to avoid harder blows. In 1862 he believed that a compensated and gradual process of black freedom was preferable and, he hoped, politically acceptable in the border states and with conservative supporters of the war in the North.

Regardless, on September 22, 1862, Lincoln crossed the Rubicon on emancipation when he issued the preliminary Emancipation Proclamation; there would be no backing down from this decision. Lincoln anxiously waited to see what the reaction to the proclamation would be in the border states and in the North. A major test for the Emancipation Proclamation, along with Lincoln's management of the war, would come in the fall congressional and state elections. One month later, when the old Congress reconvened, border state representatives and their northern Democratic allies made a final attempt to prevent the issuance of the proclamation on January 1.

■

The Struggle over Emancipation

Although Lincoln hoped otherwise, a chorus of denunciation erupted in the border states after he announced his preliminary Emancipation Proclamation. Earlier, in April 1862, when the District of Columbia emancipation bill passed Congress, Anna Ella Carroll, of a prominent Maryland family, visited the White House and warned Lincoln of dire consequences if he violated his promise not to interfere with slavery where it existed. Carroll, who had freed her own slaves, also wrote Lincoln, "Be not deceived, Mr. President, because the Union men of the South sustain you, in your efforts to suppress and maintain the integrity of the Constitution, that they will submit to the abolition of slavery, by the government." She predicted that if he agreed to the District bill, the war would be extended "for months, it may be, for years," and the rebels would secure "a reinforcement of at least fifty thousand fighting men" from the border states.[1] Even after Lincoln signed the bill, Carroll did not give up her crusade against emancipation; she denounced General David Hunter's May 9, 1862, proclamation freeing slaves in his military district. On July 14 Carroll wrote Lincoln and pleaded with him to veto the Second Confiscation bill in order to save the Republic from "social and servile wars, when anarchy and despotism, must take the place of Constitutional Liberty." She contended that "Abolitionism and the republic" could not coexist in the United States. Carroll also predicted that if the Confiscation bill became law, European nations would intervene on the side of the rebels. After Lincoln issued the preliminary Emancipation Proclamation, she unsuccessfully lobbied him for the colonization of freed slaves in British Honduras (today's Belize).[2]

Although Lincoln's proclamation did not dictate the end of slavery in their states, border state politicians and newspaper editors hotly claimed that the pronouncement would herald slavery's unraveling in their communities. They also charged that emancipation would lead to the imposition of black equality on the South. These Unionist spokesmen accurately predicted that northern "abolitionist" troops, particularly New Englanders, would seize upon the proclamation to begin freeing border state slaves who entered Union lines, regardless of their owners' loyalty.

Conflict had already erupted between loyal border slaveholders and army provost marshals and other federal officers over fugitive slaves. Maryland masters and their supporters, citing their property rights as loyal citizens, carried on a running battle with federal officials for the return of slaves who had fled to freedom in the District of Columbia and to army camps. As early as the summer of 1861, Congressman Charles B. Calvert, a large slaveholder, complained to Lincoln that the federal "camps in Maryland and Virginia [were] filled with slaves from Maryland." He told the president, "[It is] the duty of the Government to put a stop to such violations of our rights by arresting all fugitives and delivering them to their rightful owners." Although Calvert expressed his satisfaction with Lincoln's (verbal?) response to his complaint, he later wrote the president that the practice had continued and was "having a prejudicial effect on the Union cause" in Maryland.[3]

On May 19, 1862, about 100 slaveholders of nearby Prince George's County descended on the White House and demanded that General James S. Wadsworth, commanding in the District of Columbia, demonstrate more vigor in returning fugitive slaves. Lincoln promised the slaveholders that he "would take their representations into consideration, and see that no injustice was done."[4] On June 11 he arranged for Wadsworth to return the slaves of Maryland Unionists to their owners, but not those of the state's secessionists. The fugitive slaves of rebels presumably would be freed, since they had entered the recently free District of Columbia.[5]

After the passage of the Second Confiscation Act in July 1862 and the issuance of the preliminary Emancipation Proclamation in September, the promise to return the slaves of loyal Maryland owners was more often ignored than enforced by the army's provost marshals. Antislavery officers like Wadsworth, who were more numerous in the eastern armies than in the West, maintained a higher standard for loyalty than did most Maryland and other border state Unionists. The officers' requirements for loyalty included opposition to slavery and support for federal intervention in civil affairs to suppress "traitors" and ensure that only reliable Unionists could vote and hold office. Antislavery officers often ignored the complaints of local Unionists regarding fugitive slaves on the grounds that such slaves came from rebel owners and were therefore subject to confiscation and federal protection.

Disturbing reports soon reached Lincoln that armed bands of Marylanders were pursuing and recapturing fugitive slaves in the District of Columbia. Provost Marshal LaFayette C. Baker wrote Lincoln on September 30, 1863, "It is well known to you Sir, that large numbers of slaves, owned in Maryland [and] actuated by a supreme desire to participate in the blessings of freedom enjoyed by their fellows in this District, are daily, almost hourly making attempts to escape from their Masters and fly for refuge to this City." Baker informed the president, "Parties of slaves, men women & children, have been pursued within the bounds of this District, have been fiercely assailed and shot down or remorselessly beaten, and the survivors shut up in prisons or conveyed across the Potomac within the protecting arms of the rebel confederacy."[6] Lincoln's response to Baker's report, if any, has not been found. However, federal authorities, probably with Lincoln's approval, soon put a stop to the slave-catching raids from Maryland into the District.

Outrage over the preliminary Emancipation Proclamation proved greater in Kentucky than in any other border state.[7] Earlier, in December 1861, Kentuckians had expressed their proslavery fervor when Secretary of War Simon Cameron in his annual report to the president made the startling recommendation that slaves should be freed and armed. An unnamed but reputedly prominent Kentucky Unionist defiantly informed Whitelaw Reid, a Republican journalist, that Cameron's suggestion, if approved, "would destroy the Union party" in his state "and fuse the whole people into one homogeneous rebel mass." He also predicted that a "general emancipation of all slaves of rebels" would "end in the wildest anarchy" in all the southern states. This Unionist told Reid, "There is no reasoning about this matter" with Kentucky whites. "Reason hasn't anything to do with the nigger."[8]

Lincoln recognized the unsettling effect that Cameron's antislavery recommendation would have on the Union in the other border states as well as in Kentucky if it remained in the report. The president immediately ordered its deletion. For other reasons as well, mainly Cameron's incompetence, Lincoln soon removed the Pennsylvanian from office and sent him to Russia as the American minister. Radical Republicans and abolitionists, who had praised Cameron's effort to begin the process of freedom in the South, condemned Lincoln's action as another example of his wrongheaded border state policy. Wendell Phillips, the brilliant Massachusetts orator, reflected radical Republican anger over Lincoln's modification of Cameron's report when he exclaimed to a Boston audience, "If we had a man for President, or an American, instead of a Kentuckian, we should have had the satisfaction of attempting to save the Union instead of Kentucky."[9]

The president must have anticipated the hostile reaction that his preliminary Emancipation Proclamation would have in Kentucky. Soon after he issued the document in September 1862, even the Reverend Robert J. Breckinridge, a supporter of the president, pronounced the proclamation unwise and certain to undermine loyal sentiment in the state. Union speakers at a large protest rally in Frankfort in October angrily denounced Lincoln's action.[10] On October 3 George D. Prentice's *Louisville Daily Journal* announced, "There is not a paper or prominent politician in Kentucky that does not deeply regret and deprecate the President's proclamation, though all may believe that it will be wholly inoperative so far as its objects are concerned."

Despite the *Journal*'s prediction that the proclamation would be ineffective, Prentice and other white Kentuckians understood its real meaning: a major step had been taken toward emancipation, one that would eventually have an impact on the border states as well as on the Confederate states. Nonetheless, not wanting to antagonize the president or give greater comfort to the rebels, the *Journal* admitted that the proclamation "was well intended" by Lincoln. The newspaper blamed "Northern fanatics" for the rise of radical antislavery sentiment and denounced antislavery zealots for charging border state opponents of the proclamation with sympathy for the rebellion. The *Journal* editor indignantly—and disingenuously— told "abolitionist fanatics," "It is not a paramount regard for slavery that has prompted our comments upon the President's proclamation; it is a paramount regard for the Union, the Constitution, and the welfare and prosperity of the whole country"; such, he insisted, was the real basis for Kentuckian concern.[11] Emancipation, the editor claimed, would destroy, not save, the Republic of the Founders.

Lincoln had promised that he would issue the Emancipation Proclamation on January 1, 1863. By that time, Congress would have convened and voters would have had an opportunity to react to the proclamation at the polls. Lincoln's opponents expected the fall elections to create a backlash in the North against the proclamation. Although the newly elected congressmen would not take their seats until December 1863, border state members and other opponents of emancipation in the old Congress believed that if the voters repudiated Lincoln's party in the fall elections, they would be able to gain enough support to cause the president to forgo issuing the proclamation.

Before the fall 1862, elections and Congress's convening in December, border state Unionists faced an immediate and formidable military threat from rebel forces. The war had heated up in the border region during the summer of 1862. An unopposed raid in July by Confederate general John Hunt Morgan that almost reached Cincinnati caused "a stampede in Kentucky," as Lincoln put it.[12] One month later the stampede would be even greater. Confederate armies under Generals Edmund Kirby Smith and Braxton Bragg poured into Kentucky in an effort to free the state from Union control. Even Senator Garret Davis and other prominent Unionists took positions in the federal lines to protect Lexington.[13] General Smith in September brushed aside General Lew Wallace's forces and captured Lexington and Frankfort, sending Governor James F. Robinson, who had replaced Beriah Magoffin on August 18, fleeing to Louisville. General Bragg installed a Kentucky provisional government at Frankfort on October 4, but the Confederates immediately abandoned the state capital when a large Union force from Louisville approached the town. On October 8 a major battle occurred at Perryville in central Kentucky that went far toward deciding the fate of the state. Neither the Confederates under Bragg (Smith failed to join him in time) nor the federals under General Don Carlos Buell could claim a victory. However, after the battle, Bragg's and Smith's armies withdrew to Tennessee. Kentucky had been saved for the Union, though the Bluegrass State had not seen the last of General Morgan's raiders.

In Missouri, General Sterling Price's Confederate army had been driven south in late 1861 by General Samuel R. Curtis's Union forces. On March 7–8, 1862, Curtis's outnumbered army smashed a Confederate force under General Earl Van Dorn at the battle of Pea Ridge inside Arkansas. However, Missouri remained the target of rebel incursions. During the summer of 1862, Confederate raiders entered the state, gaining recruits and creating alarm among Unionists. A Confederate force defeated a small Union army at Newtonia in southern Missouri in October and stayed in the state until repulsed at Springfield in January 1863. As an offshoot of the military operations, guerrilla activity flared in the state. Claiming to be Confederates, guerrillas and bushwhackers terrorized Unionists as well as others, and they would continue their depredations throughout the war and even after it. Tension mounted between the federal military and Missouri civil authorities over the failure to stop the rebel raids and guerrilla violence. Areas of the state seemed headed toward anarchy.

Governor Hamilton Gamble blamed General Curtis, who had replaced General Henry W. Halleck as department commander, for the failure of federal forces to suppress the rebels and restore law and order. Gamble had frantically written Postmaster General Montgomery Blair in September 1862, "An army is approaching us from the South the size of which is represented to be very large." The governor, conveniently forgetting that Curtis had saved the state during the winter of 1861–1862, claimed that the general was incompetent and demanded that Blair "help us to get clear of Curtis."[14] The Iowa general's antislavery proclivities, expressed mainly in his protection of fugitive slaves, had exacerbated the conflict between the two men and their subordinates. Curtis wrote Lincoln reporting that though he refused to return the slaves of rebels, he was honoring the requests of truly loyal masters for their fugitive slaves.[15] Still, it was a petty difference over the authority to remove officers of state troops that finally got Lincoln involved in the conflict between the general and the governor.

In November 1862, Gamble, after Curtis refused to acknowledge his authority over the state officers, rushed to Washington to lay his complaints before the administration.[16] Although the War Department supported Curtis, the president sided with the governor in his control of Missouri's military forces, but he rejected Gamble's demand that Curtis be replaced in command. Lincoln also permitted Curtis to remove high-ranking state military officers. Soon after the meeting with the governor, Lincoln vented his frustration on having to decide such "a mischievous question." The president told Attorney General Edward Bates, "While it is proper that the question shall be settled, I do not perceive why either Gov. Gamble, or the government here, should care which way it is settled. I am perplexed with it only because there seems to be pertinacity about it. It seems to me that it might [go] either way without injury to the service."[17]

The political situation in Missouri would continue to trouble Lincoln, complicating the ability of Union authorities to suppress the rebel-inspired disorders in the state. The bitter divisions between the Gamble conservatives who controlled the state provisional government and the radicals who supported Curtis "tormented" Lincoln "beyond endurance," as he lamented to a group of Missouri Unionists on May 15, 1863.[18] The dissension also complicated support for emancipation in the state.

The Civil War clearly had reached a critical stage by the fall of 1862. With important elections scheduled for November, Lincoln's preliminary Emancipation Proclamation, though desirable in retrospect and supported by the majority of the president's party, had compounded the difficulties of suppressing the rebellion. The fate of the Union, national Republicans feared, hung in the balance. General Robert E. Lee's September invasion undertaken to "redeem" Maryland (and for other reasons) created the greatest alarm in the North, especially in the Northeast. Deeply concerned about the imminent threat that Lee's army posed to his state as well as to neighboring states, Governor Andrew Curtin of Pennsylvania, joined by two other northern governors, hurriedly issued a call on September 14 for Union governors to meet in Altoona, Pennsylvania, on the twenty-fourth. Contrary to what many contemporaries and some historians have claimed, Lincoln's preliminary Emancipation Proclamation on September 22 did not prompt the call for the meeting; Curtin's appeal was sent out one week before the president's announcement. At the time of the proclamation, Lincoln later remarked to Congressman George S. Boutwell of Massachusetts, "I never thought of the meeting of the governors at Altoona and I can hardly remember that I knew anything about it."[19] The president's emancipation initiative, however, became an important subject of discussion and dispute when the governors met two days after Lincoln issued the proclamation.

On September 24 twelve Union governors and a representative of Governor Oliver Morton of Indiana assembled in the Logan House parlor in

CHAPTER SIX

Altoona for the conference on the war. Several governors, for various reasons, did not attend the meeting. Only two slave state governors participated: Augustus W. Bradford of Maryland and Francis H. Pierpont of the rump Union government of Virginia. Suspecting that radical northern governors would push an antislavery agenda at the conference and facing an immediate military threat in their states, Governors Gamble of Missouri and James F. Robinson of Kentucky stayed at home, as did Democratic governor William Burton of Delaware. Attorney General Bates had earlier telegraphed Gamble warning him not to attend the meeting. "Go not," Bates told his brother-in-law. "Whatever the design, the end is revolutionary." In an explanatory letter to Gamble, the attorney general, as he was prone to do, charged that the conference owed its origins "to the leaders of the extreme wing of the Republican party," namely, the abolitionists.[20] The purpose of the Altoona conference was not to advance a radical agenda, as Bates claimed, but to shore up support for the war during this period of military crisis and faltering morale in the North. Nonetheless, a handful of New England governors, led by John A. Andrew of Massachusetts, wanted the conference to press Lincoln to abandon his conservative border state policy and issue a sweeping emancipation proclamation that would free all slaves.

The Union governors at Altoona moved quickly to squash the rumors that they plotted a radical coup; they did so by choosing the conservative Bradford to chair the meeting. Although the proceedings were supposedly secret, reports soon filtered out that two issues had created vigorous debate in the conference: emancipation and the failure of General George B. McClellan to destroy Lee's army after the battle of Antietam in Maryland one week earlier. Governor Andrew "harangued" the governors for an hour on the need for a strong statement on emancipation, for a reorganization of Lincoln's cabinet, and for the dismissal of McClellan, who, the governor charged, was incompetent and soft both on slavery and the rebels. Andrew announced, probably to the amusement of most of the governors who knew otherwise, that John C. Frémont would be an excellent replacement for McClellan. Governor Curtin and Ohio governor David Tod defended McClellan on the grounds that he had saved Maryland and Pennsylvania from Lee's powerful army and should not be removed at this critical juncture in the war. Bradford also informed the group that the general had "the perfect and unqualified confidence" of Unionists in his state. The Maryland governor, whose son was an officer in the Confederate army, took issue with the arguments advanced in favor of emancipation and specifically denounced Lincoln's proclamation of two days earlier.

By the end of the one-day conference, Governor Andrew had acquiesced in the majority's moderate position. He was given the task of drafting an address to President Lincoln that expressed the views of all the governors, except for Bradford, who predictably objected to an endorsement of the Emancipation Proclamation.[21] The address pledged the governors to "the most loyal and cordial support" of the president in the conduct of the war. It resolutely announced, "[Lincoln's] rightful authority and power, as well as the constitutional powers of Congress, must be rigorously and religiously guarded and preserved, as the condition on which alone our form of government and the constitutional rights and liberties of the people themselves can be saved from the wreck of anarchy or from the gulf of despotism." As governors, they promised to cooperate "always in our own spheres with the National Government" and to "continue in the most vigorous exercise of all our lawful and proper powers, contending against treason, rebellion, and the public enemies [until] the rebel foe shall yield a dutiful, rightful, and unconditional submission." The governors recommended that Lincoln issue a call for an additional force of no fewer than 100,000 men from the states to aid in the work of suppressing the rebellion.[22]

The Union governors devoted half of the address to expressing their "heartfelt gratitude" and justification for Lincoln's proclamation promising freedom on January 1 to "all persons held to service or labor as slaves in the rebel States." They also endorsed Lincoln's action in establishing "martial law or military governments" in occupied southern states to protect loyal citizens against "rebellious traitors." The governors predicted, "The decision of the President to strike at the root of the rebellion"—slavery—"will lend new vigor to the [Union] efforts and new life and hope to the hearts of the people," and, they went on, "[We] believe that the policy now inaugurated will be crowned with success [and] will give speedy and triumphant victories over our enemies."[23]

A committee consisting of Governors Tod, Andrew, and Pierpont delivered the Altoona address to the president in Washington. Lincoln enthusiastically approved the address because the governors endorsed his emancipation initiative (except for Bradford), pledged continuing support for his war policies, and recommended a call for more troops. He was also pleased that they had ignored the radical demand for a reorganization of the cabinet and of the military command.[24] Lincoln expressed his thanks to the governors "for all they had done and for all they had promised to do to help the General Government in this great crisis." Finally, the president praised the governors for giving their "hearty approbation" to his preliminary Emancipation Proclamation.[25]

In an attempt to gain Bradford's support for the address, Lincoln briefly delayed its printing and circulation and had Secretary of State William H. Seward give the governor's wife a pass to visit her rebel son behind the lines.[26] The ploy did not work, and Lincoln, without the Maryland governor's endorsement, had the address printed and sent out for the signatures of all of the Union governors, including those who did not attend the Altoona conference. All of them signed except for the four border state executives and the Democratic governor of New Jersey. Even military governor Andrew Johnson of Tennessee either signed or had his name affixed to the document, despite the fact that at this time he disapproved of Lincoln's antislavery policy. Union newspapers published the address, and northern editors, except for Democratic zealots, expressed their approval of it. Many border state conservatives, though reluctant to endorse the document because of its sanction of the Emancipation Proclamation, expressed relief that a radical statement had not been adopted at Altoona.[27] The governors' approval of a radical document, similar to what Andrew wanted, would have further alienated the border states at a critical time in the war and hurt the Republicans, especially in the lower North.

In addition to the northern governors, Republican leaders praised Lincoln's promise to end slavery in the insurrectionary states (except in districts that elected congressmen before January 1 and in the whole state of Tennessee). Vice President Hannibal Hamlin prophetically wrote Lincoln on September 25, 1862, that the Emancipation Proclamation, when issued on January 1, would "stand as the great act of the age." Frederick Douglass, who had been critical of Lincoln's border state policy and his inaction on slavery, now applauded the president for his decision to free the slaves in the rebellious South. It was a step in the right direction, he concluded. Douglass wrote in his newspaper, "Abraham Lincoln may be slow," but once he had issued his freedom proclamation, he would not retract it. Hamlin predicted, "It will be enthusiastically approved and sustained and future generations will, as I do, say God bless you for the great and noble act."[28]

Despite the support of Hamlin, Douglass, and other Republicans, Lincoln knew of the pitfalls that the Emancipation Proclamation faced. He wrote the vice president, "While I hope something from the proclamation, my expectations are not as sanguine as are those of some friends." While acknowledging the "commendation" of friendly northern newspapers and "distinguished individuals" for the proclamation, Lincoln remarked, "The time for its effect southward [had] not come. . . . Looked soberly in the face," the reaction to the proclamation "is not very satisfactory. . . . The North responds to the proclamation sufficiently in breath; but breath alone kills no rebels." Methodist clergyman and editor John McClintock later reported that Lincoln, probably in 1864, expressed a similar doubt to him when he issued the proclamation and said that he "feared its effects upon the border states." Nevertheless, he recalled Lincoln saying, "Yet I think it was right. I knew it would help our cause in Europe, and I trusted in God and did it."[29]

The fall 1862 state elections proved an important test for Lincoln's anti-slavery proclamation and for the war itself. As always, local issues and old political rivalries also played a role in the contests. Lincoln's party carried the upper North, where support for emancipation and for a vigorous conduct of the war was strong. Republicans, however, suffered defeats in the lower northern states where elections were held (elections were not held in even-numbered years in Ohio and Pennsylvania); in New York the Democratic candidate, Horatio Seymour, won the gubernatorial race. The Republican setbacks, including their loss of the Illinois and Indiana legislatures, occurred in part because of the president's proclamation. Northern demoralization as a result of the seemingly unending carnage on the battlefield also contributed to the Democratic opposition's success at the polls. In addition, Lincoln's suspension of the writ of habeas corpus on September 24 in cases involving resistance to military enlistments aided the Democrats, though the governors at Altoona had endorsed his action.

Despite the losses in several northern states, Republicans retained a majority in Congress. The Democrats, however, received a net gain of thirty-four members, which suggested to them that their opposition to Lincoln's war policies, including emancipation, had swung the elections in their direction. In Illinois and Indiana, where no gubernatorial elections occurred, the new Democratic majorities in the legislatures soon moved to undermine the Republican war effort.[30]

Although Lincoln had been warned by Republican leaders of the dire political consequences of his preliminary Emancipation Proclamation, he refused to admit that it had contributed to his party's losses in the fall elections.[31] He blamed the defeats on the minority status of the Republican Party, the determination of the Democratic opposition to win, the vilification of the administration in its own party newspapers—he mainly meant the radical press—and "certainly, the ill-success of the war."[32]

Fortunately for Lincoln and the Republicans, Kentucky and Maryland, where opposition to emancipation and to military violations of civil liberties was strongest, did not hold state and congressional elections in the fall. Otherwise Lincoln's party setbacks would have been greater and would have further emboldened opposition to the administration in the North. These two states had held elections for Congress in the summer of 1861 before emancipation became an issue that inflamed voters. The 1862 election results, however, brought good news for Lincoln in Missouri. There, staunch Unionists—some of whom favored emancipation—won seven of the nine seats in Congress. Furthermore, the state convention had met in June 1862 and provided for the continuance of the provisional government until 1864; Gamble remained as governor.[33] The new congressmen, however, would not take their seats in Washington until December 1863. When Congress met in late 1862 and early 1863, most of the lame-duck Missouri representatives were present and continued to oppose Lincoln's antislavery policy. On the other hand, the state's Union voters elected to the legislature a majority that favored the president's plan of gradual emancipation with federal compensation for the slaveholders, a proposal that had been tabled by the state convention during the summer.

From Washington, U.S. Senator John B. Henderson of Missouri joined the emancipationists in urging the new state legislature to adopt the president's gradual, compensated emancipation proposal so as to salvage something from the impending wreck of slavery. Henderson, an erstwhile conservative, warned, "We cannot secure [our] interest in slave property by closing our mouths and ears in Missouri whilst events here are daily demonstrating to all who take time or pains to think at all that if this war continues (and I think it will continue long enough to accomplish this end) slavery will be forever destroyed in the United States."[34] Gamble, who had earlier opposed any movement toward abolition, now also endorsed Lincoln's compensation plan; he did so not because of any moral opposition to slavery but because, like Henderson, he believed that the war had made emancipation inevitable and that the state should seize the opportunity for federal compensation before it was too late. Many white Missourians, including Gamble, agreed with Frank Blair that black colonization was a solution to the perceived race problem after slavery.[35]

Debate over emancipation in Missouri widened the political division among state Union leaders. By late 1862 a militant minority of radicals had emerged in Missouri; they were sometimes called "Charcoals," which was a spin-off of the earlier epithet "Black Republicans." The Charcoals, or radicals, wanted the state to abolish slavery outright and not pursue the chimera of federal compensation and black colonization. At first they were led by B. Gratz Brown, former editor of the *Saint Louis Missouri Democrat* and cousin of Frank Blair. However, the two cousins, having helped save the state for the Union in 1861, soon parted ways. The Charcoals referred to conservative emancipationists like Gamble as "Claybanks" because of their apparently ambiguous or colorless position on slavery and their unwillingness to pursue draconian policies against rebel supporters. The German American community in Saint Louis was the center of radical strength in the state.

When the new Missouri General Assembly met in December 1862, Governor Gamble recommended that it adopt the president's plan of gradual emancipation and seek congressional funding for it. In his annual message to Congress on December 1, Lincoln had revived his compensation plan in the form of a proposed constitutional amendment.[36] But dissension over the issue immediately erupted in Missouri, with the radicals on the left opposing gradual emancipation and the proslavery members on the right rejecting any move against slavery. In the end, a majority could not be mustered for Gamble's—and Lincoln's—proposal, and the General Assembly adjourned.

The battle over state emancipation would resume in the spring of 1863 when Gamble called for the state convention to reconvene on June 15 to achieve "some scheme of Emancipation." Despite his wishes, Lincoln found himself drawn ever more tightly into the internecine conflict between the conservatives and the radicals. The factional struggle in Missouri became enmeshed not only in emancipation but also in divisions over loyalty, civil liberties, and the relationship of the military to civil authorities. How the struggle played out would have important consequences for emancipation and security in the state.

CHAPTER SIX

After Lincoln issued his preliminary Emancipation Proclamation in September 1862, Maryland's Union leaders, like those in Missouri, gradually and grudgingly began to consider a way to end slavery with the least possible disruption to the social and economic system and, perhaps more important, to their notions of race control and public support for the war. They also knew that Lincoln in nearby Washington had a keen interest in the state's affairs. Although the proclamation did not apply to the border states, the president wanted Marylanders to adopt a plan of emancipation, preferably gradual emancipation, that would include federal compensation if Congress was willing. Many Maryland Unionists, like those in Missouri, recognized that the war was rapidly undermining slavery, with blacks fleeing to freedom in the District of Columbia, to army camps, and northward. It had become a constant battle for slaveholders to retrieve their slaves in the national capital, where their complaints had been increasingly ignored by an unsympathetic president and federal military officers.

By 1863 Governor Bradford, who had opposed the antislavery resolution at the Altoona governors' conference in September 1862, saw the handwriting on the wall for the extinction of slavery. However, not until months after Lincoln had issued the final Emancipation Proclamation on January 1 did Bradford endorse state action to end the "peculiar institution." Postmaster General Blair quietly recommended to friends in his home state that they should support a gradual plan of emancipation, along with the colonization of blacks. Henry Winter Davis, an enemy of the Blairs in Maryland politics, had emerged as the leader of a minority that demanded immediate emancipation. Davis, who would soon become a vitriolic spokesman for the radical Republicans in Congress, had become incensed by the president's support for the Blairs. He also denounced Montgomery Blair's colonization scheme as a delusion.[37] At the same time, the proslavery faction of Unionists, soon a dwindling minority, had powerful spokesmen in lame-duck senator Anthony Kennedy and Representative John W. Crisfield, a large slaveholder and a talented states' rights politician. After rejecting Lincoln's compensation plan earlier and before they committed the state to emancipation, Maryland Unionists wanted assurances from Congress that the federal government would provide the funds to compensate loyal slaveholders for the loss of their chattels. They would soon be disappointed.

Delaware's political leadership proved more hostile to the Emancipation Proclamation than neighboring Maryland Unionists. Proud of the fact that theirs was the first state to ratify the Constitution of 1787, as well as imbued with an inferiority complex because of the state's increasing political insignificance, Delaware's elite recoiled at any slight to their rights, including the right to own slaves. They had developed considerable political skill in defending their rights, and while maintaining allegiance to the Republic of the Founders, they perceived themselves as southerners, not northerners. Elected in the fall of 1862 on a platform opposing Lincoln's policies, the new legislature in January denounced the president's proclamation and his suspension of the writ of habeas corpus on September 24, 1862. The legislators connected the two presidential actions "as a flagrant attempt to exercise absolute power under the plea of military necessity [and] an artful device by persons in authority for the subversion of our form of Government, and the establishment of another in its stead."[38] The newly elected governor, William Cannon, however, soon found himself in hot water with the General Assembly when he expressed support for emancipation.

From their seats in the U.S. Senate, Willard Saulsbury and James A. Bayard, the scion of an influential Delaware family, launched an attack on the Emancipation Proclamation. They charged that under the proclamation their state would be flooded with the freed slaves of rebels, creating racial conflict and severe social problems. Saulsbury on the floor of the Senate defiantly declared that, though opposed to secession, he was "a southern man," a slaveholder, and he asserted, "Slavery as it exists in this country is right, justified by the laws of God and man, and I would not abolish it upon one foot of soil where it now exists." He would keep Delaware "a slaveholding State now and forever."[39]

Saulsbury rose to demagogic heights in his criticism of the president's actions and, in the process, rained down personal abuse on Lincoln's head. The senator characterized Lincoln as a tyrant who had acted in perfect disregard of the Constitution and the rights of the people. The president, Saulsbury claimed, was surrounded by those who flattered him and easily persuaded him of the disloyalty of his critics. He proclaimed Lincoln "a weak and imbecile man; the weakest man that I ever knew in a high place; for I have seen him and conversed with him, and I say here, in my place in the Senate of the United States, that I never did see or converse with so weak and imbecile a man as Abraham Lincoln, President of the United States." Understandably outraged by such language on the floor of the Senate, the Republicans passed a resolution declaring that Saulsbury's attack on the president was "a clear violation" of the rules of order. The Delaware senator angrily repeated his charge against Lincoln and announced that he would not "be deterred from the expression of my opinion by any blackguardism that can be uttered on this floor" in defense of the president, whereupon Vice President Hamlin, who was presiding, directed the sergeant at arms to usher him from the chamber. Later, a chastened—and sober—Saulsbury was permitted to return after he apologized for bringing a pistol to the Senate floor.[40]

Not all Delawareans opposed the Emancipation Proclamation, nor did they agree that the president was a tyrant. In addition to Governor Cannon, who had little authority, some Unionists in the northern part of the state praised Lincoln for acting against slavery in the South. Abolitionist Anna M. Ferris of Wilmington wrote in her diary on January 1, 1863, "Today the final Proclamation of Emancipation was issued by the President! Will it be merely a decree of the Government, that may fall to the ground, or is it a decree of the Almighty that will live through the future? It is impossible to say, we can only pray that events may confirm it."[41]

Lincoln could ignore the popgun attacks by the Delaware legislature and its U.S. senators, though they contributed to the propaganda barrage against emancipation and doubtless gave encouragement to the rebellion. But he had to take notice of the opposition to his proclamation in other border states. In Kentucky, conservatives like John J. Crittenden and George D. Prentice and Lincoln friends like Robert J. Breckinridge and Joshua Speed continued to warn the president against issuing the final Emancipation Proclamation lest it derail the pacification of the state.[42] Hamilton Gray, claiming to represent "the real unconditional Union Men of Kentucky," wrote Lincoln that though he did not personally object to the "obliteration" of slavery as a consequence of military operations, Kentuckians saw it differently: "The people of Kentucky do not look upon your Proclamation as a 'Military Necessity,' but as a speculative measure against the rebels not warranted by the Constitution and laws, and if practically carried out will be more calamitous to both races . . . than the rebellion." Like other border state spokesmen, Gray predicted that if the slaves were freed in the rebel states, "they [would] at once, make their way to the loyal or border States, and there become a pest to Society, an expense upon the public or be driven beyond the bounds by the bayonet, or exterminated."[43]

Another serious concern for Lincoln was the impact that the Emancipation Proclamation might have on border state troops and their commanders, particularly in Kentucky. After the issuance of the preliminary Emancipation Proclamation in September, many Kentucky troops, along with a smaller number from the other border states, left their regiments and either went home or joined the rebels. Some, perhaps even most, later rejoined their units. One Kentucky regimental commander announced in the newspapers that he would return all fugitive slaves in his camp to their masters, whether Unionist or rebel.[44] Brigadier General Jeremiah T. Boyle, commanding in western Kentucky, ordered federal troops in his district not to interfere with slavery in any way. Boyle was a Kentucky slaveholder himself, but, ironically, he was also one of the fiercest Unionists in the state and went out of his way to impose severe punishment upon rebels, though not to the extent of divesting them of their slaves. Blacks from the Confederate South who had followed General Buell's army to the counties near Louisville in 1862 were routinely rounded up by the sheriffs and sold into slavery. Buell proved more committed to protecting slave property than any commander in the West. Not until 1863—and after Buell's removal from command for military reasons—did the army in this military department officially end the policy of returning fugitive slaves.[45]

Slaves in Kentucky, Missouri, and Maryland, having learned of Lincoln's preliminary Emancipation Proclamation and assuming that it applied to them, sought freedom in Union camps. However, they were not always welcomed; indeed, slaves of loyal masters were usually returned to slavery, except in Maryland. In the army camps, border state fugitives from slavery joined blacks fleeing from the rebel states. In Kentucky, northern officers who attempted to protect black "contrabands" found themselves afoul of civil authorities who insisted on enforcing all state laws regarding slavery. In late 1862, a Lexington jury indicted Colonel William L. Utley of a Wisconsin regiment for refusing to return slaves to their owners. Utley appealed directly to Lincoln to intervene in his case; at the same time, Kentucky Supreme Court Justice George Robertson sought the president's intervention on the side of the aggrieved slaveholders.[46] Other instances of conflict between federal officers and local authorities in Kentucky over fugitive slaves rarely reached the president's desk. Robertson in his appeal admitted to Lincoln that he owned one of the five slaves sheltered by Utley. The president's initial reaction to the appeal was to scribble a note to the justice, whom he knew personally, expressing in strong language his opposition to the return of fugitive slaves, even those of Union owners. Ignoring his policy of respecting the property of border state loyalists, Lincoln admonished Robertson, "Do you not know that I may as well surrender this contest, directly, as to make any order, the obvious purpose of which would be to return fugitive slaves?"[47]

Upon reflection, Lincoln did not send the inflammatory note to Robertson. But a few days later, in a more moderate tone, he wrote the justice and, remarkably—and singularly—offered him out of his own pocket "any sum not exceeding five hundred dollars" for the freedom of his slave in Utley's camp.[48] Robertson indignantly rejected the offer and informed Lincoln that his purpose in the case was a matter of principle: "It was solely to try the question whether the civil or the military power is Constitutionally supreme in Kentucky." He expressed regret that Lincoln did not answer his question regarding the legitimacy of the military's protection of fugitive slaves. "Your silence," Robertson impertinently wrote the president, "may be so interpreted as to work harmfully" on the Union cause in the state. "Unless the robbery of union men by miscalled and misplaced union soldiers be soon stopped, I fear the deplorable consequences in Kentucky," he told Lincoln. "I feel sure that the union can never be restored or made harmonious and permanent by a war" against slavery.[49]

After Lincoln refused to intervene in the case, Robertson pressed a civil suit against Utley for payment for his slave. Incredibly, the case survived the Civil War and emancipation. Finally, in 1871 a federal court in Wisconsin ruled that the former Union colonel must pay Robertson more than $900 for his loss. However, Congress in 1873 relieved Utley of the obligation by directing the secretary of the treasury to pay the amount.[50]

Concerned about the opposition in his native state to the Emancipation Proclamation, Lincoln on November 21, 1862, met with a group of "unconditional Union Kentuckians" to encourage support for his antislavery decision. According to a report in the *New York Tribune*, the president informed them that "he would rather die than take back a word of the Proclamation of Freedom, and he dwelt upon the advantages to the Border States of his scheme for the gradual abolishment of Slavery." The Kentuckians warned Lincoln against hasty or radical action by the government on emancipation. The president urged them to return home and bring the emancipation issue "fairly before the people" of the state for their approval of his compensation plan. As a means to this end, the Unconditional Unionists pledged "to start two Emancipation journals in Kentucky to counteract the influence of the Louisville papers, and when the proper time comes," they promised to have several prominent Kentuckians canvass the state on behalf of black freedom. Lincoln ignored the hint that a federal printing contract should be given to the proposed antislavery newspapers in order to sustain them.[51]

Prentice's *Louisville Daily Journal* reacted in cold fury when the report of the meeting appeared in the *Tribune*. Any "handful of Kentucky men" attempting to establish an "abolitionist paper" in the state would "not be welcomed" by the people, the editor indignantly declared. "No person of common sense, who has been recently in this State," he wrote, "believes or can for one moment believe that our people are becoming reconciled to the emancipation proclamation. Everybody knows that they are *not*; everybody knows that the policy in question is odious to the last degree." The *Journal* editor asserted that radicals in the president's party had pushed him, probably against his will, to issue the Emancipation Proclamation. Still, the editor admitted that Lincoln was "an honest and good man" who understood that he must be supported by Kentuckians in order to "crown himself with success and glory" in the war.[52]

When Congress met in December 1862, Republicans in the House of Representatives introduced a resolution on the fifteenth proclaiming Lincoln's impending antislavery proclamation "a war measure . . . warranted by the Constitution." The resolution passed by a vote of 81 to 53, with most border state members, joined by northern Democrats, opposing it. George P. Fisher of Delaware and John W. Noell of Missouri were the only border state representatives voting for the resolution.[53]

The Senate did not debate the proclamation, probably because conservative Republicans Orville H. Browning, James R. Doolittle of Wisconsin, James Dixon of Connecticut, and Edgar Cowan of Pennsylvania, in addition to border state and northern Democratic senators, would oppose it. The Republican majority probably did not want to risk an embarrassing defeat for the antislavery cause by raising the question. Furthermore, the president seemed determined with or without a congressional endorsement to fulfill his promise to issue the final Emancipation Proclamation on January 1. Browning, who was born, raised, and educated in Kentucky, reflected the position of the conservative Republicans when he met with Lincoln and bluntly told him that his emancipation and habeas corpus proclamations in September "had been disasterous [*sic*]" to them in the fall elections and would continue to hurt the party. He explained, "Prior to issuing them all loyal people were united in support of the war and the administration. . . . But the proclamations had revived old party issues—given [Democrats] a rallying cry—capitol [*sic*] to operate upon" against the Republicans. Browning recorded in his diary that the president "made no reply" to him.[54]

The repulse of the Union army in the bloody battle at Fredericksburg, Virginia, in mid-December provided additional strength to the conservative argument against the issuance of the Emancipation Proclamation on January 1. Browning and his conservative friends pleaded with Lincoln not to issue the proclamation at this critical stage of the war, or at least to wait until the military situation had improved.[55] Some antislavery stalwarts feared that the president would falter and not sign the proclamation. Lincoln, however, followed his own maxim that a promise, once made, must be kept. His promise to issue the Emancipation Proclamation was one of those occasions—and Lincoln remained determined to keep it, despite his concern that it could damage support for the war.[56]

One day after the House passed the resolution supporting the impending proclamation, border state representatives caucused on the issue and selected a committee to meet with the president. The committee consisted of John J. Crittenden of Kentucky, John W. Crisfield of Maryland, and William A. Hall of Missouri. Their purpose in requesting the conference, as they told Lincoln, was to represent "the true situation" in the border states and to "suggest remedies for the removal of the evils under which they [were] laboring, and the public mischief to which they [might] give rise."[57] The border representatives mainly meant the "mischief" that the Emancipation Proclamation would cause. Border state Unionists, especially in Kentucky, were also becoming increasingly concerned about the military's violations of state laws and judicial authority, and these issues were apparently raised in the conference.[58]

No record has been found of what transpired in the December 18 meeting of the president and the border state representatives. Lincoln, however, must have failed to provide the committee with the "remedies" that they sought. One day after the meeting, Crisfield, who prided himself on his knowledge of constitutional issues, took to the floor of the House of Representatives and delivered a harsh attack on the president and the Republicans. Insisting that he was a true Unionist, Crisfield assailed Lincoln's antislavery policy as unconstitutional; in addition, he condemned the Republican spirit of intolerance, comparing it with that in the repressive rebel states. "One of the worst symptoms of the present times is the intolerance of adverse opinion," he told his colleagues. "Inflamed by the excitements of the times, men cannot conceive, or will not admit, the possibility of anything wise or patriotic which does not happen to run in the channel of their own thoughts. Difference is held to be little less than treason," he exclaimed. Nonetheless, the Maryland congressman charged, the president's position that emancipation was necessary to suppress the rebellion and preserve the Union, if sustained, would lead to despotism: "Once admitted as a power belonging to this Government, [necessity] swallows up all other powers, and resolves everything into the mere discretion of the individual who may happen to wield its mighty energies. This is the definition of despotism."[59]

Lincoln ignored Crisfield's criticism and the warnings of Browning and others not to issue the Emancipation Proclamation. On January 1, 1863, he signed this historic charter of freedom. As he had promised in the preliminary Emancipation Proclamation in September, the final document freed slaves in the insurrectionary states. However, as he had also promised, the proclamation exempted occupied districts where elections had been held for Congress (two districts in New Orleans and one in Virginia). It also exempted all of Tennessee, even though it was largely occupied by Confederates, because of opposition to the proclamation by Unionists in the eastern part of the state.

An enduring and unfortunate myth is that the Emancipation Proclamation had no immediate effect because it applied only to states controlled by the Confederacy. Actually, in addition to those slaves who had fled to Union camps earlier and became "contraband" of war (General Benjamin F. Butler's famous term), there were many blacks who achieved freedom soon in federally controlled areas of the Confederate States that had not been exempted from the final document. These included parts of eastern North Carolina, the Mississippi Valley, the Shenandoah Valley of Virginia, and the Sea Islands of Georgia and South Carolina. Sad to say, the newly freed slaves were usually forced to work for the army and on plantations leased to northerners while suffering in dreary settlements.[60] For many black males, Lincoln's proclamation also opened the door, though it was a

CHAPTER SIX

controversial one, for their recruitment in the army and validated their long-standing, informal service in the navy.

Although the Emancipation Proclamation did not prove to be the revolutionary or radical decree that conservatives feared, many in the border states remained defiant. On the eve of his issuance of the proclamation, Lincoln received a disturbing message from Major General Horatio G. Wright, commander of the Department of Ohio. The message reportedly conveyed reliable intelligence of a strong movement in the Kentucky General Assembly to secede from the Union if the president signed the proclamation. Wright wrote that Governor Robinson intended to issue an address favoring secession to the legislature. The general planned to bring several northern regiments into the vicinity of Frankfort and "to arrest all members of the Legislature voting for" or speaking for an "ordinance of secession, and also all State officers favoring it." He asked his superiors in Washington to approve his proposed action.[61]

On January 7, 1863, Lincoln, through General in Chief Halleck, replied to Wright's message. The president agreed that Wright could move northern troops into the Frankfort area but said he should arrest only those legislators who voted for secession and state officials who supported them. He warned the general that, whatever action became necessary, he should use his authority "with great discretion."[62] Wright followed the advice; he found no compelling cause to arrest any legislator.

On the same day that Halleck sent the president's instructions to Wright, Lincoln turned down the request of Kentuckian Green Adams for federal arms to equip a "special force" in the state to suppress guerrillas and repulse rebel raiders like General Morgan. The president bluntly explained his reason in a letter to Adams: "The changed conduct towards me of some of [the state's] members of congress, and the ominous out-givings as to what the Governor and Legislature of Kentucky intend doing, admonish me to consider whether any additional arms I may send there, are not to be turned against the government." Two days earlier, Garret Davis, in a speech on the U.S. Senate floor in support of the special military force for the state, claimed that whenever Morgan and other raiders entered Kentucky the number of secessionists increased dramatically. Davis estimated that at this time "fully one third of the population" of the state were "disloyal."[63] Lincoln was understandably concerned about placing weapons in the hands of potential rebels; however, he told Adams, "This may clear up on the right side," which would permit the arming of the special force. Despite the fact that some Kentucky troops had left the army after he issued the preliminary Emancipation Proclamation, the president now felt encouraged: "So far as I can see, Kentucky's sons in the field, are acting loyally and bravely, God bless them! I can not help thinking the mass of her people feel the same way."[64]

Governor Robinson, a conservative Unionist, soon gave Lincoln reason to believe that Kentucky would not attempt secession because of the Emancipation Proclamation. In his message to the Kentucky General Assembly on January 8, 1863, the governor reaffirmed his state's commitment to the Union, though he took the occasion to launch a blistering attack on the Emancipation Proclamation. Like other border state leaders, he made the obligatory charge that the proclamation was unconstitutional and certain to create social disorder. Robinson contended that Lincoln's antislavery policy was a slap in the face to Kentuckians, who had sacrificed greatly for the Union cause and who expected to be protected in all of their rights. He declared, "The saddest and most deplorable effect of [Lincoln's] proclamation will be to fire the whole South into one burning mass of inextinguishable hate and study for revenge, and to utterly destroy all hope for restoring the Union."[65]

Like Crisfield of Maryland and other border state spokesmen, Robinson criticized Lincoln for using "military necessity" as justification for issuing the proclamation. "If military necessity is not to be measured by constitutional limits," as Lincoln seemed to claim, "we are no longer a free people," Robinson argued. The governor reminded the legislature that a change in the slavery system would require a state constitutional convention, a change, however, that he did not recommend. Citing the frequency of military arrests and intervention in the state, Robinson complained of the unequal treatment that Kentucky had received at the hands of federal authorities—a frequent complaint of border state officials. He also objected to what he considered the unjust criticism of Kentucky by neighboring western state leaders. The governor wanted the legislature to issue a strong protest against the federal government's violations of constitutional rights, namely, the gross injustice of the Emancipation Proclamation and the military arrests and incarceration of peaceful citizens. Despite his polemic against Lincoln's antislavery policy and the actions of military authorities in the state, the governor did not threaten secession if Kentucky's grievances were ignored.[66] The presence of Wright's troops in Frankfort and the prospect of military intervention could have caused him to reaffirm clearly Kentucky's loyalty to the Union.

The *Louisville Daily Journal* applauded Robinson's message and called on the General Assembly to approve his recommendations. This influential newspaper was also careful to proclaim the state's loyalty to the Union. On January 19, James Speed wrote his brother Joshua, who was visiting his friend Lincoln in Washington, "The rabid members [of the legislature] are coming to their senses. Time is working wonders. . . . So far, I am in no fear for Ky." James Speed believed that the sitting legislature would "remain true & loyal." But, he cautioned, "what may come from the August [state] elections, God only knows."[67] Joshua Speed delivered his brother's report to Lincoln.

The General Assembly agreed with Robinson, and on March 2, after a long, vigorous debate, it adopted a series of resolutions protesting the state's many grievances against the federal government. The legislature emphatically pronounced the Emancipation Proclamation "unwise, unconstitutional, and void." As James Speed had predicted, it did not threaten armed resistance or secession if Lincoln persisted in enforcing the proclamation. The legislature, however, announced, "[It] recognizes a manifest difference between the administration of the government and the government itself—the one is transitory, limited in duration only to that period of time for which the officers [were] elected by the people; . . . the other is permanent, intended by its founders to endure forever." The Kentucky General Assembly meant that it would support the Lincoln government in its prosecution of the war, while hoping that the Republicans would soon be defeated at the polls and the Emancipation Proclamation revoked. Meanwhile, the legislature promised to exercise "its right to differ in opinion with the National Executive" and to continue its "solemn protest against" his antislavery policy and other allegedly illegal actions.[68]

Lincoln's promise of compensation in the preliminary Emancipation Proclamation of September 22, 1862, to states that chose to end slavery had been partly designed to reduce opposition in the border states to his antislavery initiative. In his annual message to Congress on December 1, 1862, Lincoln repeated the offer and elaborated on it. The proposal, in the form of a constitutional amendment containing three articles, would provide federal bonds to states that agreed to abolish slavery completely by 1900. The president maintained, "Without slavery the rebellion could never have existed; without slavery it could not continue." Lincoln advanced in one of the articles the old voluntary colonization proposal for the freed slaves. He apparently thought that even a small emigration of blacks to the Caribbean basin, which was the preferred area for colonization, would relieve some of the racial fears in the border and northern states engendered by emancipation.[69] Based on his long-time support for colonization—and his relatively conservative racial views—Lincoln probably sincerely believed that both races would benefit from the resettlement of blacks in a tropical land, though he did not consult blacks as to whether they wanted to emigrate. Lincoln, however, had acknowledged in his famous speech at Peoria on October 16, 1854, the existence of logistical barriers to shipping large numbers of blacks to foreign countries and settling them there.[70]

The president told Congress that the articles in the proposed amendment were "intended to embody a plan of . . . mutual concessions." He predicted, "If the plan shall be adopted, it is assumed that emancipation will follow, at least, in several of the States." Lincoln admitted, "Emancipation will be unsatisfactory to the advocates of perpetual slavery; but the length of time" for its completion, 1900, "should greatly mitigate their dissatisfaction." He insisted, "The time spares both races from the evils of sudden derangement—in fact, from the necessity of any derangement—while most of those whose habitual course of thought will be disturbed by the measure will have passed away before its consummation. They will never see it." The "derangement" that Lincoln seemed most concerned about related to whites. Like many of his contemporaries, he assumed that blacks would suffer from a quick transition to freedom. In proposing a constitutional article providing for voluntary resettlement, he concluded that freed blacks would benefit by separation from the old southern slave society, since they then would no longer face white racial discrimination and hostility. Lincoln announced, "I cannot make it better known than it already is, that I strongly favor colonization. And yet I wish to say there is an objection urged against free colored persons remaining in the country, which is largely imaginary, if not sometimes malicious."[71]

Any plan of compensation and colonization, as Lincoln well knew, depended upon congressional funding. Increasingly, radical Republicans in

Congress and in the press had come to oppose colonization as wrong and impractical. Frederick Douglass, a native of Maryland's Eastern Shore who had escaped slavery as a young man, was stunned by the president's continued support for colonization. He believed that Lincoln was delusional, though sincere, in advocating black resettlement in a foreign land.[72] One border state congressman, Henry Winter Davis of Maryland, joined radicals like Senator Charles Sumner of Massachusetts in denouncing the president's proposal. After the issuance in September of the preliminary Emancipation Proclamation containing Lincoln's colonization scheme, Davis declared in a speech at Newark, New Jersey, "There are some, and the President is among them, who labor under the delusion that you can free the Negroes and send them off to a foreign land. The thing is an impossibility; and if it were practicable, it would not be desirable." Davis argued, "The lands of the Southern States must be cultivated, and the Negroes will remain there, and will have to cultivate them." Furthermore, he said, it would be impossible financially and physically to remove 4 million blacks from the country.[73]

The colonization scheme soon failed after a disastrous attempt by a land speculator, encouraged by Lincoln and partly financed by the federal government, to settle a black colony on an island off Haiti in 1863. After this failure, the president, to the relief of radical Republicans and the dismay of many Unionists in the border states, abandoned colonization as impractical and as something that freed blacks did not want.[74]

For staunch antislavery proponents, the president's recommendation to compensate slaveholders for their slaves, as contained in his proposed constitutional amendment, flew in the face of the Emancipation Proclamation. But in Lincoln's mind, the compensation offer would actually run parallel to the implementation of the proclamation in the rebel states and would grease the wheels for the state-controlled, gradual end of slavery that he had proposed to the border states. Almost everyone who gave serious thought to the issue must have realized that national approval of the president's compensation proposal, in the form of a constitutional amendment, was virtually impossible to achieve. The amendment would require a two-thirds vote of Congress to initiate and ratification by three-fourths of the states, actions that could not occur within a reasonable period of time. On another occasion, Secretary of the Navy Gideon Welles confided to his diary, "[The president] has often strange and incomprehensible whims; takes sometimes singular and unaccountable freaks."[75] Lincoln's proposal of a constitutional amendment to compensate slaveholders if they freed their slaves was one of those instances.

Lincoln, however, did not abandon his earlier border state compensation proposal. In December 1862, he buttonholed Senator Henderson of Missouri and argued for compensation as part of a broader effort to end slavery. He told the senator, "Why can't you make the border State members see it? Why don't you . . . take pay for your slaves from the Government? Then . . . we can go ahead with emancipation of slaves in the other States by proclamation and end the trouble."[76]

Henderson, like Governor Gamble, had warmed to the idea of compensated emancipation since Lincoln had advanced the proposal in March 1862. After talking to the president, he dutifully gave notice in the Senate that he intended to introduce a bill to provide $20 million for the implementation of the president's plan in Missouri. One day later, Representative Noell, also of Missouri, gave a similar notice in the House.[77] On January 6, 1863, Noell preempted Henderson by introducing his compensation bill for Missouri. The bill passed the House by a vote of 83 to 50, with five border state members supporting it.[78] Nine border representatives voted against the bill, and several were absent. The opposition to the measure came mainly from northern Democrats, who objected to any change in the Union purpose of the war and probably also to the expense involved in funding compensation.

Lincoln expressed his delight with the House's approval of the Missouri compensation bill. At Henderson's prompting, he sent an urgent message to General Curtis, commanding Union forces in Missouri, where debate in the legislature raged over the state's position on compensation. "I understand there is considerable trouble with the slaves in Missouri," Lincoln told Curtis. "Please do your best to keep peace on the question for two or three weeks, by which time we hope to do something here towards settling the question, in Missouri."[79] Lincoln was referring to the effort in Congress to enact the compensation bill.

The Missouri funding bill, however, became stymied in the Senate over the amount to be paid for each slave and over a deadline for the completion of emancipation. Finally, on February 12, an amended bill passed the Senate by a vote of 23 to 18, with only Henderson of the border states supporting it. It provided for funding based on $200 per freed slaves. The amount was $100 less than in the District of Columbia emancipation bill, an important point of contention for border state members. The Senate bill also established a short deadline of July 4, 1865, for the completion of freedom. The bill went back to the House, where the dilatory parliamentary tactics of three proslavery Missouri conservatives and northern Democratic representatives prevented its consideration until February 25. When the session ended, the bill had not come to a vote. A similar scheme of compensated emancipation for Maryland, introduced on January 19 by conservative Republican John A. Bingham of Ohio, met a similar fate.[80] On March 2 the Kentucky legislature reacted to the failure of the Missouri and Maryland funding bills by emphatically reaffirming its earlier rejection of Lincoln's compensation scheme.[81]

Realistically, after these defeats, the proposal for compensated emancipation was dead, though Lincoln briefly revived the idea when he met two years later on February 3, 1865, with Confederate peace commissioners at Hampton Roads, Virginia. There, the president surprisingly expressed his belief that the northern people would support federal compensation for slaves in order to end the war quickly and, by implication, to aid the South's economic and social recovery. Although the conference failed, a few days later Lincoln drafted a bill to be introduced into Congress to provide U.S. bonds for rebel states that ceased their insurrection and returned to the Union by July 1. He submitted the proposed bill to his cabinet for consideration. With Union victory and the abolition of slavery in sight, cabinet members unanimously opposed the measure, and the president, after expressing his disappointment, dropped the scheme.[82]

Thus ended the president's efforts, begun in 1862, to secure border state approval of a gradual, compensated plan for eradicating the inhumane institution that Lincoln had long morally opposed but had had trouble finding constitutional authority to act against. The proposal for state-initiated, as opposed to federal, emancipation had failed in 1862–1863, not only because of border state opposition but also because of the Republican-controlled Congress's refusal to commit funding to compensate slaveholders, though it had done so for emancipation in the District of Columbia. During the last two years of the war, Lincoln continued to face criticism in the border states for the Emancipation Proclamation, but it was not as harsh as earlier. Gradually opinion toward emancipation underwent a change in Missouri and Maryland, though not appreciably in Kentucky, where traditional ties with Virginia and the lower South had instilled in both slaveholders and nonslaveholders a more intense support for slavery than existed in the other border states. Unionists, even including some Kentuckians, came to accept the reality of emancipation as a war measure to suppress the rebellion. This was precisely the argument that Lincoln had made for issuing the proclamation and which he would repeat in his last annual message to Congress on December 6, 1864. Furthermore, border state whites concluded that even without federal antislavery policies, the "mere friction and abrasion" of war, as Lincoln had told their congressmen in July 1862, would doom slavery. By late in the war, the main concern of a large number of border state whites had become the social and racial effects of emancipation, though, to be sure, slaveholders, a relatively small minority of the white population, resented the impending property and labor losses that they would suffer with the end of slavery. At the same time, border state whites of all classes insisted that the states, not the federal government, should determine the status of blacks in freedom.

Lincoln in 1863–1864 still faced strong political opposition in the border states. His decision, as authorized by Congress in the Second Confiscation Act (July 1862) and reaffirmed in the Emancipation Proclamation, to permit black recruitment into the federal army ignited a firestorm in the border states. Furthermore, a continuing conflict between local civil and military authorities also threatened to disrupt the gains that had been made in the pacification of these states. Although historians have concluded that the border states had been safely secured for the Union by late 1861, opposition to emancipation, black troops, military intervention in civil affairs, and disruptions created by the war, as well as the growing perception among dominant conservative Unionists that radical Republicans had gained control in Washington, continued to perplex and create trouble for the president. The radicals, these Unionists believed, were determined on a social and political revolution in the South that would vitiate the Constitution and establish a "consolidated" government in Washington. As the war entered another critical phase in 1863, Lincoln would be sorely tested in his efforts to maneuver through the political, military, and racial minefields that existed in the border states.

CHAPTER 7

■

Resistance in Kentucky,
1863–1865

On July 9, 1862, Kentucky senator Garret Davis, a slaveholder, rose in the U.S. Senate and defiantly responded to a radical Republican proposal for the recruitment of black troops. "Do you expect [those of us in the border states] to give our sanction and our approval" to former slaves serving in the army? he asked northern Republicans? "No! No! We would regard" the authors of any such proposal "as our worst enemies, and there is no foreign despotism that could come to our rescue that we would not joyously embrace before we would submit to any such condition of things as that. But before we invoked this foreign despotism, we would arm every man and boy that we have in the land, and we would meet you in a death struggle to overthrow together such an oppression." Davis, who often employed hyperbole in his speeches, contended, "If this Union cannot be preserved by the white man . . . there are no conditions upon which it can be saved." He predicted, "If you put arms in the hands of the Negroes and make them feel their power and impress them with their former slavery, wrongs, and injustice . . . you will whet their fiendish passions, make them the destroying scourge of the cotton States, and you will bring upon the country a condition of things that will render restoration hopeless." The Kentucky senator, however, found no fault in employing blacks as laborers for the army, though he would not free them.[1] Davis had fired the opening salvo against the proposal for arming blacks. It would become a major issue in the border states, especially Kentucky, after Lincoln authorized the military recruitment of former slaves in his Emancipation Proclamation on January 1, 1863.

The debate on July 9, 1862, that triggered Senator Davis's outburst focused on a provision in the Second Confiscation bill directing the president to accept blacks into the army. Due to the opposition from the border states as well as from Lincoln and conservative Republicans, the final bill, as described in chapter 5, only authorized the president "to employ as many persons of African descent as he may deem necessary and proper for the suppression of the rebellion." Fearful of losing Kentucky and possibly other border states, as he had admitted, Lincoln for several months refused to sanction black recruitment into the army. He approved the army's use of blacks as laborers, but not as soldiers. As Davis had suggested, border state loyalists did not object to African American laborers in the army, as long as they were not fugitive slaves. Nonetheless, by the time Lincoln issued his Emancipation Proclamation, several thousand former slaves were serving in federal military units in the lower South and in Kansas.

The Emancipation Proclamation fully authorized the reception of blacks "into the armed service of the United States to garrison forts, positions, stations, and other places, and to man vessels of all sorts."[2] The need to replace the tremendous losses of white troops at Antietam, Perryville, Fredericksburg, and other bloody battlefields during the last months of 1862 must have contributed to the president's approval of African Americans as soldiers. Lincoln, however, still hesitated to sanction the use of blacks in military operations.

On January 10, 1863, ten days after signing the Emancipation Proclamation, Lincoln called Secretary of War Edwin M. Stanton and Secretary of the Navy Gideon Welles to the White House for consultation on the recruitment of blacks. The president wanted the two men to "do what [they] could for the employment of the contrabands [black refugees], and as the rebels threatened to kill all caught with arms in their hands, to employ them where they would not be liable to be captured." He suggested to Stanton that blacks within Union lines "could perform Garrison duty at Memphis, Columbus [Kentucky], and other places and let the [white] soldiers go on more active service."[3]

Two days later, Pennsylvania radical Thaddeus Stevens sparked a heated debate in the House of Representatives when he introduced a bill to recruit 150,000 black soldiers. John J. Crittenden immediately denounced the proposal and predicted that Kentuckians would not permit officers recruiting blacks to set foot in the state.[4] Lincoln's friend Orville H. Browning, who had recently been replaced in the Senate, somberly predicted that if the bill passed, the Union would "lose Ky, Tennessee, Maryland and Missouri" and that "the restoration of the Union [would] no longer be possible."[5] After an amendment passed to exclude the slaves of Unionists from recruitment, the bill received the approval of the House, with the usual opposition by conservative and Democratic members from the border states and the North. But the Senate committee, which was in the process of drafting conscription legislation to fill the depleted army ranks, refused to consider Stevens's bill. Instead, the committee recommended to Congress an enrollment bill designed to prepare for the national conscription of all able-bodied men between the ages of twenty and forty-five. The bill did not explicitly exclude blacks from its provisions.

Border state members demanded assurances that under the enrollment bill the military could not recruit blacks. With that in mind, Davis in the Senate offered an amendment to the bill directing, "No Negro, free or slave, shall be enlisted in the military, marine, or naval service of the United States." After a long speech by Davis in support of the amendment, his colleague, Senator Lazarus W. Powell, called for the yeas and nays on it, a tactic designed to win the support of some Republicans who might not want to be identified politically with a measure arming blacks. The ploy failed because the northern senators realized a greater political need in their states—to find replacements for white troops, who had lately suffered heavy casualties in the war. By a vote of 23 to 12 the Davis amendment went down to defeat. All the border state senators voted for it. Powell then introduced an amendment to the enrollment bill providing "that no person of African descent shall be commissioned or hold an office in the Army of the United States." This time, several conservative Republicans sided with the border state senators. By a vote of 18 to 17, Powell's amendment passed.[6] On March 2, 1863, the enrollment bill, as amended, received the approval of Congress, and President Lincoln signed it the next day.[7]

The passage of the Enrollment Act moved Lincoln to a greater sense of urgency for the recruitment of blacks in the army. He also began to reconsider his policy of limiting black soldiers to garrison and post duties. Acting quickly in late March, he ordered the raising of African American troops along the Mississippi River. On March 25 Secretary of War Stanton dispatched Adjutant General Lorenzo Thomas on an inspection tour of federal posts along the river. Lincoln, in addition to giving Thomas specific instructions to ensure that the contrabands received proper treatment, directed him to arrange "for the organization of their labor and military strength." The president did not authorize the recruitment of African Americans in the border states, but free blacks in these states were soon serving as enlisted men in northern units. Stanton told Thomas that Lincoln "[wanted] it to be understood that no officer in the U.S. service [would be] regarded as in the discharge of his duties" if he failed to carry out the directive to enlist and organize blacks in the army.[8]

One day after Stanton dispatched Thomas to the Mississippi Valley, Lincoln wrote military governor Andrew Johnson of Tennessee, "The colored population is the great *available* and yet *unavailed* of, force for restoring the Union." Marking the letter *"Private"* lest its disclosure inflame white racial passions in Tennessee and the border states, the president told Johnson, "The bare sight of fifty thousand armed, and drilled black soldiers on the banks of the Mississippi, would end the rebellion at once. And who doubts that we can present that sight, if we but take hold in earnest?" Although Lincoln might not have admitted it, the reverse could also have been true. If a large number of African Americans were in arms, rebels could have been joined by thousands of infuriated white recruits from the border states who would be anxious to save their communities from what they feared would be a racial conflagration. The president asked Johnson to aid in the recruitment of blacks, adding, "if you *have* been thinking of it."[9] Johnson, a hero among border state Unionists, especially old Democrats, refused to "take hold" in raising black troops for the Union army.

The greatest opposition to black recruitment came from Kentucky. White Unionists in the state, joined by Confederate sympathizers, threatened serious consequences if Lincoln forced black enrollment on them. Mary E. Van Meter of Bowling Green declared that the Lincoln government's recruitment of slaves in the army would be "one of the greatest outrages . . . ever heard of in the history of nations." Other Kentuckians echoed a similar view. George D. Prentice's *Louisville Daily Journal* carried on an unrelenting and hyperbolic campaign in 1863 and 1864 against the arming of blacks. The editor starkly predicted that a reign of terror would occur in Kentucky and in the other slave states if weapons were placed in the hands of the former slaves. Black soldiers would "sweep throughout the South to despoil and ravage as their own mad and savage passions [were] aroused and infuriated by blood-shed." Albert G. Hodges, editor of the *Frankfort Commonwealth*, who would later meet with Lincoln on the issue yet ultimately supported him in the election of 1864, warned that black recruitment would severely "retard the enlistment of white soldiers" in the Union army. The *Lexington Observer and Register* thundered that arming the former slaves would be an ominous step toward fastening black equality upon the country, "more speedily than was hoped for even by the most radical Abolitionist."[10]

Nonetheless, in June 1863 Colonel James B. Fry, in charge of conscription in the War Department, ordered the enrollment of Kentucky blacks for the draft. General Jeremiah T. Boyle, who commanded the military district of Kentucky, anxiously telegraphed Fry and pleaded with him to see Lincoln and have the order rescinded. Boyle informed Fry that the enrollment applied only to the 4,130 free black males in Kentucky, of whom only about one-eighth would be drafted under the current rules. "If you gained these," Boyle told Fry, "you will lose more than ten thousand—you will revolutionize the State and do infinite & inconceivable harm. [It] will meet with decided opposition for the peace and quiet of the Country."[11] General Ambrose E. Burnside, the overall commander in the department, wired Lincoln on June 26, one day after Boyle's message, and also asked for the revocation of the order.[12]

Lincoln, who seems to have overlooked the seriousness of the controversy, immediately assured Burnside, "There is nothing going on in Kentucky on the subject . . . except an enrolment." However, he promised, "Before anything is done beyond this, I will take care to understand the case better than I now do."[13] Upon receipt of the president's telegram, Burnside wrote Lincoln (he also telegraphed Stanton) and elaborated on the reasons why the enrollment of Kentucky blacks would be a great mistake. Burnside agreed with Boyle that if black men were drafted in Kentucky, the small number obtained "from the free-black class . . . [would] lose a much larger number of good white volunteers and give the secret enemies of the Government a weapon to use" against military conscription. The white people of Kentucky, Burnside told Lincoln, "are ready and willing to stand the draft if necessary," provided blacks were not enrolled. He reported, however, "We draft slaves for labor continually," which the army needed.[14]

The president referred Burnside's appeal to Stanton, pointedly noting, "I really think" the matter "is worth considering."[15] Having failed to receive a reply from the War Department on the issue, General Boyle on July 4, 1863, sent an urgent message to Colonel Fry reporting that bands of guerrillas were organizing throughout Kentucky with the purpose of preventing the enrollment of African Americans. He warned that a revolution threatened the state. Finally, on July 22, the War Department realized the danger to the Union cause in the state and acted by temporarily suspending black enrollment in Kentucky.[16]

At the same time, Lincoln increased pressure on his commanders along the lower Mississippi River to recruit blacks. Concluding that enough was not being done in this regard, the president on July 21 told Stanton, "I desire that a renewed and vigorous effort be made to raise colored forces along the shores of the Missippi [sic]." He asked Stanton again to dispatch General Thomas to facilitate the work. Lincoln followed this directive with similar instructions to General U. S. Grant, who had recently opened the lower Mississippi River to Union control and increased the area for the recruitment of blacks freed by the Emancipation Proclamation. African American troops, the president informed Grant, "[are] a resource which, if vigorously applied now, will soon close the contest. It works doubly, weakening the enemy and strengthening us."[17]

Grant agreed. "I have given the subject of arming the Negro my hearty support," the general wrote Lincoln. "This, with the emancipation [proclamation] is the heavyest [sic] blow yet given the Confederacy."[18] Also during the summer, Stanton, with the president's cautious approval and despite conservative opposition, had authorized the organization of an African American regiment of sappers and miners in Maryland—the first black regiment organized in the border states.[19]

This recruitment effort, inspired by the president, heightened the fears of white Kentuckians that the War Department's July 22 suspension of the black enrollment for conscription in the state would soon be lifted. White Unionists worried that such action would open the door for the freeing and military recruitment of their own slaves. On October 19, 1863, Kentucky's new governor, Thomas E. Bramlette, received a report that the War Department would soon issue an order for the recruitment of African Americans in the border states. Bramlette immediately telegraphed Lincoln to request that the suspension of the order as applied to his state should be continued.[20] Actually, Lincoln had already exempted the Bluegrass State from the re-

quirement for the enlistment of black troops, but he retained it for Delaware, Maryland, and Missouri.[21] Kentucky's relief would be short-lived.

In addition to the ongoing dispute in Kentucky over emancipation and the
enlistment of blacks in the army, a divisive state election occurred during
the summer of 1863. The overzealousness of military officers attempting to
prevent the disloyal from voting and the arrests of rebel sympathizers kept
political passions high and raised the distinct possibility that Kentucky
might yet try to join the Confederacy. As early as January, Unionist
William C. Goodloe of Richmond, Kentucky, reported to former Congressman Green Adams, "We are to have a desperate struggle in Kentucky this
year." He wrote that some of the state leaders, influenced by the recent
Copperhead election victories in the West (today's Midwest), were wavering in their support for the Union. In February, Jesse W. Fell, the president's
Illinois associate, after a visit to Kentucky wrote a friend in Washington,
"The denunciation of Mr. Lincoln, and his emancipation policy, in this
state, is *bitter and universal*. Kentucky loyalty means, '*loyalty to Slavery*,'"
not to the Union. Fell predicted that the 20,000 additional Kentucky
troops recently authorized by Congress would within six months be "fighting *against* instead of *for* the Union."[22]

The political campaign for the August 3, 1863, election began in February while the General Assembly was in session debating action on Lincoln's
emancipation policy and issues relating to civil liberties. Staunch states'
rights members, a minority in the legislature, issued a call for a "National
Democratic" convention to meet at Frankfort on February 18 for the purpose of adopting a platform and nominating candidates for state offices.
On that day, approximately 200 delegates from forty counties assembled in
the state capital's Metropolitan Hall. Immediately, Colonel E. A. Gilbert,
backed by troops from his Ohio regiment, marched into the building and
announced that he had received information that "a large number of rebel
spies and emissaries were present." He then took the names of all the delegates. After permitting the convention to organize, Gilbert abruptly broke
up the meeting and directed the delegates to go home and refrain from all
"seditious and noisy conversation." The list of names, he lamely explained,
"might be of great importance . . . in certain contingencies" in the future.[23]
Outraged by Gilbert's high-handed action, a committee of the National

Thomas E. Bramlette, Union governor of Kentucky. A former colonel of a Kentucky regiment, Bramlette was elected governor in 1863 and, though he acquiesced in emancipation, he became a bitter foe of black recruitment, military intervention, and Lincoln's suspension of the writ of habeas corpus in the state in 1864. Bramlette was active in the futile effort by border state conservatives to form a coalition with national Democrats on a war platform to defeat Lincoln's reelection in 1864. Courtesy of the Kentucky Historical Society, Frankfort, Kentucky.

Democracy drew up a strong protest and asked the General Assembly to sustain them.[24]

Despite fears that Gilbert might prorogue the legislature and arrest its members, the state senate passed a resolution denouncing the colonel's intervention. General Quincy A. Gillmore, commanding troops in central Kentucky, however, supported Gilbert. He explained, "The political status of Kentucky is by no means secure, and I deem it sounder policy to arrest at once the organization of the rebel element, before it attained such impetus, strength, and character as would demand, six months hence, the exercise of force to retain the State in constitutional obedience."[25] Wisely, Gilbert took no further action.

Meanwhile, the majority in the General Assembly, who were less prone to extremism than were the National Democracy, issued a call for a convention of the "Union Democracy of Kentucky" to meet in Louisville on March 18 to prepare for the August election.[26] The leaders of the new party were not Democrats, as the name implied, but old Union Whigs like Prentice and Crittenden. The use of the word "Democracy" was designed to gain the support of former Democrats and thereby show solidarity with the war effort while opposing Lincoln's antislavery policies and military intervention in the state.

When the approximately 1,000 delegates from 103 counties gathered in Louisville for the Union Democracy convention, a controversy immediately erupted. Former congressman James A. Cravens of Indiana opened the proceedings with a Copperhead speech in which he assailed not only Lincoln but also the war itself. He was hooted down by the delegates and strongly advised to return to Indiana.[27] After order was restored, the convention nominated Joshua F. Bell for governor. Bell, an ex-Whig, had been defeated for governor in 1859 by Democrat Beriah Magoffin.

The convention adopted a series of resolutions affirming their unstinting loyalty to the Union and insisting, "The present causeless and wicked rebellion should be crushed by the whole power of the Federal Government." They protested, however, against the Emancipation Proclamation, referring to it as "unwise, unconstitutional, and void." The delegates also denounced "the extension of martial law over States where war did not exist, and the suspension of the writ of habeas corpus as unwarranted by the Constitution, tending to subordinate civil to military authority and to subvert constitutional and free government." They repeated the General Assembly's earlier declaration that a difference existed "between a transitory administration," like Lincoln's, which was "limited to an official term," and the federal government itself, "which [was] permanent, and intended by its founders to endure forever."[28]

Bell declined the Union Democracy nomination on the grounds that his private affairs "demanded his whole attention" because of the war. On May 1 the party's state central committee selected Thomas Elliott Bramlette to replace Bell. A forty-six-year-old former Whig judge, Bramlette in 1861 had defied Governor Magoffin's neutrality proclamation and raised a Union regiment. Although he had served with distinction, Bramlette resigned his commission as a colonel in 1862 over a command dispute and accepted an appointment by Lincoln as the U.S. district attorney for Kentucky.

Bramlette opened his campaign for governor at Carlisle on June 23, 1863, with a resounding Union speech. He boldly announced that he did not oppose the Emancipation Proclamation because, he reminded the crowd, it applied only to those areas in rebellion, not the border states, and because, as Lincoln had argued, it would help win the war. Bramlette ridiculed the objections to the recruitment of black troops by telling his audience that "in the beginning of this strife in New Orleans," the rebels "heralded it abroad that they had already organized two negro regiments to fight the Yankees." Furthermore, Bramlette declared, "the first act in the Tennessee rebel legislature was the organization of free negro regiments."[29] This statement might have been rhetorical, designed to minimize the significance of the black enrollment issue in the campaign. Whether or not it was rhetorical, Bramlette soon retreated from his comment on black recruitment. In a speech at Louisville on July 18, he praised the resolutions of the Union convention that had denounced military interference in civil affairs, and he hailed "the [triumph] of conservative sentiment" in the recent northern elections. Bramlette also condemned "the radical measures of the Federal administration," presumably including the organization of African American troops.[30] After becoming governor on September 2, 1863, he became an outspoken foe of black recruitment in Kentucky.

A group of dissident Democrats, who were upset with Bramlette's strong war position and his approval of the Emancipation Proclamation, put forward states' rights icon Charles A. Wickliffe for governor. Calling themselves "Peace Democrats" in emulation of the western Copperheads, who had been successful in the Indiana and Illinois elections in the fall of

1862, they excoriated Lincoln for his antislavery policy and for the inclusion of blacks in the Enrollment Act of March 1863. They also called for an end to the war. The Peace Democrats nominated a full slate of state and congressional candidates.[31] The Union Democrats repeatedly charged that the Peace Democrats were secessionists in sheep's clothing—unfairly, though some were probably rebel sympathizers. In fact, the Peace Party gained much of its support from angry and ardent states' rights men, not secessionists.

William C. Goodloe, nephew of the flamboyant radical Cassius Clay, excitedly informed Lincoln that Wickliffe and the Peace Democrats advocated withholding men and money for the prosecution of the war. Bramlette derided Wickliffe and the Peace Democrats as "the no-more-men and no-more-money secessionists." Goodloe reported that rebels were taking advantage of the confusion among Unionists on the war to create discontent. (Former Whigs like Prentice, who never liked their association with the Democratic name, began referring to the Union Democracy as simply the Union Party.) Goodloe asked the president to order General Burnside, the department commander, to suppress the Peace Democrats.[32] Although the Wickliffe threat concerned Lincoln, as well as conservative Unionists like Joshua Speed and Prentice, the president wisely refrained from intervening.[33] His interference in the election would have further inflamed passions and gained support for the Peace Party.

On the other hand, state and military authorities needed no prompting from Lincoln to take action to ensure a Union Party victory. On July 10, 1863, Governor James F. Robinson issued a proclamation requiring the "oath of loyalty" for all voters; the test oath law had been enacted by the General Assembly in 1862 over Governor Magoffin's veto. The oath was a version of the so-called ironclad oath mandated for federal officials. It required voters to swear that they had never supported the rebellion or given aid or comfort to it. Those taking the oath had to understand that if they violated it, they would face "death or other punishment by the judgment of a Military Commission."[34] The oath, which Robinson personally opposed, was too draconian for many conservative Unionists. They particularly disliked the part requiring severe punishment for those who might have earlier supported secession, changed their minds, and then perjured themselves by taking the oath. Even Lincoln had little use for such an oath, though he did not intercede against it in Kentucky or in the other border states where it was applied. He told Secretary of War Stanton that, as a matter of principle, he disliked an oath that required a man "to swear he *has* not done wrong." He explained, "It rejects the Christian principle of forgiveness on terms of repentance. I think that it is enough if the man does no wrong *hereafter*."[35]

General Burnside, still smarting from the president's revocation of his suspension of the antiwar *Chicago Times* in June, issued an order on July 31 declaring that Kentucky election officials would be held "strictly responsible" to the military if they permitted disloyal persons to vote. A Burnside subordinate in the western part of the state ordered, "Any voter, judge, or clerk of elections, or other person, who may evade, neglect, or refuse compliance with the order, will be arrested and sent before a military commission." Still, Burnside announced that the purpose of the military at the polls was "to aid the constituted authorities of the State in support of the laws and of the purity of suffrage" as set forth in Robinson's proclamation. The general justified his intervention on the grounds that "a rebel force" under General John Hunt Morgan had invaded Kentucky "with the avowed intention of overawing the judges of elections, of intimidating loyal voters . . . and forcing the election of disloyal candidates."[36] Morgan's July 1863 raid—his second in the state—had swept through Kentucky into southern Ohio. The flamboyant Morgan had military objectives in mind; only tangentially was the incursion designed to create disruptions at the polls. By the time Burnside issued his July 31 proclamation, the raid had collapsed, and Morgan and most of his men had been captured.[37]

Issued three days before the election, Burnside's order had little effect on the outcome of the contest. Bramlette and the Union Party won an overwhelming victory. In the governor's race, Bramlette captured 68,306 votes to Wickliffe's 17,389, and the Union Party won all nine seats in Congress and gained a comfortable majority in the General Assembly. The total vote in the gubernatorial election represented 60 percent of the votes cast in the 1860 presidential election. The 40 percent decline from 1860 was due mainly to the thousands of Kentuckians serving in the Union and Confederate armies in the South and the inevitable social dislocations caused by the war. The Union Party's impressive victory could be largely attributed to the repulse of Morgan and to the dramatic successes of the Union armies at Gettysburg and Vicksburg in early July. Burnside's election order and the presence of troops at the polls, however, gave "a color of plausibility to the pretence made by the Wickliffe party, that they were defeated by bayonets," the *Cincinnati Commercial* reported.[38]

CHAPTER SEVEN

Both staunch Kentucky loyalists and President Lincoln celebrated the Union Party's success. The *Louisville Daily Journal* hailed the victory and boasted, "There never was more fairness, more justice, more freedom in the election, than was practiced and accorded by the friends of the Union last Monday."[39] Lincoln crowed in a letter to his wife, Mary, who was visiting in New York, "Old Mr. Wickliffe got ugly, as you know, ran for Governor, and is terribly beaten." In addition, the president wrote Mary that Congressman John W. Menzies, "who, as we thought, behaved very badly last session of Congress," had been defeated by Green Clay Smith, an ardent Unionist.[40] As Lincoln probably realized, the election, while sustaining the Union cause in the state, was not a victory for his antislavery policies, though a small faction of emancipationists had surfaced in the state in 1863. Only the death of Crittenden on July 26 put a damper on the Union Party triumph; it also diminished the border states' conservative influence in Washington.

For the purpose of evaluating the importance of the Union Party's victory, Lincoln asked former congressman Green Adams whether "the aggregate vote" Bramlette received was "a clear majority of the largest vote ever cast in Kentucky." He cited the state total of 146,216 in the presidential election as the largest and calculated that "73,109 would be a clear majority of it."[41] The vote for Bramlette exceeded the president's "clear majority" by 12,586, which constituted Lincoln's concept of a democratic body politic in the election.

If Lincoln expected smooth sailing in Kentucky with Bramlette at the helm, he was soon disappointed. On one important point, however, the new governor agreed wholeheartedly with the president—the suppression of the rebellion. In assuming office on September 2, 1863, Bramlette emphatically announced, "Kentucky will, with unwavering faith, and unswerving purpose, stand by and support the Government in every effort to suppress the rebellion and maintain the Union." Unstated by Bramlette and other Union leaders in Kentucky was the prospect that, unlike what might be their fate in the North, defeat in the war, they believed, would result in the state joining the Confederacy, which then would place Unionists at the tender mercies of victorious rebels. Still, Bramlette, who would soon emerge as a leading border state governor, warned that Kentucky's "devotion to constitutional liberty [would] equally impel her to oppose . . . all unconstitutional, all wicked, unwise, or hurtful measures of policy." Bramlette insisted that opposition to Lincoln's policies should be done through lawful means. Kentucky, he declared, sought "a restored Union—not a reconstructed Union" as Senators Charles Sumner and Benjamin F. Wade demanded. Bramlette, as well as other conservatives and Democrats, wanted the South restored "upon a constitutional basis," code words for the restoration of the Republic as it had existed before the war, though with the political proscription of rebel leaders. The new governor in his inaugural address did not mention emancipation, the recruitment of black troops, or military arrests and trials, crucial issues that would continue to plague Kentucky's relations with Lincoln and with military authorities.[42]

In his first message to the legislature in December 1863, Bramlette again declared that every Kentuckian should be loyal to the federal government. Differences on policies with the Lincoln administration, he announced, should not be made "an excuse for relaxing our efforts to sustain the Government and suppress the Rebellion." Bramlette asked the General Assembly to adopt a hard line toward "those who rejoice or exult over rebel invasions and guerrilla raids." He recommended that the legislature "provide proper preventive, as well as punative [sic] remedies, for every form of treasonable action," whether "acts or words which tend to promote or encourage rebellion." The governor also maintained that aiders and abettors of the rebellion "should be held accountable for all the injuries inflicted by their fellow accomplices in treason."[43] However, he did not specifically call for property assessments on secessionists for damages, a policy that General Boyle had instituted in some counties in early 1863, despite Senator Powell's strong protest to Lincoln. At that time, the president wrote Boyle that an assessments policy against rebel property, "though just and politic in some cases," was "so liable to gross abuse, as to do great injustice in some others and give the government immense trouble."[44]

Bramlette in his December 1863 message to the General Assembly announced, "The State and Nation can exist with or without slavery." He maintained that "the Government was not formed for the *purpose* of preserving or destroying" slavery; it was created, he contended, "to perpetuate to the latest time the blessings of free government to the Anglo-American." Thus, he concluded, "It is not, therefore, opposition to slavery which constitutes the danger to free government, nor the advocacy of it. But the danger lies in the effort of those who would make the life of the government subordinate to the status of the negro. It is as revolutionary and disloyal to subordinate the government to the question of his freedom, as to the question of his enslavement."[45]

The issue of black recruitment in the state, however, soon tested the faith of Bramlette and Kentucky Unionists in Lincoln and the national government. A few days after delivering his message to the General Assembly, Bramlette received a report from a Captain Edward Cahill that he had been ordered to recruit "free colored men" in Kentucky in order to meet an unspecified state conscription quota. On December 10 the governor angrily reminded Cahill that Lincoln had exempted Kentucky from the recruitment of African Americans and that therefore the captain had no right to enlist them in the state. He also wrote General Boyle that black recruitment in Kentucky would not be tolerated. "Summary justice," Bramlette told Boyle, "will be inflicted upon any who attempts such unlawful purpose."[46]

One month later, Bramlette learned that a "recruiting post for negroes" had been authorized by the War Department and established at Paducah. He immediately wrote a long letter to Lincoln protesting the army's violation of the state law that prohibited the enlistment of noncitizens (blacks). The governor demanded that the president "take prompt action to remove this evil . . . and thus save me the necessity . . . of arraying the civil powers of the State against" the federal officers who "have been sent to violate our laws." Since Kentucky had exceeded its military quota with white troops, Bramlette told Lincoln, "there exists no apparent necessity, and no just pretence for the Federal authorities violating and trampling under the foot of power the laws of Kentucky." "We must be treated either as *loyal* or *disloyal*."[47] The Kentucky legislature unanimously endorsed the governor's position and demanded that Lincoln remove from the state's borders all camps for the recruitment of black troops.[48]

Lincoln turned Bramlette's letter over to Secretary of War Stanton for his response. In a report to the president on February 8, 1864, Stanton made the case for African American enlistments, specifically in the border states, from which, he said, most black troops must necessarily come. He stretched the truth when he wrote that the other border states in enforcing the Confiscation Act of 1862 had sanctioned the use of blacks in the military.[49] Actually, these states had only endorsed the confiscation of the slaves of rebel masters and their employment as army laborers, not as soldiers. Unionists in Maryland, Missouri, and Delaware had objected to the recruitment of black troops, but, unlike the Kentuckians, not to the extent of threatening nullification.

Apparently Lincoln did not respond to Stanton's report or Bramlette's February 1, 1864, letter. Congress, however, on February 24, almost one year after the passage of the Enrollment Act, took the matter into its own hands when it enacted a bill, which Lincoln approved, requiring federal enrollment boards to proceed "without delay" to make available for army enlistments all eligible slaves.[50] Congress provided Unionist owners with an indemnity of $300 for each slave enlisted and freed.

Kentucky could no longer evade black recruitment. Federal officers and agents from northern states immediately flooded the state to recruit African Americans. Some of these agents came to fulfill conscription quotas for their states, thereby reducing the pressure on their communities to enroll whites. Just as quickly, Bramlette sent another protest to the president, even stronger than the one of February 1. Suggesting that he had been betrayed by Lincoln on the issue, the governor declared that his hope "for the sympathy and cooperation of the Administration" could not "survive the attempt to inflict this wrong upon us." He told the president, "Kentuckians will obey willingly any law requiring their services in defence of their Government, . . . but they will not obey a law that violates their Constitutional rights as Citizens [and] dishonors them by preferring the slave to the loyal Kentuckian." Bramlette warned Lincoln, "Do not sow to the winds—least you reap the whirlwind" by sanctioning the recruitment of black troops.[51]

On March 13 the governor called several prominent Unionists, including Protestant minister Robert J. Breckinridge, to Frankfort for a conference the next day on the course that he should take in the crisis. A dispute later arose between the conservative Bramlette and the "radical" Breckinridge on what had occurred in the meeting. It seems clear, however, that Bramlette wanted a strong statement calling for resistance to or even legislative nullification of the federal decision to recruit black troops. On the day before he issued the call for the meeting, the governor telegraphed William C. Goodloe, another "radical," "If the President does not upon my demand stop the Negro Enrollment[,] I will."[52] Breckinridge believed that the governor's position was "a scheme to bloodily baptize Kentucky into the Confederacy," with rebel troops entering the state to join the uprising. This was not Bramlette's intent. Although his fears about black recruitment were exaggerated, Bramlette believed that his actions in opposing it would forestall disorders and prevent the state from falling to the rebels. Nevertheless, a proclamation of defiance, which the governor proposed, would have further inflamed Kentuckians and could easily have led to armed resistance, pitting the governor's poorly equipped militia against undermanned though armed federal units in the state. Some of the federal troops in the state were also Kentuckians, who conceivably would have sided with the governor. The consequences of the proposed proclamation would clearly have been detrimental to the peace and stability of Kentucky—and even the Union.

After several hours of intense debate in the meeting, cooler heads prevailed, and Bramlette agreed to issue a watered-down proclamation calling for public restraint, despite, he said, the rightful "indignation" of Kentuckians over black enrollment. The final proclamation declared that all opposition should be made "by legitimate appeals to the constituted tribunals of the Government; and through the ballot-box." Bramlette also decided to go to Washington and appeal in person to Lincoln regarding the state's position on African American troops and other issues.[53]

Governor Bramlette took with him Albert G. Hodges, editor of the *Frankfort Commonwealth*, and former Senator Archibald Dixon, both conservative Unionists. The Kentuckians arrived in Washington in late March 1864 and met with Lincoln on the twenty-sixth. Bramlette, calmer than he had been in Frankfort, began by laying out to the president Kentucky's objections to black recruitment, the interference of antislavery officers with slaves in the state, and what he claimed was an unfair calculation of the state's quota of men in the army. The president began by remarking "that he was apprehensive that Kentuckians felt unkindly toward him in consequence of not properly understanding the difficulties" that he faced.[54] After a discussion of the governor's concerns, Lincoln, as he told Browning, asked the Kentuckians "to let him make a little speech to them, which he did and with which, he said, they were much pleased."[55] Later, at Hodges's request, the president put what he had stated in a letter and sent it to the *Commonwealth* editor. He also added a paragraph that was not in his "little speech." Hodges, who warmly approved of Lincoln's sentiments, published the letter, an action that the president must have anticipated when he wrote it. Although only two typed pages in length, the so-called Hodges letter has become a minor classic in Lincoln lore. It revealed Lincoln's long-held opposition to slavery and his frustrating efforts to jump-start emancipation during the war. In the added paragraph to Hodges, Lincoln expressed his belief in God's purpose to end "the great wrong" of slavery, a point that he passionately repeated in his second inaugural address.[56]

The Hodges letter, however, failed to describe the agreements on the issues raised by Bramlette in the conference. After the meeting, Lincoln told Attorney General Edward Bates that "the arrangement with Gov Bramlette . . . seemed to be satisfactory all around."[57] The president sent a note to Secretary of War Stanton pronouncing the governor's requests "reasonable" and directing him to give Bramlette "a full hearing" and to do his best "to effect these objects." One purpose, the president wrote, was to please the governor "as far as practical" when drafting or enlisting Kentucky blacks in the army, as provided for by act of Congress. Whatever action was taken, Lincoln said, the enrollment in Kentucky should be "free from colateral [sic] embarrasments [sic], disorders, and provocations." He informed Stanton that the War Department should reduce the state's quota of troops to take into account the number of Kentuckians serving in the rebel army.[58]

Following the president's directive, Stanton and the War Department attempted to satisfy Bramlette on the issue of black recruitment. The War Department provided that "when any county filled its quota" for troops, "in any way, no further recruiting of negroes should be permitted" in the county, except where the master and slave both concurred. Stanton and his subordinates agreed with the governor that "all recruiting should be strictly limited to the regularly appointed officers for that service; and that those engaged without authority, or [in] sending out bodies of troops to gather up negroes by force" and putting them in camps, "should be arrested and summarily punished." Blacks who were recruited "should be removed to camps outside of the State, for organization and instruction." General Stephen G. Burbridge, who had replaced Boyle in command of the District of Kentucky, was ordered to carry out the new policy.[59]

Lincoln had made a good impression on both Bramlette and Hodges. The governor returned to Kentucky and reported that both Lincoln and Stanton "manifested the most cordial readiness to bestow upon the people of Kentucky every favor which, under the existing laws, could reasonably be demanded." The president, Bramlette said, expressed "a desire to avert . . . the recurrence of those calamities to which, as a Border State, [Kentucky has] been subjected."[60] But the *Louisville Daily Journal*, the leading newspaper in Kentucky, denounced the president's letter to Hodges as the most "explicit enunciation of the doctrine of absolutism that Mr. Lincoln has ever before made." The president's statement in the letter, the *Journal* contended, that "measures, otherwise unconstitutional, might become lawful, by becoming indispensable to the preservation of the constitution," was outright tyranny. The paper declared, "[It is] the most unworthy declaration that ever emanated from the chief magistrate of a free country. If it does not awaken the people to a due sense of the peril which the government must encounter from the re-election of Mr. Lincoln" in the fall, "words cannot awaken them." The Lincoln doctrine, if not successfully challenged, the *Journal* concluded, would result in "the destruction of the republic."[61]

The Lincoln-Bramlette agreement on black recruitment, as well as the governor's support of the president, proved short-lived. Some Kentucky counties did not immediately meet their quotas with white troops, whereupon General Burbridge, though a slaveholder, issued an order on April 18, 1864, opening the whole state to black enlistments in the army.[62] Complaints soon reached Lincoln that, as he told General Thomas, "our military are seizing negroes and carrying them off without their own consent, and according to no rules whatever, except those of absolute violence." He telegraphed Thomas, "Look into this & inform me, and see that the making soldiers of negroes is done according to the rules." Thomas promised to "take immediate measures to prevent a recurrence of any acts of violence" by officers enrolling blacks.[63] He also transferred the overall responsibility for the recruitment from Burbridge to General Augustus L. Chetlain and directed that "as early as possible colored troops [should] be used," instead of whites, "for recruiting purposes."[64]

Lincoln probably understood that his Emancipation Proclamation, though it did not apply to the border states, provided a powerful stimulus for black males to enlist in the army in these states. Enlistment meant freedom, not only for themselves but eventually for their families.[65] Indeed, freedom was occurring within local communities as the slave system disintegrated during the last year of the war, despite the efforts of state authorities and slaveholders to prevent it. For blacks, the novelty of fighting for the Union and of freedom in distant armies soon wore off and was replaced by the need to stay home to advance the collapse of slavery in their communities and to aid their families in the transition to freedom. But army recruiters—mainly white northerners—had an insatiable appetite for this new source of manpower. In order to meet or exceed their quotas, recruiters revived the practice of seizing blacks, freeing them from slavery, and, paradoxically, forcing them into the military. Furthermore, "bounty scalpers" from northern states entered Kentucky and, with a small amount of money, enticed slaves to enlist in the northern states' black units; in some cases, they became substitutes for conscripted whites. The bounty scalper received a hefty commission for each slave that he enlisted.[66]

Not until early 1865 did Lincoln learn of these violations of the "rules" for African American recruitment. When a complaint reached him that a Captain John Glenn, commanding a post at Henderson, Kentucky, was, as Lincoln put it, "forcing Negroes into the Military service, and even torturing them—riding them on rails and the like—to extort their consent" to enlist, he angrily telegraphed the captain, "[This] must not be done by you, or any one under you." Lincoln ordered the officer, "Answer me on this." No record has been found that Captain Glenn answered the president.[67] About the same time, the president received a similar complaint from Maysville, Kentucky. He sent a sharp note to Stanton directing him to enquire into the matter and "stop it if true."[68] On February 27, 1865, the War Department finally ordered the punishment of officers and others who were guilty of forcing blacks into the army.

By the end of the war, 23,703 Kentucky blacks had enlisted in "colored" regiments credited to the state (an undetermined number had joined regiments in Ohio and other states). This represented 57 percent of black men aged eighteen to forty-five, both free and slave, and was a higher percentage than in any other state; only Louisiana could claim a larger number of African American soldiers in the Union army. By comparison with Kentucky, Maryland provided 8,718 (28 percent); Missouri, 8,344 (39 percent); and Delaware, 954 (25 percent).[69]

Although Governor Bramlette at first expressed his approval of the black recruitment agreement reached with Lincoln in March, he soon denounced the War Department for failing to correct the abuses of its officers.[70] In addition, General Burbridge became a target of the governor's wrath as well as that of other conservative Unionists for ordering a system of trade permits that, Bramlette charged, became "a most shameful and corrupt system of partisan political corruption and oppression" that hurt Kentucky farmers. This scandal became known as the Great Hog Swindle, in which favored government agents received a monopoly on the shipment of Kentucky hogs. When the governor sent a secret report to the president explaining the details of the "swindle," Lincoln immediately ordered the revocation of this most egregious feature of the trade system.[71]

Bramlette also appealed directly to the president about the tyrannical conduct of General Eleazer A. Paine, commanding in western Kentucky. Paine, whom Lincoln had known in Illinois, reportedly had created a "reign of terror" in his district and had summarily executed forty-three persons. Bramlette preferred charges against the general, including corruption and the mistreatment of both Unionists and rebel sympathizers. Lincoln ordered General Burbridge to send a military commission to investigate the charges. The commission brought in a devastating report against Paine. The general was removed from command, and though he later faced court-martial on lesser charges, he received only a reprimand for his appalling actions in the Bluegrass State.[72] The governor also complained to Lincoln about the practice of military authorities in assuming the right "at pleasure to make [property] assessments upon the citizens and enforce the payment of heavy fines without a hearing."[73] Although the president had earlier cautioned General Boyle about possible abuses in the assessments policy, he took no action to end it in Kentucky. (He later overturned a similar policy in Missouri.)

Military misconduct, arrests, and trials, combined with white hostility to black recruitment, inflamed white Kentuckians and created conditions that Unionists predicted would lead to a violent confrontation between state and federal authorities. Defiant speeches and newspaper articles contributed mightily to the crisis atmosphere in Kentucky in 1864. Contributing to the tension and apprehension in the state, as well as elsewhere, was the fact that the war had become a stalemate during the summer and with the approach of the critical fall presidential election. Earlier in the year, Colonel Frank Wolford, a wounded Union hero of the fighting in southern Kentucky and Tennessee, assailed Lincoln in a speech at Lexington on March 10; he specifically encouraged Kentuckians to defy the president on the issue of black troops. Alarmed Unionists reported to the president that Governor Bramlette had been in the audience during the speech and "by his manner manifested positive approval" of it. These Unionists claimed that Wolford stirred rebellious sentiment by advocating "resistance to the supreme law and authorities of the land."[74]

Army authorities, probably at General Burbridge's instigation, did not wait long after Wolford's Lexington speech to arrest the colonel and dispatch him to Tennessee for a military trial on charges of disloyalty. Before the trial began, Lincoln, unwilling to make a political martyr of Wolford, ordered his release, discharge from the army, and return to Kentucky. Wolford was not to be silenced. Along with Lieutenant Governor Richard T. Jacob, he followed with even more vituperative attacks on Lincoln and his policies. In a four-hour harangue at Lebanon, Kentucky, Wolford proclaimed the president a "tyrant, usurper, and fool." The army officer on the scene sought to arrest him but backed off when the crowd threatened violence if he were to do so.[75]

Wolford also announced that Bramlette had authorized him to raise state troops to be enlisted for six months for the purposes of opposing black recruitment and the military's intervention in local affairs.[76] Radical Unionist Goodloe wrote to Congressman Green Clay Smith, "If the president does not stop the recruiting of these six months men—we shall have civil war in Kentucky in ninety days." He claimed, "The whole State Administration to day is for putting down the National Administration." Smith, as Goodloe requested, gave the letter to Lincoln, who simply noted that he had seen it.[77]

On June 27, 1864, Burbridge's officers again arrested Wolford. This time Burbridge sent him to Washington for a military trial on a vague charge of inciting opposition to the government and its war policies. Lincoln met with Wolford on July 7 and drafted a parole that the Kentuckian signed. The parole permitted Wolford to return to Louisville and await trial on the promise that he would "abstain from public speaking, and every thing intended or calculated to produce excitement."[78]

On July 17 Lincoln, still wanting to avoid a trial that could give the popular Wolford a forum and further inflame political passions in Kentucky, offered another parole to Wolford. The president pledged to drop all charges against him if he promised that he would do nothing "to hinder, delay, or embarrass the employment and use of colored persons" in the military. The former Union colonel refused to sign the parole because, as he indignantly wrote Lincoln on July 30, "I cannot bargain for my liberty, and the exercise of my rights as a freeman, on any such terms. I have committed no crime." Wolford went on to charge Lincoln with exercising arbitrary power by causing him "to be arrested and held in confinement contrary to law," not, he added, "for the good of our common country, but to increase the chances of your re-election" and that of the Republican

Party. With an overblown rhetorical flourish that Lincoln could hardly have appreciated, Wolford exclaimed, "No Sir! much as I love liberty, I will fester in a prison, or die on a gibbet, before I will agree to any terms that do not abandon all charges against me, and fully acknowledge my innocence."[79]

The president had not received Wolford's July 30 letter before U.S. Judge Advocate General Joseph Holt ordered him to Washington to face charges. But when Lincoln learned of Holt's order, he telegraphed Wolford and directed him to remain in Louisville pending a further study of his case.[80] Believing that the Republican government had no intention of dropping the charges, Wolford took to the stump again, denouncing the administration's policies and calling for the defeat of Lincoln in the forthcoming election. He threw his support to the Democrats in the fall election and became an elector for George B. McClellan. Not until after the presidential election did Burbridge, who had been straining at the bit to silence Wolford, find it politically safe to arrest him again, along with Lieutenant Governor Jacob, who had campaigned against Lincoln and the Republicans. The final chapter in the Wolford case, as well as that of Jacob, would be written after the election.

The presidential campaign of 1864 deeply divided millions of Americans like few other contests in the nation's history; nowhere was this greater than in the border states. For Lincoln and the Republicans, the fate of the Union was at stake. In Kentucky, conservative Unionists, states' rights Democrats, and rebel sympathizers, though differing on the war, agreed in their vigorous opposition to Lincoln and the Republicans. The question for dominant conservatives like Bramlette and Prentice was, should they align with the Democrats of the North, or should they quixotically seek the formation of a new national conservative party led by old Whigs who supported the war but opposed the perceived radicalism of the Republican Party? Only a relatively small minority of Kentuckians favored Lincoln as the only hope for success in the war. In most cases, they had reluctantly decided to support emancipation, but not black recruitment. The most notable Lincoln backers in the Bluegrass State were Robert J. Breckinridge and the more conservative Speed brothers. But even the Reverend Breckinridge recoiled at the prospect of associating with the radical Republicans of the North. As temporary chairman of the convention of the National

Union Party (the Republican Party renamed), on June 7, 1864, Breckinridge exclaimed to the delegates, "As a Union party I will follow you to the ends of the earth. . . . But as an Abolition party—as a Republican party—as a Whig party—as a Democratic party—as an American party, I will not follow you one foot."[81]

In an effort to gain the advantage over both the Republicans on the left and the states' rights Democrats on the right, conservative Unionists in March 1864 called for a convention of like-minded delegates to meet on May 25 in Louisville. Led by old Whig activists, the delegates retained the official designation of the Union Democratic Party as a gesture of bipartisanship in order to attract Democrats, mainly those who had voted for Stephen A. Douglas in 1860. Supporters of Lincoln also called for their convention to meet on May 25 in Louisville. By meeting at the same time, their leaders, who referred to themselves as Unconditional Unionists, hoped to persuade many of the conservative Unionists to support the president on a platform endorsing emancipation and to join them in sending delegates to the National Union convention in Baltimore. They were soon disappointed. The conservatives heard speeches by Wolford and others blasting Lincoln and condemning the enlistment of blacks in the army. Wolford promised that if the military attempted to interfere with the election, "Bayonet would be met with Bayonet," and he admonished his friends to prepare for the conflict. His remarks, according to an observer, were "highly applauded" by the delegates, making unlikely an Unconditional Unionist–conservative fusion.[82]

The conservative Unionist, or "Union Democratic," convention, chaired by James Guthrie, former treasury secretary in the Franklin Pierce administration and president of the Louisville and Nashville Railroad, proceeded to appoint delegates to the national Democratic convention scheduled to meet in Chicago later in the summer. They concluded that in order to defeat Lincoln and the Republicans, northern Democrats who had supported Douglas in 1860 would be willing to fuse with border state conservatives on a platform supporting the war on the basis of the Union only, leaving emancipation and other issues to the states. Old Whigs like Prentice envisioned the selection of former president Millard Fillmore as the coalition's candidate for president. Responding to criticism in the *Washington Daily Chronicle* and other Republican newspapers, conservatives emphatically denied that they supported the Copperhead (peace) wing of the northern Democratic Party.[83] The Unconditional Unionists, though dismayed by the turn of events in the conservative convention but still hopeful of a merger, accommodated to political realities in the Bluegrass State and rejected a resolution endorsing Lincoln. Instead, they quietly selected delegates to the Baltimore convention with the understanding that they would vote to nominate Lincoln.[84]

The Wickliffe Democrats of 1863, proclaiming that they alone were true to the old states' rights Democratic Party, met on June 28, 1864, in Louisville. After hearing speeches from Senator Powell and other states' rights Democrats, the delegates adopted a peace platform. Meeting at a time when the armies of Grant and William Tecumseh Sherman appeared stymied in the South and when battlefield casualties were mounting, the delegates pronounced Lincoln's attempt at coercion of the Confederate States "an act of suicidal folly." They also denounced the presumed effort by Lincoln and the federal government "to strike down State sovereignty," elevate "the African race to citizenship," and organize blacks "into standing armies to control white men." The Democrats also demanded that Lincoln revoke Burbridge's order barring the *Cincinnati Enquirer* and the *Chicago Times* from the state. Both were Copperhead newspapers. Finally, the convention appointed delegates to the national party's convention in Chicago.[85] This meant that Kentucky would have two delegations in the Democratic convention—the conservative Unionist and the Wickliffe (peace) Democrat.

To so-called Unconditional Unionists and to military commanders like Burbridge, Kentucky, by the summer of 1864, seemed on the verge of rebellion. Contributing to their fears, as well as to those of conservatives, was another Confederate raid, this one in June, by General Morgan, who swept through Lexington and as far as Cynthiana in northern Kentucky before being repulsed by Union troops. Morgan's audacious raid spawned increased guerrilla activity and lawlessness in the state. On June 21 General Sherman, the overall commander in the region, ordered General Burbridge to take "determined action" to suppress the guerrillas, whom he characterized as "wild beasts, unknown to the usages of war." Sherman, then campaigning in northern Georgia, specifically instructed Burbridge to round up all men and women who had given aid to the guerrillas and send them south. On the Missouri-Kansas border it was already army policy to execute bushwhackers and guerrillas as soon as they were captured and to remove rebel families from the afflicted counties.[86]

By July, even Lincoln, despite his intention to respect Kentucky's laws and civil authorities, had concluded that he must take extraordinary action to preserve the peace and forestall a rebel insurgency in the Bluegrass State. Western governors, deeply concerned about the resurgence of Copperhead strength in their own states, pleaded with the president to have the army suppress rebel sympathizers in neighboring Kentucky. Governor John Brough of Ohio wrote Secretary of War Stanton, "You must change policy in Kentucky. . . . Nothing but a vigorous application of [the] Maryland policy" of military control "will save Kentucky, and the longer that is delayed the more dangerous Kentucky becomes" to the Union.[87]

On July 5 the president boldly acted by suspending the writ of habeas corpus and establishing martial law in the state. Citing the congressional act of March 3, 1863, that granted him the authority to suspend the writ "whenever in his judgment the public safety may require it," Lincoln announced that the deplorable situation in Kentucky necessitated its suspension. He explained that "on several occasions" recently the "insurgents . . . in large force" had entered the state, and "not without aid and comfort furnished by disaffected and disloyal citizens of the United States." These incursions, the president declared, had "not only greatly disturbed the public peace but [had] overborne the civil authorities and made flagrant civil war, destroying property and life." Furthermore, "combinations [had] been formed" in Kentucky "with a purpose of inciting" civil war within the state, "and thereby to embarrass the United States armies now operating . . . in Virginia and Georgia" under Grant and Sherman. Lincoln insisted, however, that the suspension of the writ of habeas corpus and the imposition of martial law would not "interfere with the holding of lawful elections, or with the proceedings of the constitutional legislature of Kentucky or with the administration of justice in the courts of law." These civil functions, he informed Kentuckians, would continue unimpeded as long as they did not "affect the military operations" of the federal armies.[88] The president's promise, made in distant Washington, regarding restrictions on the martial law that he had proclaimed in the Bluegrass State proved a slender reed against the zealousness of military officers like General Burbridge.

Burbridge's officers immediately began rounding up and jailing "disloyal" citizens. In addition to the earlier imprisonment of Lieutenant Governor Jacob, Burbridge and his officers arrested Chief Justice Joshua F. Bullitt and local political leaders suspected of "treason." The military authorities on August 11 abruptly exiled to Canada almost forty citizens of western Kentucky, including women and children. On July 16 Burbridge decreed that for every Unionist murdered by guerrillas, four partisan prisoners would be executed. During the months that followed, scores of guerrillas reportedly fell to army firing squads or hangings. Rebels retaliated in kind.[89] Burbridge soon gained the epithet "the Butcher" and became the most vilified person in the history of the state.

Despite Lincoln's admonition against military interference in political campaigns, Burbridge, before the state election on August 1, purged conservative Alvin Duvall's name from the polls for judge of the Court of Appeals, the only important state office to be filled. At the last minute, however, the conservatives gleefully trumped the general's action by placing former chief justice George Robertson on the ballot against M. M. Benton, the Unconditional Unionist candidate. Though only 6,541 voters dared to defy military intimidation to cast their ballots, Robertson handily won the election.[90]

As expected, the Breckinridge-led Kentucky delegation in the National Union (Republican) convention in Baltimore in June cast their ballots for the Abraham Lincoln–Andrew Johnson ticket. They also supported the resolution, urged by Lincoln, calling for a constitutional amendment abolishing slavery everywhere in the United States. The seating of the Missouri radicals instead of the conservative delegation, along with the party's antislavery platform, increased the determination of conservative Unionists in Kentucky, Maryland, and Delaware and also of like-minded men in the North to seek an alignment with the Democrats in the presidential election. (See chapter 9 for the seating of the Missouri radicals.) The *Saint Louis Daily Missouri Republican* told its readers that the proceedings in the Baltimore convention indicated that Lincoln and his party had abandoned all pretense of moderation and conciliation and said that conservative Unionists must seek an accommodation with other anti-Republican elements.[91] Before they agreed to a merger, conservatives demanded two important concessions from their old political foes: The Democrats must support a war platform and must put an old-line Whig on the ticket.

With such a fusion in mind, many old Whigs, who had never warmed to General McClellan, the leading Democratic candidate, began to beat the drums for former president Fillmore to head the presidential ticket. Several border state conservatives and Congressman John Todd Stuart of Illinois, who had introduced a young Lincoln to law and to Whig politics, urged Fillmore to become a candidate. On July 2 George Read Riddle of Delaware, who had replaced James A. Bayard in the Senate, also, at the request of several colleagues (probably border state congressmen), wrote Fillmore asking him to run for president. Fillmore replied that he had "no desire under any circumstances to be president again." He informed Senator Riddle that he supported McClellan "as the conservative Union candidate" for the office but said that he would not take part in the campaign.[92]

By the time the Democrats met in Chicago in late August, the growing war-weariness in the North, with no end in sight to the fighting, had greatly strengthened the party's Copperhead wing. This meant that the Copperheads, led by Clement L. Vallandigham of Ohio, who had returned from exile, would oppose any Democratic compromise with border state Unionists or other conservatives who supported the war. They also plotted against McClellan's candidacy with the intent of putting one of their own at the head of the party's ticket. Peace Democrats, however, ultimately accepted the general as the party's standard-bearer, believing that despite his support for the war, they could control him when he became president.[93]

When the border state Unionists arrived in Chicago in late August, they still had hopes that they could play a decisive role in the convention. They believed that the delegates could be persuaded to adopt a platform supporting the war but leaving emancipation to the states. Realizing that McClellan would win the presidential nomination, the conservatives expected the convention to choose an old-line Whig for vice president, preferably from the border states. A border state selection, they believed, would undercut the National Union Party's choice of southern Unionist Andrew Johnson of Tennessee as Lincoln's running mate.[94] (Many northerners, including Lincoln, considered Tennessee, with its relatively large Union population, to be a border state.)

The Kentucky conservative delegation planned to nominate Governor Bramlette for vice president, but on the eve of the convention he wrote James Guthrie that he would not be a candidate. The governor explained, "A series of vexatious and annoying acts have been inflicted upon the people of Kentucky" by Lincoln and federal authorities (he meant the suspension of the writ of habeas corpus and the establishment of martial law). These acts, Bramlette insisted, "[were] intended to provoke some inconsiderate and hasty action upon my part . . . which might furnish an excuse for seizing military possession of the State and crushing the civil authorities. I seriously fear that if I were to be nominated by the Convention it would be the signal for renewed efforts by a malevolent fanaticism to utterly destroy the peace and security" of Kentucky and would "incite a condition of affairs dangerous to our national security. To avoid all pretence or excuse for such inflictions I desire my name withheld, or, if presented, withdrawn."[95] With the nation bitterly divided over the stalemated war and the fall elections looming on the horizon, Bramlette's letter to Guthrie reflected the anxiety and bitter divisions that had come to characterize political affairs in Kentucky and elsewhere by the summer of 1864.

On August 28, the day before the opening of the Democratic convention in Chicago, the conservative Unionists, reportedly consisting of delegates from thirty-two states, held a "consultation" meeting in the city. It was really a preconvention that was designed to publicize their reasons for opposing Lincoln and demonstrate to Democrats that conservatives also favored peace, but not at the expense of the Union. One sympathetic newspaper reported, with apparent exaggeration, that between 25,000 and 30,000 enthusiastic people attended the meeting. The conservatives adopted an address to the public charging that Lincoln had "proved himself wholly unfit for the high station" he held. His failings were extensive, they claimed: "He has declared his intention to change the character of the war from the single object of upholding the Government to that of a direct interference with the domestic institutions of the State." Among other transgressions, they said, "[he] has suppressed the freedom of elections in the Border States by taking military possession of the polls. He has stricken down the freedom of the press where rebellion did not exist." The conservative Unionist address assailed the president for his "refusal to listen to terms of peace upon the simple basis of the Union and the Constitution, and by the prostitution of all the powers of the Government to the bane purpose of forcibly securing his own re-election." Before the meeting adjourned, the conservatives endorsed McClellan for president and William B. Campbell, a former Whig governor of Tennessee and a hero of the Mexican-American War, for vice president.[96] They believed that on a war platform and with a McClellan-Campbell ticket, a conservative-Democratic coalition could win in November.

When the Democratic convention met the next day, both the Kentucky conservative and peace delegations were seated, but with only one-half vote for each delegate. The convention cheered the conservative Unionist address as it was read from the floor, but it had little influence on the proceedings. Vallandigham and the Copperheads had seized control of the convention, and brushing aside resolutions supporting the war, they adopted a peace platform that pronounced the conflict a failure. The platform demanded that "immediate efforts be made for a cessation of hostilities, with a view to an ultimate convention of states" for the purpose of restoring the Union as it had been before the war. This meant that slavery, though seemingly dying as a result of the war and Lincoln's policies, would receive a new lease on life in many areas of the South. The Democratic delegates dutifully nominated McClellan for president, despite a lack of Copperhead enthusiasm for him; however, they chose a peace Democrat, Congressman George H. Pendleton of Ohio, for vice president.

The peace platform of the Chicago convention stunned conservative Unionists and Democrats who supported the war, despite McClellan's labored repudiation of its cease-fire provision. The outrage among war supporters in the border states became greater soon after the adjournment of the convention when the electrifying news of General Sherman's capture of Atlanta, preceded in August by the navy's capture of Mobile Bay, Alabama, swept the country. After a long period of anguish and doubt for northerners and border state loyalists, victory for the Union at last seemed in sight under Republican leadership. The *Baltimore American*, which had supported the conservative effort to fuse with the Democrats, immediately denounced the Chicago platform and, though admitting that Lincoln had made grievous errors, threw its support behind the president in the election.[97]

Marylander John Pendleton Kennedy, a distinguished man of letters who had served in Fillmore's cabinet, hotly pronounced the Democratic platform "perfectly detestable—cowardly, false and treacherous." McClellan's "nomination by such a body of men" who drew up the war-failure platform, Kennedy wrote a friend, "totally disables [him] from any useful service in this crisis even if he should be elected," a view that Lincoln and members of his cabinet shared. Kennedy declared that he had little faith in Lincoln, but contrary to what border state Unionists like Bramlette and Senator Garret Davis had charged, Kennedy did not think the president was "a tyrant, or at all likely to overthrow the government." "My complaint," he said, "is that he does not prosecute the war with vigor—that he is often too lenient and compliant with the influences" around him. Kennedy, however, chose not to vote in the election.[98]

Other border state conservatives who were appalled by the defeatist platform of the Democrats reluctantly declared their intention to vote for Lincoln. The public support for the president by Governor Augustus W. Bradford, Union gubernatorial candidate Thomas Swann, and Charles C. Fulton of the *Baltimore American*, as well as by Montgomery Blair, influenced Maryland conservatives to back the president in the election. This support occurred despite the presence in the Republican campaign of Henry Winter Davis, a radical and a political enemy of the Blairs in state politics. Davis, an unrelenting critic of the president in the House of Representatives, only grudgingly campaigned for Lincoln.

On the other hand, some border state leaders, having committed themselves to the anti–Republican Party position, swallowed their opposition to the Democratic war-failure platform and supported McClellan. They insisted that McClellan would be more effective than Lincoln in restoring the Union, a weak argument at best. They also believed that as president the Young Napoleon would control Vallandigham and the Copperheads in his party, an even weaker argument. Reverdy Johnson of Maryland spoke in the North as well as in Maryland for McClellan; however, he carefully refrained from alluding to the Democratic peace platform. In a September 16 public letter to McClellan supporters in New York, Johnson, who in 1861 had defended the president's suspension of the writ of habeas corpus in Maryland, declared that he had lost all hope of a successful termination of the rebellion while Lincoln was in office. The Maryland senator listed numerous reasons for the president's failure, including "his unsteadiness in any policy, . . . his ignorant and mischievous interference with our military campaigns, . . . his frequent and nearly fatal changes of commanders, . . . his permitting military interference with elections, [and] his justifying arrests without specifications of charges." The election of McClellan, Johnson predicted, would lead to a quick restoration of peace and reunion.[99]

In supporting McClellan, the *Washington National Intelligencer*, like Johnson, focused on "Mr. Lincoln's Record" of failure rather than on the Democrat platform. The editor, James C. Welling, put the best face possible on McClellan's less than sterling military record. At the same time, he lambasted Lincoln's "military tyranny" in Kentucky and in the West (Midwest) and also his alleged support of the ironclad loyalty oath for Maryland voters. Welling frequently cited conservative hero Fillmore's opposition to

Lincoln and the Republicans. In a September 28, 1864, letter to a friend, which was printed in the *National Intelligencer* and in other anti-Republican newspapers, Fillmore wrote that he looked "upon the election of Gen. McClellan as the last hope for the restoration of the Union, an honorable peace, and the security of personal liberty."[100]

In Missouri, the conservative *Saint Louis Daily Missouri Republican* insisted that the general's pledge to restore the Union if elected did not conflict with the peace plank in the Democratic platform. Indeed, the editor argued, in a fine piece of rationalization, that if McClellan, a more sympathetic candidate than Lincoln, won, the Confederate masses would insist that their leaders make peace on the basis of reunion alone.[101] He conveniently ignored the fact that the Confederates would view a cease-fire preparatory to peace negotiations as an admission of Union defeat. Republicans and most border state Unionists, including Missourians, understood that this would be the outcome of a cease-fire.

The threat of widespread violence and military suppression plagued the presidential campaign in Kentucky, more so than in any other state. The president's suspension of the writ of habeas corpus in the state in July and General Burbridge's repressive measures inflamed conservative Unionists and Wickliffe peace Democrats alike. Federal army officers and Unconditional Unionists often identified opponents of Lincoln and the Republicans as Confederate sympathizers who, they claimed, gave aid and comfort to rebel guerrillas and other lawless groups. Burbridge promised to suppress all newspapers that were published "in the interest of the rebellion"; however, he apparently only prohibited the circulation of two newspapers in the state, one of which was the Copperhead *Cincinnati Enquirer*. Refusing to be intimidated by the military, conservative speakers and editors heatedly denounced Lincoln and Burbridge for their "tyrannical" acts. Prentice's *Louisville Daily Journal* labeled Lincoln "the chief tyrant of the country" and maintained, "His movements against the rebellion have been a series of the most wretched military mistakes, stupidities, and blunders on record." The *Journal* even assailed Lincoln for his presumed indifference to the cruel treatment of Union soldiers in rebel prisons. Although Prentice did not write all the editorials, including that one, he did control their content.[102]

The *Louisville Daily Journal* also leveled its editorial guns on Lincoln's vice presidential candidate, Andrew Johnson. The editor characterized the Tennessee military governor as "the meanest, vilest, most unscrupulous, most malignant, and most contemptible of all [Lincoln's] sub-tyrants, satraps, underlings" in the South. The *Journal*, which as a Whig newspaper had old scores to settle with the Democrat Johnson, specifically denounced the Tennessean for requiring a stringent loyalty oath for voting in the 1864 election in his state. Like other conservative Unionists who supported the war but not Lincoln, the *Journal* ignored the Democratic peace platform. Conservative speakers for McClellan included the top political leaders in the state: Governor Bramlette, Senator Garret Davis, former governor James F. Robinson, Lieutenant Governor Richard Jacob, and Frank Wolford. These speakers received campaign points from the *Louisville Daily Journal*.[103] The Wickliffe (peace) Democrats, in counties where they had the freedom to campaign, joined in the vitriol against Lincoln. Although Bramlette and the conservative Unionists distanced themselves from the Copperheads of the North and the peace party in their own state, they did not object when the Wickliffe faction fused their McClellan electoral slate with the conservative ticket.

Bramlette had a one-sided, jaundiced view of voter intimidation in the state. He believed that Burbridge and his officers alone were attempting to suppress a free ballot in the election. The governor ignored reports of violence and intimidation against Lincoln supporters perpetrated in some cases by Kentucky troops, whom an assistant inspector general of the army characterized as "merely a uniformed mob."[104] Robert J. Breckinridge and a few other Lincoln champions, sometimes in the face of threats of violence, campaigned in the state for the president. Breckinridge also stumped Ohio for Lincoln.

On September 3 Bramlette shot off a sharp letter to Lincoln, forcefully protesting against Burbridge and his underlings' interference in the election. He informed the president, "The course pursued by many of those intrusted [*sic*] with Federal authority in Kentucky [has] aroused the determined opposition to your re-election of at least three-fourths of the people." The governor attacked Lincoln for permitting the question of slavery "to obstruct the restoration of national authority." Suggesting that the president should abandon his antislavery policy, Bramlette declared that Kentuckians were "not willing to sacrifice a single life or imperil the smallest right of free white men for the sake of the Negro." Furthermore, he denounced Lincoln for treating Kentucky as "a rebellious and conquered province" by imposing martial law on the state. At stake in the matter, Bramlette angrily told the president, was "how much a brave and manly people [would] bear rather than revolt against their Government." He insisted that "a change of policy [was] essential to the salvation of our country."[105] No reply from Lincoln to Bramlette's letter has been found.

For Lincoln, a fine line existed between harsh criticism and statements encouraging rebellion. Lincoln seemed to believe that Bramlette had crossed that line, but if he had acted to stifle Bramlette, he could have expected serious consequences for the Union cause in Kentucky and also for Republican candidates, including himself, in the national election. Bramlette, for his part, refused to admit that his strong denunciation of Lincoln and the national government's policies and actions would encourage rebellion. If for no other reason, the governor did not want a civil war in the state that could place Unionist lives and fortunes in the hands of the Confederates.

Nothing in the anti-Republican campaign of 1864 in Kentucky exceeded the harsh editorial that appeared in the *Louisville Daily Journal* on November 2, six days before the election. The writer, probably associate editor Paul R. Shipman, exclaimed that the presidential election would be "the beginning of our deliverance from the 'valley of the shadow of death,' or it [would be] the beginning of the end of the Republic." The *Journal* proclaimed, "On that day, either the voice of *the people* will command the restoration of the constitution, or the voice of a *minority*, who are blinded and inflamed by demagogic falsehoods . . . will overrule, by fraud and violence combined, the voice and the will of a majority." The editor charged, "The Jacobin abolition faction," if victorious, "[will] prolong the war . . . until every family shall have yielded up its members to slaughter; and will maintain themselves in their infernal career over our prostrate liberty and Union by the power of a Negro army!" The *Journal* implored Kentuckians to go to the polls "on this great day of trial [and] let there be no laggards, no cowardly skulking, no desertion from the post of duty."[106] The Confederate press could not have been more graphic in its vilification of Lincoln and the Republicans.

On October 17 Governor Bramlette issued a proclamation warning the military against interfering with the November 8 election. He directed the sheriffs to arrest and hold for jury indictments individuals, presumably including military officers, who violated the state election laws. Bramlette also instructed election officials to shut down the polls if they were unable to hold a free election. The governor's proclamation strengthened the authority of local officials in the election and reduced the threat of military interference, though rebel guerrillas and rogue Kentucky troops still kept some Lincoln supporters from the polls.[107]

In one of the most divisive and important elections in American history, Lincoln and the Republicans won a critical victory on November 8.[108] McClellan carried only Kentucky, Delaware, and New Jersey. Kentucky voters gave McClellan by far the largest margin of popular votes in the three states; he received 64,301 votes to Lincoln's 27,786 in the state. McClellan even won Kentucky's soldiers' vote; in other states, "Father Abraham" easily captured this vote.[109]

Fearing disorders in the aftermath of the election, General Burbridge moved quickly to arrest three prominent conservatives whom he charged with inciting insurrection. All three men—John B. Houston, Lieutenant Governor Richard T. Jacob, and Frank L. Wolford—had ended the campaign with "incendiary" speeches against Lincoln and the military for interfering in the election. On election day, Burbridge began by arresting Houston and ordering him banished from the state. The next day, the general informed Bramlette that in taking Houston into custody he had exercised the authority delegated to him by the president to suppress disloyalty where civil officials refused to act. Bramlette rushed to the Frankfort telegraph office and sent a message to Lincoln strongly protesting against the seizure; he claimed that it had occurred "for no other offence" than opposition to Lincoln's election. The governor told Lincoln, "Surely [you] cannot sanction this ostracizing of loyal men who honestly opposed you."[110]

Lincoln facetiously replied to Bramlette that if Houston's campaign against his election had been the reason for his detention, he "should have heard of more than one arrest in Kentucky on election day." He continued, "If however, Gen. Houston has been arrested for no other cause than opposition to my re-election Gen. Burbridge will discharge him at once." The president sent a similar message to Burbridge, who in turn telegraphed Lincoln that the governor had misinformed him about the case. Houston, the general said, had been taken into custody because his "influence & speeches have been of a treasonable character." Burbridge, however, did not explain the nature of the treason. Nonetheless, he agreed to release Houston and permit him to return to his home, under a bond promising "not again to oppose the Govt." Burbridge took the opportunity to lecture Lincoln: "A vigorous policy against rebel sympathizers in this State must be pursued & if I have erred I fear I have made too few arrests instead of too many."[111]

Undeterred by the president's intervention in the Houston case, Burbridge on November 9 ordered the arrests of Jacob and Wolford and also Paul R. Shipman of the *Louisville Daily Journal*, whose articles, the general charged, had promoted treason. Burbridge directed that the three men be sent through Confederate lines.[112] He later ordered the arrest of Joshua F. Bullitt of the Kentucky Court of Appeals on the same grounds. Bramlette again appealed to the president to intervene and reverse Burbridge's action. Admitting that Jacob and Wolford (he apparently did not know of Shipman's arrest) had used intemperate language during the campaign, Bramlette told Lincoln that they had been falsely accused of giving aid and encouragement to treason. The governor denounced Burbridge for "pursuing a course calculated to exasperate and infuriate rather than pacify and conciliate" and said, "His whole course for weeks past has been such as was most calculated to inaugurate revolt and produce collisions" with the people. "My utmost powers," Bramlette claimed, "have been taxed to frustrate the evils of [Burbridge's] course, and preserve peace and order. I have thus far succeeded." However, he warned, "[I] shall need your cooperation to attain" peace and respect for civil authorities in the state and to defeat "the blunderings of [Burbridge's] weak intellect and over-weaning vanity."[113]

In addition, the governor forwarded to Lincoln the petition of several prominent Unionists, including the president's friend Joshua Speed, attesting to Jacob's loyalty. They especially asked that the lieutenant governor not be sent to the Confederacy, where, they said, he had no friends. The petitioners failed to mention Burbridge's detention of Wolford.[114]

Bramlette also dispatched Hodges of the *Frankfort Commonwealth*, who had supported Lincoln in the election, and General Samuel G. Suddarth, commander of the governor's state militia, to Washington to report to the president on the situation in Kentucky. They met with Lincoln on November 22 and informed him that in addition to guerrilla bands infesting many neighborhoods, the main problem in the state was General Burbridge. Lincoln asked the two Kentuckians, "How would Genl. Burnsides suit the people of Kentucky" as a replacement for Burbridge? Hodges promptly replied that the change "would be hailed with joy by the great mass of the Union people of the State." They sanguinely predicted that it would guarantee Kentucky's ratification of the abolition amendment, soon to be debated in Congress and strongly supported by Lincoln. Finally, Hodges, the recipient of Lincoln's famous antislavery letter of April 4, 1864, told the president, "There are thousands of good Union men in Kentucky, who went off with the Chicago [Democratic] concern—wish to come back—many have already come back, and will give your administration a hearty support." But, he said, Lincoln must stop the military's intervention in the civil affairs of the state.[115] The president, however, did not direct the army to cease its involvement in civil matters, nor did he revoke his July 5 suspension of the writ of habeas corpus. Not until several months after the war were the last vestiges of martial law ended in Kentucky and the privilege of the writ restored.[116]

After the meeting with Hodges and Suddarth, Lincoln telegraphed Bramlette and informed him that he and Secretary of War Stanton would try "to devise means of pacification and harmony for Kentucky," adding, "We hope to effect [it] soon, now that the *passion-exciting* subject of the election is past."[117] Lincoln, however, soon received disturbing news that contradicted the favorable reports of Bramlette, Hodges, and others on political and social conditions in Kentucky. One report indicated that Kentucky was about "to inaugurate a second rebellion," followed by a declaration of independence.[118] After a tour of the state in December 1864, E. D. Ludington, an assistant inspector general in the army, somberly informed Secretary of War Stanton, "A large majority of Kentuckians to-day are undoubtedly disloyal." He explained that while "many people avowed their devotion to the Union" during the first two years of the war, "the moment that the Government attempted to draft men or enlist Negroes, the true feeling of these people were evinced. They resisted our officers, and became more violent in their denunciations of the administration than the original rebels." Ludington told Stanton, and probably by extension Lincoln, "There is scarcely any security for person or property" in the state. "In nearly every county guerrillas are destroying the property and taking the lives of all who have been, or now are, in the U.S. armies. The citizens are so bitterly arrayed against each other as to afford immunity, if not assistance, to these desperadoes, for each party is glad to see men of the other [party] murdered."[119] Although conditions in Kentucky were indeed disturbing, Ludington probably exaggerated the pervasiveness of the disorders.

Ludington called for the removal of both Governor Bramlette and General Burbridge. Bramlette, he contended, could not restore law and order. The governor "prefers union to rebellion," but, Ludington wrongly claimed, "he knows his people are disloyal, and so qualifies his Unionism" by assailing the government and its policies. If Bramlette continued "to array himself against the Administration, there should be no hesitancy in superseding him." Burbridge, Ludington said, "is now heartily hated by a majority of the people," and did not have the "capacity [or] character" to command the military in Kentucky. Ludington concluded that only troops from other states could put down the guerrillas and rebel sympathizers in the state.[120]

Fearful Unconditional Unionists dispatched petitions to Lincoln describing a doomsday scenario if the government released Lieutenant Governor Jacob and the other political prisoners. The petitioners charged that Jacob "did not content himself with the utterance of opinions; . . . he indulged in violent threats." According to these Unionists, in a speech at New Albany, Indiana, across the Ohio River from Louisville, the lieutenant governor declared that "Kentucky had tolerated the election of Mr. Lincoln once; she would not do so a second time." Speaking in Louisville on the night before the election, Jacob reportedly "named Union men in the city who would have to leave" if McClellan won the election. "The devoted friends of the administration [had] demanded his arrest, and General Burbridge [had] obeyed their wishes," the petitioners reported. William C. Goodloe and Charles Eginton wrote the president that "the evil influence" exercised by Jacob and other conservative leaders "[rendered] it more dangerous for Union Men now than at any previous period" during the war. These two Unconditional Unionists, or radicals by Kentucky standards, maintained, "Kentucky is to day more disloyal than Tennessee & but for the military force here, no loyal man could remain in the state. If severe measures are not used towards the leaders—we shall have an out breake [sic] here in sixty days."[121]

Robert Breckinridge also demanded that Lincoln sustain Burbridge's action in arresting Jacob, Wolford, Bullitt, and Shipman. The release of these men, Breckinridge claimed, would crush the Union cause in Kentucky. The reverend charged that "the relapsed portion of the Union party," headed by Bramlette, had betrayed Kentucky and the Union. He advised the president to ignore Bramlette and act only through federal officers in the state. "The alternative," he said, "is anarchy and bloodshed."[122] Bullitt was later released at Memphis by the army, but when a furious Burbridge sought his rearrest, he fled to Canada. The fate of Shipman is unknown.

When Congress met in December 1864, Senator Powell introduced a resolution demanding that the president provide information on the arrests and detentions of Jacob and Wolford, which the Kentuckian characterized as a "gross violation" of their rights. After the Republicans added an amendment to the Powell resolution requesting, not demanding, the information, the resolution overwhelmingly received the Senate's approval.[123] Meanwhile, Burbridge had secretly banished Jacob through the Confederate lines. The lieutenant governor eventually made his way to Richmond, Virginia, where on December 26 he wrote Lincoln and appealed for permission to reenter the Union. The only charge that could be brought against him, Jacob told the president, was that he had vigorously opposed his reelection.[124]

After his receipt of Jacob's appeal and the Senate's request for information on the Kentucky prisoners, the president directed General Grant to permit the lieutenant governor to pass through the Union lines to visit Lincoln in Washington. On January 18, 1865, Lincoln interviewed Jacob and released him to return to Kentucky. He told Jacob, "I decide nothing as to the right or wrong of your arrest, but act in the hope that there is less liability to misunderstanding among Union men now than there was at the time of the arrest."[125] On January 31 Lincoln sent a message to the Senate containing the documents in the military arrests of Jacob and Wolford. Five days later, Jacob made a hero's return to the state senate, where he resumed the position of presiding officer. Undaunted by his experience and unswayed by Lincoln's hope that he would cease his agitation, the lieutenant governor in a speech on the senate floor denounced Burbridge and those who had arrested and banished him to the Confederacy. Wolford, who earlier had vowed to "fester in a prison" until his innocence was acknowledged, was quietly released from his captivity in Covington, Kentucky, across the Ohio River from Cincinnati.[126] After the war he remained active in politics, serving as state adjutant general and in Congress for two terms during the 1880s.

Governor Bramlette and the conservative Unionists soon succeeded in their efforts to have Burbridge removed from command in the state. The final chapter in the Bramlette-Burbridge conflict began in mid-February 1865 when the general disbanded the governor's state military forces. Both a Kentucky congressional delegation and a legislative delegation visited Lincoln and informed him that federal troops in the state under Burbridge's command could not suppress the growing guerrilla threat. They argued that an expansion of the state militia was essential to success, which, they said, necessitated Burbridge's removal.[127]

Fearful that Lincoln would replace Burbridge with a conservative general, a delegation of Kentucky Unconditional Unionists also visited the president and lobbied for the appointment of the controversial General Benjamin F. Butler. Lincoln reportedly told them, "You howled when Butler went to New Orleans. Others howled when he was removed from command. Somebody has been howling since at his assignment to military command. How long will it be before you, who are howling for his assignment to rule Kentucky, will be howling to me to remove him?"[128]

On February 23, 1865, the president replaced Burbridge with General John M. Palmer, a native of Kentucky and an old political associate of Lincoln in Illinois. Palmer reputedly was "a good conservative general." Lincoln also asked the Kentucky legislature to submit a plan for raising state troops to aid federal units in subduing the guerrillas and pacifying the countryside. A correspondent of the *Cincinnati Daily Gazette* ruefully remarked that the president had abandoned the "Radical party" in Kentucky and had thrown his support to the conservatives who had bitterly opposed him.[129]

Most white Kentuckians hailed General Palmer's arrival, none more so than Bramlette. The governor immediately wrote Lincoln, "Maj Genl Palmer is with us—every shade of opinion seems to center in harmony with his appointment. The good you have done to Kentucky, and to our National Cause by giving us Genl Palmer, will exceed your most sanguine hopes." He confidently predicted, "Your Administration will no longer be presented in a false light to our people, by the wrongful acts of others"; he meant Burbridge and his subordinates.[130]

Even the *Louisville Daily Journal* moderated its opposition to Lincoln and expressed an understanding of the unprecedented difficulties that he had had to confront. On inauguration day, March 4, 1865, the editor (probably Prentice) remarked, "[Lincoln's] administration during the last four years may have, and doubtless has been marked by acts unwise and ill-timed, but it should be remembered, never since the government was framed has the Presidential office been encumbered by exigencies at once so novel and perilous as those which, from the inception of Mr. Lincoln's administration, have embarrassed his official labors." Perhaps recalling the

Journal's acerbic attacks on Lincoln during the 1864 campaign, the editor promised, "When we have reason to differ from him we shall endeavor to differ kindly."[131]

Governor Bramlette in his message to the General Assembly on January 6, 1865, also reflected a desire to put hostility to the Lincoln administration behind him and aid in carrying out the measures of the federal government. With this in mind, Bramlette recommended to the legislature that it should follow the example of Maryland and Missouri and provide for state emancipation (see chapters 8 and 9 for Maryland's and Missouri's actions on slavery). But, the governor said, emancipation should be accompanied by compensation to slaveholders and the colonization of blacks. In the General Assembly, the debate on emancipation became heated and long. In the end, conservative Unionists, joined by Wickliffe Democrats, defeated all resolutions providing for emancipation.[132]

The antislavery debate erupted again in early February over the proposed Thirteenth Amendment. Both Kentucky's U.S. senators, Garret Davis and Lazarus Powell, along with six of the state's nine members of the House of Representatives, voted against the antislavery amendment when Congress initiated it on January 31.[133] Bramlette urged the amendment's ratification, but with the proviso that the U.S. Treasury pay the state $34 million for the freed slaves. On the grounds that slavery in Kentucky existed "only as a nominal institution," the *Louisville Daily Journal* called for its ratification. The *Journal* maintained that the General Assembly should insist that Congress provide compensation to loyal owners of an amount not exceeding $300 for each slave enlisted in the Union army.[134] Finally, the New England–born Prentice, after years of defending the institution, announced in his newspaper that the death of slavery would end "the most fruitful source of political strife in America" and open the door for the future prosperity of Kentucky.[135]

Still, the majority in the General Assembly remained opposed to the amendment's ratification. Although recognizing that the war had doomed slavery, some members of the legislature voted against the amendment because, they argued, it would provide constitutional justification for federal intervention to protect blacks in freedom. Despite an effort to attach a compensation proviso to the amendment, the Kentucky legislature rejected it by a vote of 21 to 13 in the Senate and 56 to 28 in the House.[136] Bramlette, who at the last moment had pleaded with the legislators to ratify the freedom amendment, reported the disappointing news to Lincoln.[137]

General Palmer also expressed his disappointment with Kentucky's failure to ratify the Thirteenth Amendment. He signified his displeasure by closing "certain negro jails" (slave pens) in Louisville. Palmer followed this decision with an order on March 12 freeing the wives and children of black soldiers, which had been legislated by Congress on March 3 and approved by Lincoln. In this order, the general also announced that he expected "the loyal men and women of Kentucky [to] encourage colored men to enlist in the army" and to recognize "them as upholders of their Government and defenders of their homes." Although Palmer relaxed military interference in civil affairs, his action to free blacks cast a pall over his relationship with state conservatives and Wickliffe Democrats.[138] The bare bones of slavery unfortunately continued in Kentucky until December 1865, when the Thirteenth Amendment finally became a part of the Constitution, freeing the last slaves in the state.

The increased guerrilla activity in Kentucky, which was often tied to the effort to maintain slavery and race control, created deep concern for the president in early 1865, despite the success of Generals Grant, Sherman, and George H. Thomas in bringing the Union close to victory on the battlefield. A Kentucky supporter of emancipation criticized his fellow citizens for tolerating the guerrillas in order, he said, to hold on to the mirage of slavery: "Guerrillas sweep your State, killing citizens, burning your houses and robbing you of your property to save the Negro. A rebel Senator stated on the floor of the Kentucky Senate that these guerrillas were doing their deeds of darkness for that very purpose."[139] Indeed, the *Richmond Sentinel*, reputedly the organ of Jefferson Davis, in February 1865, as the Confederacy tottered toward defeat, encouraged rebels in Kentucky, Missouri, Tennessee, and elsewhere to carry on guerrilla warfare if the Confederacy "should not be able to maintain large regular armies in the field." The *Sentinel* admonished the guerrillas not to save the "craven submissionists . . . from the horrors of this new mode of warfare," calling them "more obnoxious than the Yankees" and charging, "They [should] be its first victims. Let them recollect the treatment of captured tories in the Revolution of 1776, and take warning from their fate."[140]

Kentucky's home-grown guerrillas needed no encouragement from Confederates in Richmond to engage in such violent tactics. Many of them had served with Morgan in his raids through Kentucky in 1863 and 1864 and had been cut off from their commands. Forming bands of between twenty and seventy-five men, they pillaged and terrorized the countryside. Guerrillas in some cases temporarily occupied towns, and they captured trains and steamboats. Some of the bands split up and became hardened outlaws and bushwhackers, robbing and plundering without regard to the allegiances of the people. By early 1865, their brutal exploits filled the columns of the *Louisville Daily Journal* and other newspapers in Kentucky and nearby states.

Vulnerable black troops became a special target of the guerrillas. The most egregious incident occurred about twenty miles from Louisville, near Simpsonville, on January 24, 1865. A band of fifteen guerrillas, including one "black scoundrel," after robbing the town, surprised a spread-out group of African American soldiers who were driving a herd of 900 government cattle from Camp Nelson to Louisville. The soldiers' commanding officer had remained in town drinking whiskey and threatening the inhabitants; the other officers, except for one lieutenant riding at the front of the herd, had stopped at houses on the road. The guerrillas attacked the rear of the column, killing thirty-five black soldiers, some of them after they had surrendered. Other soldiers escaped after incurring serious wounds.[141]

The most notorious of the guerrillas operating in Kentucky were William C. Quantrill, of Missouri infamy, and Marcellus Jerome Clarke. Quantrill and his band of about thirty renegades, seeking an area for their exploits where they would not be easily recognized, entered the state in early January 1865. They began plundering and murdering until May 10, when Quantrill was wounded and captured. He died in a Louisville federal prison on June 6.[142] Jesse and Frank James, who had ridden with him in Missouri and Kansas, did not follow Quantrill into Kentucky; they remained relatively safe at home in western Missouri, where they prepared for their legendary life of crime after the war.

Clarke had participated in General Morgan's raids into Kentucky and Ohio. At the battle of Cynthiana on June 12, 1864, Clarke, a native of Kentucky, received a wound and was left behind to recuperate. He remained in Kentucky, where he led guerrilla attacks on Unionists. His notoriety prompted the *Louisville Daily Journal* to single Clarke out for ridicule by referring to him as a girl named "Sue Mundy." The name stuck. Finally, in mid-March 1865 Clarke's guerrilla career ended when he was captured by federal troops, classified as a prisoner of war, and taken to a prison in Louisville. The military authorities, anxious to set a public example, insisted on trying Clarke as a guerrilla, though he maintained that he was a Confederate officer. In his brief trial before a military commission, Clarke claimed that he had not committed one-tenth of the outrages that had been charged to him. The commission refused to permit witnesses who, Clarke contended, would have placed him elsewhere at the time of the Simpsonville massacre of black troops, the most serious charge against him. Found guilty of murder and sentenced to be hanged, Clarke was given only a few hours to prepare for his fate. Before a large and raucous crowd in Louisville on March 15, Sue Mundy, only twenty years of age, calmly went to the gallows.[143]

As the war entered its final weeks, General Palmer took vigorous action to end the guerrilla violence. When he arrived in Kentucky on February 18, he conferred with Governor Bramlette and secured his cooperation in suppressing the guerrillas, a collaboration that had not existed between the governor and General Burbridge. Bramlette acquiesced in Palmer's use of black troops for guard and local duty, and the general on his part highly recommended that the War Department authorize the governor to raise five regiments of white troops "to quiet public apprehension." Palmer sought and obtained additional mounted troops, which, he reported, were "indispensable" to ending the guerrilla threat.[144]

Although Palmer did not condone summary executions, cavalry units often shot or hanged bushwhackers as soon as they were captured. The *Louisville Daily Journal* had earlier warned against such hasty justice, pointing out that not all persons who seized horses and clothing were desperadoes. "These things," the *Journal* pointed out, "are undoubtedly done to a considerable extent on both sides."[145] By May 1865, most of the guerrilla bands had been suppressed; however, lawlessness continued to afflict the countryside. Blacks became special objects of violence, and opposition to bona fide black freedom existed long after the war. The intrastate hostilities, pitting communities and families against each other, would be slow to heal in Kentucky and would make the restoration of law and order difficult.

The shocking murder of Abraham Lincoln on April 14 erased much of the bitterness toward him in Kentucky. Conservatives and some defeated Confederates joined with Unconditional Unionists to deplore the assassination and to reconsider Lincoln's importance in the war. Governor Bramlette issued a proclamation calling on Kentuckians to observe a day of mourning on April 19 for the fallen president. He declared, "Let every church bell be tolled throughout the Commonwealth; and on that day let all business be suspended and all business houses be closed, the public offices closed, and draped in mourning." At a mass meeting in Louisville on April 18, which was preceded by a three-mile-long procession of mourners, Bramlette addressed the crowd and apologized for his and other Kentuckians' repeated criticism of Lincoln during the war. "He was right and we were wrong," the governor frankly admitted. Bramlette solemnly predicted, "The name and cause of Mr. Lincoln will go down to future ages as part of the record of our country" during this revolutionary time. General Palmer, shaken by the tragic event in Washington, also spoke and admonished Kentuckians to remain calm and to continue the work of restoring peace. "The wicked need not rejoice nor the patriotic despond," he told the crowd. "The Government will still go on, and as great as the calamity is, the country will accomplish its high destiny" in the future.[146]

Kentucky, however, would long be troubled by the bitter memories of the internecine sectional conflict. The "Lost Cause" legend of Confederate rightness and nobility against an antagonistic and powerful North dominated by radicals became the accepted version of the war for thousands of Kentuckians, as well as for southerners in the former Confederate states. It has often been said, though perhaps half in jest, that Kentucky remained in the Union and opposed Lincoln's policies, waiting until after the war to join the defeated Confederacy. Kentuckians honored the heroes of the rebel cause and, after a brief interval, elected many of them to political office. Indeed, former Confederates became the driving force in the Democratic conservative coalition that opposed the Republican Party and black political rights during Reconstruction. As the historian of the Lost Cause in Kentucky memory has written, "Confederate credentials soon became almost a precondition for election" in the state. Former governor Bramlette, who was not a Republican, lamented after the war that the "old Union element" had been forced "to surrender to the defeated" rebels.[147] Kentucky became a Democratic state and would remain so well into the twentieth century, a political transformation that Whig icon Henry Clay and his disciple, Abraham Lincoln, would have found troubling.

CHAPTER 8

■

Union and Emancipation Triumphant: Maryland

In early 1863 Thomas Swann, a former Baltimore mayor and conservative Maryland Unionist, announced in a meeting of the Union State Central Committee, "We are in the midst of a revolution. We could not bring slavery back if we desired it." On March 28, 1863, the *Easton (Md.) Gazette* echoed this view when it declared, "Slavery is doomed, the question is how it should be eliminated."[1] This would have been a startling and risky declaration to make in Maryland before Lincoln signed the Emancipation Proclamation. But the war was producing a remarkable change in Unionists' attitudes toward slavery in the Old Line State. Although the proclamation did not apply to Maryland, it gave impetus to the movement to end slavery in the state. Prominent Unionists like Governor Augustus W. Bradford, former governor and now senator Thomas H. Hicks, and Senator-elect Reverdy Johnson, in addition to Swann, in 1863 began to reconsider their earlier, defiant opposition to emancipation. No doubt they were influenced by Lincoln's emancipation policy on the grounds that it was a war measure designed to strike at the heart of the rebellion, as well as by his warning that the "peculiar institution" could not survive the war and that it would be to their pecuniary interest to end slavery while federal compensation was possible.

A minority faction in the Union Party who described themselves as Unconditional Unionists—others referred to them as radicals—launched a movement in February 1863 for immediate emancipation. They called for the election of like-minded congressional and legislative candidates in the fall elections. Congressman Henry Winter Davis of Baltimore, who had begun the war as a conservative and who as late as December 1861 had condemned "the abolition assault in Congress on slavery," became the main spokesman for these radicals.[2] Lincoln's close ties with the Blairs, Davis's political enemies in Maryland politics, had made him an opponent of the president and a friend of radical Republicans in Congress. Most Unconditional Unionists, however, shunned identification with abolitionists or with congressional radicals like Senator Charles Sumner of Massachusetts and Representative Thaddeus Stevens of Pennsylvania. They denied that they favored black political equality, a frequent charge leveled against them. Both the conservative Unionists and the radical Unconditionals agreed that only the state, not Lincoln or Congress, could constitutionally end slavery in Maryland. Furthermore, they also agreed that emancipation should be initiated by a state convention and properly ratified by the voters.

Despite the momentum generated by Lincoln's Emancipation Proclamation, serious obstacles to black freedom in Maryland developed in 1863. In the eastern plantation counties, a strong resistance to ending slavery under any terms was led by Senator Anthony Kennedy and Representative John W. Crisfield. The failure of Congress in early 1863 to fund compensated emancipation for Maryland and Missouri also strengthened the proslavery forces. In addition, the state Union Party was divided over the timing of emancipation. The control of the Union Party, military campaigns and arrests in the state, and the recruitment of black troops also complicated the effort to abolish slavery.[3]

General Robert E. Lee's invasion of Maryland in late June 1863 created a crisis atmosphere and diverted attention from the emancipation issue. Baltimore, with its wealth and military resources, was believed to be Lee's main target, and fears gripped the state regarding the violence and ruin that his army would bring to the area.[4] As it turned out, Baltimore was not an objective of the Confederate army, though if Lee had won a series of victories elsewhere, he could have easily placed the city in his sights. Lee had several objectives in mind as he moved north. He wanted to disrupt the Army of the Potomac's plans for a summer offensive, relieve the Virginia countryside of the burden of provisioning two armies while the crops grew, replenish his own army's commissary, and encourage the growing northern desire for a negotiated peace, which, Lee believed, would secure Confederate independence.[5]

While Lee's main army moved northward through Frederick, Maryland, and toward southern Pennsylvania, General J. E. B. Stuart's dreaded cavalry entered Maryland near Rockford on June 28, beginning a spectacular raid around the Union army that became an ongoing controversy in the history of Lee's failure in the Gettysburg campaign. The raid took Stuart within twenty miles of Baltimore. Moving into north-central Maryland, Stuart encountered no resistance in the state until he reached Westminster on June 29. There, a detachment of Delaware cavalry momentarily delayed his effort to rejoin the main Confederate army in Pennsylvania. Stuart had already left Maryland when Union general Robert C. Schenck on June 30, from his headquarters in Baltimore, imposed martial law in the city and in the eastern counties. Schenck did little to soften his action when he announced that all civil government functions would continue, as long as they did not interfere with "the predominant power" of the military authority.[6]

Schenck, of Ohio, had served four terms as a Whig in the U.S. House of Representatives, including one as a colleague of Lincoln. In 1860 he had campaigned for Lincoln in Illinois and Ohio. In 1862, Schenck proved to be a capable second-tier army commander in Virginia; however, at the second battle of Bull Run on August 30, he received a severe wound. In September, although Schenck was unfit for field duty, the president placed him in command of the Middle Department. Before assuming command, Schenck returned to Ohio, ran for Congress against the Copperhead Clement L. Vallandigham, and won. As was the rule then, he did not take his seat until December 1863.[7]

Following General Schenck's orders of June 30, 1863, provost marshals and other army officers, driven also by their fears of a fifth column operating in eastern Maryland, began rounding up and incarcerating suspected rebels. The military arrested eighteen citizens when they attended the funeral of a Confederate soldier killed at Gettysburg. Schenck's officers even briefly took into custody Baltimore women who had given food and refreshments to Confederate prisoners en route to imprisonment in Fort McHenry. The arrests continued throughout the summer, with 361 detainees being confined in July alone. Almost all of those held by the military were later released after taking the loyalty oath.

Schenck also ordered the suppression of the *Baltimore Republican and Argus* for publishing "The Southern Cross," a famous poem that "breathed a strong Southern spirit." He banished both the publishers and the editors to the South on penalty of imprisonment if they returned. For good measure, the general suspended and seized the houses of three Baltimore arts and literature clubs on the grounds that they had given "countenance, encouragement, and aid to the unnatural and causeless rebellion." (Some of the members had opposed the war but apparently had not conspired against the Union.) On July 3 Schenck issued an order that Independence Day should be observed in every house and place of business in Baltimore by the display of the American flag. "If there be any spot where it does not appear," he announced, "its absence there will only prove that patriotic hearts do not beat beneath that roof."[8] Schenck, still suffering from his battlefield wound, which might have influenced his judgment, had overreacted to the secessionist threat in eastern Maryland and to the electrifying events associated with Lee's invasion. Whether Lincoln took notice of his political friend's actions at this time is unknown, but he soon became involved in the controversial recruitment of Maryland slaves by Schenck's subordinates.

Simultaneous with the military's action in arresting "traitors," the War Department began to enroll black troops in Maryland and in the other border states during the summer of 1863. This effort inevitably created white opposition and threatened the emancipation movement in Maryland by arousing racial fears. The decision to enlist blacks, one observer anxiously noted, "occasioned much excitement in the State," though it did not trigger the threatening levels of criticism it did in Kentucky.[9] On June 30, 1863, Schenck telegraphed Lincoln that he had 4,000 blacks at work on fortifications in the Baltimore area, and he asked the president for permission to enroll them as a regiment of sappers and miners. These blacks were either free or had been confiscated by the army from rebel masters.[10] When he received no immediate reply, Schenck on July 4 sent the president another message informing him that if the black laborers were not enlisted and organized as soldiers, he would discharge most of them from work on the fortifications. Schenck informed Lincoln that the African American laborers expressed a willingness to enlist. He reported also that as many as 200 blacks on the state's Eastern Shore wanted to join the army.[11]

Spurred to action by Schenck's second telegram, Lincoln on July 6, through Secretary of War Edwin M. Stanton, authorized the organization of the Baltimore regiment into the federal army.[12] Stanton appointed

Colonel William Birney, the son of the famous abolitionist and former Alabama planter James G. Birney, to enroll the regiment and placed him under Schenck's command with the authority to enlist free African Americans.[13] Hoping to mitigate the opposition of Maryland whites to black recruitment, the War Department agreed to credit the recruits to the state's conscription quota, as it later did in the other border states.[14] The concession, however, did little to appease whites on the issue, particularly in eastern Maryland.

In addition to recruiting African Americans from among the free black population, the army took in Maryland slaves, including some of Unionists, who fled from their masters in order to enlist. While General Schenck was absent in the North, Colonel Donn Piatt, who was left in command in Baltimore, gave Colonel Birney the authority to enlist the slaves. When Governor Bradford heard that Birney had enrolled fugitive slaves, he rushed to Washington and demanded that the president halt the practice. Lincoln assured the governor that no orders had been issued for the enlistment of slaves; however, he promised to study the matter and notify Bradford of his "conclusion."[15]

Meanwhile, Stanton had learned that Piatt, an erstwhile antislavery journalist, was enrolling slaves without the approval of the War Department. He summoned the colonel to Washington for an explanation. Piatt found Stanton at the Executive Mansion with Lincoln and Secretary of the Treasury Salmon P. Chase. According to Piatt, who that night wrote an account of the meeting, the president threatened him with dismissal from the army for authorizing the recruitment of the Maryland slaves. Piatt intimated that if dismissed, he would appeal to the public to sustain him. Lincoln, according to the colonel, went into a "rage" (doubtless an exaggeration) and directed him to countermand his order as well as he could. Piatt recorded that he "was saved cashiering" from the army "through the interference of Stanton and Chase, and the further fact that a row over such a transaction at that time would have been extremely awkward" for the administration. Later, in the 1880s, Piatt wrote that he did not blame the president for the unpleasant incident, since Lincoln understood, he said, "what has taken years for us to discover and appreciate"— that the Union could not have been saved if he had acted prematurely on his antislavery principles.[16]

The enrollment of slaves, however, continued. Governor Bradford in a long letter to Lincoln on September 28, 1863, again complained that, hav-

CHAPTER EIGHT

ing heard nothing further from him on the matter, he found the recruitment "all the more reprehensible if pursued without [the president's] express authority." Bradford cited one case in which a government steamer had been sent upriver in eastern Maryland with an armed guard and under cover of darkness to recruit slaves, including those of Unionists. Loyal owners, Bradford told Lincoln, should be "fully compensated" for their losses. He warned that Maryland would "not see her property of any kind wrested from her by armed force, with no emergent military necessity" and without a proper procedure for its implementation. The governor informed the president, "No policy adopted by the Government since the commencement of the Rebellion has ever awakened such unequivocal opposition" in the state as the seizure of the slaves of Unionists for military service and other purposes. Bradford sent Senator Hicks and Reverdy Johnson to Washington to deliver the letter to Lincoln.[17]

Surprised by Bradford's alarming letter, the president summoned the governor to meet with him on October 3.[18] After the conference, Lincoln had the War Department issue specific rules, as Bradford demanded, for the recruitment of African Americans not only in Maryland but also in Missouri and Tennessee (Kentucky, as previously mentioned, was exempted temporarily from the enlistment of blacks). The War Department explained that "the exigencies of the war [required] that colored troops should be recruited" in the border states. Essentially, the rules, in the form of a general order, provided that free African Americans, slaves of Unionists with the written consent of their owners, and slaves of rebels even without their masters' approval could be enlisted in the army. A compensation, not to exceed $300 for each slave, would be given to willing loyal owners, who must take "an oath of allegiance to the Government of the United States" in order to receive payment. The order provided that "all persons enlisted into the military service [should] forever thereafter be free." It also announced that the president would appoint a board of three men in each state to investigate the claims of those loyal owners who contended that their slaves had been recruited against their will.[19]

However, the complaints of Maryland planters continued. Lincoln soon received a report that African American troops on a steamboat were landing along the Patuxent River in eastern Maryland and bringing arms and uniforms for slaves without regard to their owners' allegiance. White planters in the county, led by Congressman Charles B. Calvert, petitioned the president for the immediate removal of the soldiers. They complained to Lincoln, "Our white citizens are without arms, or any means of defending themselves, [or] their homes and property" against the armed blacks, many of whom, they said, were "our escaped slaves."[20]

On October 21, 1863, the planters' delegation delivered the petition to Lincoln in the White House. The president told them that blacks in Maryland "might be recruited by consent of masters, as they had been in the Army of the Cumberland" in Kentucky, "but he did not wish to effect the object in any rude or ungentlemanly manner." Lincoln immediately telegraphed General Schenck demanding to know why African American troops had been sent up the Patuxent River. Echoing the complaint of Calvert and the planters, the president told Schenck that the black soldiers, "by their presence, with arms in their hands, [were] frightening quiet people, and producing great confusion."[21]

On the same day, Schenck telegraphed Lincoln that the Maryland delegation had "grossly misrepresented matters." Colonel Birney, the general explained, "went, under my orders to look for a site of a camp of instruction and rendezvous for colored troops." Schenck said that Birney had landed recruiting squads under white officers at several places along the Patuxent. These squads, he insisted, were "under special instructions, good discipline," had "harmed no one," and operated in an area of "rabid secessionists." He begged the president not to "intervene and thus embolden" the rebels.[22]

Lincoln was not completely persuaded by Schenck's explanation, and he glumly concluded that the general and his subordinates by their actions had damaged the prospects of the emancipation candidates in the fall legislative elections. Lincoln's secretary John Hay recorded in his diary, "[While] the President is in favor of the voluntary enlistment of negroes with the consent of their masters & payment of the price," General Schenck's "favorite way (or rather Birney's whom Schenck approves) is to take a squad of soldiers into a neighborhood & carry off into the army all the able-bodied darkies they can find without asking master or slave to consent." "The fact is," Hay quoted Lincoln as saying, "Schenck is wider across the head in the region of the ears, & loves fight for its own sake, better than I do."[23]

The president also summoned the general to the White House for a meeting on the controversy. After this conference, violations of the War Department's and Lincoln's recruitment rules became less frequent. The issue over African American enrollments in Maryland, as well as in the other

Augustus W. Bradford, elected governor of Maryland in 1861 on the Union Party ticket. Bradford served as chairman of the Union governors' conference on the war at Altoona, Pennsylvania, in September 1862, but refused to sign the final document because it contained an endorsement of Lincoln's preliminary Emancipation Proclamation. He repeatedly complained to Lincoln about the military's violations of state laws, black recruitment in the state, and the administration's discriminatory treatment of Maryland in relation to the northen states. Courtesy of the Brady-Handy Collection, Prints and Photographs Division, Library of Congress, Washington, DC.

border states, however, did not completely die. In January 1864, newly elected Senator Reverdy Johnson on the floor of the U.S. Senate denounced the continuing activities of black recruiting squads who raided communities and freed slaves regardless of the loyalty of the owners.[24]

In May 1864, Governor Bradford complained to the president about an "outrage in Dorchester County" in which black troops under a white officer had gone through the communities and "compelled every male negro boy they could find, free and Slave—old men & boys to go with them at once, and took them off in spite of all remonstrance from the Negroes themselves or any body else." Bradford reported, "Outrages of this complexion have become somewhat chronic in portions of our State, and . . . all complaints on the subject have so far failed to secure any redress."[25] Although Lincoln called for a War Department investigation of the Dorchester County incident, the matter apparently died a silent death.[26]

In neighboring Delaware, Governor William Cannon sought to reduce opposition to federally mandated black recruitment by proposing to the General Assembly that the enrollment of African Americans was a way to meet the state's conscription quota. The Democratic-controlled legislature rejected the proposal and warned that African American recruitment would incite blacks to "insurrection and murder." Nonetheless, almost 1,000 Delaware blacks, both free and slave, ultimately served in the Union army.[27] Delaware and other border state white soldiers generally accepted the presence of blacks in the army, but in segregated units. As historian Chandra Manning has written, Union soldiers abandoned their initial opposition to black enlistments when they realized the value of African Americans in fighting the rebels. Nonetheless, the contributions of black soldiers to the Union cause "did not wholly dislodge white soldiers' racial prejudices" or gain their support for black equality.[28]

Despite complications created by the controversy over black recruitment, Maryland Unionists eagerly prepared for the fall 1863 election of a legislature that would decide whether to call a state convention to consider emancipation and other changes in the state constitution. The election would also determine the state's new membership in the U.S. House of Representatives and fill two minor state offices. It soon became clear that the Union Party of 1861–1862 had divided over emancipation, at least on how to accomplish it. Leaders in the party also differed on support for the

Lincoln administration. Meeting separately, both the Unconditional Unionists, radical by Maryland standards, and the conservatives, with exceptions like proslavery congressman John W. Crisfield, endorsed candidates for the legislature who supported a state convention to debate emancipation. The Unconditionals, in an address to the people on September 16, declared that Maryland "should legally and constitutionally abolish the institution at the earliest period compatible with the best interests of the State." They announced that their candidates for the legislature favored immediate emancipation. In addition, the radicals generally approved the measures of the Lincoln government in its efforts to put down the rebellion, including the use of black troops; however, they declared, loyal owners should be compensated for their loss.[29]

The conservatives, who viewed themselves as the true Union Party, also issued an address to the people of the Old Line State. They denounced "the radical views" and "ultra spirit" of the Unconditionals, particularly their insistence on immediate and unqualified emancipation. While supporting the call for a convention, the address admitted that conservatives were divided over how emancipation should take place. "Upon one point, however, there is entire accord," the address announced, "and that is, that the safety and integrity of this Union rises above every other issue; . . . and the authorities of the Government, whether slavery is recognized or not, must be sustained in putting down this rebellion." Unlike the Unconditionals in their address, the conservatives in theirs did not endorse the Lincoln administration or the recruitment of black troops. The conservatives also charged the radicals with seeking to obtain immediate emancipation without regard to the laws of the state. They suggested that freedom for slaves should be only "a side issue" until the rebellion had been suppressed.[30]

General Schenck created another side issue on October 27, 1863, when he issued an inflammatory election order designed to ensure a true Union and emancipation victory. He justified his action by contending, "It is known that there are many evil disposed persons, now at large in the State of Maryland, who have been engaged in rebellion . . . or have given aid or comfort" to the enemy and whose presence "[will] embarrass the approaching election [and] foist enemies of the United States into power." Schenck directed that provost marshals and other military officers arrest all such persons "hanging about, or approaching any poll" on election day. He also instructed his officers to "support the judges of election" in requiring a stringent loyalty oath of anyone who might be challenged, despite any contrary state law. Judges of election who refused the aid of military officers "in carrying out this order" were to be reported to his headquarters in Baltimore.[31]

A storm of protest greeted Schenck's election order. On the day before it was issued, Thomas Swann, conservative chairman of the Union State Central Committee, and others had an inkling of Schenck's action. Swann hurriedly wrote Lincoln that "a suspicion [had] taken possession of the minds of many loyal Union voters . . . that the election . . . [would] be attended with undue interference on the part of persons claiming to represent the wishes of the Government." Swann asked the president for his position on military intervention in the Maryland election. "An expression of opinion on your part," he told Lincoln, "would [promote] a fair expression of the public voice" in the election.[32]

The president replied to Swann that he trusted that there was "no just ground for the suspicion" of outside interference in the election. "I am somewhat mortified [that] any doubt" existed regarding his commitment to free elections, he told Swann. "I wish all loyal qualified voters in Maryland & elsewhere, to have the undisturbed previlege [sic] of voting at elections; and neither my authority, nor my name can be properly used to the contrary."[33]

On October 31 Governor Bradford, having learned of Schenck's order, called on Lincoln to explicitly revoke it. The governor wrote, "From my knowledge of your sentiments," expressed earlier at a White House meeting, "I cannot but think" that the order had been issued "without your personal knowledge." Bradford insisted that "any military interference" in the Maryland elections or in prescribing a test oath for voting "was justly obnoxious to the public sentiment of the State." Echoing a complaint that other border state Unionists had made, the governor contended that military or federal subversion of the election laws of loyal states, including Maryland, was blatantly discriminatory. He pointed out, "Highly important elections have recently taken place in [northern] States" without interference by the government. The governor reminded the president that at least one of the candidates in these states, Vallandigham in Ohio, "was considered so hostile to the Government" that he was banished from the country. Yet hundreds of thousands of Ohioans had voted without objection by federal authorities. Bradford insisted that all the legislative candidates in his state, with the possible exception of two or three in one election district, were loyal.[34]

After receiving the governor's protest, Lincoln summoned Schenck to the White House for a meeting on the matter. He directed that until they met, Schenck should issue no order in relation to the election. Before leaving Baltimore for Washington, the Ohio general telegraphed Secretary of War Stanton and informed him that his election order had already been issued. If it were revoked, Schenck unconvincingly predicted, "we lose this State" in the election.[35] After his meeting with the general, Lincoln immediately reported to Bradford that Schenck had assured him that violence would inevitably occur unless prevented by his provost guards. The general told the president that at some polls "Union voters [would] not attend at all, or run a ticket unless they [had] some assurance of protection." Lincoln informed Bradford that the loyalty oath for voters as required in Schenck's order seemed reasonable. He pointed out to the governor that Missouri had a test oath for voting and holding office, and, by implication, Maryland should also have one. "Your suggestion that nearly all the candidates are loyal, I do not think quite meets the case," Lincoln said. "In the struggle for the nation's life, I can not so confidently rely on those whose elections may have depended upon disloyal votes. Such men, when elected, may prove true; but such votes are given them in the expectation that they will prove false."[36]

Lincoln also denied that Maryland had cause to claim mistreatment, compared to Ohio and other states, in the national effort "to keep peace at the polls, and to prevent the persistently disloyal from voting." He could not refrain from recalling, "It is precisely what Gen. [John A.] Dix did when your Excellency was elected Governor" in 1861. Bradford later pointed out that this was not the case because General Dix's order had reinforced the state's election law, not overturned it. Although Lincoln approved two of the three parts of Schenck's election decree, he disallowed the section directing provost marshals and other military officers to arrest all suspicious persons near the polls. He explained that the provision was not wrong in principle, but that it made the military the sole judge of who should be arrested and thus liable for abuse. In conclusion, the president assured the Maryland governor that Schenck had the president's "strict orders" that "all loyal men may vote, and vote for whom they please."[37]

Even before receiving Lincoln's letter, Governor Bradford on November 2 drafted a proclamation to the people of Maryland denouncing Schenck's "extraordinary order" and, in effect, invalidating it. As he had complained to Lincoln, Bradford told Marylanders that the Old Line State, though as loyal as the northern states, had been outrageously subjected to military interference in its election. In a statement similar to Kentucky governor Thomas E. Bramlette's later actions in the 1864 election when faced with a military intervention, Bradford in his proclamation reminded Maryland's judges of election that they were "clothed with all the authority of Conservators of the peace" and should act accordingly. The governor admonished these officials that despite the intimidating presence of Schenck's provost officers, they should "summon to their aid any of the executive officers of the county, and the whole power of the county itself, to preserve order at the polls and secure the constitutional rights of the voters." Furthermore, they alone had the authority to determine the right of any person to vote under the laws of the state, "undeterred by any order to provost marshals to report them to 'Headquarters.'" Bradford promised the election judges, "Whatever power the State possesses, shall be exerted to protect them for anything done in the proper execution of its laws."[38]

Incensed by Bradford's defiance and challenge to his election order, Schenck immediately suppressed the governor's proclamation until after the election on November 4. He issued his own proclamation reminding army officers of their earlier instructions from his headquarters. The general directed them to "firmly and faithfully" enforce his election order but to avoid entering "into political discussions," a directive that flew in the face of his own action in speaking on behalf of Unconditional Unionist candidates. Although the presence of the military at the polls intimidated many voters, Schenck was partly correct when he noted, "There still remain at large" in Maryland "a very considerable number who are more or less actively engaged in aiding and encouraging Rebels in arms." Schenck insisted that he had drafted his election decree only after receiving "a great number of letters, petitions, and appeals in person, from respectable and loyal citizens" imploring him to issue such an order.[39]

Governor Bradford, having received Lincoln's letter of November 2 that promised a fair election, sent a blistering response to the president in which he reminded him of Schenck's election order and forcefully repeated his earlier arguments against it. Although acknowledging that Lincoln had "modified" the part of the directive granting provost officers the authority to make arrests at the polls, the governor pointed out to the president that the power of the military "to prevent all disturbance or violence" near the voting places had been left intact. Bradford claimed that this power would be subject to abuse because several army officers were also candidates in the election. Finally, he wrote, "I find no allusion in your Excellency's letter to the fact adverted to in mine that no Military intervention or test oath was ordered in either of the late important elections" in Ohio and Pennsylvania. Bradford found it "difficult to see what reliance" the president "could have reposed on such a candidate" as the Copperhead Vallandigham in Ohio and then go on to discriminate against loyal candidates in Maryland.[40] Lincoln, who wisely was adverse to prolonging a quarrel, did not respond.

Early in the 1863 campaign, the Unconditional Unionists had captured control of the state Union League, a militant organization that supported the war. The Union League had begun in the North in 1862 and grew rapidly in Maryland in 1863. Consisting of Unionist activists in the state, the league had the benefit in the campaign of talented outside speakers such as radical Republicans Salmon P. Chase and future president James A. Garfield of Ohio. In the state, Henry Winter Davis (usually referred to by his middle name, Winter); John A. J. Creswell, a rising star in the faction; and General Schenck, who in December would replace Vallandigham in Congress, spoke for the Unconditional Unionists and the Union League. Schenck's chief of staff, Donn Piatt, also did yeoman work for the Unconditional Unionists in the campaign. In a speech at Baltimore on October 28, 1863, Winter Davis announced that the suppression of the "traitors" in Maryland had largely occurred; now, he contended, the primary issue in the election was the alignment of the state with the progressive "principle, feeling, and institutions [of] our great free sisters of the North." This bond could be achieved, Davis said, by the voters' endorsement of immediate emancipation.[41]

Many ardent emancipationists feared a proslavery success in the November election, particularly after the issue became entangled in the recruitment of black troops and the growing political divisions among Union leaders. Nicholas Brewer, a concerned circuit judge in Annapolis, reported to Lincoln on October 31 that "a very large proportion of those who call themselves Union men" in the lower counties were proslavery and would join with the "bitter secessionists" or Democrats to defeat the Unconditional Unionist candidates. Brewer exaggerated when he told the president that Bradford's election proclamation, before its suppression by Schenck, in effect meant "the inauguration of open resistance to the Government."[42]

Conservative Unionist leaders like Bradford and Reverdy Johnson, most of whom now supported gradual emancipation with federal compensation, did not actively participate in the campaign. One conservative campaigner, Postmaster General Montgomery Blair, in an ill-tempered speech at Rockville, Maryland, turned his rhetorical guns on Winter Davis and his radical friends in Congress. Although supporting emancipation—and black colonization—Blair outrageously charged that the radicals "would make the manumission of the slaves the means of infusing their blood into our whole system by blending with it 'amalgamation, equality, and fraternity.'"[43] Issued as a pamphlet, the Rockville speech created a sensation and damaged Blair's political standing in Washington and Maryland; it made the radicals more determined than ever to force him from the cabinet. The vitriol in the postmaster general's speech dismayed Lincoln, who told John Hay that Blair wanted him to become involved against Davis in the Maryland campaign. Lincoln refused, explaining, "Davis is the nominee of the Union convention & as we have recognized him as our candidate, it would be mean to do anything against him now."[44]

Lincoln, however, clearly did not warm to the Maryland radical. When Winter Davis met with the president to lobby for Piatt as Schenck's replacement in Maryland, Lincoln bluntly refused. The president told Davis that he regarded the political division in Maryland as a personal dispute and one in which he should not become involved. Davis angrily walked out of Lincoln's office and told his cousin, Supreme Court Justice David Davis, that the president had been "thoroughly Blairized."[45] Winter Davis later brought his formidable talents to bear in Congress against Lincoln. He attempted to defeat the president's mild reconstruction policy for the South, and he also sought to secure for Congress "an authoritative voice in . . . prescribing the foreign policy of the United States."[46] In both cases, he failed.

Despite the division in the Maryland Unionist camp, the antislavery cause gained an important victory in the November 1863 elections to the legislature. Supporters of a state convention to end slavery in some fashion captured fifty-seven of the ninety-six seats in the General Assembly. Those supporting emancipation also won four of the five congressional contests and the two state offices filled in the election. One of the congressional victors was Winter Davis, who recaptured the seat in the House of Representatives that he had lost in 1861.[47] Only 52,344 Marylanders voted, as compared to 92,502 in the 1860 presidential election. Many potential voters, who presumably, in the main, would have cast their ballots for proslavery candidates, refused to take Schenck's loyalty oath. Others, fearing intimidation or arrest by the military, stayed away from the polls. Thousands of 1860 voters were serving in the armies in the South and were unable to vote. The predicted armed confrontations between citizens and Schenck's provost marshals did not occur, nor was there significant violence on election day.

Conservative Unionists, however, immediately complained to Lincoln, through Postmaster General Blair, that legitimate votes had been rejected and that the military had arrested alleged "traitors" at the polls. Crisfield, who vehemently opposed emancipation and who lost his congressional seat by 1,300 votes, reported that U.S. cavalry units in his southeastern district had intimidated voters and kept many of them from the polls. In Somerset County alone, he charged, squads of five to thirty cavalry troops took control of the polls. In one election district, reported Crisfield, the officer in command "pulled from his pocket" the ticket of Crisfield's opponent and announced that "no other [ticket] was to be voted that day." In the Princess Anne district, Captain Charles C. Moore of the Third Maryland Cavalry stood at the entrance of the polls and required each prospective voter to take the loyalty oath prescribed by Schenck. Furthermore, Moore questioned some voters about their loyalty and political opinions. Crisfield's son and others were barred from voting, though they were willing to take the oath. The district election judges informed Moore that they did not approve of his "mode of conducting the election," whereupon Moore arrested the officials and dispatched them under guard to Baltimore. That evening, General Henry H. Lockwood released the judges. Crisfield, who witnessed Moore's actions, claimed that altogether 350 voters in the Princess Anne district had been denied the right to vote. He wrote Blair, who gave the letter to the president, "Public indignation is very highly aroused, and will not be appeased, unless the proceedings of these military officers be disavowed and rebuked" and assurances given "that the outrage is not to be repeated."[48]

Upon reading Crisfield's letter, the president ordered an investigation of Moore's actions. He promised to "call any such officer to account" for improper conduct at the polls. At Lincoln's request, Crisfield obtained sworn statements from the election judges in the district and submitted them to the president. Lincoln, after receiving the statements, directed Schenck to try Moore by a military commission for his arrest of the election officials and for preventing Crisfield's son from voting. Much to Crisfield's dismay, but not to his surprise, the commission, appointed by Schenck, exonerated Moore of the charges.[49]

Lincoln also became involved in the vexatious case of the military arrest and imprisonment of Thomas G. Pratt, former governor and former U.S. senator, on election day. At the time of General Benjamin F. Butler's occupation of Annapolis in April 1861, Pratt, according to Circuit Judge Brewer and other hostile witnesses, had urged armed resistance to the Massachusetts troops.[50] When the ex–Whig governor appeared at the polls to vote in 1863, he refused to take Schenck's loyalty oath, though he insisted that he had never supported secession and had merely opposed federal violations of state laws. Pratt was immediately arrested and sent to Schenck's headquarters. He obtained an interview with the general, who brusquely informed him that he had been detained because his refusal to take the oath "was such an act as caused a suspicion of [his] disloyalty to the Government."[51]

Schenck dispatched Pratt to Fort Monroe in Virginia, where he was to be sent through the lines to Richmond. From his cell in Fort Monroe, Pratt bombarded Secretary of War Stanton, Postmaster General Blair, and Governor Bradford with appeals for his freedom. Pratt's son-in-law, Daniel Clark, also rushed to Washington and pleaded with Lincoln to intervene in the case. When Stanton indicated his opposition to Pratt's release, Lincoln decided that the former governor should remain at Fort Monroe and not be banished to the Confederacy.[52] After holding Pratt for a few weeks, the military freed the former governor and permitted him to return to Maryland.

In neighboring Delaware, Schenck on November 13 issued an election order similar to the one for Maryland, though without the threat of arrests at the polls. At stake in the 1863 election was Delaware's only seat in the U.S. House of Representatives. Governor Cannon, unlike Governor Bradford, supported Schenck's order and cooperated in the dispatch of troops, ironically from neighboring Maryland, to monitor the polls. The governor, who had been elected in 1862 as a conservative Unionist, wrote President Lincoln that the contest in Delaware was between the enemies of the government and the Unionists. He maintained that it required a federal military presence to ensure the success of the latter.[53] A large number of

Delawareans did not agree with Cannon that troops were required to maintain loyalty in the state. They also opposed his support of emancipation. Conservatives and Democrats met and agreed to boycott the election because of the "military occupation" of the state. As a result of the boycott and the intimidating presence of troops, only thirteen votes were cast against Cannon's candidate for Congress.[54]

Governor Bradford, Maryland's new U.S. senator Reverdy Johnson, and Kentucky senators Lazarus W. Powell and Garret Davis refused to let die the issue of military intervention in the fall 1863 elections in the border states. In his message to the newly elected Maryland legislature on January 7, 1864, Bradford described the abuses that had occurred in the state even before the polls opened. The documents regarding these abuses, the governor announced, "present a humiliating record, such as I had never supposed we should be called upon to read in any State, still less in a loyal one like [ours]."[55] In a Senate speech Johnson attacked the methods used by the military in the Eastern Shore counties to win the election for candidates supporting immediate, uncompensated emancipation. Furthermore, he claimed that John A. J. Creswell, the Unconditional Unionist candidate for Congress in the district, owed his seat to "as great an outrage as ever was perpetrated upon freemen." A stickler for lawful procedures, Johnson told the Senate that he personally favored Creswell over his proslavery opponent Crisfield, but he reported that men of "stern and rigid loyalty" were arrested miles from the polls and, along with others, were thrown into the old slave prison in Baltimore.[56]

Garret Davis, who had become increasingly extreme in his denunciation of Lincoln and antislavery Republicans, took to the floor of the Senate on January 5, 1864, and proposed eighteen resolutions condemning the administration, including its military intervention in Maryland. The Kentucky senator thundered, "The present Executive Government of the United States has subverted . . . in the loyal States, the freedom of speech, the freedom of the press, and free suffrage, the Constitution and laws of the States, the civil courts and trial by jury." He also attacked Lincoln's Proclamation of Amnesty and Reconstruction, issued on December 8, 1863, which, though lenient to former rebels, required the abolition of slavery for the restoration of the southern states to the Union. Davis contended that Lincoln's object in his so-called Ten Percent reconstruction plan was "to give adventurers in his party control of the polls in the South, backed by the bayonet." The new governments would "then form bastard constitutions to abolitionize their States" and enact black equality. Davis exclaimed that "the people of the North and the South ought to revolt against their war-leaders, and take this great matter into their own hands" and that they should "elect members to a national convention of all the States, to terminate a war that . . . threatens the masses of both sections with irretrievable bankruptcy, and infinite slaughter." The convention would then "restore the union and common government upon the great principles of liberty and compromise devised by Washington and his associates."[57]

Three days later, an outraged Republican senator, Henry Wilson of Massachusetts, offered a resolution to expel Davis from the Senate. He charged the fiery Kentuckian with "advising the people of the United States to treasonable, insurrectionary, and rebellious actions against the Government of the United States, and of a gross violation of the privileges of the Senate."[58] Not surprising, border state conservatives opposed the Republican effort to expel Davis. Senator Reverdy Johnson, though regretting that the Kentucky senator had offered the resolutions, argued that Davis's criticism of the president was no more censurable than that indulged in earlier by radical Senator John P. Hale of New Hampshire. The Maryland senator also cited a myriad of American and English precedents for such legislative vilification of an administration.[59]

Faced with probable expulsion, Davis on January 26 sent a note to the Senate disclaiming any intention in his resolutions "to incite the people of the United States to revolt against the President of the United States." His purpose, he insisted, "was to exhort the whole people, North and South, to terminate the war by a constitutional settlement of their difficulties and reconstruction of the Union." Although some Republicans still wanted Davis expelled, Senator Wilson, sobered by the precedent that the removal might establish in the Senate, accepted the Kentuckian's explanation and withdrew his expulsion resolution. Davis's hostile resolutions were then laid over and never considered by the Senate.[60]

The border state demand for congressional action to prohibit military interference in state elections grew in early 1864. Retiring senator James A. Bayard of Delaware on January 26 charged that the elective franchise had been "trodden under foot" in his state and that citizens had been arrested for attempting to vote. He declared that the army's intervention had occurred despite the fact that the courts were open and added, "At no period has there existed the semblance of a conspiracy or combination to resist the authority of the United States." Bayard also denounced Schenck's test oath for voting in Maryland and Delaware.[61]

It was left to Kentucky senator Powell to introduce a bill to prohibit the military from interfering with elections in the Union states unless appealed to by state authorities to prevent violence. Under the proposed bill, military officers, soldiers, and seamen found guilty of intervening at the polls or attempting to influence the outcome of an election would be subject to imprisonment for two to twenty years. However, the Republican-dominated Senate Committee on Military Affairs recommended the bill not be approved. This rejection did not deter Senator Powell; on March 3, 1864, he brought the proposal to the Senate floor as a personal bill. The Kentucky senator presented extensive documentary evidence, especially for Maryland, to demonstrate the need to curb military interference in elections in the Union states. He overreached, however, when he charged that Lincoln's "meddling" in the 1863 Maryland contest by supporting Schenck and his subordinates was "the harshest usurpation against the loyal people of [any] State." Powell denounced the Military Affairs Committee for asserting in its report that Governor Bradford's proclamation overruling Schenck's election order was illegal. Furthermore, Powell said, several members of the committee (apparently conservatives) had informed him that they had not had an opportunity to read the report before it was presented to the Senate.[62]

Republicans, not wanting to alienate the border states and also concerned about the precedent of military involvement in loyal states' elections, gave Powell a half loaf on the issue. They agreed to a bill that prohibited military interference in Union elections. The bill, however, permitted the employment of troops to "repel the armed enemies of the United States or to keep the peace at the polls," presumably with or without the governor's approval. The revised bill passed Congress in June 1864 with border state members voting for it.[63]

Despite Bradford's outrage over military interference in the 1863 election and despite having earlier likened emancipation to treason, in his January 7, 1864, message to the new General Assembly the Maryland governor called for "immediate measures" to end slavery. Although a large majority in the legislature favored a state convention to abolish the institution, a lively debate erupted over the timing of emancipation. Most of the legislators agreed that the convention's work should be submitted for the approval of the loyal voters in the forthcoming fall election. Those members who supported gradual emancipation, however, sought to delay voter action on an antislavery amendment to the state constitution until November 1865; others, including staunch proslavery advocates, urged an even longer postponement. The legislators were also divided over compensation for slaveholders, particularly by the state. Some members still hoped that the federal government would finance emancipation. This prospect had become unrealistic after Congress adjourned in 1863 without approving compensation bills for Maryland or Missouri. The General Assembly easily agreed on a provision that prohibited military or federal intervention at the polls; if any such did occur at a voting place, the legislature authorized the governor to order a new election for that precinct. Finally, on February 9, the General Assembly provided for an election on April 6 to determine whether a convention should be called. At the same time, in case of its approval, delegates to the convention were to be elected and assembled on April 27. Only voters who could take a stringent loyalty oath could participate in the convention election.[64]

As the April 6 election approached, Unconditional Unionists worried that the state convention would be defeated by a coalition of proslavery supporters and conservatives opposed to immediate emancipation and also to the oath for voting. The opposition's charge that they advocated "black equality"—a typical campaign ploy in the election—inflamed passions during the brief canvass. In a speech on April 1, 1864, in Baltimore, Winter Davis, the most active spokesman for the Unconditional Unionists, poured scorn on the proslavery charge that he and his faction supported black equality. The proslavery advocates, Davis declared, raised the issue of black equality "to delude" the people, but he was confident that it would not work. "It is one of the paltry, dirty tricks to cheat men who they [incorrectly] suppose are fools enough to be cheated." The radical congressman told his sympathetic audience, "I am perfectly content that the negro shall be equal with [his opponents], but not with me or my friends." Taking a page from Lincoln's ridicule of Stephen A. Douglas at Charleston, Illinois, in the 1858 senatorial campaign when the Little Giant raised the bugbear of black equality, Davis exclaimed, "In my judgment, they that are afraid of marrying a negro woman had better go to the Legislature and pe-

CHAPTER EIGHT

tition for a law to punish them if they are guilty of that weakness."[65] The issue for Winter Davis in the election was the eradication of slavery in Maryland, a cause that he believed would fail in 1863–1864 if proslavery leaders succeeded in tying black civil and political equality to emancipation. It should be remembered that Davis had earlier joined a corporal's guard of border state Unionists in exposing the chimera of black colonization that border state conservatives and some northern Republicans supported.

Still, hostility to the radical Winter Davis caused antislavery friends of Montgomery Blair, Davis's nemesis, to contemplate opposing the convention. Charles C. Fulton, editor of the *Baltimore American*, wrote Blair and asked him to curb his friends' antagonism toward Davis as a matter of necessity in order to win the election.[66] Although Blair favored a state convention to end slavery, Fulton had asked too much of him in requesting him to advise his supporters to cooperate with Davis and his faction in the campaign.

No one worried more about the divisions among Maryland emancipationists than Abraham Lincoln. On March 7, 1864, he wrote Creswell, recently elected to Congress, that he was "very anxious for emancipation to be effected in Maryland in some substantial form." Lincoln admitted, "My expressions of a preference for *gradual* over *immediate* emancipation, are misunderstood" and probably had caused divisions. "I had thought the *gradual* would produce less confusion, and destitution, and therefore would be more satisfactory; but if those who are better acquainted with the subject, and are more deeply interested in it prefer the *immediate*, most certainly I have no objection to their judgment prevailing." Lincoln went on to say that his wish was "that all who [were] for emancipation in any form" would "co-operate, all treating all respectfully, and all adopting and acting upon the major opinion." The president added that he "dreaded . . . the danger that by jealousies, rivalries, and consequent ill-blood" the election on emancipation would be lost, a point he repeated to Missouri antislavery champions. Fearing, however, that he would be charged with interfering in the election, Lincoln asked Creswell not to make the letter public, but he said that "no man representing" him as he had stated in the letter would be " in any danger of contradiction" by him. The president addressed the letter himself and marked the envelope "*Private.*" Creswell honored Lincoln's wishes; he also returned the letter and envelope for the president's file.[67]

Ten days later, Lincoln again wrote Creswell. This time he said that his wish for the success of emancipation in the state no longer needed to be a secret. He announced, with Maryland in mind, that a decision for emancipation "would aid much to end the rebellion." "Hence," he said, "it is a matter of national consequence, in which every national man may rightfully feel a deep interest. I sincerely hope the friends of the measure will allow no minor consideration to divide and distract them" from the task at hand.[68]

In the same month, March, Lincoln appointed General Lew Wallace to command the Middle Department in Maryland and Delaware. Before assuming command in Baltimore, Wallace visited the president to express his appreciation for the appointment. As the general was leaving the room, Lincoln called him back and declared, "Ah, Wallace, I came near forgetting that there is an election nearly due over in Maryland, but don't you forget it." Wallace next visited Secretary of War Stanton who warned him that the Middle Department had been "a graveyard for commanders." When Wallace reported that the president had admonished him not to forget about the Maryland election, Stanton bluntly responded, "Nor must you forget it." Stanton reminded him, "The last Maryland legislature passed an act for an election looking to the abolition of slavery in the state by constitutional amendment," adding, "The President has set his heart on the abolition of slavery in that way; and mark, he don't want it to be said by anybody that the bayonet had anything to do with the election. He is a candidate for a second nomination. You understand?"[69]

Stanton's suggestion that Lincoln's political interest was a primary motive in his efforts to secure emancipation in Maryland does not completely ring true. As early as 1862, when no personal political interest was at stake, Lincoln advanced his controversial compensation scheme designed to secure emancipation in Maryland and in the other border states. Pressure from radicals in his party had had little influence on him when he revoked the emancipation proclamations of Generals John C. Frémont and David Hunter in 1861 and 1862. Lincoln's main motivation in seeking border state emancipation was his belief, however unrealistic, that the war would be dramatically shortened if slavery was ended in the border states. As he had said on several occasions, a decision by the border states to abolish slavery, even gradually with an established deadline, would disabuse the rebels of the notion that these states would join them in the insurrection. Without border state support, Lincoln believed that the rebels would recognize that they faced inevitable defeat; they then would have no choice but to give up the fight against the Union.

Lincoln's long-held moral opposition to slavery, which he had repeatedly expressed, also influenced his efforts to secure emancipation in the border states as well as his decision to issue the Emancipation Proclamation. His abhorrence of slavery was probably not as intense and was certainly not as militant as that of the northern abolitionists; unlike Lincoln, they did not have constitutional restraints on their antislavery efforts. Still, Lincoln wanted to see slavery placed en route to "ultimate extinction," a position that he had taken before the war. If slavery were ended, according to Lincoln, there would be no reason for sectional conflict in the future.

General Wallace, the son of an early Indiana governor and possessed of some political savvy, in his meeting with Stanton informed the secretary of war that he "understood" the antislavery and political purposes in his appointment to command in Maryland and Delaware. "Anyhow," he told the secretary, "I want [Lincoln] renominated and elected."[70] Neither Lincoln nor Stanton talked to Wallace about his purely military responsibilities in the Middle Department, responsibilities that would become highly important when Confederate general Jubal Early raided the state three months later on a daring push toward Washington.[71]

Stanton also advised Wallace to see Schenck, now a member of Congress, about affairs in Maryland. Schenck's experience in Maryland, particularly in the eastern counties, had left him embittered and contemptuous of the people. "Your troubles will have origin altogether in Baltimore," he told Wallace. "The questions of the war divided the old families, but I was never able to discover the dividing line." Schenck complained that when he had "put a heavy hand on one of the Secessionists, a delegation of influential Unionists" like Reverdy Johnson "hurried to the President, and begged the culprit off." "The most unfortunate thing in connection with the department and its management," Schenck said, "is that it is only a pleasant morning jaunt by rail from Baltimore to Washington"; there, complaints could be personally made to Lincoln and others in the administration.[72]

Schenck informed Wallace, "Baltimore is headquarters for a traffic in supplies for the rebel armies, the extent of which is simply incredible." With apparent exaggeration, he declared that the illicit trade had been left "entirely to the women," who he said were "cunning beyond relief [belief?], and bold on account of their sex." And, he complained, "When the fair culprits are caught . . . the President always lets them off. They promise him not to do it again, and [they] come away laughing at the 'Old Ape.'"[73]

Fortified with his instructions from Lincoln and Stanton and also by Schenck's biased assessment of the situation in eastern Maryland, Wallace arrived in Baltimore two weeks before the state convention election in April. He immediately received reports claiming that "persons disloyal to the Government of the United States [were] candidates for the Constitutional Convention." In addition, Unconditional Unionists petitioned Wallace for troops to protect them at the polls, despite the fact that under the law only the judges of election could call on the military if violence was threatened. Wallace soon proved more skillful in managing affairs than Schenck had been. He decided to meet with Governor Bradford for an opinion regarding the petitions and the extent of the election officials' authority vis-à-vis the military. Aware that the other military commanders had largely ignored Bradford, Wallace demonstrated his good faith by going to the governor's office at Annapolis for the meeting. The general found Bradford to be "a plain, farmer-like, undemonstrative person [who] held himself well . . . as became a chief of one of the original colonies."[74]

The meeting went well. Wallace agreed that the state's laws were sufficient to ensure against voting by disloyal elements and against interference by troops in the election. He also accepted Bradford's stipulation that all the petitions for the posting of soldiers at the polls should be sent to the governor, who would then ask in writing for their stationing within one mile of the doubtful precincts. Wallace gave orders that his troops could only approach the polls if summoned by election judges for assistance. On the controversial point of challenging voters, Bradford and Wallace agreed that the judges would administer the oath to those whose loyalty was questioned, upon the penalty of prosecution for perjury in the state courts if the oath was taken falsely. A slight difficulty in the agreement arose when Wallace sought to prevent the candidacy of E. G. Kilbourn for a seat in the convention. Kilbourn, the speaker of the state house of representatives in 1861, had been arrested and imprisoned for opposing the war, but he had been released in time to stand for election to the 1864 convention. The budding conflict over Kilbourn's eligibility was amicably settled when he withdrew from the campaign.[75] Even Winter Davis expressed his approval of the election arrangement between the general and the conservative governor. He wrote Wallace, "Now freedom is secure" in the state, and "soon the rebellion will be as prostrate everywhere as its *cause* [slavery] is in Maryland."[76]

The news from Maryland on the eve of the convention election delighted Lincoln. He summoned Wallace to Washington to congratulate him on his success in managing the volatile situation in the state and to discuss the forthcoming election with him. Arriving on the next train, Wallace was received "most cordially" by the president. "I sent for you," Lincoln informed the general, "to say that I watched the boiling of the kettle over in Maryland, and I think you managed it beautifully." Lincoln explained, "It was a good thing, that getting Governor Bradford between you and the enemy [Davis?] in Congress. Winter Davis is happy over it." Lincoln admonished the young general (he was thirty-six years of age), "Keep right along now, and get Davis and the governor together. And—yes, yes—be fair, but whenever there is a doubt with a benefit in it, don't fail to give the benefit where it will do the most good. You'll do it, I know. That's a good fellow."[77]

The president then sent Wallace to see Stanton, with a note summarizing their conversation and adding that he expected "the benefit of all doubts" in the general's actions to go "to the emancipationists." The usually gruff war secretary shook Wallace's hand "warmly," praised him, and announced, "They can't say now that we used the bayonet in the election. If the governor did, that's a different thing. Nobody will deny his right to use it."[78]

As expected by Lincoln and Stanton, the convention election on April 6, 1864, occurred largely without trouble. Many, however, did not vote because they could not take the ironclad oath required by the General Assembly in February. Although Wallace blanketed the proslavery Eastern Shore with detachments to be available in case election judges called for their assistance, only in one district of the state, at Rockville near Washington, did Bradford, as the Maryland law required, order a new election because of military interference. Even a leader of the proslavery forces commended Wallace "for the judicious arrangement of his troops" and for their behavior.[79]

The convention forces swept to victory in the election. Out of a total of 51,117 votes, a majority of 31,593 supported the call for a convention. This was a similar number of votes as cast in the November 1863 contest, but 26,056 fewer, understandably so, than the last prewar state election of

1859. Of the ninety-six delegates elected, sixty-one supported emancipation; however, a division still existed between those who favored immediate abolition and those who wanted to delay the process. Some emancipationists remained hopeful of obtaining federal compensation for loyal slaveholders. Although the issue for state compensation was raised, few of the elected delegates wanted to burden Maryland taxpayers with paying for it.[80]

On April 18, before the convention met on the twenty-seventh, President Lincoln made a quick trip to Baltimore, ostensibly to participate in the ceremony opening the Maryland Sanitary Fair to aid the troops. However, an important reason for his visit was to encourage support for emancipation and to applaud the progress that Baltimore had made for the Union since early 1861. "The change in Baltimore," Lincoln declared in his address at the fair, was "part only of a far wider change." He explained, "When the war began, three years ago, neither party, nor any man, expected it would last till now. Each looked for the end, in some way, long ere to-day. Neither did any anticipate that domestic slavery would be much affected by the war. But here we are; the war has not ended, and slavery has been affected—how much needs not now to be recounted. So true is it that man proposes, and God disposes."[81]

Lincoln at Baltimore also commented on the meaning of liberty and how its definition might differ with parties; one person's liberty might be another person's tyranny, he said. "Hence we behold the processes by which thousands are daily passing from under the yoke of bondage, hailed by some as the advance of liberty, and bewailed by others as the destruction of all liberty. Recently, as it seems, the people of Maryland have been doing something to define liberty." Lincoln meant that they were coming down on the right side of the definition of liberty—freedom for the slaves.[82]

Disturbed by "the painful rumor, true I fear," of the rebel massacre of 300 black troops and their officers at Fort Pillow, Tennessee, Lincoln took the occasion in his Baltimore address to recount his decision to use "colored troops" in the war. He knew that the enrollment of blacks in the army had become a contentious issue in Maryland as well as in the other border states. "Upon a clear conviction of duty I resolved to turn that element of strength to account," he announced; "and I am responsible for it to the American people, to the christian world, to history, and on my final account to God. Having determined to use the negro as a soldier, there is no way but to give him all the protection given to any other soldier. The difficulty is not in stating the principle, but in practically applying it," including what action should be taken if reports of a massacre at Fort Pillow indeed proved true.[83]

When the Maryland convention met at Annapolis, a Committee on the Declaration of Rights was formed, and on May 12 it presented a majority and a minority report to the delegates. In addition to a number of changes in the old constitution, the majority report proposed an article to end slavery immediately. The minority report accepted most of the recommendations but objected to the "sudden, violent, and most mischievous destruction of the relation of master and slavery."[84] The convention debate over the emancipation article consumed more than a week in June. The opposition desperately raised every conceivable argument to defeat immediate emancipation, focusing on property rights, the ruin that would follow abolition, and, in lieu of state financial support, the unwillingness of Congress to provide compensation for the slaveholders. They echoed the fears of the Delaware elite (see chapter 6) that free blacks from other states would flood Maryland, creating severe social and racial problems. As a concession to the minority, the convention appointed a committee to talk to Lincoln and request federal money to reimburse loyal slaveholders for the loss of their slaves.[85] Nothing came of the effort; by this time the day for congressional consideration of compensation, which Lincoln had fervently sought in 1862, had passed.

On June 30 the Maryland convention adopted the immediate emancipation article by a vote of 53 to 27, subject to ratification by the loyal voters in the fall election. But military events soon required the delegates to take a quick recess and seek safety before completing work on the new constitution. On July 6 startling news reached Annapolis that a Confederate force of almost 15,000 men under General Early had crossed the Potomac near Sharpsburg, beginning a major raid into Maryland designed to relieve pressure on General Lee's army, then engaged with General U. S. Grant's forces near Petersburg, and if possible to capture Washington. In a spin-off operation usually forgotten in the history of this dramatic raid, General Early dispatched a Maryland cavalry brigade under General Bradley Johnson, a native of Frederick, Maryland, and a Princeton graduate, to cut Union communications in the Baltimore area, dash to the southern tip of the state, and free thousands of Confederate prisoners at Point Lookout. It was a tall order, bound to fail, but Johnson's men did ride around Baltimore, creating panic. The Confederates briefly occupied communities in the region, burned bridges, and destroyed Governor Bradford's home in retaliation for the Union army's destruction of former Virginia governor John Letcher's estate. Early's main army also destroyed the Blair family house at Silver Spring, Maryland.[86]

Alarmed by the Confederate invasion, General Wallace left Baltimore and hurriedly organized an ad hoc force to impede General Early's movement toward Washington. Wallace, with approximately 7,000 men, encountered Early's larger force near Frederick along the Monocacy River. In the battle on July 9, the Confederates defeated Wallace's small army, but the action delayed by one day Early's planned assault on Washington, thereby providing time for the preparation of the capital's defenses and for the arrival of reinforcements from Grant's army in Virginia. An attack by the Confederates on the outskirts of Washington on July 12 failed, and Early had no choice but to retreat and recross the Potomac at Leesburg, Virginia.

In the aftermath of Early's raid and expecting another Confederate incursion into western Maryland, General Hunter, commanding in the area, ordered the arrest, seizure of property, and banishment to the Confederacy of all (presumed) secessionists and all those who had given aid to the rebel raiders. Hunter's order sparked sharp protests to Washington by conservative Unionists in the Frederick area. Writing for "a large number of prominent Union citizens of Frederick," George R. Dennis, a colonel in a Maryland home brigade, informed Montgomery Blair that the order had created "an unhappy and distracted state of affairs, destructive to our interest as a community, and of no practical benefit to the Government." Hunter's military decree, Dennis reported, had undermined much of the fervor for the Union in western Maryland. He asked Blair to see the president and request that he either revoke or modify the general's order.[87] After receiving other protests, Lincoln on August 3 suspended the order, which prompted Hunter, no stranger to controversy, to submit his resignation as regional commander. On August 8 the general was granted a leave of absence preparatory to his removal from command on August 29.[88]

The Maryland constitutional convention reassembled on September 6, after a long recess that was partly dictated by the need for the delegates and others to settle their nerves and recover from the Confederate raids. By a vote of 53 to 25, the delegates approved the new constitution that included the emancipation article. They scheduled October 12–13 for the vote on the document's ratification.[89] Like the General Assembly earlier, the convention required a stringent loyalty oath for voters. It also provided that loyal Maryland troops could cast ballots in the field. The vote would occur within three weeks of the critical national election in November that, in addition to choosing a president, congressmen, and state officers, would have a bearing on final emancipation in the South and in the border states. The National Union, or Republican, platform, at Lincoln's urging, contained a plank advocating an amendment to the U.S. Constitution abolishing slavery in all the states.

As the campaign for the state election climaxed in the early fall, opposition to the constitution grew. In addition to the lingering proslavery sentiment in Maryland, opposition developed because of the restrictive voter qualification article adopted by the convention.[90] A reaction to Winter Davis's radicalism, even within the Unconditional Unionists ranks, had flared, further weakening support for the constitution. Davis had launched a bitter attack on Lincoln because of his pocket veto in July of the Wade-Davis reconstruction bill designed to overturn the president's restoration policy for the rebel states. He also had intrigued to replace Lincoln as the Republican candidate for president, which upset many Unionists in view of the Copperhead (Democrat) threat in the national election.[91] To restore harmony, Unionists repudiated Davis's leadership and conceded control of their party to the conservatives. Conservative Unionist Thomas Swann, on a platform supporting emancipation, received the party's nomination for governor in the election.

Winter Davis, with his political strength in decline, did not run for re-election. Nonetheless, he took to the stump to campaign for the constitution and, unenthusiastically, for Lincoln in the presidential election. Davis's conservative rival, Montgomery Blair, also campaigned for the president and for the ratification of the constitution, even after he had been forced out of the cabinet to satisfy the radicals in the Republican Party. The president expressed doubts, however, fearing that neither Davis nor Blair would be effective in the canvass because of their "bad temper" toward their opponents. Worried that the constitution would fail, Lincoln told John Hay, perhaps only half seriously, that if Winter Davis "and the rest" could "succeed in carrying the state for emancipation," he would be "very willing to lose [its] electoral vote."[92]

Sensing blood in the water, the proslavery forces issued an address to the voters lambasting the stringent oath for voting and condemning the emancipation article, ostensibly on the grounds that it failed to provide compensation for slaveholders.[93] The *Washington National Intelligencer*, which still exercised influence among old-line Whigs in Maryland, entered the campaign on the side of the opposition to the constitution. In a long editorial on October 1, it excoriated the test oath and charged that many Union voters would refuse to undergo an interrogation at the polls, as required by the convention for those suspected of disloyalty.[94] Senator Johnson, though supporting emancipation, also denounced the oath but encouraged Unionists to swallow their pride, if challenged, and take it under protest.[95]

General Wallace on September 20 inadvertently contributed to the opposition cause by ordering the suppression of the *Baltimore Evening Post* on the dubious grounds that he wanted to prevent attacks on the newspaper's office. The editors and proprietors immediately wrote Lincoln and demanded that he revoke the order. They insisted that the real reason for the general's high-handed action was the *Evening Post*'s strident criticism of the constitution and also its support of George B. McClellan for president. Two representatives of the newspaper immediately visited the president and delivered a letter of protest from Senator Johnson. Lincoln, however, refused to intervene in the controversy.[96]

Lincoln soon received a disturbing report that the constitution—and thus emancipation—was in trouble. William L. W. Seabrook, commissioner of the U.S. Land Office in Maryland, visited the president and told him that the constitution's ratification was "very doubtful." Startled by the information, Lincoln, as Seabrook vividly recalled, exclaimed, "You surely do not mean that," and he expressed his doubts that the constitution would fail. However, when Seabrook attempted to explain, Lincoln became agitated. Several times the president declared, "You alarm me, sir! you alarm me." He declared, "I fear you and others of our friends in Maryland are not alive to the importance of this matter and its influence upon the conflict in which we are engaged. The adoption of your Constitution abolishing slavery will be equal to a victory by one of our armies in the field." It would be, he said, "a notification to the South" that slavery would not survive the war. When Seabrook rose to leave, Lincoln put his hand on his shoulder and said, "I implore you, sir, to go to work and endeavor to induce others to go to work for your Constitution, with all your energy. Try to impress other unionists with its importance as a war measure, and don't let it fail!"[97]

CHAPTER EIGHT

With the ratification of the constitution in doubt, its supporters held a "Grand Mass Meeting" in Baltimore on October 10, two days before the election. Because of "local dissensions," the organizers of the "Free Constitution" rally decided "to rely exclusively" upon outside speakers at the rally. The chairman of the committee, Henry W. Hoffman, wrote Lincoln on October 3 and invited him to attend and speak. "We are convinced that your presence on the occasion would insure it's [sic] success both as to harmony and point of numbers" in the election. In case he could not come, Hoffman asked Lincoln to write a letter "expressive of the deep interest which we know you feel in regard" to the election's outcome; it "would be productive of the greatest good."[98]

Lincoln did not attend the Baltimore rally. Instead, he wrote a statement to be read at the meeting emphatically expressing his support for the ratification of the constitution. "I presume the only feature of the instrument, about which there is serious controversy," he told Hoffman, "is that which provides for the extinction of slavery. It needs not to be a secret, and I presume it is no secret, that I wish success to this provision. I desire it on every consideration. I wish all men to be free." The president also declared that he wished "the material prosperity of the already free," which he was sure "the extinction of slavery would bring." Furthermore, he declared, "I wish to see, in process of disappearing, that only thing which ever would bring this nation to civil war." He closed by announcing, "I shall be gratified exceedingly if the good people of the State shall, by their votes, ratify the new constitution." Hoffman wrote Lincoln that when the statement was read at the rally, it received "the unbounded applause of the many thousands assembled." "The new constitution," he predicted, "will be adopted."[99] Although the president's statement probably aided the cause in Baltimore, as Hoffman claimed, its effect on the remainder of the state was problematic. Already the lines had been tightly drawn on the issue of emancipation, which many Marylanders, with good reason, believed was the most important one in the history of the Old Line State.

Despite his suppression of the *Baltimore Evening Post*, General Wallace followed Lincoln's and Stanton's earlier warnings to avoid the appearance of military intervention in the election on the constitution. On October 4 the general sent strict instructions to his troops regarding their conduct and duties during the two days of the election. In Baltimore, where rowdyism often imperiled political contests, Wallace announced that he "particularly desired to avoid the slightest demonstration looking to military interference." He directed, "In no case must bodies of armed soldiers be allowed to approach the polls, except to put down an outbreak for which the police are insufficient, and then the mayor must first apply to you for assistance for that purpose." Wallace informed his officers that troops should be sent only to districts "in which the judges of election have formally solicited military protection" and that the troops should be assigned "purely to protect and support the judges of election in enforcing the law regulating the exercise of the voting privilege." Unless requested by the judges, troops must "under no circumstances" interfere at the polls or act to disperse crowds or arrest persons. Officers, he said, "must not even post their detachment within one mile of the polls."[100] Wallace's election directive contrasted sharply with General Schenck's arbitrary intervention in the 1863 contest.

In an extremely close election on October 12–13, Maryland voters approved the free-state constitution. Although both sides complained of election irregularities, including intimidation of voters, only one significant violation occurred. In Caroline County, the election judges refused to permit 200 men to vote, though they reportedly had expressed their willingness to take the loyalty oath. By a 10 to 1 margin, soldiers, who could now vote in the field, cast their ballots for the constitution. Their votes, which were not known for a few days, decided the election.[101] The final vote was 30,174 for the constitution to 29,799 against it—a razor thin victory of 375 votes for freedom.[102] The total vote represented an increase of 8,856 over the April election on the constitutional convention and delegates to it.

Upon hearing the news of the Maryland election results, a jubilant Lincoln proclaimed to an antislavery visitor, "It was a victory worth double the number of electoral votes of the state because of its moral influence."[103] The president made a similar point to other visitors on October 18. The next day he told a group of Marylanders that he regretted that emancipation in their state—and by inference other border states—had not occurred "two years sooner," when he had offered slaveholders compensation for their slaves. "I am sure [it] would have saved to the nation more money than would have met all the private loss incident to the measure."[104] Lincoln was still holding on to the far-fetched notion that the abolition of slavery in the border states would have produced an early end to the rebellion. Such a course would have signaled to the seceded states,

CHAPTER EIGHT

he believed, that they could not depend on the border states for help, and they would have surrendered the fight.

Several days later, blacks in the District of Columbia celebrated the victory at a large Washington church. Carrying torches and displaying Union Party banners, they marched to the White House, where their "loud and repeated cheers brought out the President." He responded by telling the celebrants, "It is no secret that I have wished, and still do wish, mankind everywhere to be free. And in the State of Maryland how great an advance has been made in this direction. It is difficult to realize that in that State, where human slavery has existed for ages . . . by the action of her own citizens[,] the soil is made forever free." Lincoln expressed his belief that emancipation would "result in good to the white race as well as to those who [had] been made free by this act," though he admitted, "Some may thereby be made to suffer temporary pecuniary loss." He closed with an admonition to blacks that mildly reflected the paternalistic, though well-meaning, racial attitudes of even the most progressive whites of the time. "I hope that you, colored people, who have been emancipated," Lincoln advised, "will use this great boon which has been given you to improve yourselves, both morally and intellectually."[105]

Despite Lincoln's profession that the success of emancipation in Maryland was worth double the electoral votes of the state, he plainly wanted the electoral votes of the Old Line State. On October 19, when a group of "loyal Marylanders" came to the White House to compliment him on the success of his emancipation policy in their state, Lincoln's attention had already turned to the presidential election in November. After expressing his congratulations to "Maryland, and the nation, and the world" upon the state's emancipation, he devoted much of his response to reminding his visitors of what was at stake in the presidential election. He voiced his confidence that the American people would reject the Democratic siren call of "immediate peace" and instead "preserve their country and their liberty" by supporting the war at the polls.[106]

Lincoln's chances of winning Maryland's electoral votes, along with those of neighboring Delaware, had been problematic. Antipathy to the Republican Party, though not as strong as in Kentucky and even in Delaware, lingered in the Old Line State. In changing the name of the party to the National Union Party in the convention at Baltimore in June, Republicans did not dissolve the hostility to them among Maryland conservatives. Radical leaders in Congress like Winter Davis, Benjamin F. Wade, Thaddeus Stevens, and Charles Sumner were viewed by conservatives as revolutionaries determined to impose black equality and a "consolidated" government on the country. Many Maryland Unionists had little faith that Lincoln would or could withstand the radicals in his party; furthermore, along with old Union Democrats, they still remembered the president's violations of civil liberties early in the war. On the other hand, they could not forgive McClellan for the direct role that he had played in the arrests and imprisonment of Maryland officials and legislators in 1861. These conservatives, as did conservatives in the other border states, also questioned whether Lincoln could bring the war to a speedy and successful conclusion. Nonetheless, their commitment to the struggle to preserve the Union and defeat the rebels trumped all other considerations for them in the 1864 presidential election. Gubernatorial candidate Swann summarized the position of the conservative supporters of Lincoln when he declared, "The path to peace lies across the battlefield" of the South, and not in the election to the presidency of a failed general, McClellan, on a defeatist platform.[107]

Maryland radicals, though still a minority in the Unionist ranks, had increased in number during the emancipation campaign. They identified with the Unconditional Unionist faction. Although they supported Lincoln as the party's candidate, Winter Davis and the radicals found him insufficiently radical and feared that he would be willing to accept a compromise peace after the election. They worried that Lincoln, despite his support for a constitutional amendment to end slavery everywhere in the country, would leave blacks to the tender mercies of returning rebels after the war. The president had already made clear his approval of state apprenticeship systems for young blacks after emancipation, which radicals viewed as an attempt to maintain slavery. Radicals also vehemently objected to his mild plan of amnesty and reconstruction, or "restoration" as Lincoln preferred, for former Confederates.

In campaigning for Lincoln, Maryland radicals repeatedly charged that McClellan's supporters, whether Democrats or conservatives like Senator Johnson, were Copperheads and traitors to the Union. Radicals claimed that as president McClellan would be under the influence of the Copperheads and upon assuming office would arrange a cease-fire with the rebels. This, they insisted, would inevitably mean Confederate independence. The forced resignation in September of Blair from the post of postmaster general had helped Winter Davis and other Maryland radicals overcome some of their concerns about Lincoln. Still, after Lincoln won the election, Davis wrote, "The people now know Lincoln and voted for him to keep out worse people—keeping their hands on the pit of the stomach the while! No act of wise self-control—no such subordination of disgust to the necessities of a crisis and the dictates of cool judgment has ever before been exhibited by any people in history."[108]

Whatever the truth of Davis's biased conclusion, Lincoln swept to victory in Maryland and in the nation. He captured 40,153 votes to McClellan's 32,739 in the Old Line State. Swann, who was aligned with Lincoln and also with both Unionist factions, won the governorship by a similar majority over the Democratic candidate. Swann's coalition captured three of the five seats in the U.S. House of Representatives. It also retained control of the state legislature, though by only a slim margin in the senate.[109] Swann hailed Lincoln's election and congratulated the president on his success in winning Maryland's electoral vote. "With freedom proclaimed, and the [Union] party upon a footing of harmony," he wrote Lincoln, "we may promise you a cordial support during your new term."[110]

Encouraged by the president, the old Congress on January 31, 1865, initiated the Thirteenth Amendment abolishing slavery. Lincoln immediately sent it to the states for ratification. All but one of the Maryland members in the House of Representatives voted for it. Senator Johnson also supported it while still holding out a false hope that slaveholders would be compensated by the federal government for their losses. Johnson and Robert Wilson of Missouri were the only border state senators voting for the amendment.[111] Senator Hicks, who favored the amendment, was dying and unable to vote. The Maryland General Assembly ratified the freedom amendment, though it declared that Congress should compensate the former owners for the freed slaves.[112]

Troubles in Maryland, however, did not end with the approval of the state constitution and the Lincoln and Swann victories in the November election. Many "evil-disposed persons," General Wallace complained on November 9, 1864, were intent on "obstructing and nullifying . . . the emancipation provision of the New Constitution [by] availing themselves of . . . the ancient slave code of Maryland, as yet unrepealed." He cited the continued enforcement of the apprentice law as one evasion. In some counties, the general noted, law officers had prevented the freedpersons from appealing to the courts for protection. Wallace, who was no longer under political restraints—and without consulting Lincoln—issued an order placing the former slaves "under special military protection" until the Maryland legislature could provide for their security. He established "a freedmen's bureau" for the Middle Department and placed Major William M. Este, his aide-de-camp, in charge. Wallace directed district provost marshals to assist Estes in protecting and aiding blacks. The general's freedmen's bureau would be financed by fines and donations, but where these fell short, Estes could levy "contributions" on "avowed rebel sympathizers" in Baltimore.[113]

Wallace's action had a limited effect, and after three months his freedmen's bureau gave way to the federal Bureau of Refugees, Freedmen, and Abandoned Lands, also known as the Freedmen's Bureau. Black education became the main permanent contribution of this much-maligned agency. After the demise of the Freedmen's Bureau in Maryland in 1868, discriminatory state laws and municipal ordinances replaced the old slave codes.[114]

After his reelection, Lincoln became involved in the old, vexatious quarrel between Montgomery Blair and Winter Davis over federal patronage in Maryland. The president had repeatedly pressed the two antagonists to put aside their differences and cooperate in matters of federal offices, but to no avail.[115] Blair, who had been politically sacrificed by Lincoln in September to appease the radicals in his party, expected the president to reward him after the election. The former postmaster general wanted control of federal offices in his state. He also sought the president's support for him or one of his friends for a Senate seat. Like Davis, Blair had made many political enemies, and his influence among conservatives like Governor Bradford and Governor-elect Swann had declined since his ill-tempered speech at Rockville in 1863. The president disliked Davis, though he believed (incorrectly) that the brilliant congressman might lessen his hostility to him after the election. At the same time, Lincoln was grateful to the Blairs for their unstinting support of his administration.

Any hope that Lincoln might have had for avoiding the Maryland patronage squabble ended one month after the election when Blair approached him and asked that he remove Henry W. Hoffman, a Davis associate, from his position as collector of the port of Baltimore. Hoffman owed his appointment, one of the most lucrative under federal patronage, to Secretary of the Treasury Chase. Lincoln attempted a ploy to satisfy

Blair without offending the Davis faction. He told Blair that he would place a position in the Spanish mission in Madrid at his disposal so he could offer it to Hoffman, who in turn would resign as collector of the port. If Hoffman agreed, Hicks, who was sick, would resign from the Senate and fill the post of collector. This scenario, Lincoln hoped, would permit the Maryland General Assembly's selection of Blair to the Senate.[116]

Blair immediately realized that Hoffman would never resign the collectorship for a foreign mission. He stormed into Secretary of the Navy Gideon Welles's office and exclaimed that Lincoln had betrayed him to his enemies in Maryland and in Congress. Welles, a friend of Blair, advised him to confront the president and demand Hoffman's removal. Two days later Blair finally saw Lincoln and proceeded to unload his pent-up anger on the president, accusing the radicals of trying to destroy him. Taken aback by Blair's vitriol, the president admonished him, "It is better not to be led from the region of reason into that of hot blood, by imputing to public men motives which they do not avow." In the meeting, Lincoln declined to provide Blair with any satisfaction regarding Hoffman.[117]

When Senator Hicks died in February 1865, Lincoln privately favored Blair to replace him, but he refused to make known his wishes because, as Welles unfairly claimed, powerful influences "controlled him against his will." These influences, according to the navy secretary, included not only the Davis faction but also Treasury Department officials in Washington and Maryland. They were supported, Welles said, by Chase and Stanton, both of whom had often crossed swords with Blair in the cabinet. At any rate, the Maryland General Assembly selected Congressman Creswell, a compromise candidate, to take Hicks's seat. Winter Davis, not satisfied with the outcome, continued his attacks on the president and his policies, though his congressional term had expired. Irritated by Davis's conduct and probably feeling guilty that he had not aided Blair earlier, Lincoln, finally in early April, removed Hoffman as collector of the Baltimore port. He also asked Senator Creswell to meet with Swann and submit to him a list of federal appointments for Maryland, including the collectorship. On April 14, the last day of his life, Lincoln accepted the Swann-Creswell slate of appointees.[118]

The assassination of the man who had navigated the treacherous political waters in the border states en route to saving the Union and ending slavery sent shock waves through the nation. Marylanders, who, like most border state citizens, had voted against Lincoln in the 1860 election, who had rioted against his call for troops in April 1861, and who had resisted his antislavery policies, now overwhelmingly mourned his death. Anna M. Ferris in neighboring Delaware reflected in her diary the shock and pain of so many people in Maryland and in her state upon the news of the assassination: "We laid down last night with a sense of peace and happiness long unknown. We awoke this morning to a consciousness of horror & grief never known before! It is really dreadful to write the words that express such a horrible crime—the President has been assassinated! No words can possibly express the feeling it creates." Some people could not believe that such a horrible event had occurred in America, a republic of constitutional processes specially created, they thought, to avoid such political horrors. Thomas F. Bayard, a leading Delaware Democrat, wrote that "this foul murder" of a public official in America was "disgraceful and horrible" and "unknown" in the country. "Assassination is un-American," Bayard declared.[119]

On April 21 Marylanders turned out in large numbers when the funeral train passed through the state on the long circuitous route that would take Lincoln's body to Springfield for burial. At Baltimore, where the train stopped for five hours and where in February 1861 Lincoln had secretly slipped through the city to avoid an assassination plot, thousands of people gathered to view his body at the Merchants' Exchange building. Only one-fifth of those who had waited since dawn succeeded in paying their solemn respects. On every Baltimore street, crowds of African Americans, "the saddest of the sad," according to an observer, watched the carriage pass. That afternoon the funeral train continued its mournful journey and entered Pennsylvania, where the coffin was taken to the state capitol in Harrisburg and opened.[120]

The martyred Lincoln now occupied a special place for Marylanders in the pantheon of American heroes. His policies, while often opposed by them as well as by those who fought in the Confederate army, had achieved the main war objective that most Maryland citizens wanted—the preservation of the Union. Although violations of civil liberties had occurred with Lincoln's support or acquiescence, the war had been prosecuted without serious or long-term damage to the rights of citizens, traditional federal-state relations, constitutional government, or local institutions. The major changes, of course, to Maryland institutions and lifestyles was the destruction of slavery, the albatross around the neck of the state that had retarded its political, social, and economic progress. Lincoln had successfully nudged Maryland Unionists toward emancipation, and in October 1864 the Old Line State had become the first border state to abolish slavery. This success had been achieved without confirming white fears that abolition would create a social revolution, since white supremacy and discrimination against blacks continued. Lincoln, a son of the conservative border country, had accomplished the enormous task of suppressing the greatest threat to the Republic, southern secession, and bringing about the end of the nation's colossal blemish—slavery. The price, however, had been high in terms of casualties and social and economic dislocations. It would be left for others, in Maryland and elsewhere, during Reconstruction and beyond, to pursue Abraham Lincoln's vision of equality, progress, and true democracy in America.

■

Union and Emancipation Triumphant: Missouri

On January 4, 1863, six members of the Missouri delegation in Congress called on Lincoln at the White House. They came to ask him to prohibit General Samuel R. Curtis from interfering in the civil affairs of the state. Curtis in September 1862 had replaced Henry W. Halleck as commander of the Department of Missouri after "Old Brains" became general in chief of the Union armies. The Missouri congressmen specifically wanted Lincoln to end the military's abusive enforcement of tax assessments on rebel supporters, which, they said, was also often levied on unoffending citizens. In addition, the Missouri congressmen protested the increased interference of Curtis's provost marshals in the civil and judicial affairs of the state.[1] Four days earlier, Union governor Hamilton Gamble had written Lincoln demanding that he revoke the assessments imposed on the citizens. In doing so, Gamble inaccurately reported that he had succeeded in restoring peace and civil government in the state, and he argued that no need existed for the federal military's intervention in local affairs.[2]

At the same time, radical Unionists, or Charcoals, urged Lincoln to sustain Curtis and the army's assessments policy as a means to punish rebel sympathizers and those who aided local guerrillas. Gamble, they charged, was weak and too lenient on enemies of the Union. Furthermore, they told the president that he had been misled by Gamble about conditions in the state and the success of his military forces, known as the Enrolled Missouri

Militia and commanded by General John M. Schofield. B. Gratz Brown, a radical leader and an ardent emancipationist, also informed the president that while Curtis acted "openly in the interests of Freedom," the governor, "no matter what professions he [might] make at Washington, [was] secretly in the service of Slavery."[3] Charles D. Drake, a Saint Louis lawyer and a rising star in the radical firmament, warned Lincoln that, whatever he had heard from the governor, "the disloyal element in Missouri [had] not yielded a jot of its spirit" and could only be controlled by the power of the federal military. The success of the northern Democrats in the fall 1862 elections and the opposition to the Emancipation Proclamation had increased defiance of the Union in the state, Drake wrote the president. "I solemnly assure you that never has the spirit of hatred to the Union been more resolute in this State than now." Drake bluntly blamed Lincoln for contributing to the deplorable situation in Missouri by his "kind-heartedness" and forbearance toward the rebels.[4]

On January 5, 1863, the day after his meeting with the state's congressmen, Lincoln wrote Curtis reminding him, "I am having a good deal of trouble with Missouri matters." Denying any desire to intervene in the state's affairs, the president asked the general to confer with Governor Gamble on the assessments issue and on "other Missouri questions." However, Lincoln did not await the action of the two men; on January 20 he had Secretary of War Edwin M. Stanton suspend military assessments throughout the state. The president also sought to enlighten Curtis on the reasons for the Unionist divisions in the state. "One class of friends believe in greater severity, and another in greater leniency, in regard to arrests, banishments, and assessments," he said. "As usual in such cases, each questions the other's motives. On the one hand it is insisted that Gov. Gamble's Unionism, at most, is not better than a secondary spring of action—that hunkerism, and a wish for political influence, stand before Unionism, with him. On the other hand, it is urged" by supporters of the governor "that arrests, banishments, and assessments are made more for private malice, revenge, and pecuniary interest, than for the public good." Lincoln told Curtis, "Gov. Gamble is an honest and true man," and by acting with him, he said, the Missouri issues could be resolved.[5]

Lincoln sent Gamble a copy of his letter to Curtis. The two Union leaders met, but they failed to reach an agreement on the key issues that disturbed civil-military relations in the state, mainly the control of Missouri troops and the system of provost marshals. Curtis, a former Republican congressman of Iowa, reported to the president that despite conservative claims, he was diligent in protecting the property of Unionists, including their slaves but not those of rebels. Curtis said that he had been careful to prevent the fugitives of loyal owners from entering his camps. The general insisted, however, "The Slave power will be respected" in Missouri, "but it cannot lead in this Department."[6]

Concerned that the president's support of him was slipping, Gamble on February 4, 1863, wrote Lincoln and demanded that he "manifest publicly whatever confidence" the president had in him. The claims of Curtis's radical friends in Washington that his Unionism was "but a secondary motive of [his] action" had especially offended Gamble. The governor again defended his record as a true Unionist and reminded Lincoln that when he "took office the Union men were oppressed and outraged all over the State," but now, he said, "they are organized and feel that the strength is with them."[7] (Gamble was still technically the provisional governor of Missouri, having been appointed to the position by the state convention in 1861.) The president wisely did not respond to Gamble's demand for a public statement of support; it would have inflamed radical opposition to Lincoln in the state.

Meanwhile, Lincoln had become entangled in another Missouri hubbub that largely divided along radical-conservative lines. On December 19, 1862, General Curtis expelled Samuel B. McPheeters, a prominent minister of the Pine Street Presbyterian Church in Saint Louis, from his pastorate and ordered him out of the state because of "unmistakeable [sic] evidence of sympathy with the rebellion."[8] The general's provost marshal seized the church's records and appointed three church members to fill the pulpit. McPheeters, a native of Raleigh, North Carolina, and a graduate of the University of North Carolina and the Princeton Theological Seminary, immediately wrote Attorney General Edward Bates, a friend, and sought his support. With Governor Gamble's blessings and those of the conservatives in his church, McPheeters rushed to Washington to present his case in person to secure the president's revocation of the expulsion order. He brought with him documents designed to demonstrate that he had done nothing to warrant Curtis's action.[9]

On December 27 McPheeters, along with Bates, met with Lincoln. He showed the president the documents in his case, including the loyalty oath that he had taken as required of all pastors by the Union state convention. McPheeters argued that the charges of disloyalty against him stemmed from the failure of radical members of his church to have him express his views on the war; if he had done so, he said, it would have violated his pastoral responsibility to stay out of politics. When he refused, McPheeters told Lincoln, the disaffected members demanded that General Curtis issue the expulsion order. McPheeters reported to the president that a few days before Curtis ordered his banishment, the *Saint Louis Missouri Democrat*, the organ of the radicals, published an article charging him with supporting the rebellion. The article was signed by the three parishioners whom Curtis's provost marshal later appointed to manage the affairs of the church.[10]

After listening to McPheeters's appeal, Lincoln informed the minister that he had received letters from Saint Louis Unionists supporting Curtis's expulsion order. According to McPheeters's account of the meeting, the president remarked, "If this order should be revoked it would be considered a secession triumph" by many Unionists. In a revealing aside, probably prompted by the recent crushing defeat of the Union army at Fredericksburg, Lincoln despondently declared that he did not know that the rebellion "would be put down." He "doubted if the Government had the power to suppress it" and added that "the means that were necessary, it seemed, the country would not allow." The president then switched back to the situation at hand in Missouri and commented, "It is doubtful, from all I can learn, whether the United States or Jeff. Davis have [the] most authority in St. Louis." On the issue of McPheeters's loyalty, Lincoln stated, "I presume if you were in Jeff. Davis' dominions you would preach and pray differently from what you do here," a conclusion that the minister challenged. "No sir," McPheeters indignantly declared, "I conduct the worship of God's house without reference to human government. I hold that there are two kingdoms—both ordained of God—the State and the Church. I recognize in you the chief officer of the United States [with whose] duties I do not interfere."[11]

Attorney General Bates came to McPheeters's defense in the meeting and argued that the minister had violated no law, nor had he acted in a way hostile toward the government. At this point, Lincoln softened his attitude and announced that he did not see any reason for Curtis's issuance of the expulsion order. He wrote out a message to the general suspending the order until, he said, "you hear from me again."[12] As McPheeters left the room, Lincoln turned to him and remarked, "There [is] a difficulty in knowing what to do with such cases, very much like the difficulty that [Shakespeare's] Shylock had in knowing how to get the pound of flesh without the blood."[13]

Stunned by the president's message suspending McPheeters's expulsion, Curtis immediately wrote Lincoln defending his action and asking the president to restore his order. In a separate letter of explanation, he protested that Lincoln permitted McPheeters and others "to carry everything to you, even before seeking redress elsewhere."[14] The general still insisted that the minister was disloyal, but as evidence of it, Curtis only cited the pastor's refusal to pray for the president, a charge that McPheeters had denied. Curtis claimed, "This man is evidently a bad rebel doing injury here, and his removal [is] universally approved by Union men." He reported, "Some of the most reliable men of the city"—he mainly meant those in the radical faction—"express surprise at the influence rebel sympathizers have at Washington." Curtis contended, "Rebel priests are dangerous and diabolical in society," and he admitted that he had expelled McPheeters as an example of the consequences for those ministers who expressed sympathy for the rebellion.[15] The general also sent a leading Saint Louis attorney, who was also a member of McPheeters's church, George P. Strong, to deliver the letter to Lincoln and argue for the president's reinstatement of the expulsion order.[16]

Lincoln stood by his suspension of the general's order. He wrote Curtis that the military's case for McPheeters's expulsion was unsubstantiated; it was based, he declared, on the flimsy charges that the minister did not pray for the president and the government and that he had "a rebel wife & rebel relations." At the same time, Lincoln expressed his belief that McPheeters did indeed sympathize with the rebels, but, he told Curtis, he should not be "exiled upon the suspicion of his secret sympathies." Nonetheless, the president left the matter with the general, who, he said, was "on the spot," and told him, "If, after all, you think the public good requires his removal, my suspension of the order is withdrawn." In closing, Lincoln made an important point regarding the military or the federal government's involvement with the churches. "The U.S. government," he wrote, "must not . . . undertake to run the churches. When an individual, in a church or out of it, becomes dangerous to the public interest, he must be checked; but let the churches, as such take care of themselves. It will not do for the U.S. to appoint Trustees, Supervisors, or other agents for the churches."[17]

The McPheeters controversy, which had received national attention, did not easily go away. Although the banishment order had been suspended and he had returned to Saint Louis, McPheeters and his conservative friends petitioned Curtis for his reinstatement as pastor of the Pine Street Presbyterian Church. Curtis indicated his willingness to accommodate McPheeters, provided he could satisfactorily answer a series of questions designed to establish his loyalty. As he had done before, the reverend refused to answer the political questions because, he argued, they would compromise his position as a minister and also the church's relationship with the government.[18] Angered by that response, the general refused to reinstate McPheeters as the minister of the church. On April 3, 1863, Curtis wrote Lincoln explaining the reasons for his decision and asking for further instructions on the issue. He maintained that his questions to McPheeters sought to ascertain only his loyalty, not his religious sentiments. Curtis sarcastically commented that McPheeters's "idea of a [government] assault on the Divinity of Christs [sic] Church [was] quite too refined for my intellectual comprehension."[19]

There is no evidence that Lincoln answered Curtis's letter. He might not have read the letter or he might have simply forgot it.[20] In December 1863 McPheeters and his friends, including Governor Gamble, again appealed to the president to revoke the suspension order. Lincoln expressed surprise that the matter had not been resolved; he had assumed that Curtis had obeyed his January 2, 1863, instructions, although he had given the general the authority to reinstate the suspension if he believed that it was necessary. The president also chided McPheeters's petitioners for their failure to specify what "ecclesiastical rights" had been withheld from the minister. "Is it not a strange illustration of the condition of things," Lincoln remarked, "that the question of who shall be allowed to preach in a church in St. Louis, shall be decided by the *President of the United States*?" He thought that the controversy over McPheeters's status should have been settled in a cooperative way by the two sides, not by someone in Washington, least of all the president.[21] Although irritated by the Missourians, Lincoln on December 31, 1863, restored McPheeters's "ecclesiastical rights," and in early 1864, the minister resumed the pastorate of the Pine Street Presbyterian Church.[22]

By February 1863 it had become clear to Gamble and to Missouri's conservative Unionists, or "Claybanks" that Curtis had cast his lot with their

Charles D. Drake, firebrand spokesman of the Missouri radicals and a harsh critic of Lincoln and conservative Unionists. He was the leader in the Missouri convention that abolished slavery in early 1865 and disfranchised rebels and their supporters in the state. After the war, Drake served in the U.S. Senate. Courtesy of the Brady-Handy Collection, Prints and Photographs Division, Library of Congress, Washington, DC.

radical adversaries. Curtis's alignment with the Charcoals created a growing demand by conservatives like U.S. Senator John B. Henderson for the general's removal from command in the state. In Washington, Attorney General Bates, who was Gamble's brother-in-law, and Missouri's conservative congressmen joined in the chorus against Curtis. In late February Henderson spoke to Lincoln and, according to the senator, persuaded the president "to think positively [about] the removal of Curtis"; Lincoln, however, expressed difficulties in finding an acceptable replacement. Henderson's motivation in demanding the general's replacement was not altogether pure. He admitted to Bates that if he could secure Curtis's removal, it would increase his influence in the state legislature, where he expected to be a candidate for election to the U.S. Senate.[23] (Henderson had been appointed to the U.S. Senate by Governor Gamble in 1862 to replace a senator who had gone south to join the Confederacy.) On one important point Henderson agreed with the radicals: he favored the recruitment of black troops, a policy that, as in other border states, a majority of Missouri whites vehemently opposed when it was launched in early 1863.[24]

By March 10, 1863, Lincoln thought that he had worked through the difficulties of finding an acceptable replacement for General Curtis. He selected the aging General Edwin V. Sumner to command the Department of Missouri.[25] Sumner, however, died en route to Missouri, and Curtis remained in temporary command. Curtis's radical supporters and others now began a campaign for his retention as the department commander. Sixty-four members of the General Assembly petitioned the president on behalf of the general. "His administration has given satisfaction to the unconditional Union Men," they told Lincoln. Moreover, they "deemed the present a most injudicious time to make a change in this Department" because of the forthcoming reconvening of the state convention to consider emancipation.[26]

A delegation of the president's friends from Illinois, including O. M. Hatch and Jesse K. Dubois, visited Saint Louis in late March and appealed to Lincoln to retain Curtis in command. "The Emancipation struggle now going on in Missouri is well known to you," they wrote, "and it is all important that some one in sympathy with that effort, should be in command."[27] The radical Henry T. Blow, a new member of Congress from Missouri, informed Lincoln that General Curtis had "administered this Department in a manly, prudent & satisfactory manner [and had] been both friendly and generous towards Govr. Gamble," who, however, had maintained an "unrelenting [hostile] spirit towards every one" who disagreed with or opposed him. General Francis J. Herron, the youngest major general in the Union army, leaped over his superiors and appealed directly to the president for the retention of Curtis. He claimed that Curtis had the unanimous support of both officers and men in the department.[28]

Drake, who pulled no punches in his attacks on Gamble and conservative Unionists, wrote Lincoln that Curtis had saved Saint Louis and Missouri from a rebel invasion and should be retained in command. He claimed, "St. Louis is full of traitors, daily & hourly contriving ways & means to aid the rebel cause, and watching & waiting continually for the advent of 'Price's Army,' that they may rise and take their revenge." Drake again blamed the president for the troubles in Missouri. "Your natural clemency is doing harm that I am sure you do not intend, and perhaps are not aware of," he told Lincoln. "The warmest partizan that aided in your elevation to the Presidency has no more confidence in your patriotism than I have, nor any more earnest purpose to uphold you," but, Drake frankly asserted, "your leniency is weakening the heart of the nation. . . . Mr President, I tell you that your tenderness toward rebels and their sympathizers is one of the serious difficulties which the nation has to contend; and it is particularly felt in Missouri." He demanded that Lincoln permit the military authorities "to deal with rebels as they deserve." As it stood, Curtis and his provost marshals, Drake declared, were afraid to move against rebel sympathizers because they had "reason to apprehend a countermand from Washington." "It is trying enough," Drake complained, "to be outspokenly loyal here, without finding traitors screened and encouraged by the kind-heartedness of the nation's Chief."[29]

Whatever Lincoln thought of Drake's assessment of the situation in Missouri and of his national leadership, he knew that he would receive no peace at the hands of the radicals unless he abandoned Gamble, which he would not do. He probably also knew that the surge of partisanship in the state, triggered by the controversy over Curtis, now threatened the emancipation movement in the reconvened state convention.

Meanwhile, Senator Henderson had returned to Missouri and, predictably, found further evidence for the removal of Curtis. He reported to Lincoln that "much angry excitement" existed against the general because he permitted army camps to become sanctuaries for the slaves of loyal masters. In addition, Henderson told the president that outside Saint Louis "a most terrible prejudice" had developed against Curtis on account of his alleged involvement in cotton speculation. "This of itself is enough to damn any man." Furthermore, the senator said, because Curtis and Gamble were at cross-purposes, "I believe if [the general] remains, the Gov. will resign. If he does, I fear in the excited state of affairs here" that the rebels "will seize upon it as a pretext for new operations against the Government," which might succeed. Henderson predicted, "The simple removal of Genl Curtis will . . . be worth fifty thousand men" toward the pacification of Missouri.[30] (Lincoln later absolved the general from the cotton speculation charge, though some of his officers were deeply engaged in the seizure and sale of this valuable commodity.)

Other conservative Unionists also sought to enlighten the president on the calamitous consequences of keeping Curtis in command. "Revolutionaries" like Drake and B. Gratz Brown of Saint Louis, they claimed, had been empowered by Curtis's command of the department. Samuel T. Glover, a political confidant of Lincoln in Missouri and a Claybank, warned the president that the Charcoals had organized a party in the state determined upon the immediate abolition of slavery by the military and the disfranchisement of all men who opposed them. "[These] Revolutionaries have derived their influence almost wholly from the terror created by the military," Glover, with considerable exaggeration, reported to Lincoln. Already, he wrote, provost marshals were issuing "deeds of emancipation" to slaves without regard to the loyalty of their owners. "The belief [has been] fixed on many minds that the Provost Marshalls [sic] were soon to abolish slavery regardless of law or constitution." In an appeal to Lincoln's political instincts, Glover informed the president that the radicals were organizing to oppose him in the presidential election. He said that "they continually inveighed against [Lincoln's] administration" and proclaimed Secretary of the Treasury Salmon P. Chase "the very hope of the country." Chase surrogates, Glover told Lincoln, had been appointed as treasury agents in the state for the purpose of preparing the ground for the secretary's candidacy. Glover warned the president, "The good of the country requires this [revolutionary] movement to be checked. But while the military influence upholds it nothing can stand in its way." On May 2, 1863, Gamble echoed these sentiments and implored Lincoln, "Take Curtis away from here," asking him to give the command to someone who would suppress the radical publications that were "most contemptuous [of Lincoln's] administration."[31]

Caught in the middle of the bitter factional feud in Missouri, Lincoln, as was his practice, hesitated to act in the Curtis case until he had thought carefully about it. Finally, on May 11 he made his decision. He informed Secretary of War Stanton that he could see "no other way to avoid the worst consequences" in Missouri than to relieve General Curtis and appoint General Schofield to the command of the department.[32] Lincoln knew that Schofield, a conservative, was acceptable to Governor Gamble and his political supporters. Hoping that Schofield would appreciate the difficulties of the situation, Lincoln in making the appointment explained to him, "[I] did not relieve Gen. Curtis because of any full conviction that he had done wrong by commission or omission. I did it because of a conviction in my mind that the Union men of Missouri, constituting, when united, a vast majority of the whole people, have entered into a pestilent factional quarrel among themselves, Gen. Curtis, perhaps not of choice, being the head of one faction, and Gov. Gamble that of the other." This characterization of the political divisions in Missouri would come back to haunt Lincoln when his statement became public. He told Schofield that after trying to moderate the conflict, it became worse, until, he said, "I felt it my duty to break it up some how; and as I could not remove Gov. Gamble, I had to remove Gen. Curtis."[33]

The president admonished Schofield, "Undo nothing merely because Gen. Curtis or Gov. Gamble did it; but . . . exercise your judgment, and do *right* for the public interest." He instructed his new department commander to let his "military measures be strong enough to repel the invader and keep the peace, and not so strong as to unnecessarily harass and persecute the people." With typical Lincolnesque reasoning, he advised Schofield, "If both factions, or neither, shall abuse you, you will probably be about right. Beware of being assailed by one, and praised by the other." Schofield assured Lincoln that he would follow his advice, and he acknowledged that his greatest task would be in dealing with the two antagonistic Unionist factions.[34]

Curtis's removal and Schofield's appointment brought down on Lincoln's head the wrath of the Missouri radicals and their friends elsewhere. Upon news of the president's decision, radicals held a mass protest meeting in Saint Louis. German Americans, as they had done for Frémont in 1861, turned out in large numbers to voice their strong disapproval of the change in the military command. Many of them, having escaped oppression in Germany, naturally identified with the radical antislavery movement in Missouri and passionately opposed the Confederate oligarchy. However, they increasingly viewed Lincoln as too conservative on slavery and too willing to please Gamble and his Missouri friends.

Charles Drake headed a committee in the radical meeting that telegraphed Lincoln demanding he suspend the appointment of the conservative Schofield until he heard from them. Angered by the committee's effrontery and frustrated by his dealings with the state's Unionists, Lincoln immediately replied, "It is very painful to me that you in Missouri can not, or will not, settle your factional quarrel among yourselves. I have been tormented with it beyond endurance for months, by both sides. Neither side pays the least respect to my appeals to [their] reason. I am now compelled to take hold of the case." He did not, however, say how he would do it.[35]

Despite the difficulties in finding a replacement for Curtis, Lincoln's appointment of Schofield was a mistake. He could have left Curtis in command until he had found a successor who was not viewed by the Charcoals as sympathetic to the Claybanks. Lincoln could have selected a more politically sensitive senior general (for example, John A. Dix of New York), who might have been able to secure the cooperation of the more reasonable members of both Unionist factions.

The Saint Louis meeting of radicals adopted a series of resolutions calling for Curtis's restoration to command and also for immediate emancipation in Missouri. They dispatched James Taussig, a Saint Louis attorney, to lay the resolutions before the president. Taussig's meeting with the president proved testy, with Lincoln venting his frustration on him. According to Taussig's account, which the radical *Saint Louis Missouri Democrat* printed on June 9, 1863, Lincoln declared that he found the "dissensions" in Missouri "due solely to a factious spirit which is exceedingly reprehensible." "The two parties," he said, "ought to have their heads knocked together. Either [party] would rather see the defeat of their adversary than that of Jefferson Davis." The president contended that "this spirit of faction" in the state was the reason for the defeat of the congressional bill in February 1863 to compensate Missouri slaveholders for the loss of their slaves, a measure that he "strongly desired."[36]

Lincoln was wrong in attributing the failure of the compensation bill to Missouri's factionalism. The defeat of the bill occurred because of congressional divisions over funding and the delaying tactics of members who opposed it (see chapter 6). The president startled Taussig when he informed him, "The Union men in Missouri who are in favor of gradual emancipation represented his views better than [the radicals] who are in favor of immediate emancipation." Rejecting the demand for Curtis's reinstatement, Lincoln told Taussig that he had appointed Schofield "with a view, if possible, to reconcile and satisfy the two factions." He said that he had given

Schofield "instructions not to interfere with either party, but to confine himself to his military duties," a rather tall order for any commander in Missouri.[37]

The publication in the radical *Saint Louis Missouri Democrat* of Lincoln's May 27 confidential letter to General Schofield created instant trouble for the president. Upset by this breach of secrecy, Schofield demanded an explanation from the editor, William McKee, on how he had obtained the letter and why he had printed it. McKee refused to answer, whereupon Schofield arrested him, but he immediately paroled him pending military proceedings against him. The radicals wasted no time in denouncing the arrest as "an insult to the supporters of the Union."[38] When Lincoln learned of McKee's arrest, he wrote the general expressing his regret for the action and his fear that it had lost the general "the middle position" that Lincoln had wanted him to hold. He told Schofield, "I care very little for the publication of any letter I have written"; however, Lincoln asked the general to "spare me the trouble this is likely to bring," which suggested that he really did care about it. Schofield complied and suspended all military proceedings against McKee. The general never found out who had obtained Lincoln's May 27 letter, but he suspected that it was a subordinate of General Curtis, to whom the president had indiscreetly sent a copy and who had cause to embarrass him.[39]

The disclosure of the president's May 27 letter to Schofield also provoked an indignant response from Governor Gamble. The governor took great offense at Lincoln's assertion that the Union men of Missouri had become engaged in "a pestilent factional quarrel among themselves" and that he, Gamble, headed one of the factions. He wrote Lincoln "that the language of your letter when writing about the Governor of one of the United States [was] unbecoming your position." Gamble denied that he headed a faction, and Lincoln probably regretted that he had made the assertion. The irate governor asked, and himself answered, nine questions designed to remind Lincoln of his actions in saving the state for the Union. He concluded his protest by telling the president, "Your insult published over the land was most underserved" and that it was grossly unfair to him.[40]

Knowing its contents, Lincoln refused to read Gamble's "cross letter" because, as he wrote the Missouri governor, "I am trying to preserve my own temper, by avoiding irritants, so far as practicable." However, when he wrote Schofield on May 27, Lincoln told Gamble, "I was totally unconscious of any malice, or disrespect towards you, or of using any expression which should offend you, if seen by you."[41] The president's explanation seems to have calmed down the hypersensitive governor, who probably realized that he could ill afford to carry on a quarrel with the president while he confronted a serious challenge to his authority from the radicals in the state.

The Missouri state convention meeting in June 1862 had debated Lincoln's proposal for federal, compensated emancipation, only to reject it by a large majority. After the convention adjourned in December and Lincoln issued his Emancipation Proclamation, pressure mounted for the state to reconsider the question of emancipation. Wanting to act before it was too late to salvage something from the collapse of slavery, which was more at risk in Missouri than in neighboring Kentucky, Governor Gamble called for the convention to reconvene on June 15, 1863, at Jefferson City for the purpose of adopting "some scheme of Emancipation." Gamble resumed the chairmanship of the convention and, taking his cue from Lincoln's comment to Taussig, introduced a proposal for gradual, federal, compensated emancipation designed to end slavery by July 4, 1876, fittingly on the centennial anniversary of the Declaration of Independence.[42]

In introducing his emancipation plan, Gamble was also influenced by a conversation that former governor Austin A. King had had with Lincoln in the spring and that was recalled by King in a speech at Lexington, Missouri, three weeks before the convention met. After praising Gamble as "a conservative man," the president related to King an anecdote about confronting a rattlesnake in order to demonstrate that gradual emancipation was the best policy for ending slavery in Missouri. Lincoln said that "if he met a rattlesnake in his path, and he had a stick in his hand, his first impression would be to kill it; but if he found one in the bed between his children he would pursue a different course, for by killing the snake he may injure the children; therefore he would take a more gentle way to get the snake out before he killed it. The same with slavery; he was satisfied that immediate emancipation would be detrimental to the interest of the State."[43] Lincoln had used the rattlesnake analogy in a speech at Hartford, Connecticut, on March 5, 1860, when he argued that the ultimate extinction of slavery could be achieved constitutionally by preventing its expansion into the territories.[44]

The weakness in Gamble's compensated emancipation resolution in the state convention soon became apparent. Congress, as Lincoln noted, had already failed to enact a federal compensation bill for Missouri, a prerequisite for many delegates before they would support Gamble's resolution. Even if the convention had approved compensation in principle, delegates probably would have quibbled over the amount per slave to be paid to the slaveholder. A growing number of delegates, mainly radicals, now favored immediate emancipation as the only practical way to rid the state of the institution that had caused the war and that kept the rebellion alive. With that in mind, Drake, the radical leader in the convention, offered a substitute to the Gamble proposal that would provide for emancipation by January 1, 1864, and without compensation. But even Drake, at least at this time, was not prepared to extend civil rights to blacks. He included in his substitute resolution a provision for a temporary apprenticeship system "sufficient to avoid any serious inconvenience to those interests with which slave labor is now connected, and to prepare emancipated blacks for complete freedom." A vitriolic debate erupted over the two proposals, culminating in the formation of a nine-member committee on emancipation with Gamble as the chairman. Only one member of the committee could be clearly identified as a radical.[45]

At this junction in the debate, General Schofield arrived in Jefferson City for the purpose of observing the convention's work and providing any assistance that he could give the members. He quickly discovered that the delegates wanted assurances from Lincoln that he would support the conservative plan for gradual emancipation. The delegates had probably read Taussig's newspaper account of his interview with the president in which Lincoln expressed his preference for the adoption of a timetable for the abolition of slavery. They also wanted to know if Lincoln would prohibit the military from interfering with slavery during the period of transition to final emancipation. Schofield, a supporter of gradual emancipation, immediately telegraphed the president on June 20, 1863, asking for authority to pledge the federal government's backing for the convention's plan. The general insisted that the answer to the question was of "vital importance to the peace of Missouri," although he did not explain why.[46]

Lincoln responded in a carefully worded letter to Schofield. The letter was delivered quickly and by special messenger. The president wrote, "Desirous as I am, that emancipation shall be adopted by Missouri, and believing as I do, that *gradual* can be made better than *immediate* for both black and white, except when military necessity changes that case, my impulse is to say that such protection would be given." The president admitted that he could not "know exactly what shape an act of emancipation may take"; he would leave the details of the process to the state. Lincoln, however, thought that the time for its implementation "from the initiation to the final end, should be comparatively short, and the act should prevent persons being sold, during that period, into more lasting slavery." He also desired that the military in Missouri should not be used "in subverting the temporarily reserved legal rights in slaves during the progress of emancipation." He reminded Schofield, and thus the convention delegates, that he had "very earnestly urged the slave-states to adopt emancipation," adding, "and it ought to be, and is an object with me not to overthrow, or thwart what any of them may in good faith do, to that end."[47]

The president in his letter to Schofield satisfied the Gamble conservatives by endorsing their policy of gradual emancipation. In so doing, he missed an opportunity to press for an immediate end of slavery by the state convention. Lincoln clearly remained influenced by his long-held and paternalistic view that phased emancipation was best for blacks and, probably not incidentally, for the white community also. Even after he threw his support in 1864 behind a constitutional amendment to abolish slavery throughout the nation, he apparently still thought that a temporary apprenticeship system for young blacks under white tutelage was acceptable, even if not desirable.[48]

Lincoln's support for gradual emancipation, combined with his removal of General Curtis from command, understandably infuriated Missouri radicals and increased their determination to gain control of the state and impose a stringent settlement on rebels and also abolish slavery. The radicals now doubted that the president was capable of winning the war, ending slavery in America, and ensuring a true reconstruction settlement in the South. For the radicals, it was the security of the Republic and its ideals that were at stake, not revolution, as their conservative opponents charged. They would soon be found intriguing with like-minded radicals, both inside and outside Congress, in an effort to thwart Lincoln and replace him as the Republican presidential candidate in 1864.

Drake expressed the disillusionment of many Missouri radicals with the president when he harshly wrote him on July 31, 1863, "You have given your confidence to Gov. Gamble, who represents a faction, & turn away from those who represent the loyal masses. . . . I assure you that your known sympathy with Gov. Gamble is, in fact, sympathy with the disloyal people of Missouri, however little you so intend it." Drake warned Lincoln not to do "so great a wrong as to disregard any longer the opinions and wishes of [Missouri's] loyal people." He promised that the Unconditional Unionists would "engulf Gamble, Slavery, & disloyalty in a common grave, from which there will be no resurrection."[49] Drake followed up with a speech at LaGrange on August 19 in which he unfairly characterized Lincoln "as a Tyrant and a Dictator" because of his "tyrannical interference with the [state] convention through his agent Schofield." The comment was reported to the president, who later alluded to it when he met with Drake and a group of Missouri and Kansas radicals at the White House.[50]

Despite the growing opposition of Drake and the radicals to gradual emancipation, the Missouri state convention's committee on emancipation reported to the floor a proposed ordinance designed to meet the president's concerns and secure the support of a majority of the delegates. After a bruising debate in which both the radicals and the diehard proslavery delegates vehemently denounced it, the ordinance passed the convention by a vote of 51 to 30. The ordinance probably stretched the intention of Lincoln's statement in his Schofield letter that the transition period to freedom for all slaves should be "comparatively short." It provided for a process of emancipation to be completed by July 4, 1870, not 1876, as Gamble had originally proposed. However, blacks up to the age of twenty-three and those over the age of forty would remain for a time as apprentices under the control of their former masters, a concession to proslavery whites and other conservatives who feared the social and racial consequences of young freed blacks and who still wanted their labor. In effect, the ordinance, if implemented by the legislature, would extend indefinitely a form of slavery into the postwar era.[51]

The convention rejected the demand of the radicals for a referendum on the ordinance. Gamble concluded that its defeat at the polls, with proslavery men defiantly voting with the radicals, would renew the debate over emancipation and, not incidentally, work against the political advantage of his conservative faction. The governor, however, made the reasonable argument that a fair election could not be held in some parts of the state because of intense guerrilla activity and Confederate raids.[52] Senator Henderson assured the president that though there would be no referendum, "nine tenths of the people every-where in the State are disposed to acquiesce" in the ordinance "abolishing slavery prospectively." Henderson, who favored immediate emancipation, admitted, "The ordinance is not exactly as I would have had it, but it is better than I expected, and secures all that the true friends of the Government ought to ask. The point gained is, that . . . our internal peace is put beyond peradventure."[53] Lincoln seemed to agree; he expressed no objection to the ordinance, the timing for the completion of emancipation in Missouri, or the apprenticeship arrangement.

Drake and the Missouri radicals refused to accept the state convention's approval of the gradual emancipation scheme and its failure to proscribe those who were pro-Confederate. After the convention adjourned, the radicals, styling themselves "Unconditional Union men" and reportedly consisting of representatives from four-fifths of the counties, held a meeting in Jefferson City on September 1. They organized for the purpose of securing a reversal of the state convention's actions. The radicals also sought to contest the "reactionary influences" of Governor Gamble and General Schofield, who, they unfairly contended, had encouraged rebel sympathizers and bushwhackers. They adopted a resolution demanding that the legislature call a new state convention to effect immediate emancipation and disfranchise all who had taken up arms against the Union or in any way or at any time supported the rebellion. In addition, the resolution denounced Lincoln's "delegation . . . of the military power to a provisional State organization," whose "whole tendency," they said, was "to throw back the people under the control of the pro-slavery party" and prolong "a reign of terror throughout a large section of the State." The massacre on August 21, 1863, of 200 men and teenage boys in Lawrence, Kansas, by 450 Missouri partisans under William C. Quantrill provided grim evidence for the radicals and also for many conservative Unionists that Gamble and Schofield had tragically failed to restore law and order in Missouri. The radical convention called for Gamble's resignation as governor and insisted that the president replace Schofield with a different general, preferably Benjamin F. Butler. The delegates predicted that Butler would conduct "a vigorous prosecution of the war" in the military department.[54]

Outraged by the Lawrence massacre and the increase of guerrilla activity in Missouri, the radicals demanded the arming of blacks "to kill rebels," a federal policy that Schofield at first disapproved of but ultimately supported. Although begun in 1863, black enlistments in the state initially fell short of federal expectations. By February 1864 only 3,700 African Americans had enrolled in the army in Missouri.[55] By the end of the war, 8,344 blacks had enlisted in Missouri regiments; an undetermined number had joined free state units.[56] As in the other border states, white Unionists in Missouri, with the exception of the radicals, opposed black recruitment.

Before the radical convention adjourned, the delegates appointed a committee of one person from each county to visit Lincoln and present their grievances to him.[57] They also heard Drake, who would lead the delegation to Washington, make an intemperate speech that was soon published and circulated around the state. Drake devoted most of his speech to vilifying Gamble and the conservative Unionists. The fiery radical leader, who Lincoln ironically noted had earlier fervently opposed abolition, now charged that the governor had advanced the gradual emancipation ordinance in the state constitution as a ruse to preserve slavery.[58]

Having received a preview of the radicals' complaints, Lincoln was ready on September 30 for the "little army," as he described the Missouri delegation of about seventy men who marched into the White House. Some rough-looking Kansas Jayhawkers (border warriors), including Senator James "Jim" H. Lane, joined the Missourians in the meeting. As Lincoln informed John Hay on the day before the confrontation, he would "stand by" the Missouri state convention's ordinance on gradual emancipation and would also continue his support of General Schofield. "I think I understand this matter perfectly," he said, "and I cannot do anything contrary to my convictions to please these men, earnest and powerful as they may be."[59] Hay took careful notes on the session with the radicals, which provide the historian and student of the Civil War with a revealing record of one of the most contentious meetings of the Lincoln presidency.

Drake began the meeting by reading an address outlining the radicals' complaints. When he had finished, Lincoln announced that he would give careful consideration to their concerns, but, he told them, "there are some matters" that he had already decided. He informed the delegation that he would not interfere with Governor Gamble's authority under the laws of Missouri, as they demanded, and he reminded them that Gamble was the legitimate and loyal governor of the state. In response to their complaint about the state militia, Lincoln declared that Gamble had every right to enroll a military force as long as it did not operate independently of the federal government. He pointed out that on several occasions he had refused permission for the governor to transfer these troops to the exclusive control of the state. He said that both Gamble and the radicals had objected to his characterization of the troubles in Missouri as a "pestilent factional quarrel." The governor, Lincoln told the group, had written him complaining so bitterly of that expression that he had declined to read the letter.[60]

Lincoln chastised the Missouri radicals for what he called their "vague denunciations" of General Schofield, which were "so easy to make and yet so unsatisfactory." He challenged them to prove that the general had "disobeyed orders": "Show me that he has done something wrong & I will take your request for his removal into serious consideration." Regarding the charge that Schofield had muzzled the radical press (this occurred apparently in only one case, when the general arrested William McKee of the *Saint Louis Missouri Democrat*), Lincoln informed the delegation, "When an officer in any department finds that a newspaper is pursuing a course calculated to embarrass his operations and stir up sedition and tumult, he has the right to lay hands upon it and suppress it, but in no other case." The president indicated that he had approved Schofield's arrest of McKee. A member of the delegation shouted, "[But] we thought" that the suspension of the writ of habeas corpus and the suppression of the press were "to be used against the other side." "Certainly you did," Lincoln snapped. "Your ideas of justice seem to depend upon the application of it."[61]

The president then turned to the radicals' insistence "upon adherence to . . . the proclamation of Emancipation as a test of . . . political friendship." He reminded the delegates that the proclamation did not apply to Missouri and told them, "The Proclamation can therefore have no direct bearing upon your state politics. Yet you seem to insist that it shall be made as vital a question as if it had. You seem to be determined to have it executed there." A delegate interjected, "We think it a national question" that should be applied to the border states as well as the rebel states. Lincoln, who had become increasingly annoyed with the attitude of the radicals, responded to the delegate, "You are then determined to make an issue with men who may not agree with you upon the abstract question of the propriety of that act of mine." Declaring that he had given more thought to the proclamation "than probably any one" of the men before him, Lincoln asserted, "[I] believe it to be right and expedient."[62]

Lincoln expressed his disappointment with the radicals' resistance to the convention ordinance providing for the gradual end of slavery. He told the Missouri delegation that their opposition endangered "the success of the whole advance towards freedom." Although Lincoln acknowledged that he still favored a process of gradual abolition, he reaffirmed to the group, "The mode of emancipation in Missouri is not my business." Drake and the radicals must have found this comment by Lincoln contradictory in view of his approval of the Gamble convention's antislavery ordinance. He admonished the radicals to go home and work with other antislavery men to make "emancipation a final fact forever."[63]

In his meeting with the Missourians, Lincoln gave a rare public response to critics, including Drake and his friends, who had repeatedly charged him with tyranny. He firmly announced, "I do not intend to be a tyrant. At all events I shall take care that in my own eyes I do not become one. I shall always try and preserve one friend within me, whoever else fails me, to tell me that I have not been a tyrant, and that I have acted right. I have no right to act the tyrant to mere political opponents." Nonetheless, Lincoln told the delegation, "I must make a dividing line some where, between those who are the opponents of the Government and those who only oppose peculiar features of my administration while they sustain the Government." He said, "Where political opponents do not in any way interfere with or hinder military operations, I have judged it best to let them alone." Lincoln cited General Ambrose E. Burnside's controversial arrest and order exiling Clement L. Vallandigham as a necessary action on the grounds that the Ohio Copperhead had become a "political enemy of the government [and] dangerous in a military point of view."[64]

The president lectured the radical delegation on the terrible effects of civil war on the political and social fabric of a people. "In a civil war," he began, "one of the saddest evils is suspicion. It poisons the springs of social life. It is the fruitful parent of injustice and strife." Lincoln applied that general principle to the situation that he faced in their state: "Were I to make a rule that in Missouri disloyal men were outlawed and the rightful prey of good citizens as soon as the rule should begin to be carried into effect I would be overwhelmed with affidavits to prove the first man killed under it was more loyal than the one who killed him." Lincoln declared that it was "impossible to determine the question of the motives that govern men, or to gain absolute knowledge of their sympathies."[65]

A delegate again interrupted the president and blurted out, "Let the loyal people judge" who were true Unionists. "And who shall say who the loyal people are?" Lincoln asked. "You [radicals] ask for the disfranchisement of all disloyal people: but difficulties will environ you at every step in determining the questions which will arise in that matter." The president argued, "A vast number of Missourians who have at some time aided the rebellion will wish to return to their homes and resume their peaceful avocations. Even if you would, you cannot keep them all away." He insisted that the radicals "stand by" the Missouri laws on the eligibility of voters until they were properly altered by the state.[66]

Senator Lane, the champion of the Kansas Jayhawkers, asked the president, "Do you think it sufficient cause for the removal of a General, [if] he has lost the entire confidence of the people?" Lincoln replied that it would be "a sufficient cause." Lane quickly asserted, "General Schofield has lost that confidence," and just as quickly, Lincoln replied, "You being judge!" The delegates, "all crying in chorus," according to John Hay, backed Lane's condemnation of Schofield. Lincoln answered, "I am in possession of facts that convince me that Gen Schofield has not lost the confidence of the entire people of Missouri."[67] He did not, however, reveal those "facts."

Lane refused to give up on his demand for Schofield's removal. He told the president that Quantrill's recent massacre and sack of Lawrence was "solely due to the embicility [sic] of Gen. Schofield" and that all the people wanted him replaced as the department commander. Lincoln replied that, as to raids like the one on Lawrence, they "could be done by any one making up his mind to the consequences, and could no more be guarded against than assassination," explaining, "If I make up my mind to kill you for instance, I can do it and these hundred gentlemen" in the room "could not prevent it. They could avenge but could not save you."[68]

The radicals and the president ended the meeting still deeply divided. Lincoln later remarked to Hay, "The Delegation on the whole disappointed me badly." Hay himself concluded that the Missourians had presented their "cause" in an "incoherent, vague, abusive, prejudiced" fashion. They unfortunately chose for their spokesman Drake, who "covered the marrow of what they wanted to say in a purposeless mass of unprofitable verbiage," Hay wrote.[69]

Drake, as chairman of the delegation, remained in Washington until October 10, unsuccessfully seeking an interview and a written response from Lincoln to the radicals' address. Before he left town, Drake wrote the president and made "an earnest entreaty for the favorable consideration" of their grievances. With a critical state judicial election forthcoming on November 3, Drake told Lincoln that if he yielded "to the wishes of the Conservatives" and retained Schofield in command, he would "discourage the loyal men of Missouri, and give such an impulse to their opponents as may result in our defeat." But on the other hand, he said, "A contrary decision on your part will probably lead to a triumphant result in our favor." Drake intimated that if Lincoln supported Schofield and the Claybanks "at the expense of his friends," he would pay a political price.[70]

Actually, the president had already written his reply to Drake and the Missourians, but he waited until they had left town before mailing it to them in Saint Louis. He obviously did not want another confrontation with the delegation. Lincoln's response, written on October 5, mainly reiterated, though in more precise language, what he had said in the September 30 meeting. He reminded Drake and the radicals, "We are in civil war. In such cases there always is a main question; but in this case that question is a perplexing compound—Union and Slavery. It thus becomes a question not of two sides merely, but of at least four sides, even among those who are for the Union, saying nothing of those who are against it." Lincoln then delineated the "sides" vis-à-vis the Union and slavery in the conflict, and he insisted that all were loyal and sincere in their convictions.[71]

As he had done in the meeting with the Missouri radicals, the president in his reply described how the war had caused blood to grow hot and had forced "thought . . . from old channels into confusion." Because of the war, he said, "Deception breeds and thrives. Confidence dies, and universal suspicion reigns. . . . Each man feels an impulse to kill his neighbor, lest he be first killed by him. Revenge and retaliation follow. And all this . . . may be among honest men only." Lincoln told Drake and the radicals, "These causes amply account for what has occurred in Missouri" since the beginning of the war.[72] Within this context, the president again defended his general and affirmed "with confidence that no commander of that Department," which included Kansas and Arkansas as well as Missouri, had, "in proportion to his means" and the difficulties that he faced, "done better than Gen. Schofield." He praised Schofield for his dispatch of "a large general force to the relief of Gen. Grant, then investing Vicksburg, and menaced from without by Gen. [Joseph E.] Johnston." Schofield, the president insisted, had done the right thing in replacing the federal troops with Governor Gamble's Missouri Enrolled Militia, despite opposition from the radicals.[73]

Lincoln also absolved Schofield from any wrongdoing in prohibiting the Kansas Jayhawkers from pursuing "the Lawrence murderers" into Missouri. "I am well satisfied," he explained, "that the preventing of the threatened remedial raid into Missouri, was the only safe way to avoid an indiscriminate massacre there, including probably more innocent than guilty. Instead of condemning, I therefore approve what I understand Gen. Schofield did in that respect."[74]

Drake wrote Lincoln, lamenting that many in his delegation would "return to a border state filled with disloyal sentiment." He also issued a warning: "If upon their return there the military policies of your administration shall subject them to risk of life in the defense of the government and their blood shall be shed—let me tell you, Mr. President, that their blood shall be upon your garments and not upon ours."[75]

Lincoln's new instructions to Schofield, dated October 1, 1863, the day after the meeting with the radical delegation, directed that since no organized rebel military force existed in the state, the general's principal duty was to use his troops, "as far as practicable, to compel the excited people to leave one another alone." The president instructed him, "Only arrest individuals, and suppress assemblies, or newspapers, when they may be working *palpable* injury to the Military in your charge; and, in no other case will you interfere with the expression of opinion in any form, or allow it to be interfered with violently by others. In this, you have a discretion to exercise with great caution, calmness, and forbearance."[76]

The president reminded Schofield of his mission to "expel guerrillas, marauders, and murderers, and all . . . known to harbor, aid, or abet them." Lincoln told him that he would not now interfere with the controversial (and, for many people, morally reprehensible) military order for the removal of rebel sympathizers in three western counties and a part of a fourth county. This draconian action had been taken by General Thomas Ewing and endorsed by Schofield, his superior, soon after the Lawrence massacre. Only those inhabitants who had ironclad proof of their Unionism avoided removal. (The future mother of Harry S. Truman, Martha Ellen Young, then nine years old, and her parents were part of this forced removal.)[77]

Lincoln instructed Schofield to prohibit his troops from "either returning fugitive slaves, or . . . forcing, or enticing slaves from their homes" and ordered him to prevent others from doing so. The president also addressed the concerns of Missouri Unionists about the unauthorized recruitment of black troops. He directed that no African American enlistments should be made except by orders of the general or the War Department. Finally, in regard to the forthcoming fall election, Lincoln ordered Schofield to ensure that only those eligible under the laws of Missouri, enacted by the state convention, should be permitted to vote.[78]

Predictably, Lincoln's efforts to restore the peace among Missouri's Unionist factions or to end the violence on the border came to naught. When the Drake delegation returned to the state from their meeting with the president, they issued an address to the "Radical Union Men of Missouri" reporting that their mission had failed. Branding the conservatives Copperheads who did not truly support the Union, the address called for the defeat of the Gamble-Schofield faction in the November election for a seat on the Missouri supreme court and for vacant General Assembly seats.[79]

While the Drake delegation was still in Washington, Governor Gamble sent a scathing message to the president claiming, "A [radical] party has sprung up in Missouri, which openly and loudly proclaims the purpose to overturn" the state government. He predicted, "If these Anarchists are allowed to initiate their measures of violence in this State, their revolutionary spirit will probably extend to other states and produce a conflagration which it will be impossible for the Federal Government to extinguish." Gamble demanded that Lincoln order Schofield to use "all the force under his control" to suppress these revolutionaries.[80]

On October 12 the governor followed his ill-tempered letter to Lincoln with a blistering proclamation to Missourians attacking the "corrupt and malignant" radical press that for many months, he contended, had been advocating a violent overthrow of the state government. Ignoring the specific differences between the radicals and the conservatives, Gamble warned "the good people of the State" to be on their guard against the treacherous "falsehoods of a few designing leaders" that might "lead them to their ruin." He also urged qualified voters to go to the polls in November and announced that any military interference in the election would be "regarded as an offence of the greatest magnitude" against the laws.[81] Instead of calming the political waters in the state as Lincoln fervently wished, the hotheaded governor had clearly enlarged the chasm between the conservatives and the radicals. He had also contributed to the weakening of his faction's support among middle-of-the road Unionists like Senator Henderson.

CHAPTER NINE

Other Missouri conservative Unionists also wrote the president, corroborating Gamble's charge that there was a radical conspiracy against the state government. Congressman James S. Rollins, who would emerge in January 1865 as a key player in Congress's initiation of the Thirteenth Amendment, informed Lincoln on October 8, 1863, that the radicals were engaging in "lawless acts . . . to exterminate, or drive out, all who differ from them in political sentiment." "This lawlessness," he charged, "is instigated, encouraged and applauded by the radical press and leaders. Every effort to put down this lawlessness is denounced by the radicals as *persecution of loyal men*." James O. Broadhead, Schofield's provost marshal general for the Department of Missouri and a prominent Unionist, wrote Attorney General Bates, in a letter forwarded to Lincoln, that the radicals sought to get rid of the conservative government, including the state convention: "[They] hate [Gamble] and do not hesitate to denounce him as a traitor. They are opposed to Lincoln also—but not so openly, for they still hope through him to accomplish their purposes."[82]

On October 19, 1863, Lincoln responded to both Gamble's October 1 letter and his October 12 proclamation. The president denied that there was a conspiracy to overthrow the state government as the governor claimed. Even if a few radicals attempted an uprising, Lincoln said, General Schofield had sufficient forces to prevent it. "In the absence of such violence, or imminent danger," Lincoln told Gamble, "it is not proper for the national executive to interfere; and I am unwilling, by any formal, action, to show an appearance of belief that there is such imminent danger, before I really believe there is." Although he was disappointed with Gamble, the president reinforced his support for the provisional government, declaring that it had been placed in authority "by the unanamous [*sic*] action and acquiescence of the Union people of the State." He added, "I have seen no occasion to make a distinction against the provisional government because of it's [*sic*] not having been chosen and inaugurated in the usual way. Nor have I seen any cause to suspect it of unfaithfulness to the Union," as opponents had claimed.[83] In his despair regarding affairs in the state, Lincoln lamented to Bates that he "had no *friends in Missouri*," a point that the attorney general immediately contested.[84]

General Schofield, despite Lincoln's earlier warning to avoid involvement in the "pestilent factional quarrel" in Missouri, had become increasingly antagonistic toward the radicals and convinced of their malevolent intentions. On September 20, 1863, Schofield wrote General in Chief Halleck that the radicals were a "revolutionary faction," particularly in Saint Louis where the German American element provided militant support. The radicals, Schofield charged, strove "to overthrow the State government, and change the policy of the national administration." He urged the Lincoln administration to permit him to apply "a strong remedy" against the radicals and their newspapers in Saint Louis.[85] Although the president did not give him the authority to impose a "strong remedy" in Missouri, Schofield continued his opposition to the radicals and his support for Governor Gamble's faction.

Fears that the state election in November 1863 of a Missouri supreme court judge and a legislature would produce widespread violence and intimidation at the polls proved largely unfounded. In an extremely close election, Barton Bates, the conservative son of U.S. Attorney General Edward Bates, defeated the radical candidate for the seat on the court. However, the Unconditional Union men, consisting mainly of those who supported the radicals, gained a majority in the state house of representatives, but not in the senate. When the General Assembly met after the election, a coalition of radicals and a few conservatives, who were probably supporters of Senator Henderson, secured control of both chambers and in early 1864 approved a bill calling for a new state convention to be held after the election of delegates to it in November. The main purpose of the new convention would be to undo the work of the Gamble state convention, particularly to overturn the gradual emancipation ordinance and replace it with a provision for the immediate abolition of slavery. The legislature also elected Henderson, who had made his peace with the radicals, and B. Gratz Brown to the U.S. Senate. Brown was the former editor of the radical *Saint Louis Missouri Democrat*. Charcoal support for the election of Henderson appeared necessary in order to win a majority for the convention bill.[86]

With the radical-led coalition gaining the ascendancy in the General Assembly and with Governor Gamble's health deteriorating, the pressure on Lincoln to replace General Schofield increased. Secretary of the Treasury Chase, whose ambition for the presidency could not be sated, had been cultivating the support of the Missouri radicals. He sent his agents into the state, one of whom joined the staff of the *Saint Louis Missouri Democrat*. When the Drake delegation visited Washington in late September 1863,

Chase hosted them at his house after they had met with Lincoln.[87] As a part of his strategy to win the 1864 Republican nomination, he sought the removal of Schofield, which, he believed, would endear him to the radicals not only in Missouri but also elsewhere. Chase deviously suggested to the president that the radicals (though he did not use that term to refer to them) unconditionally supported the administration, whereas their opposition "really sympathized with [the administration's] opponents and [would] finally act with them." Chase recommended that the president send Schofield "honorably to the field" and place General William Rosecrans in command of the department.[88] Lincoln probably had little difficulty in dismissing Chase's biased view of the political situation in Missouri; however, he did eventually appoint Rosecrans as department commander, mainly because he needed to find a place for the senior general after his humiliating defeat in the battle of Chickamauga near Chattanooga, Tennessee.

Lincoln might ignore Chase's self-serving opinion, but he had to take seriously the anti-Schofield opposition of such Illinois friends as Joseph Gillespie and Joseph Medill of the *Chicago Tribune*, as well as others who were not associated with either Missouri faction. Gillespie wrote the president, "Your friends incline to the belief that Schofields [*sic*] administration is not in harmony with the current of events or the ruling ideas of the people. . . . A more radical policy would at the present be more acceptable in regard to Missouri." Medill exaggerated when he reported to the president, "None but the Copperheads support Schofield & Gamble" in the West; if Lincoln did not remove Schofield from command, he warned, "it will be the worst mistake of your life."[89] William G. Eliot, a longtime antislavery minister in Saint Louis, though critical of the political methods of the Charcoals, wrote Senator Charles Sumner that Schofield, who lacked "force," could not "control the disturbed & chaotic elements of this almost revolutionary State." Eliot astutely observed that when Schofield assumed command in Missouri, "he failed to conciliate the radicals, which he might have done"; instead, he "yielded to nearly all the demands of the Conservatives." Sumner forwarded the letter to Lincoln.[90]

In December 1863 Lincoln came to the conclusion that he must replace Schofield in command. He was probably influenced by the fact that the radical-led coalition had gained control of the General Assembly and believed that he would need their cooperation to effect emancipation and the security of the state. The president now seemed to believe that Governor

Gamble and General Schofield were the main obstacles in the way of Unionist harmony in Missouri and the suppression of rebel guerrillas like Quantrill. Although Lincoln had made it abundantly clear that he did not have the authority to remove Gamble, Schofield's status as a military commander made his removal a different matter. In reevaluating the situation, Lincoln on December 10 remarked to John Hay (and perhaps to others also), "I know these Radical men have in them the stuff which must save the state and on which we must mainly rely. They are absolutely uncorrosive by the virus of secession . . . while the Conservatives, in casting about for votes to carry through their plans, are tempted to affiliate with those whose record is not clear. If one side *must* be crushed out & the other cherished there could be no doubt which side we would choose as fuller of hope for the future. We would have to side with the Radicals." But then, in a comment that historians have ignored, Lincoln denounced the radicals for the way they had treated Gamble and his supporters, who, he said, "have done their whole duty in the war faithfully & promptly [and] who when they have disagreed with me have been silent and kept about the good work." It "is simply monstrous," he continued, that the radicals treat "these men as copperheads and enemies to the Govt" and maliciously attack Governor Gamble.[91] Clearly, Lincoln still disliked the radicals and deplored their partisan methods, but he had to be guided by the new political realities in Missouri and support the radicals' efforts to secure immediate freedom for blacks, despite his preference for gradual emancipation.

Yet Lincoln hesitated to remove Schofield. He acted after receiving a disturbing report from Illinois congressman Elihu B. Washburne, who had visited Missouri. The powerful congressman informed Lincoln that Schofield "was working rather energetically in the politics of the State." The general, Washburne said, had rejected his suggestion that he "use his influence to harmonize the conflicting elements so as to elect one of each [Unionist] wing, Gratz Brown and Henderson," to the Senate. Schofield, according to Washburne, indignantly declared that "he would not consent to the election of Gratz Brown."[92] Brown himself reported to the president that the general had informed him he would oppose a new state convention proposed by the radicals in the General Assembly. "These things," Lincoln told Hay, "are obviously transcendent of [Schofield's] instructions and must not be permitted."[93]

The president summoned Schofield to Washington to explain his actions; in reality he had already decided to relieve him from command.[94]

The problem Lincoln faced, as he admitted to Secretary of War Stanton, was how to do it without creating "an additional amount of trouble." One of Lincoln's greatest strengths was his awareness of the probable consequences of his actions, especially in personnel and political matters. Nothing demonstrates better this acuity than his handling of Schofield's replacement as commander of the Department of Missouri without offending the general and his conservative supporters. He informed Stanton on December 18 of "the mode" for doing it. With the support of Senators Henderson and the recently elected Senator Brown, Lincoln said that he would ask the Senate to approve Schofield's promotion to major general; at the same time he would reassign him to an important field command. General Rosecrans would replace Schofield in Missouri, and the area west of the state would become a separate department with General Curtis in overall command, a division that the troublesome Senator Lane of Kansas had wanted.[95]

Lincoln immediately secured the approval of several Republican senators for Schofield's promotion to major general. After three meetings with Brown, he believed that the new senator would support Schofield's confirmation by the Senate. But when the nomination reached the floor of the Senate, Brown violated what Lincoln considered to be a promise by securing a postponement of the issue. Displeased by the Senate's failure to confirm the promotion, the president informed Stanton that he would resubmit the nomination at an appropriate time. Meanwhile, Lincoln followed through on his resolve to give Schofield an important field command. He ordered him to report to General U. S. Grant, who then appointed him commander of the Army of the Ohio. On May 12, 1864, the Senate finally confirmed Schofield's promotion to major general.[96] During the last months of the war, Schofield distinguished himself in the important battles of Franklin and Nashville. He ended his military career two decades later as commanding general of the U.S. Army.[97]

On January 22, 1864, General Rosecrans assumed command of the Department of Missouri. One week later, Governor Gamble, who had been plagued with illness for several years, died of pneumonia. Lieutenant Governor Willard P. Hall became governor, and though he was a conservative, he did not prove to be the political lightning rod that Gamble had been.[98] With Schofield replaced by an accommodating general, Rosecrans, and with Hall unwilling to publicly challenge the radicals, the Drake party saw Lincoln as the only obstacle to their control of the state and the triumph of their brand of Unionism in the war, including immediate emancipation and a harsh policy toward rebels and Missourians who aided them. Inspired by their new strength and by the national attention they were receiving for their antislavery efforts, the Missouri radicals issued a call for a Freedom Convention of the Slave States to meet in Louisville on February 22. The main purpose of the convention would be to press for immediate emancipation and, though unstated in the call, for the substitution of a radical candidate for Lincoln in the fall election.[99]

Delegates from Missouri, Kentucky, Tennessee, and Arkansas answered the call. Approximately seventy came from Missouri and forty from Kentucky; only a handful of representatives came from the other two states. Not all the delegates identified with the radicals. James Speed of Kentucky, a conservative who favored emancipation but not the political proscription of former rebels or the repudiation of Lincoln's leadership, convened the group in the federal building in Louisville. Drake, the main speaker, fired up the delegates with his usual vilification of rebels, Copperheads, and proslavery men.[100] A major division occurred over a resolution calling for a "National Radical Convention" to meet in Saint Louis on May 10, 1864, to form a new political party for the fall elections. Heavily weighted toward German Americans, most of the Missouri delegates favored a radical party with candidates to oppose Lincoln and the Republicans as well as the Democrats. However, almost all the Kentuckians and the other delegates wanted to stay in the Republican Party and avoid a division of the Unconditional Unionist vote in the fall. A motion in the convention to organize a new party failed by a vote of 53 to 64. Missouri radicals complained that though John J. Crittenden had died in 1863, the Kentucky delegates were still too much influenced by his conservatism.[101]

The radical Salmon P. Chase seemed at that time to be the logical candidate to challenge Lincoln as the Republican standard-bearer. At the Louisville convention, Chase supporters distributed copies of the Pomeroy Circular, a printed letter signed by Kansas senator Samuel S. Pomeroy as "Chairman, [Republican] National Executive Committee" and sent to leading Republicans.[102] The circular promoted the presidential qualifications of the treasury secretary, declared that the reelection of Lincoln was "practically impossible," and insisted that all Republicans who wanted "a change" should organize and "appeal at once to the people" before it was "too late" to save the country.[103] The Chase boomlet did not last long, but it was in full bloom when the Freedom Convention met in Louisville. Apparently believing that Chase could win the party's nomination, Drake spoke in favor of the radicals' remaining in the Republican Party and against the formation of a new party. Despite the fact that Drake was hissed by members of his own delegation, his opposition turned the tide against the resolution for a May 10 convention to organize a radical party.[104]

Some of the Missouri delegates, mainly German Americans, later joined in a movement to form a national radical party. Meeting in Cleveland on May 31, 1864, and adopting the name Radical Democratic Party, they nominated the Pathfinder, John C. Frémont, for president. Those Missouri radicals who did not bolt the Republican Party sent a delegation to the National Union (Republican) convention in Baltimore in early June, along with a contesting delegation of conservative Unionists. Realizing that Lincoln could easily win the nomination without the support of the Missouri conservative delegation, the convention seated the radicals, apparently as a gesture of goodwill to appease northern radicals who were also upset with the president. The Missouri radicals cast twenty-two ballots for U. S. Grant for president, the only votes that Lincoln did not receive.[105] A German American newspaper in Saint Louis denounced the Missourians for then voting to make Lincoln's nomination unanimous. The paper also charged that those delegates had sold out the principles of the Missouri radical party by supporting all the resolutions in the "meaningless" Republican platform. The Saint Louis German Americans who supported Frémont refused to give the Republican convention any credit for adopting a resolution calling for a constitutional amendment abolishing slavery.[106]

Before adjourning on February 23, 1864, the Louisville Freedom Convention passed a series of resolutions designed to advance the radical cause both in the border states and in the North. In anticipation of the Republican platform, the convention also called for a constitutional amendment to secure emancipation in all the states. An amendment, put forward by James Speed, that would provide compensation for loyal slaveholders was defeated. The delegates ignored the issue of black rights after emancipation, though many German Americans, having escaped repression in Europe, generally favored the right to vote and civil equality for the ex-slaves. The majority in the Louisville convention urged the revocation of Lincoln's lenient Amnesty and Reconstruction Proclamation of December 8, 1863, and, instead, advocated the disfranchisement of anyone who had taken up arms against the Union. Another resolution, which Speed and many of the Kentuckians refused to support, demanded a constitutional amendment limiting the president to one term in office, an obvious slam at Lincoln. A Republican correspondent of the *Cincinnati Gazette* reported, "The Radicals of Missouri are inveterate in their hostility to Lincoln, and positively will not co-operate with a party favoring his nomination."[107] As it turned out, the national Democrats in adopting a peace, or Copperhead, platform when they met in late August changed the dynamics in the presidential election and caused Missouri radicals, though unenthusiastically, to back Lincoln in the fall. The German Americans also fell in line behind the president after the resignation of Postmaster General Montgomery Blair, the bête noire of the radicals, and after Frémont's withdrawal from the race in September.

During the summer and fall of 1864 Missouri experienced a new and more brutal wave of guerrilla warfare and social banditry, the worst in its history. The western and northern areas of the state suffered the greatest from this reign of terror. Quantrill continued his violent activities in Missouri; he was joined in criminal infamy by William "Bloody Bill" Anderson and other merciless guerrillas. The worst incident in Missouri occurred at Centralia on September 27. Anderson with about eighty men, including Frank and Jesse James, terrorized the citizens of the town and murdered two dozen unarmed Union (Missouri) soldiers who were on a train en route to home. That did not end the Centralia massacre. Later in the day, Anderson, with reinforcements, repulsed a nearby federal force, returned to the town, and murdered and mutilated dozens of troops who tried to surrender. One month later Bloody Bill deservedly met his maker at the hands of a state militia force.[108]

General Rosecrans added to the excitement and fear in Missouri when he telegraphed Lincoln on June 2, 1864, that his agents had uncovered a plot to overthrow the government. Unwilling to submit his report of the conspiracy by express mail, Rosecrans asked Lincoln to send a staff officer to convey it to Washington. The president immediately dispatched John Hay to Saint Louis to receive the report and obtain any verbal information the general wanted to provide about the plot.[109] In his report, Rosecrans asserted that the Order of the American Knights, a secret Copperhead organization in the Midwest, had penetrated Missouri and Kentucky with the immediate objective of overthrowing the Union governments in those states. He declared that the uprising would be coordinated with Confederate military operations by Generals Sterling Price in Missouri and John Hunt Morgan in Kentucky. These incursions, Rosecrans told Hay, were designed to increase national opposition to the war in the North and to the Republicans in the fall elections. Rosecrans indicated that the Knights claimed 25,000 members in Missouri, 70,000 in Kentucky, 140,000 in Illinois, 100,000 in Indiana, and 80,000 in Ohio.[110] Lincoln, however, realistically dismissed the threat to overthrow the Union governments in the border states and in the Midwest. Still, he probably overstated the case when he informed Hay that the Order of the American Knights was merely a malicious political organization and incapable of disrupting the war.[111]

Although he did not share Rosecrans's fear of a Copperhead uprising, Provost Marshal General Broadhead, erstwhile Saint Louis lawyer and conservative Unionist, provided Attorney General Bates with a graphic description of the awful situation in the state during the summer of 1864. In a July 24 letter to Bates intended for Lincoln's eyes, Broadhead reported, "The condition of Missouri is worse to-day than it ever has been—massacres, private assassinations—burnings—plundering, thieving are more frequent now than they ever have been—the newspapers of all kinds show this and yet not the half is told." Broadhead lamented that some people were afraid to report the outrages; others were in sympathy with the assassins and plunderers. Bands of "stragglers or emissaries" from General Price's rebel army in the South had returned to prey upon the citizens, Broadhead wrote. In addition, Jayhawkers from Kansas continued to enter Missouri, ostensibly to avenge attacks on Unionists. But, Broadhead claimed, they came mainly to plunder and kill; many of their victims were unoffending citizens. According to Broadhead, Rosecrans had wrongly ordered the disarming of the citizens, both loyal and disloyal, and at the same time he had issued a proclamation admitting that the army could not suppress the widespread and brutal lawlessness.[112]

Broadhead blamed the president for removing Schofield and appointing a cast-off general, Rosecrans, to command the military department. "It is hard that Missouri," he wrote, "should be made the victim of political ambition or political malice . . . because there was no other place" for Rosecrans after his failures around Chattanooga. Undisciplined troops, Broadhead informed Bates, had also contributed to the disorders. He reported that newspaper presses had been destroyed by mobs of soldiers and partisans. "A crisis like that which is now upon us," he declared, "demands that something should be done and that speedily if Missouri is to be saved from desolation."[113]

Bates took Broadhead's letter to Lincoln, who "read it in silence and seemed deeply moved," the attorney general wrote. "But," Bates concluded, "I foresee that no good will come of it. The Prest knows what is right, as well as any man, and would be glad to *see it done*, but, unhappily, lacks the nerve to do it."[114] The attorney general failed to understand the real reason for the president's failure to aid Missouri. His armies under Grant, William Tecumseh Sherman, and other Union commanders had been stretched to the limit during the 1864 spring and summer campaigns in the South. Lincoln simply did not have the troops or the resources to restore law and order in the state.

During the fall of 1864, Missouri again became a battlefront, though not to the extent of the horrific fighting in Virginia and Georgia. General Price made another bold attempt—his last—to win the state for the Confederacy. With a ragtag force estimated at 12,000 men, Price entered southern Missouri on September 19 and began a march toward Saint Louis. He planned to benefit from increased rebel guerrilla activity in the state and from the divisions among conservative and radical Unionists. General Rosecrans later wrote Lincoln that Price had hoped the chaos generated by his invasion would turn "the election in this State for McClellan" in November and, with the aid of Illinois and Indiana Copperheads, would redeem Missouri from Union control.[115]

Price never made it to Saint Louis. The guerrillas did not join his army; they had their own vengeful and plundering agendas to pursue. At the battle of Pilot Knob below Saint Louis, Price suffered heavy losses, forcing him to turn to the west, where General Rosecrans with federal troops and local militiamen successfully confronted the decimated rebel army. On October 30 the remnants of Price's army returned to Arkansas, on the eve of the crucial national (Union) and state elections.[116] The failure of the Confederate invasion emboldened Unionists and increased voter support for the radicals, who all along had urged a hard-line policy against rebels and their sympathizers. By the end of the year, guerrilla warfare and the terror it created had waned.[117] Lawlessness, however, continued, particularly in the west, where small bands of outlaws, led by former guerrillas such as the young Jesse James, robbed and violently sought to settle personal scores.

The 1864 political campaign in Missouri began soon after the National Union (Republican) delegates returned from the Baltimore convention that had nominated Lincoln. Despite the fact that their delegation had been sacrificed as a goodwill gesture to the radical Republicans, conservative Unionists proclaimed their support for Lincoln, formed Lincoln clubs, and organized a state central committee. They also nominated Thomas L. Price (no relation to the Confederate general) for governor. The conservatives endorsed the election of a new state convention for the purpose of abolishing slavery; however, they quixotically called for the establishment of a separate area for the resettlement of freed blacks.

The radicals held a convention in Jefferson City and issued their litany of complaints against the Claybanks. They also demanded the removal of the conservative members of Lincoln's cabinet, including Attorney General Bates, and urged a more vigorous prosecution of the war. Although the radicals had been seated in the National Union convention, they refused at this time to endorse Lincoln lest they alienate the 6,000 or more German American voters who opposed the president and supported Frémont's candidacy. The radicals bypassed the controversial Charles Drake for governor and nominated Thomas C. Fletcher, a colonel in the Union army in Tennessee who had supported Lincoln in 1860.[118]

As the national campaign intensified in October, Lincoln worried that the old divisions among the factions would prevent their cooperation at the polls. Such an eventuality, he believed, would result in a victory for George B. McClellan and the Democrats in Missouri and perhaps nationally. The president learned that conservative gubernatorial candidate Price was making anti-Lincoln speeches, which, it seemed, boded ill for Unionist unity during the final weeks of the campaign.[119] Seeking more information on the uncertain political situation in Missouri and also to encourage Unionist accord in the election, Lincoln dispatched his secretary John G. Nicolay to Saint Louis to confer with both Charcoal and Claybank leaders.

As expected, Nicolay found things "in a pretty bad tangle" in Missouri. However, after consulting "with a number of gentlemen," Nicolay reported to the president that he believed the Unionist factions were "gravitating towards an understanding—temporary at least if not permanent—which [would] unite the vote of all Union men on the electoral and State ticket."[120] A conciliatory meeting of activists in the two factions was held to develop a joint ticket for the election of delegates to the new state convention that had been called by the radical-dominated legislature. The only serious difficulty occurred when several conservatives withdrew when the word "Radical" was retained in the name of the "Union" party. Otherwise, surface harmony prevailed in the coalition, despite the refusal of a county convention in Saint Louis to endorse Lincoln for president. German Americans, Nicolay wrote the president, "were yet bitterly hostile to you"; they almost certainly dominated the Saint Louis convention. Earlier, radical gubernatorial candidate Fletcher had hesitated to endorse Lincoln for fear that he would lose immigrant votes. (In addition to opposing the president's support for the Claybanks, many German Americans and also Irish Americans in Saint Louis probably remembered that Lincoln had been a Whig, a party steeped in prewar nativism, though he had never expressed anti-immigrant or anti-Catholic sentiments.) Nicolay in his report to Lincoln confidently concluded, "With the exception of very few impracticables, the Union men will cast their votes, for you, for the radical Congressmen, for the Emancipation candidates for the State Legislature and the State Convention." Nonetheless, the political divisions in Missouri remained, Nicolay told Lincoln, and, he said, "[only] time will abate the disorder" among the Unionists.[121]

As the campaign climaxed in October, even Drake campaigned for Lincoln, but outside of the state. "I have not taken the stump in this State," he explained to the president, "for I do not covet my days suddenly brought to an end by bushwhackers."[122] Much to the surprise of the McClellan supporters, the Unionist coalition held firm in the November election, though some Claybanks voted with the resurrected Democratic Party. Aided by the ballots of soldiers and by a stringent loyalty oath for voting, the coalition swept to a surprisingly easy victory in both the national and state elections. Lincoln received 71,676 votes to McClellan's 31,626 in Missouri, the largest percentage and total for the president in any of the border states. The total vote was almost 52,000 fewer than in the presidential election of 1860. The insecurity in some areas kept eligible voters from the polls, but not on the large scale that rebel sympathizers had hoped. In the first election for governor since before the war, Fletcher won a majority similar to Lincoln's, and the voters approved the referendum for a new state convention. The Unionist coalition captured three-fourths of the seats in the convention and a comfortable majority in the legislature; it also won eight of the nine seats in Congress.[123] The success of the coalition—and particularly the clear victory for emancipation, along with Maryland voters' approval of abolition—obviously delighted Lincoln. It must have bolstered his hopes that Congress, when it convened in December, would move quickly to initiate the antislavery amendment to the Constitution.

Governor Fletcher and the new Missouri state government assumed office on January 2, 1865; four days later the state constitutional convention assembled in Saint Louis. The convention wasted little time in acting to end slavery in Missouri; on January 12 it overwhelmingly passed an ordinance immediately abolishing the institution. A fanciful proposal for the state to compensate loyal slaveholders for their losses was tabled by a vote of 44 to 4.[124]

In Washington, Lincoln called Rollins, a Missouri lame-duck congressman, to the White House and sought his support for the antislavery amendment that had been introduced in Congress. Lincoln expected a close vote on it, and he needed border state support. As Rollins later remembered, the president began by reminding him, "You and I were old whigs, both of us followers of that great statesman, Henry Clay, and I tell you I never had an opinion upon the subject of slavery in my life that I did not get from him." (Lincoln was probably more antislavery by the mid-1850s than Clay ever had been.) The president informed Rollins that he was "very anxious that the war should be brought to a close at the earliest possible date." He repeated his old argument that if the border states united in support of emancipation, "those fellows down South" would see that they could not "rely upon the border states to help them." As a result, Lincoln claimed, the rebels would "give up their opposition and quit their war upon the government." He asked Rollins, a large slaveholder who had earlier vigorously opposed federal emancipation, to support the amendment. The Missouri conservative, recognizing that slavery was in its death throes and that his state was in the process of abolishing it, agreed to do so. Also, at Lincoln's urging, he consented to lobby other border state representatives to vote for it.[125]

True to his word, Rollins talked to his conservative colleagues and also spoke in support of the antislavery amendment on the floor of the House of Representatives. He succeeded, along with Lincoln, in persuading some of his border state colleagues to vote for it, despite their fears that the amendment's adoption would provide authority for federal interference in state racial matters.[126] Requiring a two-thirds majority, the Thirteenth Amendment passed Congress by a razor-thin margin, and the president sent it out to the states for ratification. As mentioned previously, Missouri and Maryland quickly approved the amendment, but Kentucky and Delaware rejected it. The amendment became a part of the Constitution in December 1865, thereby freeing the last slaves in the United States.

By February 1865, with the Union on the verge of victory in the South, Missouri no longer faced a military threat. Although guerrilla activity had declined, widespread lawlessness and a culture of violence and revenge still plagued the state. Disturbed by the continued "destruction of property and life" in Missouri, Lincoln, whose conservative fear of anarchy predated the war, made a remarkable suggestion to Governor Fletcher on how the disorders might be ended. On February 20 he wrote the new governor, "Let neighborhood meetings be every where called and held, of all entertaining a sincere purpose for mutual security in the future, whatever they may heretofore have thought, said or done about the war. Let all such meet and waiving all else pledge each to cease harassing others and to make common cause against whomever persists in making, aiding or encouraging further disturbance." Lincoln predicted, "[In] such meetings old friendships will cross the memory; and honor and Christian Charity will come in to help." He contended, "Every man, not naturally a robber or cut-throat would gladly put an end to this [lawless] state of things. A large majority in every locality must feel alike upon this subject; and if so they only need to reach an understanding one with another."[127]

Fletcher was stunned by what he considered, probably correctly, an unrealistic proposal for ending the lawlessness and violence in the state. When Fletcher hesitated in replying, Lincoln on February 27, by telegram, reminded him and promised that if the governor agreed to the plan, he would "direct the Military to co-operate."[128] Upon receipt of Lincoln's message, Fletcher telegraphed that he would "diligently, faithfully, and honestly try the policy" Lincoln suggested, but he admitted that he possessed an "utter want of confidence in its success."[129]

The governor followed with a long letter giving his reasons why the president's proposal could not succeed and, in the process, mildly rebuked Lincoln for his naïveté regarding the situation in Missouri. He wrote that for four years the state had been "infested with thousands of outlaws" who were "naturally and practically 'robbers' and 'cut-throats'" who "no good man desires to reach any understanding with." Fletcher said, "An agreement to leave 'all others alone' would be kept by the good, and only result in advantages to the men who can neither be bound by oaths nor agreements. It would but madden the true men of this State to talk to them of reliance on the 'honor' and 'christian charity' of these fiends in human shape." The governor told the president, "If you could see and fully understand what we have done and suffered in Missouri . . . you would agree . . . that we want no peace with rebels but the peace which comes of unconditional submission to the authority of the law." However, he promised Lincoln that he would meet with General John Pope, who had replaced Rosecrans in December as department commander, and General Grenville Dodge, his subordinate in Missouri, to determine "the best method of fully testing the policy suggested by you."[130]

Instead of meeting with the generals, Fletcher wrote Pope inquiring as to "the best uses of the U.S. military forces, and their relation to the present and prospective condition of this State" and its security. In a long letter on March 3, Pope told the governor that martial law, which still prevailed in Missouri, seemed "essential now to the protection of life and property and to the preservation of the State from utter lawlessness," because it seemed to be "the only law which is generally enforced." Pope, however, insisted that he was anxious for civil authorities to rapidly assume responsibility for suppressing bushwhackers and preventing returning rebel soldiers from becoming a threat to their communities. He wanted Fletcher to replace the army's provost marshals as soon as possible with "loyal and trustworthy" civil officials. Pope lectured the governor on the need for Missourians to take hold and reestablish civil authority throughout the state, thereby reducing the necessity for military intervention.[131]

Pope sent Lincoln a printed copy of his letter to the governor and submitted "a few remarks and suggestions" for the president's consideration. He told Lincoln, "So long as United States troops remain in Missouri and interfere in any manner in the affairs of the State, they will be a constant source of embarrassment, and a difficult obstacle to the renewal of civil administration. . . . Remove that source of difficulty [and the people] will soon learn, that they must depend upon themselves and their state government, as their final resort for justice," and not look to Washington as unfortunately, he brashly reminded the president, had been the case. Pope insisted that Lincoln refer all appeals from Missouri to the civil authorities in the state. He maintained that all factions in the state—radicals, conservatives, Democrats, and the "semi-disloyal"—for different reasons would approve of a gradual end of martial law. On March 19 the president, assuming that the governor concurred, endorsed the general's plan.[132]

Already, on March 7, Governor Fletcher had issued a proclamation designed primarily to satisfy the president and General Pope. He asked all citizens who had not "made themselves infamous by crime" to join with the civil government in suppressing those who persisted in "making, aiding, or encouraging any description of lawlessness." The governor "requested" the judges and justices of the peace in the state "to hold regular terms of their courts and exercise all the authority vested by law for the protection of the lives and property of the people and the preservation of the peace of the State." Fletcher instructed the judges to ask the nearest military commanders for assistance when it was necessary to suppress the lawless.[133] He admitted to friends that the proclamation would have little effect in curbing violence and lawlessness in the state; it would only aid his conservative and Democratic opponents, Fletcher said.[134]

Like the governor, the radical-controlled state constitutional convention also had little faith in a policy of reconciliation. Meeting at the time of Lincoln's conciliatory proposal, the convention, led by Charles Drake, went in the opposite direction and moved toward framing a new constitution that disfranchised everyone with the slightest tinge of disloyalty, even if the person had later sworn to support the Union. Lincoln must have concluded that the work of the convention would further aggravate political and social conditions in Missouri. But he refrained from involvement in the convention's proceedings. Under the "Drake constitution," which went into effect after a referendum on July 4, 1865, all public officers, lawyers, ministers, teachers, jurors, and corporation officers had to take a stringent loyalty oath before they could serve or practice their professions. Not until January 1, 1871, could the state legislature revoke the requirement for voting, when presumably it would be safe to do so. In two cases in 1867, the U.S. Supreme Court invalidated the oath disqualifying lawyers and ministers who had supported secession from practicing law and from preaching.[135]

The draconian provisions in the state constitution and the fierce determination of the radicals to prevent a resurgence of "rebels" and "Copperheads" to positions of influence contributed to the prolongation of Missouri's agony. For years after the war, the state remained convulsed by lawlessness and bitter political conflict, the likes of which were not seen in the other border states. Outlaws, such as the James and Younger brothers, often purporting to carry on the fight against their Civil War enemies, operated well into the postwar years. With his assassination, Abraham Lincoln at last was free of involvement in the affairs of the most troublesome state in the Union, a freedom that he would undoubtedly have relished.

■
Notes

Abbreviations Used in Notes

Annual Cyclopedia, with year designation: *Appleton's Annual Cyclopedia and Register of Important Events*. 15 vols. New York: D. Appleton, 1862–1875.

Browning Diary: *The Diary of Orville Hickman Browning*. Ed. Theodore Calvin Pease and James G. Randall. 2 vols. Springfield: Illinois State Library, 1925–1933.

Collected Works: *The Collected Works of Abraham Lincoln*. Ed. Roy P. Basler, Marion Dolores Pratt, and Lloyd A. Dunlap. 9 vols. New Brunswick, N.J.: Rutgers University Press 1953–1955. Two supplements have been published: the first by the Greenwood Press, Westport, Connecticut, in 1974 and reprinted by the Rutgers University Press in 1990, and the second by the Rutgers University Press in 1990.

Lincoln Papers: Papers of Abraham Lincoln, Manuscript Division, Library of Congress, Washington, D.C. Available at http://memory.loc.gov/ammem/alhtml/alhome.html.

OR, with series, volume, and, when necessary, part designations: *The War of the Rebellion: A Compilation of the Official Records of the Union and Confederate Armies*. 128 vols. Washington, D.C.: Government Printing Office, 1880–1901.

Rebellion Record, with volume and document designations: *The Rebellion Record: A Diary of American Events, with Documents, Narratives, Illustrative Incidents, Poetry, Etc.* Ed. Frank Moore. 12 vols. 1866–1869. New York: G. P. Putnam, 1977.

Introduction

1. Abraham Lincoln to Orville H. Browning, September 22, 1861, *Collected Works*, 4: 532.

2. As quoted in James Brewer Stuart, *Wendell Phillips: Liberty's Hero* (Baton Rouge: Louisiana State University Press, 1986), 229.

3. James Oakes, *The Radical and the Republican: Frederick Douglass, Abraham Lincoln, and the Triumph of Antislavery Politics* (New York: W. W. Norton, 2007), 162–163.

4. James Russell Lowell to Sibyle Norton, September 28, 1861, *Letters of James Russell Lowell*, ed. Charles Eliot Norton, 2 vols. (New York: Harper & Brothers, 1894), 1: 314; *Atlantic Monthly,* December 1861, 768.

5. Allan Nevins, *The War for the Union,* vol. 1, *The Improvised War, 1861–1862* (New York: Charles Scribner's Sons, 1959), 340.

6. Emancipation Proclamation, January 1, 1863, *Collected Works,* 6: 30.

7. Annual Message to Congress, December 1, 1862, *Collected Works,* 5: 530–531.

8. Abraham Lincoln to Henry T. Blow, Charles D. Drake, and Others, May 15, 1863; Lincoln to John M. Schofield, May 27, 1863, *Collected Works,* 6: 218, 234.

9. For the view that the border states were solidly in the Union camp by the end of 1861, see James A. Rawley, *Turning Points of the Civil War* (Lincoln: University of Nebraska Press, 1966), 44–45; David Herbert Donald, Jean H. Baker, and Michael F. Holt, *The Civil War and Reconstruction* (New York: W. W. Norton, 2001), 171, 175, 177; Kevin Conley Ruffner, *Maryland's Blue and Gray: A Border State's Union and Confederate Junior Officer Corps* (Baton Rouge: Louisiana State University Press, 1997), 57; Jean H. Baker, *The Politics of Continuity: Maryland Political Parties from 1858 to 1870* (Baltimore: Johns Hopkins University Press, 1973), 54.

10. William E. Gienapp, "Abraham Lincoln and the Border States," *Journal of the Abraham Lincoln Association* 13 (1992): 15–16.

11. As quoted in Robert S. Harper, *Lincoln and the Press* (New York: McGraw-Hill, 1951), 69–70.

12. For the best study of West Virginia during the Civil War, see Richard O. Curry, *A House Divided: A Study of State Politics and the Copperhead Movement in West Virginia* (Pittsburgh: University of Pittsburgh Press, 1964).

Chapter 1
The Border States and Lincoln's Election

1. Speech at Peoria, October 16, 1854, *Collected Works,* 2: 255–256. Lincoln's speech at Peoria set forth almost all his positions on slavery that would become important in his rise as an antislavery leader. See Lewis E. Lehrman's *Lincoln at Peoria: The Turning Point* (Mechanicsburg, Pa.: Stackpole Books, 2008), for an excellent account of this often-neglected address and its historical significance.

2. Abraham Lincoln to John J. Crittenden, November 4, 1858, *Collected Works,* 3: 335–336.

3. *Louisville Daily Courier,* May 26, 1860, as reported in *Southern Editorials on Secession,* ed. Dwight Lowell Dumond (1931; reprint, Gloucester, Mass.: Peter Smith, 1964), 112–115.

4. *Louisville Daily Journal,* August 22, 1860, as reported in Dumond, *Southern Editorials on Secession,* 164–167.

5. A report of Crittenden's speech can be found in the *Springfield Illinois State Register,* August 23, 1860. See also John P. Usher to Abraham Lincoln, August 18, 1860, Lincoln Papers.

6. Richard W. Thompson to Abraham Lincoln, June 12, 1860, Lincoln Papers; Instructions for John G. Nicolay [ca. July 16, 1860], *Collected Works*, 4: 83.

7. Richard W. Thompson, *To the Conservative Men of Indiana* (n.p., n.d.), in Lincoln Papers.

8. For the National Union Party convention in Illinois, see the *Springfield Illinois State Register*, August 18, 1860.

9. *Louisville Daily Journal*, October 30, 1860, as reported in Dumond, *Southern Editorials on Secession*, 198. Though Breckinridge was the southern rights candidate, he did not advocate secession if Lincoln were elected. However, after the war began, he joined the Confederacy and served both as a general and as secretary of war.

10. Harold Bell Hancock, *Delaware during the Civil War* (Wilmington: Historical Society of Delaware, 1961), 36.

11. William E. Gienapp, "Who Voted for Lincoln?" in *Abraham Lincoln and the American Political Tradition*, ed. John L. Thomas (Amherst: University of Massachusetts Press, 1986), 62.

12. Garret Davis to John J. Crittenden, December 10, 1860, as quoted in William H. Townsend, *Lincoln and the Bluegrass: Slavery and Civil War in Kentucky* (Lexington: University of Kentucky Press, 1955), 255. Davis's first name is usually misspelled as Garrett.

13. *Lexington Kentucky Statesman*, November 13, 1860, in Dumond, *Southern Editorials on Secession*, 233–235.

14. *Lexington Kentucky Statesman*, November 20, 1860, in Dumond, *Southern Editorials on Secession*, 253–255.

15. *Baltimore Sun*, December 4, 1860, in *Maryland Voices of the Civil War*, ed. Charles W. Mitchell (Baltimore: Johns Hopkins University Press, 2007), 15.

16. The quotations are in Harper, *Lincoln and the Press*, 155.

17. *Frederick (Md.) Herald*, quoted in the *Baltimore American*, November 14, 1860, in Mitchell, *Maryland Voices of the Civil War*, 16–17.

18. As quoted in William J. Evitts, *A Matter of Allegiances: Maryland from 1850 to 1861* (Baltimore: Johns Hopkins University Press, 1974), 155.

19. Harold Holzer, in his excellent recent book *Lincoln, President-Elect: Abraham Lincoln and the Great Secession Winter, 1860–1861* (New York: Simon & Schuster, 2008), 69, 510–511n103, challenges the view that Lincoln misread the surge of secession sentiment in the South.

20. Abraham Lincoln to Nathaniel P. Paschall, November 16, 1860, *Collected Works*, 4: 139–140.

21. Nathaniel P. Paschall to Abraham Lincoln, November 18, 1860, Lincoln Papers; *Saint Louis Daily Missouri Republican*, November 21, 1860, in Dumond, *Southern Editorials on Secession*, 258–261.

22. For a fine biography of Jackson, see Christopher Phillips, *Missouri's Confederate: Claiborne Fox Jackson and the Creation of Southern Identity* (Columbia: University of Missouri Press, 2000).

23. William E. Parrish, *A History of Missouri*, vol. 3, *1860 to 1875* (Columbia: University of Missouri Press, 1973), 3–4.

24. *Resolutions Adopted by the Missouri State Convention* [March 1861], Lincoln Papers; William E. Parrish, *Turbulent Partnership: Missouri and the Union, 1861–1865* (Columbia: University of Missouri Press, 1963), 13–14.

25. Lowell H. Harrison, *Lincoln of Kentucky* (Lexington: University Press of Kentucky, 2000), 126.

26. For Governor Magoffin's letter to the slave states' governors, see the *New York Tribune*, December 20, 1860.

27. As quoted in Charles B. Dew, *Apostles of Disunion: Southern Secession Commissioners and the Causes of the Civil War* (Charlottesville: University Press of Virginia, 2001), 57–58.

28. Hale's long letter to Magoffin is copied in ibid., 90–103.

29. Thomas Speed, *The Union Cause in Kentucky, 1860–1865* (New York: G. P. Putnam's Sons, 1907), 35–37; E. Merton Coulter, *The Civil War and Readjustment in Kentucky* (1926; reprint, Gloucester, Mass.: Peter Smith, 1966), 27–28.

30. Speed, *The Union Cause in Kentucky*, 26–27.

31. *Louisville Daily Journal*, January 22, 1861.

32. Ibid., January 28 and February 4, 1861.

33. See ibid., January–February 1861 issues, for the Union rallies on the state convention issue.

34. For a superb account of Maryland's antebellum political history, see Evitts, *A Matter of Allegiances*. Also important is Baker, *The Politics of Continuity*.

35. George L. P. Radcliffe, *Governor Thomas H. Hicks of Maryland and the Civil War*, Studies in Historical and Political Science 19 (Baltimore: Johns Hopkins University Press, 1901), 22.

36. *Rebellion Record*, vol. 1, doc. 16, pp. 17–18; Evitts, *A Matter of Allegiances*, 164.

37. *Rebellion Record*, vol. 1, doc. 16, pp. 17–18.

38. Hancock, *Delaware during the Civil War*, 44–45, 45n.

39. For Johnson's January 10, 1861, speech, see *Rebellion Record*, vol. 1, doc. 143, pp. 199–201.

40. George Ashmun to Abraham Lincoln, November 13, 1860, Lincoln Papers; John G. Nicolay, "Memorandum, Springfield, 15 November, 1860," in *With Lincoln in the White House: Letters, Memoranda, and Other Writings of John G. Nicolay, 1860–1865*, ed. Michael Burlingame (Carbondale: Southern Illinois University Press, 2000), 10.

41. Worthington G. Snethen to Abraham Lincoln, December 21, 1860, Lincoln Papers.

42. Joseph Medill to Abraham Lincoln, December 26, 1860, Lincoln Papers.

43. Alexander K. McClure to Lincoln, January 15, 1861, Lincoln Papers.

44. William C. Harris, *Lincoln's Rise to the Presidency* (Lawrence: University Press of Kansas, 2007), 264–266.

45. Holzer, *Lincoln, President-Elect*, 155–160.

46. Abraham Lincoln to Lyman Trumbull, December 10, 1860, *Collected Works*, 4: 149–150.

47. The standard account of the Crittenden Compromise and its fate is David M. Potter, *The Impending Crisis, 1846–1861*, completed and edited by Don E. Fehrenbacher (New York: Harper & Row, 1976), 531–532.

48. Albert D. Kirwan, *John J. Crittenden: The Struggle for the Union* (Lexington: University of Kentucky Press, 1962), 392.

49. Samuel T. Glover to Abraham Lincoln, February 5, 1861, Lincoln Papers. For other examples of border state and southern Unionist pressure on Lincoln to support the Crittenden Compromise, see Harris, *Lincoln's Rise to the Presidency*, 288–289.

50. As quoted in Michael Burlingame, *Abraham Lincoln: A Life*, 2 vols. (Baltimore: Johns Hopkins University Press, 2008), 1, 717. Professor Burlingame has persuasively made the case that Lincoln anonymously wrote many articles in the *Springfield Illinois State Journal*, and suggests that he wrote this one.

51. Abraham Lincoln to William H. Seward, February 1, 1861, *Collected Works*, 4: 183.

52. Entry for February 9, 1861, *Browning Diary*, 1: 453. The words are Browning's.

53. Speech from the balcony of the Bates House in Indianapolis, Indiana, February 11, 1861, *Collected Works*, 4: 195–196.

54. Dumond, *Southern Editorials on Secession*, 453, 460, quoting the *Louisville Daily Courier*, February 13, 1861, and the *Saint Louis Daily Missouri Republican*, February 15, 1861.

55. *Rebellion Record*, vol. 1, doc. 38, pp. 33–34.

56. Radcliffe, *Governor Thomas H. Hicks*, 47; George William Brown, *Baltimore and the Nineteenth of April, 1861: A Study of the War*, with an introduction by Kevin Conley Ruffner (Baltimore: Johns Hopkins University Press, 2001), 11–12. Brown's account was originally published in 1887.

57. Chauncey F. Black, *The Life of Abraham Lincoln from His Birth to His Inauguration as President*, attributed to Ward Hill Lamon (Boston: James R. Osgood, 1872), 526–527; Elihu B. Washburne, "Abraham Lincoln in Illinois, Part II," *North American Review* 141 (November 1885): 455, 458. Though Lamon provided the materials for *The Life of Abraham Lincoln*, Chauncey F. Black wrote the book.

58. Norma B. Cuthbert, *Lincoln and the Baltimore Plot, 1861, from the Pinkerton Records and Related Papers* (San Marino, Calif.: Huntington Library, 1949).

59. Thomas H. Hicks to William H. Seward, March 28, 1861, Lincoln Papers. Seward gave the letter to Lincoln.

60. First Inaugural Address—Final Text, March 4, 1861, *Collected Works*, 4: 262–266.

61. First Inaugural Address—Final Text, March 4, 1861, *Collected Works*, 4: 270–271.

62. Henry Watterson, *Marse Henry: An Autobiography* (New York: George H. Doran, ca. 1919), 84.

63. The Kennedy quotations are in Burlingame, *Abraham Lincoln*, 2: 66.

64. *Rebellion Record*, vol. 1, doc. 43, pp. 39–40, quoting the *Saint Louis Missouri Democrat*.

65. *Louisville Daily Journal*, March 7, 1861. For Lincoln's role in the defeat of the Force bill, see the testimony of Alexander R. Boteler in *Recollected Words of Abraham Lincoln*, comp. and ed. Don E. Fehrenbacher and Virginia Fehrenbacher (Stanford: Stanford University Press, 1996), 35.

66. *Rebellion Record*, vol. 1, doc. 43, p. 40, quoting the *Baltimore American*. The

Wilmington Delawarean could find "no policy" in Lincoln's inaugural address, and it facetiously offered a reward of $5,000 to anyone who could tell if the message meant peace or war (Hancock, *Delaware during the Civil War*, 53–54).

67. *Rebellion Record*, vol. 1, doc. 43, p. 40, quoting the *Baltimore Sun*.

68. Oscar Browsfield [?] to John J. Crittenden, March 6, 1861, John J. Crittenden Papers, Manuscript Division, Library of Congress, Washington, D.C. (microfilm).

69. *Rebellion Record*, vol. 1, doc. 43, p. 40, quoting the *Saint Louis Missouri Republican*.

70. John W. Ellis to Simon Cameron, April 15, 1861, *OR*, ser. 3, vol. 1, p. 72.

71. Claiborne Jackson to Simon Cameron, April 17, 1861, *OR*, ser. 3, vol. 1, pp. 82–83.

72. Beriah Magoffin to Simon Cameron, April 15, 1861, *OR*, ser. 3, vol. 1, p. 70.

73. Radcliffe, *Governor Thomas H. Hicks*, 52.

74. Proclamation of the Governor of Delaware, April 26, 1861, *Rebellion Record*, vol. 1, doc. 104, p. 155.

75. Message to Congress in Special Session, July 4, 1861, *Collected Works*, 4: 426.

76. As quoted in Burlingame, *Abraham Lincoln*, 2: 136. By May 9, 1861, Kennedy had renewed his support for the Union. On that day, he issued a pamphlet passionately appealing for Marylanders to stay in the Union. The border states, he said, could be the linchpin to bring about the restoration of the Union, and he predicted that in 1864 a "conservative President" would replace Lincoln in the White House. John Pendleton Kennedy, *The Great Drama: An Appeal to Maryland*, in *Union Pamphlets of the Civil War, 1861–1865*, ed. Frank Freidel, 2 vols. (Cambridge, Mass.: Belknap Press of Harvard University Press, 1967), 1: 86–101.

77. Speech of Reverdy Johnson, in Baltimore, January 10, 1861, *Rebellion Record*, vol. 2, doc. 13, p. 145.

78. Hancock, *Delaware during the Civil War*, 65.

Chapter 2
After Fort Sumter: Crisis in Maryland

1. Evitts, *A Matter of Allegiances*, 176; Brown, *Baltimore and the Nineteenth of April*, 35–36.

2. Radcliffe, *Governor Thomas H. Hicks*, 52.

3. Ibid., 52–53.

4. Ibid., 53; Brown, *Baltimore and the Nineteenth of April*, 36–37.

5. The resolutions of the Southern Rights Convention can be found in Brown, *Baltimore and the Nineteenth of April*, 37–38.

6. George W. Brown and Thomas H. Hicks to Abraham Lincoln, April 19, 1861, Lincoln Papers.

7. George W. Brown, with Thomas H. Hicks's endorsement, to Abraham Lincoln, April 18, 1861, Lincoln Papers.

8. The account of the Baltimore Riot has been pieced together from the report of Colonel Edward F. Jones of the Sixth Massachusetts Regiment, April 22, 1861; from the message of Mayor Brown to the members of the First and Second Branches of the City

Council, July 11, 1861; and from the statement of George M. Gill, July 12, 1861, *OR,* ser. 1, vol. 2, pp. 7–10, 15–21. Brown's account, *Baltimore and the Nineteenth of April,* 42–57, including documents, was also useful.

9. As quoted in Hancock, *Delaware during the Civil War,* 62–63.

10. Brown, *Baltimore and the Nineteenth of April,* 56; Radcliffe, *Governor Thomas H. Hicks,* 54–55.

11. Governor Hicks's letter to the People of Maryland, along with documents relating to the bridge-burning episode, are found in *Rebellion Record,* vol. 2, doc. 2, pp. 181–184; report of Mayor Brown to the General Assembly of Maryland, May 9 [?] 1861; message of Mayor Brown to Members of the First and Second Branches of the City Council, July 11, 1861, *OR,* ser. 1, vol. 2, pp. 12–13, 15–20.

12. Memorandum of events, April 21, 1861, in Nicolay, *With Lincoln in the White House,* ed. Burlingame, 37; Abraham Lincoln to Thomas H. Hicks and George W. Brown, April 20, 1861, *Collected Works,* 4: 340.

13. Abraham Lincoln to Thomas H. Hicks and George W. Brown, April 20, 1861, *Collected Works,* 4: 341.

14. Addison's "Memorandum" was included in a letter from H. D. J. Pratt of Baltimore to Abraham Lincoln, April 20, 1861, Lincoln Papers.

15. Brown, *Baltimore and the Nineteenth of April,* 63–69.

16. Ibid., 65–66.

17. Brown's account, written on the day of the conference, is reprinted in his *Baltimore and the Nineteenth of April,* 71–72.

18. Ibid., 72.

19. Ibid., 72, 73–74.

20. Ibid., 73.

21. General Winfield Scott to General Robert Patterson, April 22, 1861, *OR,* ser. 1, vol. 2, p. 587.

22. Reverdy Johnson to Abraham Lincoln, April 22, 1861, Lincoln Papers.

23. Abraham Lincoln to Reverdy Johnson, April 24, 1861, *Collected Works,* 4: 342–343.

24. Reverdy Johnson to Abraham Lincoln, June 17, 1861, Lincoln Papers; *Rebellion Record,* vol. 2, doc. 58, pp. 185–193.

25. Both cited in *Rebellion Record,* vol. 1, doc. 134, pp. 188–190.

26. General Orders, no. 4, April 26, 1861, *OR,* ser. 1, vol. 2, p. 602.

27. John G. Nicolay and John Hay, *Abraham Lincoln: A History,* 10 vols. (New York: Century, 1890), 4: 139–140. The date of the interview is in doubt; however, the editors of the *Collected Works,* 4: 342n, believe that it occurred on April 22, 1861. The precise quotation is also open to question.

28. Reply to Baltimore Committee, April 22, 1861, *Collected Works,* 4: 341–342. See also Nicolay and Hay, *Abraham Lincoln,* 4: 139–140.

29. Diary of Events, *Rebellion Record,* vol. 1, p. 50; John C. McGowan to Abraham Lincoln, May 6, 1861, Lincoln Papers.

30. Thomas H. Hicks to Abraham Lincoln, April 22, 1861, Lincoln Papers.

31. William H. Seward to Thomas H. Hicks, April 22, 1861, Lincoln Papers. Hicks's letter of April 22 was delivered and replied to on the same day.

32. Nelson D. Lankford, *Cry Havoc! The Crooked Road to Civil War, 1861* (New York: Viking Press, 2007), 213; Radcliffe, *Governor Thomas H. Hicks*, 60–61.

33. William L. W. Seabrook, *Maryland's Great Part in Saving the Union: The Loyalty of Her Governor, Thomas Holliday Hicks, and a Majority of Her People* (Westminster, Md.: American Sentinel, 1913), 39.

34. Radcliffe, *Governor Thomas H. Hicks*, 68–69; Message of Governor Hicks, April 27, 1861, *Rebellion Record*, vol. 1, doc. 109, pp. 159–161. In addition to Hicks, other Marylanders also advocated a position of neutrality in the war. On April 30, 1861, the *Frederick Examiner* declared, "Neutrality is our only safety. Any other policy would mean Ruin, ruin, ruin" (Evitts, *A Matter of Allegiances*, 186).

35. Abraham Lincoln to Winfield Scott, April 25, 1861, *Collected Works*, 4: 344.

36. Mark E. Neely Jr., *The Fate of Liberty: Abraham Lincoln and Civil Liberties* (New York: Oxford University Press, 1991), 7.

37. See the Lincoln Papers for the holograph original of the president's April 25 directive to Scott.

38. Entry for April 22, 1861, in *The Diary of George Templeton Strong: The Civil War, 1860–1861*, ed. Allan Nevins and Milton Halsey Thomas (New York: Macmillan, 1952), 131.

39. *New York Herald*, May 5, 1861, as reported in *Northern Editorials on Secession*, 2 vols. (1942; reprint, Gloucester, Mass.: Peter Smith, 1964), 2: 825.

40. Burlingame, *Abraham Lincoln*, 2: 91. A notable exception to the neglect by historians of the Baltimore Riot and subsequent events in rallying northern support for the war is Burlingame's recent magisterial biography of Lincoln. The president was strongly criticized for caving in to the demand of Hicks and other Marylanders that troops not be sent through Baltimore. The *New York Times* suggested that Lincoln be impeached (ibid., 2: 143).

41. Lyman Trumbull to Abraham Lincoln, April 21, 1861, Lincoln Papers.

42. Orville H. Browning to Lincoln, April 22, 1861, Lincoln Papers.

43. Edward Bates to Abraham Lincoln, April 23, 1861, Lincoln Papers.

44. Memorandum of events, April 21, 1861, in Nicolay, *With Lincoln in the White House*, ed. Burlingame, 39.

45. Abraham Lincoln to Winfield Scott, April 27, 1861, *Collected Works*, 4: 347. On July 2 the suspension of the writ was extended to New York.

46. Brown, *Baltimore and the Nineteenth of April*, 84, 87.

47. For an excellent account of the Merryman case, which became a cause célèbre of those charging Lincoln with violations of civil liberties, see James F. Simon, *Lincoln and Chief Justice Taney: Slavery, Secession, and the President's War Powers* (New York: Simon & Schuster, 2006), 186–198.

48. Abraham Lincoln to Edward Bates, May 30, 1861, *Collected Works*, 4: 390.

49. Edward Bates to Abraham Lincoln, July 5, 1861, Lincoln Papers.

50. Reverdy Johnson, "Power of the President to Suspend the Habeas Corpus Writ," n. d., *Rebellion Record*, vol. 2, doc. 58, pp. 185–193. The quotation is on page 192.

51. Message to Congress in Special Session, July 4, 1861, *Collected Works*, 4: 429–431.

52. For Merryman's fate, see Simon, *Lincoln and Chief Justice Taney*, 197.

53. Diary of Events, *Rebellion Record*, vol. 1, p. 46.

54. Speech of Reverdy Johnson, at Frederick, Maryland, May 7, 1861, *Rebellion Record*, vol. 1, doc. 143, pp. 199–201.

55. Entry for April 28, 1861, in Strong, *Diary*, ed. Nevins and Thomas, 136.

56. Radcliffe, *Governor Thomas H. Hicks*, 76.

57. Commissioners' Report to the Maryland Legislature, *Rebellion Record*, vol. 1, doc. 135, p. 190; Abraham Lincoln to Otho Scott, Robert M. McLane, and William J. Ross, May 6, 1861, *Collected Works*, 4: 358 and n; entry for May 4, 1861, in *Inside Lincoln's White House: The Complete Civil War Diary of John Hay*, ed. Michael Burlingame and John R. Turner Ettlinger (Carbondale: Southern Illinois University Press, 1997), 17–18.

58. For the House of Delegates' resolution, see Radcliffe, *Governor Thomas H. Hicks*, 82–83.

59. Maryland Resolution Passed in the Legislature, May 10, 1861, *Rebellion Record*, vol. 1, doc. 153, p. 234.

60. The quotations are from Jefferson Davis's letter to the Maryland commissioners, May 25, 1861, *Rebellion Record*, vol. 1, doc. 246, p. 362. See Radcliffe, *Governor Thomas H. Hicks*, 105, for the withdrawal of the commissioners to Washington.

61. For the election, see Charles Lewis Wagandt, *The Mighty Revolution: Negro Emancipation in Maryland, 1862–1864* (Baltimore: Johns Hopkins University Press, 1964), 17–21. My description of the political positions of the six victors in the election differs from Wagandt's.

62. Nathaniel P. Banks to Simon Cameron, June 16, 1861, *OR*, ser. 1, vol. 2, p. 690.

63. *Lew Wallace: An Autobiography*, 2 vols. (New York: Harper & Brothers, 1906), 2: 675.

64. See the Lincoln Papers for Snethen letters to Lincoln in 1860–1861.

65. Order from General Scott for the arrest of the Commissioners, June 24, 1861, *OR*, ser. 1, vol. 2, pp. 138–139.

66. Abraham Lincoln to Winfield Scott, April 25, 1861, *Collected Works*, 4: 344.

67. General Nathaniel P. Banks to the People of Baltimore, June 27, 1861, *OR*, ser. 1, vol. 2, pp. 140–141.

68. Worthington G. Snethen to Winfield Scott, June 29, 1861, Lincoln Papers.

69. Nathaniel P. Banks to William H. Seward, July 9, 1861, Lincoln Papers.

70. William H. Seward to Nathaniel P. Banks, July 5, 1861, *OR*, ser. 2, vol. 1, p. 628.

71. Nathaniel P. Banks to William H. Seward, July 9, 1861, Lincoln Papers.

72. Hancock, *Delaware during the Civil War*, 132.

73. Memorial of the Board of Police Commissioners, to the Senate and House of Representatives of the United States, n.d. [July 1861]; Memorial of the Mayor and City Council of Baltimore, to the Senate and House of Representatives of the United States, n.d. [July 1861], *OR*, ser. 1, vol. 2, pp. 144–152, 152–156 (the quotation is on page 156).

74. Memorial of the Board of Police Commissioners, to the Senate and House of Representatives of the United States, n.d. [July 1861], *OR*, ser. 1, vol. 2, p. 148.

75. Resolution of the House of Representatives, July 24, 1861; To the House of Representatives, July 27, 1861, *OR*, ser. 1, vol. 2, p. 156.

76. Radcliffe, *Governor Thomas H. Hicks*, 106–107; Brown, *Baltimore and the Nineteenth of April*, 100.

77. Proclamation of Governor Thomas H. Hicks, May 14, 1861, *Rebellion Record*, vol. 1, doc. 168, p. 245.

78. James M. McPherson, *Ordeal by Fire: The Civil War and Reconstruction*, 3d ed. (New York: McGraw Hill, 2001), 167; Ira Berlin, Joseph P. Reidy, and Leslie S. Rowland, eds., *Freedom's Soldiers: The Black Military Experience in the Civil War* (Cambridge, U.K.: Cambridge University Press, 1998), 16–17. See also Ruffner, *Maryland's Blue and Gray*, 7, 10n.

79. George B. McClellan to Simon Cameron, September 8, 1861, in *The Civil War Papers of George B. McClellan: Selected Correspondence, 1860–1865*, ed. Stephen W. Sears (New York: Ticknor & Fields, 1989), 95–96.

80. Frederick Schley to William H. Seward, September 12, 1861; Worthington G. Snethen to Seward, September 15, 1861, *OR*, ser. 2, vol. 1, pp. 595, 679.

81. George B. McClellan to Nathaniel P. Banks, September 12, 1861, in McClellan, *The Civil War Papers*, ed. Sears, 99.

82. Simon Cameron to Nathaniel P. Banks, September 11, 1861, *OR*, ser. 2, vol. 1, pp. 677–678.

83. John A. Dix to Simon Cameron, September 13, 1861, Lincoln Papers. For Henry May's release in time to take his seat in Congress, see Cong. Globe, 37 Cong., 2d Sess. (December 2, 1861), 2.

84. The documents relating to the payment controversy between Brown and Dix are found in Brown, *Baltimore and the Nineteenth of April*, 104–107.

85. Nathaniel P. Banks to Thomas H. Ruger, September 16, 1861; R. Morris Copeland to Banks, September 18, 1861, *OR*, ser. 2, vol. 1, pp. 681, 682–683.

86. Arrest and Detention of Certain Members of the Maryland Legislature, n.d., *OR*, ser. 2, vol. 1, pp. 667–676; Baker, *The Politics of Continuity*, 58 and n.

87. Neely, *The Fate of Liberty*, 75.

88. Statement Concerning Arrests in Maryland [ca. September 15, 1861], *Collected Works*, 4: 523 and n.

89. As quoted in Neely, *The Fate of Liberty*, 18.

90. Francis Key Howard to the *Maryland Times*, September 22, 1861, Lincoln Papers.

91. Copy of printed declaration with original signatures of citizens of Maryland found among the papers of F. Key Howard at the time of his arrest, n.d., *OR*, ser. 2, vol. 1, p. 676.

92. George W. Brown to the *Baltimore American*, September 22, 1861, Lincoln Papers.

93. Draft of statement by President Lincoln [November 1861], Lincoln Papers. This statement, which is not in the *Collected Works*, is incorrectly filed in September 1861 in the Lincoln Papers. Seward's response to Davis's appeal, even though Lincoln was not mentioned, indicates that the president's statement was written in November 1861.

94. Memoranda from Record Book, State Department, "Arrests for Disloyalty," n.d., *OR*, ser. 2, vol. 1, pp. 619–621.

95. Thomas H. Hicks to Nathaniel P. Banks, September 20, 1861, *OR*, ser. 2, vol. 1, p. 685.

96. Thomas H. Hicks to William H. Seward, November 12, 1861; Reverdy Johnson to Seward, November 12, 1861, *OR*, ser. 2, vol. 1, pp. 704, 704–705.

97. Brown, *Baltimore and the Nineteenth of April*, 70, 108–109; Harper, *Lincoln and the Press*, 161–162.

98. John A. Dix to Daniel Engel and William Ecker, November 1, 1861, *OR*, ser. 2, vol. 1, p. 609; Wagandt, *The Mighty Revolution*, 32.

99. Speech of Reverdy Johnson, at a Mass Meeting of Union Citizens of Baltimore County, at Calverton, Maryland, November 4, 1861; Speech of Francis Thomas in Baltimore, October 29, 1861, *Rebellion Record*, vol. 3, docs. 115, 130, pp. 252–253 (Thomas), 272–276 (Johnson).

100. For a long and revealing document arguing the southern rights position, see To the People of Harford [County], n.d., *OR*, ser. 2, vol. 1, pp. 604–608.

101. Wagandt, *The Mighty Revolution*, 32–33; Baker, *The Politics of Continuity*, 68, 70–71.

102. Reply to Delegation of Baltimore Citizens, November 15, 1861, *Collected Works*, 5: 24.

103. Draft of a Proclamation to People of Maryland [ca. January 1, 1862], *Collected Works*, 5: 86–87 and 87n.

104. Diary of Events, entry for December 4, 1861, *Rebellion Record*, vol. 3, pp. 191–192.

105. *Inaugural Address of Hon. Augustus W. Bradford, Governor of Maryland, Delivered in the Senate Chamber, Annapolis, January 8th, 1862* (Annapolis, Md.: Schley & Cole, Printers, 1862). This pamphlet is part of a collection of digital texts and images that have been created and curated by the Cornell University Library since 1992.

106. Wagandt, *The Mighty Revolution*, 36.

107. Last Public Speech, April 11, 1865, *Collected Works*, 8: 403–404.

Chapter 3
Kentucky: Experiment in Neutrality

1. William Nelson to John B. S. Todd, April 18, 1861, Lincoln Papers. Todd, a relative of Mary Lincoln, apparently was in Washington when he received the letter from Nelson. Governor Beriah Magoffin initially gave tacit approval to the recruitment of Confederate troops in the state, but he soon withdrew the permission when he committed to a policy of armed neutrality (Harrison, *Lincoln of Kentucky*, 132–133). For an excellent historiographic account of Lincoln and Kentucky, see John David Smith, "'Gentlemen, I too, am a Kentuckian': Abraham Lincoln, the Lincoln Bicentennial, and Lincoln's Kentucky in Recent Scholarship," *Register of the Kentucky Historical Society* 106 (Summer–Autumn, 2008): 433–470.

2. [A. H. Markland], *Reminiscences of Abraham Lincoln by Distinguished Men of His Time*, ed. Allen Thorndike Rice (New York: North American Review, 1889), 318–319.

3. William Nelson to John B. S. Todd, April 18, 1861, Lincoln Papers.

4. Kirwan, *John J. Crittenden*, 433–434.

5. Address of the Union State Central Committee of Kentucky to the People of the Commonwealth, Cong. Globe, 37th Cong., 2d Sess., Appendix, 81.

6. Meeting at Louisville, Kentucky, *Rebellion Record*, vol. 1, doc. 63, pp. 72–74.

7. Ibid., 74–76.

8. The description of Davis appears in Allan G. Bogue, *The Earnest Men: Republicans of the Civil War Senate* (Ithaca, N.Y.: Cornell University Press, 1981), 47.

9. Garret Davis to George D. Prentice, April 28, 1861, Cong. Globe, 37th Cong., 2d Sess., Appendix, 82–83. An abbreviated version of Davis's account can be found in Lincoln, *Recollected Words*, comp. and ed. Fehrenbacher and Fehrenbacher, 133–134.

10. Ibid.

11. Nicolay and Hay, *Abraham Lincoln*, 4: 236.

12. As quoted in Nevins, *The War for the Union*, vol. 1, *The Improvised War*, 134.

13. Proclamation of Governor Beriah Magoffin, April 24, 1861, *Rebellion Record*, vol. 1, doc. 94, pp. 144–145.

14. Ibid.

15. Harrison, *Lincoln of Kentucky*, 134.

16. Proclamation of Governor Magoffin, May 20, 1861, *Rebellion Record*, vol. 1, doc. 181, pp. 264–265.

17. Nevins, *War for the Union*, vol. 1, *The Improvised War*, 132; E. Merton Coulter, *The Civil War and Readjustment in Kentucky* (1926; reprint, Gloucester, Mass.: Peter Smith, 1966), 51–52.

18. To the People of the United States, *Rebellion Record*, vol. 1, doc. 243, pp. 350–353.

19. To the People of Kentucky, *Rebellion Record*, vol. 1, doc. 243, pp. 353–356.

20. Ibid.

21. John J. Crittenden to Winfield Scott, May 17, 1861, Lincoln Papers.

22. Ibid.

23. Coulter, *The Civil War and Readjustment in Kentucky*, 68–71. The Morehead quotation is on page 70.

24. Diary of Events, April 20, 1861, *Rebellion Record*, vol. 1, p. 35. For an excellent account of the divisions in the Breckinridge family created by secession and war, see James C. Klotter, *The Breckinridges of Kentucky, 1760–1981* (Lexington: University Press of Kentucky, 1986), chaps. 7–11.

25. Unknown, Memorandum, April 11, 1861; William Nelson to John B. S. Todd, April 22, 1861, Lincoln Papers. The April 11 date that the editors assigned to the memorandum in the Lincoln Papers was obviously an error. The memorandum was written after the war began, probably in early May. (In another place on the transcription, the editors had assigned "[April 1861]" to the document.)

26. Kirwan, *John J. Crittenden*, 436; Coulter, *The Civil War and Readjustment in Kentucky*, 89.

27. Charles A. Wickliffe et al. to Abraham Lincoln, May 28, 1861, Lincoln Papers; Kirwan, *John J. Crittenden*, 436.

28. Joshua F. Speed to "President A Lincoln," May 27, 1861, Lincoln Papers.

29. Coulter, *The Civil War and Readjustment in Kentucky*, quoting the *Frankfort Kentucky Yeoman*.

30. For a detailed account of the "Lincoln guns," see Thomas Speed, *The Union Cause in Kentucky* (New York: G. P. Putnam's Sons, 1907), 99–121.

31. Abraham Lincoln to Robert Anderson, May 7, 1861, *Collected Works*, 4: 359.

32. Abraham Lincoln to Robert Anderson, May 14, 1861, *Collected Works*, 4: 368–369; Robert Anderson to Lincoln, May 19, 1861, Lincoln Papers.

33. Memorial from W. Dennison, Richard Yates, and O. P. Morton, May 24, 1861, OR, ser. 1, vol. 52, pp. 146–147.

34. Kenneth M. Stampp, *Indiana Politics during the Civil War* (1949; reprint, Bloomington: Indiana University Press, 1978), 113–115; William Dennison et al. to Abraham Lincoln May 24, 1861, Lincoln Papers.

35. Orville H. Browning to Abraham Lincoln, April 30, 1861, Lincoln Papers.

36. Joseph Holt's Letter on the Pending Revolution, May 31, 1861, *Rebellion Record*, vol. 1, doc. 197, pp. 283–292.

37. For Joseph Holt's background and family, see Elizabeth D. Leonard, "One Kentuckian's Hard Choice: Joseph Holt and Abraham Lincoln," *Register of the Kentucky Historical Society* 106 (Summer–Autumn 2008): 373–408.

38. Joseph Holt's Letter on the Pending Revolution.

39. Ibid.

40. Message to Congress in Special Session, July 4, 1861, *Collected Works*, 4: 428.

41. Abraham Lincoln to Simon B. Buckner, July 10, 1861, *Collected Works*, 4: 444 and n.

42. Abraham Lincoln to Simon Cameron, August 17, 1861, *Collected Works*, 4: 489.

43. To the Kentucky Delegation in Congress, July 29, 1861, *Collected Works*, 4: 464 and n.

44. Beriah Magoffin to Abraham Lincoln, August 15, 1861, Lincoln Papers.

45. Entry for August 22, 1861, in Hay, *Inside Lincoln's White House*, ed. Burlingame and Ettlinger, 24.

46. Abraham Lincoln to Beriah Magoffin, August 24, 1861, *Collected Works*, 4: 497.

47. Johnson-Crittenden Resolution, in *Documents of American History*, ed. Henry Steele Commager, 8th ed. (New York: Appleton-Century-Crofts, 1968), 395–396.

48. Speech of Andrew Johnson, Delivered in the Senate of the United States, July 27, 1861, *Rebellion Record*, vol. 2, doc. 129, p. 427, quoting Senator Lazarus Powell.

49. Cong. Globe, 37th Cong., 2d Sess. (February 20, 1862), 891–892.

50. Ibid., (March 14, 1862), 1230–1232.

51. Ibid., (March 18, 1862), 1234.

52. Ibid.

53. Cong. Globe, 38th Cong., 1st Sess. (January 5, February 1, 1864), 96–97, 418–419.

54. Address of Joseph Holt, Delivered at Louisville, July 13, 1861, *Rebellion Record*, vol. 2, doc. 90, pp. 297–303. The quotations are on page 299.

55. For a revealing account of the war excitement during the summer of 1861, the

accompanying fears of Unionists in southern Kentucky, and the generational division over secession (the old generation supporting the Union and the young, the rebellion), see entries for June 20, July 2, August 1, 10, 16, 25, 29, 31, September 12, 1861, in *Josie Underwood's Civil War Diary*, ed. Nancy Disher Baird, with foreword by Catherine Coke Shick (Lexington: University Press of Kentucky, 2009), 85–96.

56. Proclamation of General John C. Frémont, August 30, 1861, OR, ser. 1, vol. 3, pp. 466–467.

57. Garret Davis to Salmon P. Chase, September 3, 1861, in *The Salmon P. Chase Papers*, vol. 3, *Correspondence, 1858–March 1863*, ed. John Niven (Kent, Ohio: Kent State University Press, 1993), 94–95.

58. As reported in *Rebellion Record*, vol. 3, doc. 18, p. 34.

59. Ibid., vol. 3, doc. 18, p. 36.

60. Joshua Speed to Abraham Lincoln, September 1, 1861, Lincoln Papers.

61. Joshua Speed to Abraham Lincoln, September 3, 1861, Lincoln Papers.

62. Robert Anderson to Abraham Lincoln, September 13, 1861, Lincoln Papers.

63. Joseph Holt to Abraham Lincoln, September 12, 1861, Lincoln Papers.

64. Nevins, *The War for the Union*, vol. 1, *The Improvised War*, 334–335 and 335n; *Rebellion Record*, vol. 1, doc. 18, pp. 33–35.

65. Abraham Lincoln to Orville H. Browning, September 22, 1861, *Collected Works*, 4: 532.

66. Abraham Lincoln to John C. Frémont, September 2, 1861, *Collected Works*, 4: 506.

67. John C. Frémont to Abraham Lincoln, September 8, 1861, Lincoln Papers.

68. Abraham Lincoln to John C. Frémont, September 11, 1861, *Collected Works*, 4: 517–518. One week after the receipt of the president's letter and before complying with the order, Frémont defiantly dispatched 200 printed copies of his original proclamation to the army at Ironton, Missouri, for distribution in the area. Lorenzo Thomas to Simon Cameron, October 21, 1861, OR, ser. 1, vol. 3, p. 543.

69. Joseph Medill to Salmon P. Chase, September 15, 1861, in *Chase Papers*, vol. 3, *Correspondence*, ed. Niven, 97–98.

70. As quoted in Doris Kearns Goodwin, *Team of Rivals: The Political Genius of Abraham Lincoln* (New York: Simon & Schuster, 2005), 394.

71. The Childs and Swisshelm quotations are in Burlingame, *Abraham Lincoln*, 2: 204.

72. Andrew Peck to Abraham Lincoln, September 19, 1861; John L. Williams to Lincoln, September 19, 1861, Lincoln Papers.

73. J. G. Roberts to Abraham Lincoln, September 17, 1861, Lincoln Papers.

74. Hamilton, Illinois, Ministers to Lincoln, October 1, 1861, Lincoln Papers. For similar examples of Christian outrage regarding Lincoln's revocation of the antislavery provision in Frémont's proclamation, see S. Hine to Lincoln, September 20, 1861; Erastus Wright to Lincoln, September 20, 1861; Mrs. E. A. Spaulding to Lincoln, September 23, 1861, Lincoln Papers. Mrs. Spaulding wrote, "Until the Peculiar Institution is abolished, Civilization is impeded, Humanity languishes and our boasted land of Freedom is a Practical Lie."

75. John L. Scripps to Abraham Lincoln, September 23, 1861, Lincoln Papers.

76. Orville H. Browning to Abraham Lincoln, September 17, 1861, Lincoln Papers.

77. Abraham Lincoln to Orville H. Browning, September 22, 1861, *Collected Works*, 4: 531–532.

78. Ibid.

79. Orville H. Browning to Abraham Lincoln, September 30, 1861, Lincoln Papers.

80. *Rebellion Record*, vol. 3, doc. 40, pp. 120–121; Abraham Lincoln to Orville H. Browning, September 22, 1861, *Collected Works*, 4: 532.

81. For the wording of the resolutions, see *Rebellion Record*, vol. 3, doc. 45, p. 129.

82. As quoted in Burlingame, *Abraham Lincoln*, 2: 204.

83. Proceedings of the convention held at Russellville, November 18, 19, and 20, 1861, *OR*, ser. 4, vol. 1, pp. 740–743.

84. William Tecumseh Sherman to General Lorenzo Thomas, November 6, 1861, *OR*, ser. 1, vol. 4, pp. 340–341.

85. General Lorenzo Thomas to Simon Cameron, October 21, 1861, *OR*, ser. 1, vol. 3, p. 548, quoting General Sherman.

86. For white troop statistics, see Lowell H. Harrison, *The Civil War in Kentucky* (Lexington: University Press of Kentucky, 1975), 95; and for blacks, Berlin, Reidy, and Rowland, *Freedom's Soldiers*, 16. Harrison's small book provides a useful survey of military operations in the Bluegrass State.

87. Oliver P. Morton to Abraham Lincoln, September 26, 1861; William Tecumseh Sherman to Lincoln, October 10, 1861, Lincoln Papers.

88. Simon Cameron to Abraham Lincoln, October 16, 1861, Lincoln Papers.

89. Joshua Speed to Lincoln, September 17, October 7, 1861; George D. Prentice, James Guthrie, and James Speed to Lincoln, November 5, 1861, Lincoln Papers. Union General Nathaniel Lyon was killed in the battle of Wilson's Creek, Missouri, in August 1861. The battle was a Confederate victory and stunned Unionists in Missouri and Kentucky.

90. Joseph Holt to Abraham Lincoln, November 2, 1861, Lincoln Papers; Lorenzo Thomas to Simon Cameron, October 21, 1861, *OR*, ser. 1, vol. 3, pp. 548–549.

91. Abraham Lincoln to Oliver P. Morton, September 29, 1861, *Collected Works*, 4: 541–542.

92. A. H. Smead [Sneed] to Abraham Lincoln, September 21, 1861, Lincoln Papers; Case of Charles S. Morehead, Reuben T. Durrett and M. W. Barr, *OR*, ser. 2, vol. 2, pp. 805–806, 816.

93. Case of Charles S. Morehead, Reuben T. Durrett and M. W. Barr; Leslie Coombs to Abraham Lincoln, November 12, 1861, *OR*, ser. 2, vol. 2, pp. 805–806, 818.

94. *OR*, ser. 2, vol. 2, p. 816. For a biographical sketch of Associate Justice Catron, see Kermit L. Hall, ed., *The Oxford Companion to the Supreme Court of the United States* (New York: Oxford University Press, 1992), 129–130.

95. George D. Prentice to Abraham Lincoln, September 24, 1861; Prentice et al. to Lincoln, n.d.; James Guthrie to Lincoln October 25, 1861; statement of Virgil McKnight, et al., n.d., *OR*, ser. 2, vol. 2, pp. 807, 811, 813, 818–819; John J. Crittenden to Lincoln, November 3, 1861, Lincoln Papers.

96. George D. Prentice to Abraham Lincoln, September 24, 1861, *OR*, ser. 2, vol. 2, p. 807; John J. Crittenden to Lincoln, November 3, 1861, Lincoln Papers.

97. Endorsement: Release of Imprisoned Secessionists [ca. September 24, 1861]; Abraham Lincoln to William H. Seward, October 4, 1861, *Collected Works*, 4: 534, 534n, 549, 549n.

98. Much of the documentary evidence in the cases of the three prisoners can be found in *OR*, ser. 2, vol. 2, pp. 805–829. James Guthrie's letter to Lincoln is on page 813.

99. John J. Crittenden to Abraham Lincoln, November 3, 1861, Lincoln Papers; Lincoln to William H. Seward, December 28, 1861, *Collected Works*, 5: 81; Crittenden to William H. Seward, December 31, 1861; Seward to Colonel Martin Burke, January 2, 1862; statement of Charles S. Morehead, January 6, 1862; Seward to John J. Crittenden, January 10, 1862, *OR*, ser. 2, vol. 2, pp. 823–824, 825, 826.

100. E. D. Webster to Charles S. Morehead, March 19, 1862, *OR*, ser. 2, vol. 2, p. 829.

101. David Rankin Barbee and Milledge L. Bonham Jr., eds., "Notes and Documents: Fort Sumter Again," *Mississippi Valley Historical Review* 28 (June 1941): 65–73. The quotations are on pages 71–72.

102. Daniel W. Crofts, *Reluctant Confederates: Upper South Unionists in the Secession Crisis* (Chapel Hill: University of North Carolina Press, 1989), 304.

103. Charles S. Morehead, *Slavery and President Lincoln's Emancipation Proclamation* (London: Saunders, Otley, 1864).

104. *A Radical View: The "Agate" Dispatches of Whitelaw Reid, 1861–1865*, edited and with an introduction by James G. Smart, 2 vols. (Memphis, Tenn.: Memphis State University Press, 1976), 1: 68; Stephen Berry, *House of Abraham: Lincoln and the Todds, a Family Divided by War* (Boston: Houghton Mifflin, 2007), has a well-researched and illuminating account of the divisions over the war in Mary Todd Lincoln's family.

105. Townsend, *Lincoln and the Bluegrass*, 284–285; Robert J. Anderson to Abraham Lincoln, September 28, 1861; James Guthrie and Robert J. Anderson to Lincoln, September 30, 1861; John Catron to William T. Carroll, October 9, 1861, Lincoln Papers.

106. John Catron to William T. Carroll, October 9, 1861, Lincoln Papers.

107. Nancy Disher Baird, "Editor's Postscript," in Underwood, *Civil War Diary*, ed. Baird, 203; Coulter, *The Civil War and Readjustment in Kentucky*, 140–141.

108. Coulter, *The Civil War and Readjustment in Kentucky*, 152.

109. Cong. Globe, 37th Cong., 2nd Sess. (May 28, 1862), 2393.

110. Ibid., (May 14, 1862), 2113.

111. Ibid.

112. Ibid.; To the Senate, May 21, 1862, *Collected Works*, 5: 227 and n.

113. Ezra J. Warner, *Generals in Blue: Lives of the Union Commanders* (Baton Rouge: Louisiana State University Press, 1964), 40.

114. Harrison, *Lincoln of Kentucky*, 195.

115. As quoted in Coulter, *The Civil War and Readjustment in Kentucky*, 152n.

116. J. B. Temple to Abraham Lincoln, August 12, 1862, *OR*, ser. 2, vol. 4, p. 378. On July 28 Temple had reported to Lincoln that recruiting for state Union regiments had come to a standstill. Lincoln Papers.

117. James F. Robinson to Abraham Lincoln, September 15, 1862; Joshua F. Speed to Lincoln, September 15, 1862, *OR*, ser. 1, vol. 16, pt. 2, p. 519.

118. Edwin M. Stanton to Jeremiah T. Boyle, September 15, 1862, *OR*, ser. 1, vol. 16, pt. 2, p. 519.

119. Jeremiah T. Boyle to Edwin M. Stanton, September 15, 1862, *OR*, ser. 1, vol. 16, pt. 2, p. 519.

120. James F. Robinson to Abraham Lincoln, October 6, 1862, Lincoln Papers.

121. Ibid.

122. Annual Message to Congress, December 3, 1861, *Collected Works*, 5: 50.

Chapter 4
Missouri: A State in Turmoil

1. Dumond, *Southern Editorials on Secession*, 500–501.

2. Napton, quoted in the introduction by Christopher Phillips and Jason L. Pendleton to *The Union on Trial: The Political Journals of Judge William Barclay Napton, 1829–1883*, ed. Christopher Phillips and Jason L. Pendleton (Columbia: University of Missouri Press, 2005), 1.

3. As reported in Thomas L. Snead, *The Fight for Missouri: From the Election of Lincoln to the Death of Lyon* (New York: Charles Scribner's Sons, 1888), 162.

4. "Our Legislature," as reported in the *Saint Louis Evening News*, April 23, 1861, *OR*, ser. 1, vol. 1, pp. 673–674. In calling the legislature into special session, Governor Jackson deliberately bypassed the Unionist state convention that had met and adjourned before the fighting in Charleston Harbor.

5. Proclamation of General William S. Harney, May 12, 1861, *OR*, ser. 1, vol. 3, p. 370. In this proclamation Harney recounted his efforts to preserve the peace in Missouri.

6. Snead, *The Fight for Missouri*, 150–151.

7. Jefferson Davis to Claiborne F. Jackson, April 23, 1861; Jackson to Leroy P. Walker, May 5, 1861, *OR*, ser. 1, vol. 1, pp. 688, 690.

8. Daniel M. Frost to Nathaniel Lyon, May 10, 1861, *OR*, ser. 1, vol. 3, pp. 5–6.

9. William E. Parrish, *Frank Blair: Lincoln's Conservative* (Columbia: University of Missouri Press, 1998), 94; George Rollie Adams, *General William S. Harney: Prince of Dragoons* (Lincoln: University of Nebraska Press, 2001), 221, 224.

10. For example, see Lincoln's speeches in his 1858 debates with Douglas: in Kansas in 1859 and at Dover, New Hampshire, on March 2, 1860, *Collected Works*, 3: 256, 265, 314, 500.

11. For an account of Frank Blair's schemes for black colonization, see Parrish, *Frank Blair*, 69–72, 138–139.

12. Ibid., 68–69, 74.

13. Ibid., 94–96; Lorenzo Thomas to Nathaniel Lyon, April 21, 1861; Simon Cameron to Nathaniel Lyon, with Lincoln's approval, April 30, 1861; Frank P. Blair Jr.

to Simon Cameron, May 4, 1861; Cameron to Blair, May 9, 1861, OR, ser. 1, vol. 1, pp. 670, 675, 679, 681.

14. As quoted in Christopher Phillips, *Damned Yankee: The Life of General Nathaniel Lyon* (Columbia: University of Missouri Press, 1990), 128. Despite Lyon's importance in the history of the Civil War, Phillips's fine account is the first scholarly biography of him.

15. Nathaniel Lyon, Memorandum for Mr. F. J. Dean, about to visit Springfield, Illinois, April 16, 1861, OR, ser. 1, vol. 1, p. 667; John G. Nicolay, Memorandum of Events, ca. April 20, 1861, Nicolay, *With Lincoln in the White House*, ed. Burlingame, 36; Parrish, *Turbulent Partnership*, 19.

16. W. W. Greene to Edward Bates, April 22, 1861; Charles Gibson to Bates, April 22, 1861; Charles Wiggins to Bates, April 24, 1861, OR, ser. 1, vol. 1, pp. 671–673.

17. As quoted in Burlingame, *Abraham Lincoln*, 2: 158.

18. Adams, *General William S. Harney*, 226–227.

19. Report of Captain Nathaniel Lyon, May 11, 1861, OR, ser. 1, vol. 3, p. 4.

20. Phillips, *Damned Yankee*, 182–183; Louis S. Gerteis, *Civil War St. Louis* (Lawrence: University Press of Kansas, 2001), 100.

21. Phillips, *Damned Yankee*, 184.

22. Snead, *The Fight for Missouri*, 165–166.

23. Report of Captain Nathaniel Lyon, May 11, 1861; Daniel M. Frost to Lyon, May 10, 1861, OR, ser. 1, vol. 3, pp. 4–5.

24. The above account has been pieced together from Gerteis, *Civil War St. Louis*, 107–110; Phillips, *Damned Yankee*, 190–193; and Snead, *The Fight for Missouri*, 171–172.

25. Phillips, *Missouri's Confederate*, 251–252; Snead, *The Fight for Missouri*, 176; Parrish, *Turbulent Partnership*, 24.

26. Proclamation of General William S. Harney, May 12, 1861, OR, ser. 1, vol. 3, p. 370.

27. *To the People of the State of Missouri*, May 14, 1861, OR, ser. 1, vol. 3, pp. 371–372.

28. Thomas T. Gantt to William S. Harney, May 14, 1861; Harney to Gantt, May 14, 1861, OR, ser. 1, vol. 1, pp. 372–373, 373.

29. Adams, *General William S. Harney*, 233–234; Parrish, *Frank Blair*, 104–105; Hamilton R. Gamble and James E. Yeatman to Abraham Lincoln, May 15, 1861, Lincoln Papers. Gamble and Yeatman apparently gave this letter to Lincoln when they met with him in the White House. The Missouri state convention would soon elect Gamble provisional governor of the state.

30. Abraham Lincoln to Francis P. Blair Jr., May 18, 1861, *Collected Works*, 4: 372–373.

31. Agreement between General Sterling Price and General William S. Harney, May 21, 1861, OR, ser. 1, vol. 1, p. 375.

32. *To the People of the State of Missouri*, May 21, 1861, OR, ser. 1, vol. 1, p. 375.

33. Samuel T. Glover to Abraham Lincoln, May 24, 1861, Lincoln Papers.

34. Lorenzo Thomas to William S. Harney, May 27, 1861, OR, ser. 1, vol. 3, p. 376.

35. William S. Harney to E. D. Townsend, May 29, 1861, OR, ser. 1, vol. 3, p. 377.

36. William S. Harney to Sterling Price, May 27, 1861; Price to Harney, May 24, 28, 29, 1861, *OR*, ser. 1, vol. 3, pp. 379–381.

37. William S. Harney to Lorenzo Thomas, May 31, 1861; Nathaniel Lyon, General Orders no. 5, May 31, 1861, *OR*, ser. 1, vol. 3, p. 381.

38. Adams, *General William S. Harney*, chap. 13.

39. Ibid., 239.

40. Albert Castel, *General Sterling Price and the Civil War in the West* (Baton Rouge: Louisiana State University Press, 1968), 23–24; Robert E. Stalhope, *Sterling Price: Portrait of a Southerner* (Columbia: University of Missouri Press, 1971), 162–164.

41. John S. Phelps to Abraham Lincoln, June 3, 1861, Lincoln Papers.

42. Phillips, *Damned Yankee*, 212–213.

43. Snead, *The Fight for Missouri*, 199–200. Although there are several versions of Lyon's dramatic words ending the meeting, historians have usually followed Snead's account.

44. Proclamation of Governor Claiborne Jackson, June 12, 1861, *Rebellion Record*, vol. 1, doc. 247, pp. 363–364.

45. Ibid.

46. General Nathaniel Lyon's Proclamation, June 18, 1861, *Rebellion Record*, vol. 1, doc. 260, p. 412.

47. Parrish, *Turbulent Partnership*, 32; Phillips, *Missouri's Confederate*, 260–262.

48. Parrish, *Turbulent Partnership*, 37; Dennis K. Boman, *Lincoln's Resolute Unionist: Hamilton Gamble, Dred Scott Dissenter and Missouri's Civil War Governor* (Baton Rouge: Louisiana State University Press, 2006), 108.

49. For the actions of the Wheeling convention and Lincoln's approval, see William C. Harris, *With Charity for All: Lincoln and the Restoration of the Union* (Lexington: University Press of Kentucky, 1997), 21–23. Congress also endorsed the work of the Wheeling convention.

50. Boman, *Lincoln's Resolute Unionist*, ix–x, 15–16; Don E. Fehrenbacher, *The Dred Scott Case: Its Significance in American Law and Politics* (New York: Oxford University Press, 1978), 265, 287.

51. The quotations are in Parrish, *Turbulent Partnership*, 46–47.

52. Inaugural of Governor Gamble, Delivered at Jefferson City, Missouri, August 1, 1861, *Rebellion Record*, vol. 2, doc. 151, pp. 458–459.

53. Proclamation of Governor Gamble, August 3, 1861, *Rebellion Record*, vol. 2, doc. 156, pp. 472–474.

54. Nevins, *The War for the Union*, vol. 1, *The Improvised War*, 309.

55. Ibid., 308.

56. John Howe to Montgomery Blair, August 4, 1861, Lincoln Papers. This letter must be misdated, since in it Howe mentioned the death of General Lyon, which occurred on August 10.

57. Phillips, *Damned Yankee*, 247–251; Parrish, *A History of Missouri*, vol. 3, *1860–1875*, 28–29.

58. Samuel T. Glover to Montgomery Blair, September 2, 1861; John Howe to Blair, August 4, 1861 (misdated), Lincoln Papers.

59. Snead, *The Fight for Missouri*, 293–294, 312.

60. Castel, *General Sterling Price,* 51–55.

61. Samuel T. Glover to Montgomery Blair, September 2, 1861, Lincoln Papers.

62. Samuel T. Glover to Abraham Lincoln, September 21, 1861, Lincoln Papers.

63. John C. Frémont to Abraham Lincoln, August 17, 1861, Lincoln Papers.

64. Frank Blair Jr. to Montgomery Blair, September 1, 1861, Lincoln Papers.

65. Montgomery Blair to Abraham Lincoln, September 4, 1861, Lincoln Papers.

66. Abraham Lincoln to David Hunter, September 9, 1861, *Collected Works,* 4: 513 and n.

67. Abraham Lincoln to Mrs. John C. Frémont, September 12, 1861, *Collected Works,* 4: 519.

68. Montgomery Blair to Abraham Lincoln, September 14, 1861, Lincoln Papers.

69. Hamilton R. Gamble to Charles Gibson, September 20, 1861, Lincoln Papers. Gibson was Gamble's nephew and agent in Washington. He evidently gave this letter to Lincoln. Although Lincoln's letter to Frémont has not been found, the general's reaction after reading it, as reported by Gamble to Gibson, suggests its substance.

70. Nevins, *Frémont: The West's Greatest Adventurer,* 2 vols. (New York: Harper & Brothers, 1928), 2: 585–589; "The Lincoln Interview: Excerpts from 'Great Events,'" in *The Letters of Jessie Benton Frémont,* ed. Pamela Herr and Mary Lee Spence (Urbana: University of Illinois Press, 1993), 264–267. Two days after his meeting with Jessie Frémont, Lincoln wrote a note to her protesting against "being understood as acting in any hostility toward" her husband. Lincoln denied her contention that Montgomery Blair had been sent to Saint Louis as an enemy of the general. Blair's mission, he said, was "to see and converse with Gen. Frémont as a friend." Abraham Lincoln to Mrs. John C. Frémont, September 12, 1861, *Collected Works,* 4: 519.

71. Josiah Bushnell Grinnell, *Men and Events of Forty Years: Autobiographical Reminiscences of an Active Career from 1850 to 1890* (Boston: D. Lothrop, 1891), 174. I am indebted to Professor Michael Burlingame for drawing my attention to this source.

72. Entry for December 9, 1863, in Hay, *Inside Lincoln's White House,* ed. Burlingame and Ettlinger, 123. Lincoln also told Congressman Grinnell that Jessie Frémont threatened that her husband would "try titles with you"; she obviously meant the presidency (Grinnell, *Men and Events of Forty Years,* 174).

73. Entry for December 9, 1863, in Hay, *Inside Lincoln's White House,* ed. Burlingame and Ettlinger, 123.

74. Montgomery Blair to Abraham Lincoln, September 14, 1861, Lincoln Papers.

75. See Schuyler Colfax to Abraham Lincoln, September 23, 1861; Timothy O. Howe to William H. Seward, October 11, 1861; Samuel J. Kirkwood to Lincoln, October 9, 1861; clipping from *Boston Evening Transcript,* September 17, 1861, Lincoln Papers; David Donald, *Charles Sumner and the Rights of Man* (New York: Alfred A. Knopf, 1970), 26. Colfax soon became speaker of the House of Representatives, Howe was a Republican senator from Wisconsin, and Kirkwood was the Republican governor of Iowa.

76. Abraham Lincoln to Orville H. Browning, September 22, 1861, *Collected Works,* 4: 533.

77. Gustave P. Koerner to Abraham Lincoln, October 8, 1861, Lincoln Papers.

78. John G. Nicolay to Abraham Lincoln, October 21, 1861; Orville H. Browning to Lincoln, September 24, 1861, Lincoln Papers.

79. Lyman Trumbull to Abraham Lincoln, October 1, 1861, Lincoln Papers.

80. Ward H. Lamon to Abraham Lincoln, October 21, 1861, Lincoln Papers.

81. Elihu B. Washburne to Abraham Lincoln, October 17, 21, 1861, Lincoln Papers.

82. John C. Frémont to Colonel E. D. Townsend, September 23, 1861; Winfield Scott to Frémont, September 23, 1861, OR, ser. 1, vol. 3, pp. 184, 185.

83. Parrish, *Frank Blair*, 124–125; Anonymous, "T-Blank," to Montgomery Blair, September 24, 1861; John F. Lee to Abraham Lincoln, September 27, 1861, Lincoln Papers.

84. Abraham Lincoln to Samuel R. Curtis, October 7, 1861, *Collected Works*, 4: 549.

85. Simon Cameron to Abraham Lincoln, October 12, 1861; Samuel Curtis to Lincoln, October 12, 1861, Lincoln Papers.

86. Simon Cameron to Abraham Lincoln, October 14, 1861, Lincoln Papers.

87. General Thomas's report, October 21, 1861, can be found in OR, ser. 1, vol. 3, pp. 540–549.

88. Entry for October 22, 1861, *The Diary of Edward Bates, 1859–1866*, ed. Howard K. Beale (Washington: Government Printing Office, 1933), 198–199.

89. General Orders, no. 18, Headquarters of the Army, Washington, October 24, 1861, OR, ser. 1, vol. 3, p. 553; Abraham Lincoln to Samuel R. Curtis, October 24, 1861, *Collected Works*, 4: 562.

90. Samuel R. Curtis to Abraham Lincoln, November 1, 1861; Leonard Swett to Lincoln, November 9, 1861, Lincoln Papers.

91. John G. Nicolay, Memorandum, 2 October 1861, a Private Paper, Conversation with the President, in Nicolay, *With Lincoln in the White House*, ed. Burlingame, 59.

92. Leonard Swett to Abraham Lincoln, November 9, 1861, Lincoln Papers.

93. Nevins, *Frémont*, 2: 618–619.

94. Samuel R. Curtis to Abraham Lincoln, November 16, 1861, Lincoln Papers.

95. John F. Marszalek, *Commander of All Lincoln's Armies: A Life of General Henry W. Halleck* (Cambridge: The Belknap Press of Harvard University Press, 2004), 109; entry for November 15, 1861, Bates, *Diary*, ed. Beale, 201.

96. Hamilton R. Gamble to Abraham Lincoln, October 31, 1861, Lincoln Papers; Order Approving the Plan of Governor Gamble of Missouri, November 6, 1861, *Collected Works*, 5: 15.

97. The approved plan has been printed in Lincoln's *Collected Works*, 5: 16–17.

98. Parrish, *Turbulent Partnership*, 84–85.

99. Henry W. Halleck to George B. McClellan, November 30, 1861, OR, ser. 2, vol. 1, pp. 232–233. Before writing this letter, Halleck had tried by telegram to obtain the authority to declare martial law. However, even before McClellan received the letter, Lincoln had granted the authority to Halleck.

100. Abraham Lincoln to Henry W. Halleck, December 2, 1861, *Collected Works*, 5: 35.

101. Henry W. Halleck to Lorenzo Thomas, January 18, 1862; Halleck to General David Hunter, February 2, 1862, OR, ser. 1, vol. 8, pp. 507–508, 829.

102. Edwin M. Stanton to James S. Rollins and Thomas L. Price, February 6, 1862, *OR*, ser. 1, vol. 8, pp. 546–547. Although Stanton cited it, the Rollins and Price letter has not been found.

103. Parrish, *Turbulent Partnership*, 85–86.

104. Hamilton Gamble to Abraham Lincoln, May 19, 1862, Lincoln Papers.

105. General Orders, no. 2, Headquarters, Department of the Mississippi, March 13, 1862, *OR*, ser. 2, vol. 1, p. 270. The Department of the West had been reorganized, first as the Department of Missouri, then as the Department of the Mississippi, the latter to include a vast area from Kansas to Ohio and southward.

106. General Orders, no. 17, Headquarters, District of Central Missouri, April 22, 1862, *OR*, ser. 2, vol. 1, pp. 281–282.

107. General Orders, no. 18, Headquarters, Missouri State Militia, May 29, 1862, *OR*, ser. 1, vol. 13, pp. 402–403.

108. For a good account of the savage guerrilla warfare on the border and its prewar background, see Michael Fellman, *Inside War: The Guerrilla Conflict in Missouri during the American Civil War* (New York: Oxford University Press, 1989).

109. Annual Message to Congress, December 3, 1861, *Collected Works*, 5: 50.

Chapter 5
Lincoln's Emancipation Initiatives and the Border States

1. Nicolay and Hay, *Abraham Lincoln*, 5: 206.

2. George Bancroft to Abraham Lincoln, November 15, 1861, Lincoln Papers; Lincoln to Bancroft, November 18, 1861, *Collected Works*, 5: 25–26.

3. Drafts of a Bill for Compensated Emancipation in Delaware [November 26? 1861], *Collected Works*, 5: 29–30. For another account of the Delaware proposal, see Allen C. Guelzo, *Lincoln's Emancipation Proclamation: The End of Slavery in America* (New York: Simon & Schuster, 2004), 57–59.

4. Hancock, *Delaware during the Civil War*, 107.

5. Entry for December 1, 1861, *Browning Diary*, 1: 512; Message to Congress, March 6, 1862, *Collected Works*, 5: 145.

6. Patience Essah, *A House Divided: Slavery and Emancipation in Delaware, 1838–1865* (Charlottesville: University Press of Virginia, 1996), 162, 166.

7. Nicolay and Hay, *Abraham Lincoln*, 5: 207–208.

8. As quoted in Guelzo, *Lincoln's Emancipation Proclamation*, 69.

9. Salmon P. Chase, Draft of message to Congress on compensated emancipation, February–March 1862, Lincoln Papers.

10. Cong. Globe, 37th Cong., 2d Sess. (February 11, 1862), 736–737; *Chicago Tribune*, February 3, 4, 1862; *New York Daily Tribune*, March 18, 1862.

11. Harris, *With Charity for All*, 34.

12. Message to Congress, March 6, 1862, *Collected Works*, 5: 144–145; Burlingame, *Abraham Lincoln*, 2: 335.

13. Message to Congress, March 6, 1862, *Collected Works*, 5: 145.

14. Ibid., 5: 145.

15. Ibid., 5: 145–146.

16. Abraham Lincoln to James A. McDougall, March 14, 1862, *Collected Works,* 5: 160–161. McDougall, however, continued to oppose the compensated emancipation plan because, as he said in a speech on March 26, Congress had no constitutional authority to provide federal funds for such a purpose (ibid., 161n).

17. *New York World,* March 7, 1862.

18. Ibid., March 8, 1862.

19. Benjamin Quarles, *The Negro in the Civil War,* 2d ed. (Boston: Little, Brown, 1969), 138; Abraham Lincoln to Horace Greeley, March 24, 1862, *Collected Works,* 5: 169 and n; *New York Tribune,* March 7, 8, 11, 1862.

20. *New York Tribune,* March 12, 1862.

21. As quoted in Burlingame, *Abraham Lincoln,* 2: 337.

22. *Washington National Intelligencer,* March 8, 1862; *New York Times,* March 8, 12, 1862; Henry J. Raymond to Abraham Lincoln, March 15, 1862, Lincoln Papers.

23. *Louisville Daily Journal,* March 8, 1862.

24. Thomas H. Hicks to Abraham Lincoln, March 18, 1862, Lincoln Papers.

25. Crisfield's account of the March 10 meeting with Lincoln (in this and the next few paragraphs) can be found in *The Political History of the United States of America, during the Great Rebellion,* ed. Edward McPherson, 2d ed. (Washington: Philp & Solomons, 1865), 210–211.

26. *Washington National Intelligencer,* October 30, 1862.

27. McPherson, *The Political History of the United States of America,* 210.

28. *Washington National Intelligencer,* March 13, 1862.

29. Abraham Lincoln to Horace Greeley, March 24, 1862, *Collected Works,* 5: 169.

30. Cong. Globe, 37th Cong., 2d Sess. (April 3, 1862), 1523.

31. Ibid., (March 12, 24, 1862), 1192, 1333. "A bloody Vendee" refers to a revolt in the province of Vendée, France, during the French Revolution that cost more than 100,000 lives before it ended in 1796.

32. Entry for January 18, 1862, *Browning Diary,* 1: 526.

33. *New York Tribune,* March 21, 1862; Annual Message to Congress, December 3, 1861, *Collected Works,* 5: 48.

34. *New York Tribune,* March 11 (quotation), 21, 1862.

35. The roll-call votes on the District of Columbia emancipation bill can be found in McPherson, *The Political History of the United States of America,* 212.

36. Guelzo, *Lincoln's Emancipation Proclamation,* 86.

37. As quoted in Oakes, *The Radical and the Republican,* 183.

38. Entry for April 14, 1862, *Browning Diary,* 1: 541.

39. In a broad legal sense, a femes-covert was a married woman.

40. Message to Congress, April 16, 1862, *Collected Works,* 5: 192 and n.

41. McPherson, *The Political History of the United States of America,* 210.

42. Cong. Globe, 37th Cong., 2d Sess. (March 26, 1862), 1371. Garret Davis on the floor of the Senate frequently referred to slaves as property and compared them to land and livestock. He argued that "slavery . . . is the normal condition in the United States" of blacks (ibid., March 24 [quotation], April 2, 1862, 1334, 1499–1502).

43. McPherson, *The Political History of the United States of America,* 213.

44. As quoted in the *Washington National Intelligencer*, June 5, 1862.

45. Montgomery Blair to A. B. Davis, April 8, 1862, Blair Family Papers, Manuscript Division, Library of Congress, Washington, D.C. (microfilm).

46. *New York World*, April 15, 1862, quoting the *Baltimore American*; *Washington National Intelligencer*, June 7, 1862.

47. Reverdy Johnson to Abraham Lincoln, May 16, 1862; Francis S. Corkran to Montgomery Blair, May 20, 1862, Lincoln Papers.

48. Harrison, *Lincoln of Kentucky*, 227–228; Boman, *Lincoln's Resolute Unionist*, 169–170.

49. *Louisville Daily Journal*, May 17, 1862.

50. Salmon P. Chase to Abraham Lincoln, May 16, 1862, Lincoln Papers.

51. As reported in the *Washington National Intelligencer*, May 20, 1862.

52. Carl Schurz to Abraham Lincoln, May 16, 1862, Lincoln Papers.

53. Abraham Lincoln to Salmon P. Chase [May 17, 1862], *Collected Works*, 5: 219.

54. Proclamation Revoking General Hunter's Order of Military Emancipation of May 9, 1862, *Collected Works*, 5: 222.

55. Ibid., 5: 223.

56. Appeal to Border State Representatives to Favor Compensated Emancipation, July 12, 1862, *Collected Works*, 5: 317.

57. Ibid., 5: 318.

58. Ibid.

59. Ibid.

60. Ibid., 5: 319.

61. Border State Congressmen to Abraham Lincoln, July 14, 1862 (Majority Response), Lincoln Papers. A few days later, this response, along with a minority report by seven representatives supporting the resolution, was printed in the newspapers.

62. Ibid.

63. Ibid.

64. Ibid.

65. Ibid.

66. Border State Congressmen to Abraham Lincoln, July 15, 1862 (Minority Response), Lincoln Papers. Horace Maynard of Tennessee gave Lincoln a separate statement supporting the resolution.

67. Isaac Newton Arnold, *The Life of Abraham Lincoln*, 4th ed., with an introduction by James A. Rawley (Lincoln: University of Nebraska Press, 1994), 251.

68. To the Senate and House of Representatives, July 14, 1862, *Collected Works*, 5: 324.

69. For the brief history of Lincoln's bill in Congress, see ibid., 5: 324–325n. Since the bill required federal appropriations, the Senate could not act on it until the House had considered and approved it. Thus the Senate did not debate Lincoln's emancipation proposal for the border states.

70. John Syrett, *The Civil War Confiscation Acts: Failing to Reconstruct the South* (New York: Fordham University Press, 2005), 21–22.

71. Henry Wilson, *History of the Antislavery Measures of the Thirty-Seventh and Thirty-Eighth United-States Congresses, 1861–64* (Boston: Walker, Wise, 1864), 115–116, 118, 129–130 (Saulsbury quotation).

72. As quoted in ibid., 114.

73. McPherson, *The Political History of the United States of America*, 196–197.

74. The roll-call votes can be found in ibid., 197. On June 25 Browning addressed the Senate for almost three hours in opposition to the Confiscation bill. Entry for June 25, 1862, *Browning Diary*, 1: 554.

75. Entry for July 1, 1862, *Browning Diary*, 1: 555.

76. See, for example, Guelzo, *Lincoln's Emancipation Proclamation*, 4–5.

77. McPherson, *The Political History of the United States of America*, 197.

78. Syrett, *The Civil War Confiscation Acts*, 53.

79. To the Senate and House of Representatives, July 17, 1862, *Collected Works*, 5: 328–330.

80. Ibid., 5: 328–329.

81. Ibid., 5: 330.

82. For an excellent account of black recruitment in the army, see John David Smith, "Let Us All Be Grateful That We Have Colored Troops That Will Fight," in *Black Soldiers in Blue: African American Troops in the Civil War Era*, ed. John David Smith (Chapel Hill: University of North Carolina Press, 2002), 1–77.

83. Remarks to Deputation of Western Gentlemen, August 4, 1862, *Collected Works*, 5: 356–357.

84. Reply to Emancipation Memorial Presented by Chicago Christians of All Denominations, September 13, 1862, *Collected Works*, 5: 420, 422–424.

85. Syrett, *The Civil War Confiscation Acts*, 55.

86. As quoted in the *Washington National Intelligencer*, September 6, 1862.

87. Parrish, *A History of Missouri*, vol. 3, *1860 to 1875*, 91–92.

88. Essah, *A House Divided*, 174–175.

89. Nicolay and Hay, *Abraham Lincoln*, 6: 121–122; entry for [July 13, 1862?], *Diary of Gideon Welles, Secretary of the Navy under Lincoln and Johnson*, with an introduction by John T. Morse Jr., 3 vols. (Boston: Houghton, Mifflin, 1911), 1: 70–71.

90. Emancipation Proclamation—First Draft [July 22, 1862], *Collected Works*, 5: 336–337.

91. Francis B. Carpenter, *Six Months at the White House* (New York: Hurd & Houghton, 1868), 21.

92. Professor Guelzo has the best account of the deliberations in the cabinet meeting of July 22 in his *Lincoln's Emancipation Proclamation*, 121–123. See also Salmon P. Chase's account. Entries for July 21, 22, 1862, in *The Salmon P. Chase Papers*, vol. 1, *Journals, 1829–1872*, ed. John Niven (Kent, Ohio: Kent State University Press, 1993), 348–352.

93. Proclamation of the Act to Suppress Insurrection, July 25, 1862, *Collected Works*, 5: 341.

94. Guelzo, *Lincoln's Emancipation Proclamation*, 130–156.

95. Ibid., 154.

96. Preliminary Emancipation Proclamation, September 22, 1862, *Collected Works*, 5: 433–435.

97. Ibid., 5: 434.

Chapter 6
The Struggle over Emancipation

1. As quoted in Janet L. Coryell, *Neither Heroine nor Fool: Anna Ella Carroll of Maryland* (Kent, Ohio: Kent State University Press, 1990), 61.

2. Anna Ella Carroll to Abraham Lincoln, July 14, October 21, 1862, Lincoln Papers.

3. Charles B. Calvert to Abraham Lincoln, July 10, August 3 (quote), 1861, Lincoln Papers.

4. Reply to Maryland Slaveholders, May 19, 1862, *Collected Works*, 5: 224 and n.

5. Entry for June 11, 1862, *Browning Diary*, 1: 549–550.

6. LaFayette C. Baker to Abraham Lincoln, September 30, 1863, Lincoln Papers.

7. Cuthbert Bullitt to Abraham Lincoln, October 1, 1862, Lincoln Papers.

8. Reid, *A Radical View*, ed. Smart, 1: 84–85.

9. Speech of Wendell Phillips in Boston, January 7, 1862, as quoted in Burlingame, *Abraham Lincoln*, 2: 239–240.

10. *Louisville Daily Journal*, October 3, 1862.

11. Ibid., October 6, 1862.

12. Abraham Lincoln to Henry W. Halleck, July 13, 1862, *Collected Works*, 5: 322.

13. Wallace, *An Autobiography*, 2: 598.

14. Hamilton R. Gamble to Montgomery Blair, September 24, 1862, Lincoln Papers.

15. Samuel R. Curtis to Abraham Lincoln, January 31, 1863, Lincoln Papers.

16. Hamilton R. Gamble to Henry W. Halleck, October 1862; Samuel R. Curtis to Abraham Lincoln, October 4, 1862, Lincoln Papers.

17. Abraham Lincoln to Edward Bates, November 29, 1862; Lincoln to Edwin M. Stanton, December 2, 1862, *Collected Works*, 5: 515–516, 538.

18. Abraham Lincoln to Henry T. Blow, Charles D. Drake, and Others, May 15, 1863, *Collected Works*, 6: 218.

19. As quoted in Josiah G. Holland, *The Life of Abraham Lincoln* (Springfield, Mass.: Gurdon Bill, 1866), 394–395. For a similar version of Lincoln's statement, see also James G. Blaine, *Twenty Years of Congress: From Lincoln to Garfield, With a Review of the Events Which Led to the Political Revolution of 1860*, 2 vols. (Norwich, Conn.: Henry Bill, 1884), 1: 439.

20. William B. Hesseltine, *Lincoln and the War Governors* (1948; reprint, Gloucester, Mass.: Peter Smith, 1972), 257–258; Parrish, *Turbulent Partnership*, 135 (quotations); Hamilton R. Gamble to Montgomery Blair, September 24, 1862, Lincoln Papers.

21. *Washington National Intelligencer*, September 27, 1862.

22. Address of loyal Governors to the President, adopted at a meeting of Governors of loyal States, held to take measures for the more active support of the Government, at Altoona, Pa., on the 24th day of September, 1862, *OR*, ser. 3, vol. 2, pp. 582–583.

23. Ibid., 583–584.

24. Nicolay and Hay, *Abraham Lincoln*, 6: 167.

25. Reply to the Delegation of Loyal Governors, September 26, 1862, *Collected Works*, 5: 441.

26. Entry for September 30, 1862, Welles, *Diary*, 1: 156.

27. *Washington National Intelligencer*, October 2, 4, 11, 1862; Address to the President, September 30, 1862, Andrew Johnson Papers, Manuscript Division, Library of Congress, Washington, D.C. (microfilm); *Boston Herald*, October 3, 1862.

28. Hamlin's quotations from Hannibal Hamlin to Abraham Lincoln, September 25, 1862, Lincoln Papers; Douglass quoted in Oakes, *The Radical and the Republican*, 197.

29. Abraham Lincoln to Hannibal Hamlin, September 28, 1862, *Collected Works*, 5: 444. For John McClintock's account, see Lincoln, *Recollected Words*, comp. and ed. Fehrenbacher and Fehrenbacher, 314.

30. James M. McPherson, *Battle Cry of Freedom: The Civil War Era* (New York: Oxford University Press, 1988), 560–561.

31. For a dire warning by John W. Forney, Republican proprietor and editor of the *Washington Chronicle* and the *Philadelphia Press*, that the party would be hurt in the fall elections by the proclamation, see Forney to Lincoln, September 26, 1862, Lincoln Papers.

32. Abraham Lincoln to Carl Schurz, November 10, 1862, *Collected Works*, 5: 493–494.

33. Parrish, *Turbulent Partnership*, 126–129.

34. Francis P. Blair Jr. to Abraham Lincoln, November 14, 1862, Lincoln Papers; Parrish, *A History of Missouri*, vol. 3, *1860–1875*, 92 (quotation), 93–94.

35. Boman, *Lincoln's Resolute Unionist*, 168, 196.

36. Annual Message to Congress, December 1, 1862, *Collected Works*, 5: 530–532.

37. Wagandt, *The Mighty Revolution*, 76–77, 84–85, 92, 94.

38. *Report of the Committee on Federal Relations Concerning the Delaware Resolutions, Accompanied with the Message of Governor Gamble, to the Twenty-Second General Assembly* (Jefferson City, Mo.: N.p., 1863). The resolutions of the Delaware legislature were apparently sent to all the Union states and printed in this report of the Missouri General Assembly. The Missouri legislators criticized the Delaware resolutions' strident attack on Lincoln. The president received a copy of the Missouri report; it can be found in his papers.

39. Cong. Globe, 37th Cong., 3d Sess. (January 27, 1863), 545.

40. Ibid., 549–550, 552.

41. As quoted in Hancock, *Delaware during the Civil War*, 128.

42. Harrison, *Lincoln of Kentucky*, 232; Coulter, *The Civil War and Readjustment in Kentucky*, 159–160.

43. Hamilton Gray to Abraham Lincoln, January 7, 1863, Lincoln Papers.

44. William B. Campbell to Andrew Johnson, November 2, 1862, *The Papers of Andrew Johnson*, vol. 6, *1862–1864*, ed. Leroy P. Graf and Ralph W. Haskins (Knoxville: University of Tennessee Press, 1983), 46.

45. Victor B. Howard, *Black Liberation in Kentucky: Emancipation and Freedom, 1862–1884* (Lexington: University Press of Kentucky, 1983), 25–26, 44. For Jeremiah Boyle's career, see Warner, *Generals in Blue*, 40.

46. William L. Utley to Abraham Lincoln, November 17, 1862; George Robertson to Lincoln, November 19, 1862, Lincoln Papers.

47. Abraham Lincoln to George Robertson, November 20, 1862, *Collected Works*, 5: 502.

48. Abraham Lincoln to George Robertson, November 26, 1862, *Collected Works,* 5: 512.

49. George Robertson to Abraham Lincoln, December 1, 1862, Lincoln Papers.

50. *Collected Works,* 5: 514n.

51. Remarks to Union Kentuckians, *Collected Works,* 5: 503–504.

52. *Louisville Daily Journal,* December 2, 1862.

53. Cong. Globe, 37th Cong., 3d Sess. (December 15, 1862), 92.

54. Entry for November 29, 1862, *Browning Diary,* 1: 588–589.

55. Entries for December 29, 1862, January 1, 2, 1863, *Browning Diary,* 1: 606–607, 609.

56. Donald, *Charles Sumner and the Rights of Man,* 96; Richard Carwardine, *Lincoln: A Life of Purpose and Power* (New York: Alfred A. Knopf, 2006), 218. Frederick Douglass was not one of those radicals who doubted Lincoln's resolve to issue the Emancipation Proclamation on January 1, 1863. He believed that the president would stand firm behind it (Oakes, *The Radical and the Republican,* 200–201).

57. John J. Crittenden, John W. Crisfield, and William A. Hall to Abraham Lincoln, December 17, 1862, Lincoln Papers.

58. Kentucky Unionists were especially upset with the military appointment of provost marshals in the state. In October, the new governor, James F. Robinson, had protested to Lincoln about the "great injury to the Union cause by an indiscreet and unjust system of arrests, adopted by Provost Marshals throughout the State." James F. Robinson to Abraham Lincoln, October 6, 1862, Lincoln Papers.

59. Cong. Globe, 37th Cong., 3d Sess. (December 19, 1862), 146–149.

60. See my article "After the Emancipation Proclamation: Lincoln's Role in the Ending of Slavery," *North and South* 5 (December 2001): 43–53.

61. Horatio G. Wright to Henry W. Halleck, December 30, 1862, *OR,* ser. 1, vol. 20, pt. 2, p. 282.

62. Henry W. Halleck to Horatio G. Wright, January 7, 1863, *OR,* ser. 1, vol. 20, pt. 2, p. 308.

63. Cong. Globe, 37th Cong., 3d Sess. (January 5, 1863), 186.

64. Abraham Lincoln to Green Adams, January 7, 1863, *Collected Works,* 6: 42.

65. *Louisville Daily Journal,* January 9, 1863.

66. Ibid.

67. James Speed to Joshua F. Speed [with endorsement by Lincoln], January 19, 1863, Lincoln Papers.

68. *Annual Cyclopedia 1863,* 563.

69. Annual Message to Congress, December 1, 1862, *Collected Works,* 5: 530–531, 534. For the historical debate over Lincoln's purpose in proposing black colonization, see Don E. Fehrenbacher, *Lincoln in Text and Context* (Stanford: Stanford University Press, 1987), 221. Fehrenbacher contended that Lincoln's colonization scheme was a "dissimulative strategy aimed primarily at the white mind rather than the black population" in order to reduce white racial apprehension about emancipation.

70. Lehrman, *Lincoln at Peoria,* 130.

71. Annual Message to Congress, December 1, 1862, *Collected Works,* 5: 530–531, 534.

72. Oakes, *The Radical and the Republican*, 193–195.

73. Henry Winter Davis, *Speeches and Addresses Delivered in the Congress of the United States and on Several Public Occasions by Henry Winter Davis of Maryland* (New York: Harper & Brothers, 1867), 305–306.

74. Entry for July 1, 1863, in Hay, *Inside Lincoln's White House*, ed. Burlingame and Ettlinger, 217.

75. Entry for January 30, 1865, Welles, *Diary*, 2: 231–232.

76. As quoted in Guelzo, *Lincoln's Emancipation Proclamation*, 230.

77. Nicolay and Hay, *Abraham Lincoln*, 6: 395–396.

78. McPherson, *The Political History of the United States of America*, 224–225.

79. Abraham Lincoln to Samuel R. Curtis, January 10, 1863, *Collected Works*, 6: 52; John B. Henderson to Abraham Lincoln [January 1863], Lincoln Papers.

80. McPherson, *The Political History of the United States of America*, 225–226; Nicolay and Hay, *Abraham Lincoln*, 6: 396–397; Blaine, *Twenty Years of Congress*, 1: 446–447. For the Senate debate on the Missouri compensation bill, see Cong. Globe, 37th Cong., 3d Sess. (February 12, 1863), 897–903.

81. *Annual Cyclopedia, 1863*, 563.

82. Abraham Lincoln to the Senate and the House of Representatives [February 5, 1865] and endorsement, *Collected Works*, 8: 260–261.

Chapter 7
Resistance in Kentucky, 1863–1865

1. Cong. Globe, 37th Cong., 2d Sess. (July 9, 1862), 3204–3205.

2. Emancipation Proclamation, January 1, 1863, *Collected Works*, 6: 30.

3. Entry for January 10, 1863, Welles, *Diary*, 1: 218.

4. Howard, *Black Liberation in Kentucky*, 47.

5. Entry for February 1, 1863, *Browning Diary*, 1: 622.

6. Cong. Globe, 37th Cong., 3d Sess. (March 2, 1863), 1446–1448.

7. For the Enrollment Act, officially known as "An Act for Enrolling and Calling Out the National Forces, and for Other Purposes," see *OR*, ser. 3, vol. 3, pp. 88–93.

8. Edwin M. Stanton to Lorenzo Thomas, March 25, 1863, *OR*, ser. 3, vol. 3, p. 100.

9. Abraham Lincoln to Andrew Johnson, March 26, 1863, *Collected Works*, 6: 149–150.

10. All the quotations in this paragraph are found in John David Smith, "The Recruitment of Negro Soldiers in Kentucky, 1863–1865," *Register of the Kentucky Historical Society* 72 (1974): 368–369, 371. Professor Smith graciously provided me with a copy of this article.

11. Jeremiah T. Boyle to James B. Fry, June 25, 1863, Lincoln Papers.

12. Ambrose E. Burnside to Abraham Lincoln, June 26, 1863, *Collected Works*, 6: 299n.

13. Abraham Lincoln to Ambrose E. Burnside, June 28, 1863, *Collected Works*, 6: 298.

14. Ambrose E. Burnside to Abraham Lincoln, June 27, 1863, *OR*, ser. 3, vol. 3, pp. 419–420.

15. Abraham Lincoln to Edwin M. Stanton, June 28, 1863, *Collected Works*, 6: 299. Lincoln was responding to Burnside's telegram to Stanton on the previous day, which repeated the same appeal that Kentucky be exempted.

16. Howard, *Black Liberation in Kentucky*, 48–49.

17. Abraham Lincoln to Edwin M. Stanton, July 21, 1863; Lincoln to U.S. Grant, August 9, 1863, *Collected Works*, 6: 342, 374.

18. U.S. Grant quoted in *Collected Works*, 6: 375n.

19. Abraham Lincoln to Robert C. Schenck, July 4, 1863, *Collected Works*, 6: 317 and n.; Edwin M. Stanton to Schenck, July 6, 1863, *OR*, ser. 3, vol. 3, pp. 470–471.

20. Thomas E. Bramlette to Abraham Lincoln, October 19, 1863, Lincoln Papers.

21. General Orders no. 329, October 3, 1863, *OR*, ser. 3, vol. 3, pp. 860–861.

22. William C. Goodloe to Green Adams, January 25, 1863; Jesse W. Fell to F. Price, February, 18, 1863, Lincoln Papers. Both letters were forwarded to Lincoln.

23. D. Merriwether et al., *To the General Assembly of the Commonwealth of Kentucky*, February 19, 1863, *Annual Cyclopedia, 1863*, 565–566.

24. Ibid., 566.

25. Gillmore quotation is in Coulter, *The Civil War and Readjustment in Kentucky*, 171–172.

26. *Annual Cyclopedia, 1863*, 566–567.

27. W. G. Brownlow to Montgomery Blair, March 25, 1863, Blair Family Papers.

28. *Annual Cyclopedia, 1863*, 567.

29. "Speech of Judge Bramlette on the Condition of the War and the Duty of Kentuckians, Delivered at Carlisle, Ky., June 23, 1863," *Louisville Daily Democrat*, July 1, 1863, copied from the *Cincinnati Commercial*, n.d. An excerpt from the speech may be found in the entry for August 7, 1863, in Hay, *Inside Lincoln's White House*, ed. Burlingame and Ettlinger, 335.

30. *Annual Cyclopedia, 1863*, 567.

31. Coulter, *The Civil War and Readjustment in Kentucky*, 174. See also Harrison, *Lincoln of Kentucky*, 179.

32. William C. Goodloe to Abraham Lincoln, June 30, 1863, Lincoln Papers.

33. For Lincoln's interest in the election, see Abraham Lincoln to the *Cincinnati Gazette*, August 5, 1863, and Lincoln to Mary Todd Lincoln, August 8, 1863, *Collected Works*, 6: 366, 372.

34. McPherson, *The Political History of the United States of America*, 313.

35. Abraham Lincoln to Edwin M. Stanton, February 5, 1864, *Collected Works*, 7: 169.

36. *Annual Cyclopedia, 1863*, 568. Burnside was also unhappy when Lincoln in May sent Copperhead Clement L. Vallandigham into exile after Burnside had had him arrested and imprisoned.

37. For Morgan's July 1863 raid, see Harrison, *The Civil War in Kentucky*, 67–69.

38. The *Cincinnati Commercial*, n.d., as quoted in the *Annual Cyclopedia, 1863*, 569. The *Annual Cyclopedia, 1863*, also gives the election results (569). A threat by General Boyle to arrest those voting for Wickliffe had little effect on the outcome of the election.

39. As quoted in *Annual Cyclopedia, 1863*, 568.

40. Abraham Lincoln to Mary Todd Lincoln, August 8, 1863, *Collected Works*, 6: 372.

41. Abraham Lincoln to Green Adams, August 22, 1864, *Collected Works*, 6: 401–402.

42. *Annual Cyclopedia, 1863*, 569.

43. *Message of Governor Bramlette, to the General Assembly of Kentucky at the December Session, 1863* (Frankfort, Ky.: Commonwealth Office, William E. Hughes, State Printer, 1863), 11–12.

44. Abraham Lincoln to Jeremiah T. Boyle, February 1, 1863, *Collected Works*, 6: 87 and n. Lincoln did not reply to Powell's protest. Lazarus W. Powell to Lincoln, February 11, 1863, Lincoln Papers.

45. *Message of Governor Bramlette*, 17.

46. *Annual Cyclopedia, 1864*, 447.

47. Thomas E. Bramlette to Abraham Lincoln, February 1, 1864, Lincoln Papers. General Thomas, who visited Bramlette and other Kentucky leaders in January, concluded, "It would be injudicious to attempt raising [black] troops in the State at present." He suspended the recruitment operations at Paducah. General Orders, no. 38, War Department, Adjutant General's Office, February 1, 1864, *OR*, ser. 3, vol. 4, p. 60.

48. *Annual Cyclopedia, 1864*, 447.

49. Edwin M. Stanton to Abraham Lincoln, February 8, 1864, Lincoln Papers.

50. Circular no. 8, War Department, Provost Marshal General's Office, March 1, 1864, *OR*, ser. 3, vol. 4, p. 146, citing the February 24, 1864, act of Congress.

51. Thomas E. Bramlette to Abraham Lincoln, March 8, 1864, Lincoln Papers.

52. Thomas E. Bramlette to William C. Goodloe, March 12, 1864, Lincoln Papers. A copy of this telegram was sent to Washington.

53. The account of the March 14 meeting has been pieced together from Coulter, *The Civil War and Readjustment in Kentucky*, 200–201, and the *Annual Cyclopedia, 1864*, 448.

54. *Annual Cyclopedia, 1864*, 448.

55. Entry for April 3, 1864, *Browning Diary*, 1: 665.

56. For a fine analysis of the Hodges letter, see Ronald C. White Jr., *The Eloquent President: A Portrait of Lincoln through His Words* (New York: Random House, 2005), 261–262, 266–275.

57. Entry for March 28, 1864, Bates, *Diary*, ed. Beale, 352.

58. Abraham Lincoln to Edwin M. Stanton, March 28, 1864, *Collected Works*, 7: 272.

59. *Annual Cyclopedia, 1864*, 448.

60. Ibid.

61. *Louisville Daily Journal*, April 27, 1864.

62. Harrison, *Lincoln of Kentucky*, 185.

63. Abraham Lincoln to Lorenzo Thomas, June 13, 1864, *Collected Works*, 7: 390 and n.

64. General Orders, no. 20, June 13, 1864, Adjutant General Lorenzo Thomas, *OR*, ser. 3, vol. 4, pp. 429–430.

65. For an account of the effect of the Emancipation Proclamation on the desire of blacks to join the army, see Berlin, Reidy, and Rowland, *Freedom's Soldiers*, 21.

66. Smith, "The Recruitment of Negro Soldiers in Kentucky," 385–387.

67. Abraham Lincoln to John Glenn, February 7, 1865, *Collected Works*, 8: 266 and n.

68. Abraham Lincoln to Edwin M. Stanton, February [7?], 1865, *Collected Works*, 8: 268.

69. Berlin, Reidy, and Rowland, *Freedom's Soldiers*, 16–17, for the state statistics on black troops in the Civil War.

70. Thomas E. Bramlette to Edwin M. Stanton, June 20, 1864, *OR*, ser. 3, vol. 4, pp. 436–438.

71. *Annual Cyclopedia, 1864*, 449–450; Coulter, *The Civil War and Readjustment in Kentucky*, 222–223.

72. A good account of the General Paine case is in Harrison, *Lincoln of Kentucky*, 208–211. Additional information on the charges against him can be found in *Annual Cyclopedia, 1864*, 449.

73. Thomas E. Bramlette to Abraham Lincoln, September 3, 1864, *OR*, ser. 3, vol. 4, p. 689.

74. E. W. Hawkins et al. to Abraham Lincoln, June 5, 1864, Lincoln Papers.

75. Statement of Joseph Odell, June 17, 1864; statement of Captain J. Bates Dickson, n.d., U.S. Senate Executive Documents, no. 16, 38th Congress, 2d Sess., 7, 24–25.

76. E. W. Hawkins et al. to Abraham Lincoln, June 5, 1864, Lincoln Papers.

77. William C. Goodloe to Green Clay Smith, May 29, 1864, Lincoln Papers.

78. Parole for Frank L. Wolford, July 7, 1864, with Lincoln's endorsement, Lincoln Papers.

79. Frank Wolford to Abraham Lincoln, July 30, 1864, Lincoln Papers; Harrison, *Lincoln of Kentucky*, 186–187.

80. Abraham Lincoln to Frank Wolford, August 4, 1864, *Collected Works*, 7: 480.

81. As quoted in David Herbert Donald, *Lincoln* (New York: Simon & Schuster, 1995), 504.

82. William C. Goodloe to Green Clay Smith, May 29, 1864, Lincoln Papers.

83. Albert G. Hodges to Abraham Lincoln, May 10, 1864, Lincoln Papers; *Louisville Daily Journal*, April 11, 1864; *Washington Daily Chronicle*, March 16, 1864; *New York Times*, May 29, 1864. For the platform of the conservative Unionist convention, see the *Washington National Intelligencer*, June 2, 1864.

84. Albert G. Hodges to Abraham Lincoln, May 27, 1864, Lincoln Papers; *Annual Cyclopedia, 1864*, 451.

85. *Annual Cyclopedia, 1864*, 451.

86. Ibid., 451–452.

87. John Brough to Edwin M. Stanton, June 11, 1864, *OR*, ser. 3, vol. 4, p. 429.

88. Proclamation Suspending Writ of Habeas Corpus, July 5, 1864, *Collected Works*, 7: 425–426.

89. *Annual Cyclopedia, 1864*, 453; James M. Prichard, "Stephen Gano Burbridge," in *Encyclopedia of the American Civil War: A Political, Social, and Military History*, ed.

David S. Heidler and Jeanne T. Heidler, 5 vols. (Santa Barbara, Calif.: ABC-CLIO, 2000), 1: 324.

90. *Annual Cyclopedia, 1864*, 453. Despite Burbridge's action, more than 1,000 conservatives and Democrats cast their ballots for Duvall.

91. *Saint Louis Daily Missouri Republican*, June 11, 1864.

92. James T. Noble to Millard Fillmore, June 9, 1864; John Todd Stuart to Fillmore, August 6, 24, 1864; James Harlan to Hiram Ketchum, September 8, 1864; George Read Riddle to Fillmore, July 2, 1864; Fillmore to Riddle, July 5, 1864, Millard Fillmore Papers, Buffalo and Erie County Historical Society, Buffalo, N.Y. (microfilm).

93. R. F. Stevens to William B. Campbell, July 29, 1864, Campbell Family Papers, Duke University Library, Durham, N.C.; Hiram Ketchum to Millard Fillmore, July 22, 1864, Fillmore Papers; Stephen W. Sears, *George B. McClellan: The Young Napoleon* (New York: Tichnor & Fields, 1988), 375–376. For an excellent account of the Copperheads during the summer of 1864 and their role in the Chicago convention, see Jennifer L. Weber, *Copperheads: The Rise and Fall of Lincoln's Opponents in the North* (New York: Oxford University Press, 2006), chaps. 5–6.

94. For the conservative demand that the Democratic convention nominate a border state Unionist for vice president to counter the Republican selection of Andrew Johnson, see A. B. Norton to William B. Campbell, June 18, 1864, Campbell Family Papers.

95. Thomas E. Bramlette to James Guthrie, August 22, 1864, in the *Washington National Intelligencer*, September 3, 1864.

96. The resolutions of the conservative Union meeting appear in the *Washington Constitutional Union*, October 20, 1864. For a report of the meeting, see the *Baltimore American*, August 29, 1864.

97. *Baltimore American*, September 1, 8, 1864.

98. John P. Kennedy to Robert C. Winthrop, September 6, 1864, Robert C. Winthrop Papers, Massachusetts Historical Society, Boston (microfilm).

99. Charles F. Brinkerhoft to Millard Fillmore, October 15, 1864, Fillmore Papers; Reverdy Johnson to New York Committee of Arrangements for a McClellan meeting, September 16, 1864, printed in the *Louisville Daily Journal*, September 30, 1864.

100. *Washington National Intelligencer*, October 1864 issues. The Fillmore quotation is in the October 4 issue.

101. *Saint Louis Daily Missouri Republican*, September 4, 13, 1864.

102. *Louisville Daily Journal*, June 11 (quotation), October 8, 18, 20, 1864. One of Prentice's sons was killed fighting for the Union, and another son served in the Confederate army.

103. Ibid., October 18, 1864 (quotation); *Nashville Daily Press*, October 1, 1864.

104. William C. Goodloe and Charles Eginton to Abraham Lincoln, November 23, 1864, Lincoln Papers; E. D. Ludington to Edwin M. Stanton, *OR*, ser. 1, vol. 45, pt. 2, p. 93.

105. Thomas E. Bramlette to Abraham Lincoln, September 3, 1864, *OR*, ser. 3, vol. 4, pp. 688–690.

106. *Louisville Daily Journal*, November 2, 1864.

107. *Annual Cyclopedia, 1864*, 453–454. See Albert G. Hodges to Abraham Lin-

coln, November 1, 1864, Lincoln Papers, on the inability of the federal forces under General Burbridge to prevent intimidation and violence against Lincoln voters.

108. For an analysis of the importance of the 1864 presidential election, see my *Lincoln's Last Months* (Cambridge, Mass.: Belknap Press of Harvard University Press, 2004), 45–48; and McPherson, *Ordeal by Fire*, 492–494.

109. *Annual Cyclopedia, 1864*, 453; William C. Davis, *Lincoln's Men: How President Lincoln Became Father to an Army and a Nation* (New York: Free Press, 1999), 219–224.

110. S. G. Burbridge to Thomas E. Bramlette, November 10, 1864; Abraham Lincoln to Burbridge, November 10, 1864, quoting Governor Bramlette, *OR*, ser. 1, vol. 39, pt. 3, p. 739.

111. Stephen G. Burbridge to Abraham Lincoln, November 11, 1864, *Collected Works*, 8: 99n.

112. Captain J. Bates Dickson to General N. C. McLean, November 9, 1864; Dickson to General Hugh Ewing, November 9, 1864, *OR*, ser. 1, vol. 39, pt. 3, p. 726.

113. Thomas E. Bramlette to Abraham Lincoln, November 14, 22, 1864, Lincoln Papers.

114. Kentucky Unionists to Abraham Lincoln, November 21, 1864, Lincoln Papers.

115. Albert G. Hodges to Abraham Lincoln, December 1, 1864, Lincoln Papers. In this letter, Hodges recalled the conversation that he and General Suddarth had had with the president on November 22.

116. Coulter, *The Civil War and Readjustment in Kentucky*, 288.

117. Abraham Lincoln to Thomas E. Bramlette, November 22, 1864, *Collected Works*, 8: 120.

118. *Cincinnati Gazette*, November 16, 1864, as reported in Coulter, *The Civil War and Readjustment in Kentucky*, 210.

119. E. D. Ludington to Edwin M. Stanton, December 7, 1864, *OR*, ser. 1, vol. 45, pt. 2, pp. 93–94.

120. Ibid., 93–94.

121. Theodore S. Bell et al. to Joseph Holt, November 22, 1864; William C. Goodloe and Charles Eginton to Abraham Lincoln, November 23, 1864, Lincoln Papers.

122. Robert J. Breckinridge to Abraham Lincoln, November 16, 1864; Thomas E. Bramlette to Lincoln, November 16, 1864; Stuart Robinson to Lincoln, December 10, 1864, Lincoln Papers. See also George W. Lewis to Lincoln, November 30, 1864, Lincoln Papers. Like Prentice's, Robert Breckinridge's family was divided on the war. He had two sons in the Confederate army; he was also the uncle of John C. Breckinridge, Confederate general and Jefferson Davis's last secretary of war.

123. Cong. Globe, 38th Cong., 2d sess. (December 20, 1864), 73, 77.

124. Richard T. Jacob to Abraham Lincoln, December 26, 1864, Lincoln Papers.

125. Abraham Lincoln to Ulysses S. Grant, January 5, 1864; Lincoln to Richard T. Jacob, January 18, 1865, *Collected Works*, 8: 198, 222.

126. U.S. Senate Executive Documents, no. 16, 38th Cong., 2nd sess.; Robert J. Breckinridge, letter to the editors, *Cincinnati Daily Gazette*, February 15, 1865.

127. *Annual Cyclopedia, 1865*, 460.

128. Reply to a Delegation of Kentuckians, January 2, 1865, *Collected Works*, 8: 195.

129. *Louisville Daily Journal*, February 14, 1865; *Cincinnati Daily Gazette*, February 21, 22, 1865.

130. Thomas E. Bramlette to Abraham Lincoln, February 18, 1865, Lincoln Papers.

131. *Louisville Daily Journal*, March 4, 1865. For the conservative reception of General Palmer in Kentucky, see the *Cincinnati Daily Gazette*, March 18, 1865.

132. *Cincinnati Daily Gazette*, January 9, 11, 1865; *Philadelphia Press*, January 9, 1865.

133. For the roll-call vote in the U.S. House of Representative on the Thirteenth Amendment, see Cong. Globe, 38th Cong., 2d Sess. (January 31, 1865), 531.

134. *Saint Louis Missouri Democrat*, February 10, 1865; *New York Herald*, February 19, 1865; *Louisville Daily Journal*, March 13, 1865.

135. *Louisville Daily Journal*, March 24, 1865.

136. Harrison, *Lincoln of Kentucky*, 243–244.

137. Thomas E. Bramlette to Abraham Lincoln, March 2, 1865; printed message of Governor Bramlette to the Kentucky House of Representatives, March 1, 1865, Lincoln Papers; Michael Vorenberg, *Final Freedom: The Civil War, the Abolition of Slavery, and the Thirteenth Amendment* (Cambridge, U.K.: Cambridge University Press, 2001), 232 and n.

138. *Cincinnati Daily Gazette*, March 18, 1865; Howard, *Black Liberation in Kentucky*, 78–79.

139. Kentucky Contributor, *Cincinnati Daily Gazette*, February 28, 1865.

140. As reported in the *Cincinnati Daily Gazette*, February 21, 1865.

141. *Louisville Daily Journal*, January 26, 1865; *Cincinnati Daily Gazette*, January 28, February 2, 1865.

142. James M. Morris, "William Clarke Quantrill," in Heidler and Heidler, *Encyclopedia of the American Civil War*, 3: 1583.

143. *Louisville Daily Journal*, March 16, 1865. For "Sue Mundy's" capture, see ibid., March 15, 1865. The *Journal* in its report of the trial and hanging admitted that Clarke was a "man of culture and gentlemanly refinement" who did not fit the stereotype of a villainous guerrilla.

144. John M. Palmer to Edwin M. Stanton, February 24, 1865, *OR*, ser. 1, vol. 49, pt. 1, pp. 763–764.

145. *Louisville Daily Journal*, January 23, 1865.

146. Harrison, *Lincoln of Kentucky*, 10–11 (quotations); Coulter, *The Civil War and Readjustment in Kentucky*, 257.

147. Anne E. Marshall, *Creating a Confederate Kentucky: The Lost Cause and Civil War Memory in a Border State* (Chapel Hill: University of North Carolina Press, 2010), 43–44. Professor Marshall kindly provided me with these pages from her book shortly before its publication.

Chapter 8
Union and Emancipation Triumphant: Maryland

1. Both quotations are in Baker, *The Politics of Continuity*, 84–85.

2. Davis, *Speeches and Addresses Delivered in the Congress of the United States*, 307; Davis quotation in Burlingame, *Abraham Lincoln*, 2: 211.

3. For a good account of the disruption of the Union Party in 1863, see Wagandt, *The Mighty Revolution*, chap. 8.

4. *Annual Cyclopedia, 1863*, 609.

5. Russell F. Weigley, *A Great Civil War: A Military and Political History, 1861–1865* (Bloomington: Indiana University Press, 2000), 237.

6. *Annual Cyclopedia, 1863*, 609. For Stuart's raid, see Mark Nesbitt, *Saber and Scapegoat: J. E. B. Stuart and the Gettysburg Controversy* (Mechanicsburg, Pa.: Stackpole Books, 1994).

7. Mitchell Yockelson, "Robert Cumming Schenck," in Heidler and Heidler, *Encyclopedia of the American Civil War*, 4: 1711–1712.

8. *Annual Cyclopedia, 1863*, 613–614.

9. Ibid., 614.

10. Robert C. Schenck to Abraham Lincoln, June 30, 1863, Lincoln Papers.

11. Robert C. Schenck to Abraham Lincoln, July 4, 1863, *OR*, ser. 1, vol. 27, pt. 3, p. 528.

12. Lincoln to Schenck, July 4, 1863, *Collected Works*, 6: 317 and n.

13. Edwin M. Stanton to Robert C. Schenck, July 6, 1863, *OR*, ser. 3, vol. 3, pp. 470–471.

14. *Annual Cyclopedia, 1863*, 614.

15. Bradford recalled the meeting in a later letter to Lincoln. Augustus W. Bradford to Abraham Lincoln, September 28, 1863, Lincoln Papers.

16. Allen Thorndike Rice, ed., *Reminiscences of Abraham Lincoln by Distinguished Men of His Time* (New York: North American Review, 1889), 495–497.

17. Augustus W. Bradford to Abraham Lincoln, September 28, 1863, Lincoln Papers.

18. Abraham Lincoln to Augustus W. Bradford, October 1, 1863, *Collected Works*, 6: 491.

19. General Orders, no. 329, U.S. Department of War, October 3, 1863, *OR*, ser. 3, vol. 3, pp. 860–861.

20. Prince George's County Maryland Citizens to Abraham Lincoln, 1863, Lincoln Papers.

21. Reply to Maryland Slaveholders, October 21, 1863; Abraham Lincoln to Robert C. Schenck, October 21, 1863, *Collected Works*, 6: 529–530, 530.

22. Robert C. Schenck to Abraham Lincoln, October 21, 1863, Lincoln Papers.

23. Entry for October 22, 1863, in Hay, *Inside Lincoln's White House*, ed. Burlingame and Ettlinger, 97.

24. Bernard C. Steiner, *Life of Reverdy Johnson* (New York: Russell & Russell, 1914), 68–69, 99.

25. Augustus W. Bradford to Montgomery Blair, with endorsement by Lincoln, May 12, 1864, Lincoln Papers. This letter was intended for Lincoln. Bradford sent it to Blair to ensure that the president read it.

26. Abraham Lincoln to Edwin M. Stanton, May 26, 1864, *Collected Works*, 7: 363 and n.

27. Essah, *A House Divided*, 179–180; *Annual Cyclopedia, 1864*, 358.

28. Chandra Manning, *What This Cruel War Was Over: Soldiers, Slavery, and the Civil War* (New York: Alfred A. Knopf, 2007), 95–96.

29. The address as well as other documents regarding the Maryland Unionists in the campaign can be found in *Annual Cyclopedia, 1863*, 617–618.

30. Ibid., 616–617.

31. General Orders, no. 53, Headquarters Middle Department, 8th Army Corps, October 27, 1863, *OR*, ser. 1, vol. 29, pt. 2, pp. 394–395.

32. Thomas Swann to Abraham Lincoln, October 26, 1863, Lincoln Papers.

33. Abraham Lincoln to Thomas Swann, October 27, 1863, *Collected Works*, 6: 542.

34. Augustus W. Bradford to Abraham Lincoln, October 31, 1863, *OR*, ser. 3, vol. 3, pp. 967–968.

35. Edwin M. Stanton to Robert C. Schenck, November 1, 1863; Schenck to Stanton, November 1, 1863, *OR*, ser. 3, vol. 3, p. 968.

36. Abraham Lincoln to Augustus W. Bradford, November 2, 1863, *Collected Works*, 5: 556–557.

37. *Collected Works*, 6: 557.

38. *Annual Cyclopedia, 1863*, 619–620.

39. To the Loyal People of Maryland, November 3, 1863, November 3, 1863, *OR*, ser. 3, vol. 3, pp. 988–990.

40. Augustus W. Bradford to Abraham Lincoln, November 3, 1863, Lincoln Papers.

41. *Annual Cyclopedia, 1863*, 623.

42. Nicholas Brewer to Abraham Lincoln, October 31, 1863, Lincoln Papers.

43. William E. Smith, *The Francis Preston Blair Family in Politics*, 2 vols. (New York: Macmillan, 1933), 2: 237–242.

44. Entry for October 22, 1863, in Hay, *Inside Lincoln's White House*, ed. Burlingame and Ettlinger, 97.

45. Wagandt, *The Mighty Revolution*, 189–190.

46. In December 1864, after an earlier failure, Winter Davis, as the chairman of the House Committee on Foreign Affairs, secured the passage of a House resolution designed to give Congress a veto over foreign affairs. The Senate, however, rejected the resolution. Cong. Globe, 38th Cong., 2d Sess. (December 20, 1864), 50–51; McPherson, *The Political History of the United States of America*, 600.

47. *Annual Cyclopedia, 1863*, 625.

48. John W. Crisfield to Montgomery Blair, November 8, 1863, Lincoln Papers.

49. Abraham Lincoln to Montgomery Blair, November 11, 1863; Lincoln to Robert C. Schenck, November 20, 1863; Lincoln to Joseph Holt, February 22, 1864, *Collected Works*, 7: 9, 26, 27n, 197n.

50. Nicholas Brewer to Abraham Lincoln, November 7, 1863; Donn Piatt to Lincoln, November 27, 1863, Lincoln Papers.

51. Thomas G. Pratt to Edwin M. Stanton, November 28, 1863, Lincoln Papers.

52. Thomas G. Pratt to Edwin M. Stanton, November 28, 1863; Augustus W. Bradford to Pratt, November 22, 1863; Daniel Clark, December 1863 (Notes on case of

Thomas G. Pratt), Lincoln Papers; Stanton to Donn Piatt, November 30, 1863; Stanton to Benjamin F. Butler, December 1, 1863, *OR*, ser. 2, vol. 6, pp. 607, 626.

53. Printed General Orders no. 59, November 13, 1863, Headquarters, Middle Department 8th Army Corps, Baltimore, Maryland, Lincoln Papers; William Cannon and N. B. Smithers to Abraham Lincoln, November 13, 1863, Lincoln Papers.

54. Hancock, *Delaware during the Civil War*, 138.

55. *Annual Cyclopedia, 1863*, 623–624.

56. Steiner, *Life of Reverdy Johnson*, 71.

57. Cong. Globe, 38th Cong., 1st Sess. (January 5, 1864), 96–97.

58. Ibid., (January 8, 1864), 139.

59. Ibid., (January 26, 1864), 348–349.

60. Ibid., 343.

61. Ibid., 342.

62. Ibid., (March 3–4, 1864), Speech of Hon. L. W. Powell, Appendix, 55–70. The quotation is on page 62.

63. Ibid., (June 23, 1864), 3192–3194; Wagandt, *The Mighty Revolution*, 187.

64. Wagandt, *The Mighty Revolution*, 190, 194–195. For documents on the legislative debate over emancipation in Maryland, see *Annual Cyclopedia, 1864*, 496–498.

65. Davis, "On Emancipation in Maryland," April 1, 1864, in *Speeches and Addresses Delivered in the Congress of the United States*, 588–589.

66. Charles C. Fulton to Montgomery Blair, March [1?], 1864, Blair Family Papers.

67. Abraham Lincoln to John A. J. Creswell, March 7, 1864, *Collected Works*, 7: 226–227 and n.

68. Abraham Lincoln to John A. J. Creswell, March 17, 1864, *Collected Works*, 7: 251.

69. Wallace, *An Autobiography*, 2: 670–672. Wallace was the future author of the famous novel *Ben Hur*.

70. Ibid., 2: 672.

71. Ibid., 2: 676.

72. Ibid., 2: 673–675.

73. Ibid., 2: 675.

74. Ibid., 2: 681–682; Lew Wallace to Augustus W. Bradford, March 30, 1864, *Annual Cyclopedia, 1864*, 498.

75. The Wallace-Bradford meeting and agreement has been pieced together from the following sources: *Annual Cyclopedia, 1864*, 498–500; Wallace, *An Autobiography*, 2: 681–683; and General John R. Kenly to Lieutenant Colonel S. B. Lawrence, April 8, 1864, *OR*, ser. 1, vol. 33, pp. 826–827.

76. H. Winter Davis to Lew Wallace, [April?] 1864, in Wallace, *An Autobiography*, 2: 683.

77. Wallace, *An Autobiography*, 2: 684.

78. Abraham Lincoln to Edwin M. Stanton, March 31, 1864, *Collected Works*, 7: 276–277; Wallace, *An Autobiography*, 2: 685.

79. Wagandt, *The Mighty Revolution*, 214.

80. *Annual Cyclopedia, 1864*, 500.

81. Address at Sanitary Fair, Baltimore, Maryland, April 18, 1864, *Collected Works*, 7: 301.

82. Ibid., 7: 301–302.

83. Ibid., 7: 302. The "rumor" of the Fort Pillow massacre proved true, but Lincoln did not retaliate against the Confederates, despite his promise in his Baltimore address to do so (ibid., 7: 303); McPherson, *Battle Cry of Freedom*, 794.

84. *Annual Cyclopedia, 1864*, 500–502.

85. Ibid., 502–503; Wagandt, *The Mighty Revolution*, 224–225.

86. For an account of Bradley Johnson's raid in the Baltimore area and his failed effort to reach Point Lookout, see Gary Baker, "Gilmor's Ride around Baltimore," *Civil War Interactive: The Daily Newspaper of the Civil War since 1996*, http://www.civilwarinteractive.com/ArticlesGilmorsRide.htm. Major Harry Gilmor commanded Johnson's vanguard.

87. George R. Dennis to Montgomery Blair, July 21, 1864, Lincoln Papers.

88. Abraham Lincoln to Edwin M. Stanton, August 3, 1864, *Collected Works*, 7: 477 and n; David Hunter to Lincoln, August 7, 1864, Lincoln Papers; Special Orders, no. 2, Department of West Virginia, August 8, 1864, *OR*, ser. 1, vol. 43, pt. 1, p. 726.

89. *Annual Cyclopedia, 1864*, 503.

90. Wagandt, *The Mighty Revolution*, 246–247.

91. For the repudiation of Winter Davis after his attack on Lincoln in the so-called Wade-Davis Manifesto, see my *Lincoln's Last Months*, 18–19.

92. Entry for September 24, 1864, in Hay, *Inside Lincoln's White House*, ed. Burlingame and Ettlinger, 230.

93. Wagandt, *The Mighty Revolution*, 248.

94. *Washington National Intelligencer*, October 1, 1864.

95. Steiner, *Life of Reverdy Johnson*, 66.

96. Joshua M. Bosley and James R Brewer to Abraham Lincoln, October 5, 1864; Reverdy Johnson to Lincoln, October 6, 1864; W. Kimmel and Joshua M. Bosley to Lincoln, October 8, 1864, Lincoln Papers.

97. Seabrook, *Maryland's Great Part in Saving the Union*, 54–56.

98. Henry W. Hoffman to Abraham Lincoln, October 3, 1864, Lincoln Papers.

99. Abraham Lincoln to Henry W. Hoffman, October 10, 1864, *Collected Works*, 8: 41; Hoffman to Lincoln, October 12, 1864, Lincoln Papers.

100. Lew Wallace to his adjutant, Lieutenant Colonel Samuel. B. Lawrence, October 4, 1864, *OR*, ser. 1, vol. 43, pt. 2, pp. 279–280.

101. Wagandt, *The Mighty Revolution*, 257.

102. *Annual Cyclopedia, 1864*, 504.

103. Lincoln, *Recollected Words*, comp. and ed. Fehrenbacher and Fehrenbacher, 355.

104. Response to a Serenade, October 19, 1864, *Collected Works*, 8: 52.

105. *Lincoln Observed: Civil War Dispatches of Noah Brooks,* ed. Michael Burlingame (Baltimore: Johns Hopkins University Press, 1998), 141–142, 267n.87. The account of Lincoln's response to the black celebrants on November 1, 1864, is not included in his *Collected Works*.

106. Response to a Serenade, October 19, 1864, *Collected Works*, 8: 52–53.

107. Baker, *The Politics of Continuity*, 109, quoting Swann.

108. Davis quoted in Allan Nevins, *The War for the Union*, vol. 4, *The Organized War to Victory, 1864–1865* (New York: Scribner, 1971), 142.

109. *Annual Cyclopedia, 1864*, 506.

110. Thomas Swann to Abraham Lincoln, November 12, 1864, Lincoln Papers.

111. Cong. Globe, 38th Cong., 2d Sess. (January 31, 1865), 531; Steiner, *Life of Reverdy Johnson*, 75, 78; McPherson, *The Political History of the United States of America*, 256–257, 590.

112. Vorenberg, *Final Freedom*, 216.

113. General Orders, no. 112, Headquarters Middle Department, November 9, 1864, *OR*, ser. 1, vol. 43, pt. 2, pp. 587–588; Wallace, *An Autobiography*, 2: 691–692.

114. Charles L. Wagandt, "Redemption or Reaction?—Maryland in the Post–Civil War Years," in *Radicalism, Racism, and Party Realignment: The Border States during Reconstruction*, ed. Richard O. Curry (Baltimore: Johns Hopkins Press, 1969), 155–156.

115. Harry J. Carman and Reinhard H. Luthin, *Lincoln and the Patronage* (1943; reprint, Gloucester, Mass.: Peter Smith, 1964), 205–212.

116. For an extended account of the Blair-Davis imbroglio after the election, see my *Lincoln's Last Months*, 79–81.

117. Entry for December 10, 1864, in Welles, *Diary*, 2: 195–196; entry for December 18, 1864, in Hay, *Inside Lincoln's White House*, ed. Burlingame and Ettlinger, 252–254; the quotation is on page 254.

118. Entry for February 21, 1865, Welles, *Diary*, 2: 243; Carman and Luthin, *Lincoln and the Patronage*, 325–326; Memorandum Concerning Maryland Appointments, April 14, 1865, *Collected Works*, 8: 411.

119. The Anna Ferris and Thomas F. Bayard quotations are in Hancock, *Delaware during the Civil War*, 160–161.

120. *Christian Advocate and Journal*, May 4, 1865.

Chapter 9
Union and Emancipation Triumphant: Missouri

1. Missouri Delegation in Congress to Abraham Lincoln [With Endorsement by Lincoln], January 1863, Lincoln Papers. The military assessments were mainly designed to support the Enrolled Missouri Militia.

2. Hamilton Gamble to Abraham Lincoln, November 17, December 31, 1862; Samuel T. Glover to Abraham Lincoln, December 7, 1862, Lincoln Papers.

3. B. Gratz Brown to John G. Nicolay, November 25, 1862, Lincoln Papers.

4. Charles D. Drake to Abraham Lincoln, January 22, 1863, Lincoln Papers.

5. Abraham Lincoln to Samuel R. Curtis, January 5, 1863, *Collected Works*, 6: 36–37; Edwin M. Stanton to Samuel R. Curtis, January 20, 1863, *OR*, ser. 1, vol. 22, pt. 1, p. 64. "Hunkerism" refers to the faction in the New York Democratic Party during the Jacksonian era that allegedly "hunkered," that is, hungered, for public office and spoils.

6. Samuel R. Curtis to Abraham Lincoln, January 31, 1863; Hamilton Gamble to Lincoln, February 4, 1863, Lincoln Papers.

7. Hamilton Gamble to Abraham Lincoln, February 4, 1863, Lincoln Papers.

8. Franklin A. Dick, the provost marshal in Saint Louis, actually issued the expulsion order under General Curtis's authority. *Collected Works*, 6: 20n.

9. John S. Grasty, *Memoir of Rev. Samuel B. McPheeters, D.D.*, with an introduction by Stuart Robinson (Saint Louis, Mo.: Southwestern Book and Publishing, 1871), 183–184.

10. Ibid., 184; Samuel B. McPheeters to Edward Bates, December 23, 1862, Lincoln Papers.

11. Grasty, *Memoir of Rev. Samuel B. McPheeters*, 184–185.

12. Abraham Lincoln to Samuel R. Curtis, December 27, 1862, *Collected Works*, 6: 20.

13. Grasty, *Memoir of Rev. Samuel B. McPheeters*, 186.

14. Samuel R. Curtis to Abraham Lincoln, January 15, 1863, *OR*, ser. 1, vol. 22, pt. 2, pp. 42–43.

15. Samuel R. Curtis to Abraham Lincoln, December 28, 1862, Lincoln Papers.

16. Samuel R. Curtis to Abraham Lincoln, December 29, 1862, Lincoln Papers.

17. Abraham Lincoln to Samuel R. Curtis, January 2, 1863, *Collected Works*, 6: 33–34.

18. Grasty, *Memoir of Rev. Samuel B. McPheeters*, 187–189.

19. Samuel B. McPheeters to Samuel R. Curtis, March 31, 1863; Samuel R. Curtis to Abraham Lincoln, April 3, 1863, Lincoln Papers.

20. Boman, *Lincoln's Resolute Unionist*, 192.

21. Abraham Lincoln to Oliver D. Filley, December 22, 1863, *Collected Works*, 7: 85–86 and 86n.

22. Grasty, *Memoir of Rev. Samuel B. McPheeters*, 198 200.

23. Entry for February 24, 1863, in Bates, *Diary*, ed. Beale, 279; Charles Gibson to Abraham Lincoln, February 23, 1863, Lincoln Papers.

24. Parrish, *A History of Missouri*, vol. 3, *1860–1875*, 104.

25. Special Orders, no. 114, War Department, March 10, 1863, *OR*, ser. 1, vol. 22, pt. 2, p. 152.

26. Missouri State Legislature to Abraham Lincoln, March 2, 1863, Lincoln Papers.

27. Ozias M. Hatch et al. to Abraham Lincoln, March 25, 1863, Lincoln Papers.

28. Henry T. Blow to Abraham Lincoln, March 22, 1863; Francis J. Herron to Lincoln, March 21, 1863, Lincoln Papers. Herron was reprimanded by the War Department for his brashness.

29. Charles D. Drake to Abraham Lincoln, April 29, 1863, Lincoln Papers.

30. John B. Henderson to Abraham Lincoln, March 30, 1863, Lincoln Papers. For other demands that Curtis be replaced, see Saint Louis Citizens to Lincoln, May 1,1863, and Hamilton Gamble to Lincoln, May 2, 1863, Lincoln Papers.

31. Samuel T. Glover to Abraham Lincoln, April 13, 1863; Hamilton Gramble to Lincoln, May 2, 1863, Lincoln Papers. For similar appeals for Lincoln to put down the "Revolutionists," see Saint Louis Citizens to Abraham Lincoln, May 1, 1863, and Congressman William A. Hall to Lincoln, April 15, 1863, Lincoln Papers.

32. Abraham Lincoln to Edwin M. Stanton, May 11, 1863, *Collected Works*, 6: 210.

33. Abraham Lincoln to John M. Schofield, May 27, 1863, *Collected Works*, 6: 234.

34. Ibid., 6: 234 and n.

35. Charles D. Drake et al. to Abraham Lincoln, May 15, 1863, Lincoln Papers; Lincoln to Henry T. Blow, Charles D. Drake, and Others, May 15, 1863, *Collected Works*, 6: 218.

36. *Saint Louis Missouri Democrat*, June 9, 1863, as quoted in Lincoln, *Recollected Words*, comp. and ed. Fehrenbacher and Fehrenbacher, 442–443.

37. Ibid., 443.

38. John M. Schofield to Abraham Lincoln, July 14, 1863; Henry T. Blow to Abraham Lincoln, July 13, 1863, Lincoln Papers.

39. Abraham Lincoln to John M. Schofield, [July 13], July 20, 1863, *Collected Works*, 6: 326, 338; Schofield to Lincoln, July 14, 1863, Lincoln Papers.

40. Hamilton Gamble to Abraham Lincoln, July 13, 1863, Lincoln Papers.

41. Abraham Lincoln to Hamilton Gamble, July 23, 1863, *Collected Works*, 6: 344.

42. Boman, *Lincoln's Resolute Unionist*, 212.

43. *Annual Cyclopedia, 1863*, 653.

44. Speech at Hartford, Connecticut, March 5, 1860, *Collected Works*, 4: 5.

45. Parrish, *Turbulent Partnership*, 143.

46. John M. Schofield to Abraham Lincoln, June 20, 1863, Lincoln Papers.

47. Abraham Lincoln to John M. Schofield, June 22, 1863, *Collected Works*, 6: 291.

48. In his reconstruction plan for the seceded states, announced on December 8, 1863, Lincoln decreed that states "which shall recognize and declare [the] permanent freedom" of blacks, "provide for their education, and which may yet be consistent, as a temporary arrangement, with their present condition as a laboring, landless, and homeless class, will not be objected to by the national Executive." Proclamation of Amnesty and Reconstruction, December 8, 1863, *Collected Works*, 7: 55. Lincoln never repudiated this position.

49. Charles D. Drake to Abraham Lincoln, July 31, 1863, Lincoln Papers.

50. Joseph A. Hay to Abraham Lincoln, September 11, 1863, Lincoln Papers; entry for September 29, 1863, in Hay, *Inside Lincoln's White House*, ed. Burlingame and Ettlinger, 89.

51. *Annual Cyclopedia, 1863*, 654–655.

52. Parrish, *Turbulent Partnership*, 147–148; Boman, *Lincoln's Resolute Unionist*, 214.

53. John B. Henderson to Abraham Lincoln, July 6, 1863, Lincoln Papers.

54. *Annual Cyclopedia, 1863*, 655.

55. For a good account of black enlistments in Missouri, see Boman, *Lincoln's Resolute Unionist*, 220–222. Many Missouri blacks had fled to Iowa and Kansas, where they enrolled in the regiments of those states.

56. Berlin, Reidy, and Rowland, *Freedom's Soldiers*, 16.

57. *Annual Cyclopedia, 1863*, 655–656.

58. Charles D. Drake, "The Wrongs to Missouri's Loyal People," in *Southern Unionist Pamphlets and the Civil War,* ed. Jon L. Wakelyn (Columbia: University of Missouri Press, 1999), 148–169.

59. Entry for September 29, 1863, in Hay, *Inside Lincoln's White House*, ed. Burlingame and Ettlinger, 89.

60. Memorandum, September 30, 1863, in *At Lincoln's Side: John Hay's Civil War Correspondence and Selected Writings*, ed. Michael Burlingame (Carbondale: Southern Illinois University Press, 2000), 57–58.

61. Ibid., 59.

62. Ibid., 60.

63. Ibid., 63–64.

64. Ibid., 63.

65. Ibid., 60–61.

66. Ibid., 61.

67. Ibid.

68. Ibid.

69. Ibid., 64.

70. Charles D. Drake to Abraham Lincoln, October 7, 10, 1863, Lincoln Papers.

71. Lincoln explained the divisions vis-à-vis the Union and slavery: "Those who are for the Union *with*, but not *without* slavery—those for it *without*, but not *with*—those for it *with* or *without*, but prefer it *with*—and those for it *with* or *without*, but prefer it *without*. Among these again, is a subdivision of those who are for *gradual* but not for *immediate*, and those who are for immediate, but not for *gradual* extinction of slavery." Abraham Lincoln to Charles D. Drake and Others, October 5, 1863, *Collected Works*, 6: 500.

72. Ibid.

73. Ibid., 6: 503.

74. Ibid., 6: 502–503.

75. Quoted in Enos Clarke, "Lincoln and the Radical Men of Missouri," reprinted in Walter B. Stevens, *A Reporter's Lincoln*, ed. Michael Burlingame (Lincoln: University of Nebraska Press, 1998), 151.

76. Abraham Lincoln to John M. Schofield, October 1, 1863, *Collected Works*, 6: 492.

77. David McCullough, *Truman* (New York: Simon & Schuster, 1992), 32.

78. Abraham Lincoln to John M. Schofield, October 1, 1863, *Collected Works*, 6: 493.

79. *Annual Cyclopedia, 1863*, 657; Parrish, *A History of Missouri*, vol. 3, *1860–1865*, 102.

80. Hamilton R. Gamble to Abraham Lincoln, October 1, 1863, Lincoln Papers.

81. *Annual Cyclopedia, 1863*, 657.

82. James S. Rollins to Abraham Lincoln, October 8, 1863; James O. Broadhead to Lincoln, September 22, 1863, Lincoln Papers.

83. Abraham Lincoln to Hamilton Gamble, October 19, 1863, *Collected Works*, 6: 526–527.

84. Edward Bates to Abraham Lincoln, October 22, 1863, Lincoln Papers.

85. John M. Schofield to Henry W. Halleck [with endorsement by Lincoln], September 20, 1863, Lincoln Papers.

86. For the election results, see *Annual Cyclopedia, 1863*, 657.

87. Entry for September 30, 1863, in Bates, *Diary*, ed. Beale, 308; Samuel T. Glover to Abraham Lincoln, April 13, 1863, Lincoln Papers.

88. Salmon P. Chase to Abraham Lincoln, October 31, 1863, Lincoln Papers.

89. Joseph Gillespie to Abraham Lincoln, October 10, 1863; Joseph Medill to Lincoln, October 3, 1863, Lincoln Papers.

90. William G. Eliot to Charles Sumner, September 4 (quotation), October 30, 1863, Lincoln Papers. Later Eliot blamed the partisanship of the radicals for the troubles in Missouri and admitted his mistake in calling for Schofield's removal. Eliot to Lincoln, December 16, 1863, Lincoln Papers.

91. Entry for December 10, 1863, in Hay, *Inside Lincoln's White House*, ed. Burlingame and Ettlinger, 125.

92. Entry for December 13, 1863, in Hay, *Inside Lincoln's White House*, ed. Burlingame and Ettlinger, 127.

93. Ibid., 127.

94. Writing three decades later of the meeting, Schofield reported that Lincoln, after hearing his explanation, declared, "I believe you Schofield; those fellows [radicals] have been lying to me again." Donald B. Connelly, *John M. Schofield and the Politics of Generalship* (Chapel Hill: University of North Carolina Press, 2006), 81.

95. Abraham Lincoln to Edwin M. Stanton, December 18, 1863, *Collected Works*, 7: 78–79.

96. Entry for December 23, 1863, in Hay, *Inside Lincoln's White House*, ed. Burlingame and Ettlinger, 129; Abraham Lincoln to Edwin M. Stanton, December 21, 1863, *Collected Works*, 7: 84 and 85n.

97. For a fine modern biography of Schofield, see Connelly, *John M. Schofield.*

98. Parrish, *A History of Missouri*, vol. 3, *1860–1875*, 106–107.

99. *Washington Daily Chronicle*, February 6, 1864; *Saint Louis Missouri Republican*, January 17, 1864; *Louisville Daily Journal*, February 25, 1864.

100. *Saint Louis Missouri Republican*, February 27, 1864; *Chicago Tribune*, March 4, 1864.

101. *Saint Louis Missouri Republican*, February 27, 1864.

102. Ibid., February 26, 27, 1864; *New Orleans Daily True Delta*, March 5, 1864.

103. J. G. Randall and Richard N. Current, *Lincoln the President: Last Full Measure*, with a new introduction by Richard N. Current (1955; reprint, Urbana: University of Illinois Press, 1991), 99; Burlingame, *Abraham Lincoln*, 2: 611–617.

104. *Saint Louis Missouri Republican*, February 27, 1864; *Nashville Daily Union*, February 27, 1864.

105. Lincoln's role in the seating of the Missouri radicals has been a subject of dispute. According to Professor Michael Burlingame, Lincoln's secretary John G. Nicolay told the Illinois delegation that Lincoln wanted the convention to seat them as a conciliatory gesture to unite the party (Burlingame, *Abraham Lincoln*, 2: 643). On the other hand, Professor Don E. Fehrenbacher has written that Lincoln, in order to avoid a divisive charge of interference in the convention's proceedings (for example, in the vice presidential nomination), did not become involved in the decision on the Missouri

delegation. Fehrenbacher, "The Making of a Myth: Lincoln and the Vice-Presidential Nomination in 1864," *Civil War History* 41 (December 1995): 273–290.

106. The *Saint Louis Missouri Republican*, June 11, 1864, gives excerpts from the German American press denouncing the actions of the Baltimore convention.

107. *Saint Louis Missouri Republican*, February 26 (quotation from the *Cincinnati Gazette*), 27, 1864; *Nashville Daily Union*, February 27, 1864.

108. For an excellent account of the brutal conflict in Missouri in 1864, see Daniel E. Sutherland, *A Savage Conflict: The Decisive Role of Guerrillas in the American Civil War* (Chapel Hill: University of North Carolina Press, 2009), 200–204. See also Fellman, *Inside War*, chap. 4, and Albert Castel and Thomas Goodrich's account of the Centralia massacre, in *Bloody Bill Anderson: The Short Savage Life of a Civil War Guerrilla* (Mechanicsburg, Pa.: Stackpole Books, 1998), 88, 94–96.

109. Abraham Lincoln to William S. Rosecrans, June 7, 8, 10, 1864, *Collected Works*, 7: 379 and n, 386.

110. William S. Rosecrans to Abraham Lincoln, June 14, 22, 1864, Lincoln Papers; entry for [June 17, 1864], in Hay, *Inside Lincoln's White House*, ed. Burlingame and Ettlinger, 204–205.

111. Entry for [June 17, 1864], in Hay, *Inside Lincoln's White House*, ed. Burlingame and Ettlinger, 207.

112. James O. Broadhead to Edward Bates, July 24, 1864, Lincoln Papers. After the war Broadhead became the first president of the American Bar Association.

113. Ibid.

114. Entry for August 5, 1864, in Bates, *Diary*, ed. Beale, 394.

115. William S. Rosecrans to Abraham Lincoln, November 15, 1864, Lincoln Papers.

116. Parrish, *A History of Missouri*, vol. 3, *1860–1875*, 113–114.

117. Sutherland, *A Savage Conflict*, 204.

118. Parrish, *Turbulent Partnership*, 184–185; *Saint Louis Missouri Republican*, June 18, 1864.

119. James B. Wright to Abraham Lincoln, October 5, 1864; D. W. Moore to Lincoln, October 5, 1864; A. B. Beller to Lincoln, October 8, 1864, Lincoln Papers.

120. John G. Nicolay to Abraham Lincoln, October 10, 1864, Lincoln Papers.

121. John G. Nicolay to Abraham Lincoln, October 18, 1864, Lincoln Papers.

122. Charles D. Drake to Abraham Lincoln, October 5, 1864, Lincoln Papers.

123. Parrish, *A History of Missouri*, vol. 3, *1860–1875*, 114–115; *Annual Cyclopedia, 1864*, 552.

124. *Annual Cyclopedia, 1864*, 553–554.

125. James S. Rollins's account of his meeting with Lincoln is found in *Conversations with Lincoln*, ed. Charles M. Segal, with a new preface by the editor and an introduction by David Donald (1961; reprint, New Brunswick, N.J.: Transaction Publishers, 2002), 362–364.

126. Harris, *Lincoln's Last Months*, 130–131.

127. Abraham Lincoln to Thomas C. Fletcher, February 20, 1865, *Collected Works*, 8: 308.

128. Abraham Lincoln to Thomas C. Fletcher, February 27, 1865, *Collected Works*, 8: 319.

129. *Collected Works*, 8: 319–320n.

130. Thomas C. Fletcher to Abraham Lincoln, February 27, 1865, *OR*, ser. 1, vol. 48, p. 997.

131. John Pope to Thomas C. Fletcher, March 3, 1865, *OR*, ser. 1, vol. 48, pp. 1070–1077.

132. John Pope to Abraham Lincoln, March 8, 1865, Lincoln Papers; Lincoln to Pope, March 19, 1865, *Collected Works*, 8: 365.

133. Proclamation of Governor Thomas C. Fletcher, March 7, 1865, *OR*, ser. 1, vol. 48, p. 1115.

134. Henry T. Blow to Abraham Lincoln, March 16, 1865, Lincoln Papers.

135. William E. Parrish, "Reconstruction Politics in Missouri, 1865–1870," in Curry, *Radicalism, Racism, and Party Realignment*, 9, 15.

Index

colonization and, 219
election arrangement of, 292–293
election of, 282–283
emancipation and, 207, 282, 297
slavery and, 289
Unconditional Unionists and, 288
Union League and, 281
Davis, Jefferson, 46, 61, 122, 127, 264,
 311, 319,
 message to, 121
 welcome from, 63
Davis, John W., 73
Declaration of Independence, 321
Delaware General Assembly, 208, 209
Delaware ratification of U.S. Constitution
 (1787), 208
Democratic Party, 12, 246, 247, 344
 anti-Republican rhetoric of, 13
 convention of, 251
 platform of, 7, 252, 253, 255
Democrats, 81
 Conservative Unionists and, 251
 Know Nothings and, 18
Dennis, George R., 296
Dennison, William, 90
Department of Kentucky, 90, 240
Department of Missouri, 153, 308, 337,
 372n105
Department of Ohio, 215
Department of the Cumberland, 108
Department of the West, 78, 98, 120,
 126, 140, 143, 147, 148, 152, 153
Dick, Franklin A., 129, 391n8
District of Columbia emancipation bill,
 169–170, 178, 179, 184, 221
 colonization and, 192
 opposition to, 172
 passage of, 194
Dix, John A., 70, 71, 74, 279, 319,
 360n84
Dixon, Archibald, 82, 239
Dixon, James, 212
Dodge, Grenville, 347
Doolittle, James R., 170, 212

Douglas, Stephen A., 15, 18, 25, 29, 78,
 97, 100, 105, 122, 123, 246, 288
 Jackson and, 22
 Missouri Democrats and, 13
 nomination of, 14
 popular sovereignty doctrine and, 12
 support for, 16
 Union Saving Committee and, 32
Douglass, Frederick, 4, 378n56
 colonization and, 219
 District bill and, 172
 Emancipation Proclamation and, 203
 slave liberation and, 103
Dover Delawarean, 18
Drake, Charles D., 316, 317, 318–319,
 322, 323, 329–330, 332, 338,
 348
 campaigning by, 344
 emancipation and, 325
 opposition of, 309, 324
 photo of, 314
 radicals and, 330, 339
 response to, 328
 speech by, 326
Dred Scott decision, 59, 60, 169
Dubois, Jesse K., 315
Durrett, Reuben T., 109, 110, 112
Dutch Blackguards, 127
Duvall, Alvin, 249, 383n90

Early, Jubal, 291, 295, 296
Easton (Md.) Gazette, 268
Economic system, 162, 207, 307
Eginton, Charles, 260
Eliot, William G., 335, 394n90
Ellis, John W., 39
Emancipation, 2, 6, 77, 145, 160, 168,
 178, 183, 187, 196–197, 204, 213,
 220, 221–222
 black equality and, 195, 289
 black troops and, 229
 border states and, 158, 162, 163,
 166–167, 169, 180, 188, 291,
 374n69